OS/2 Connectivity and Networking

J. Ranade Workstation Series

CHAKRAVARTY • *Power RISC System/6000: Concepts, Facilities, and Architecture*, 0-07-011047-6

CHAKRAVARTY, CANTON • *PowerPC: Concepts, Architecture, and Design*, 0-07-011192-8

DEROEST • *AIX for RS/6000: System and Administration Guide*, 0-07-036439-7

HENRY, GRAHAM • *Solaris 2.X System Administrator's Guide*, 0-07-029368-6

LAMB • *MicroFocus Workbench and Toolset Developer's Guide*, 0-07-036123-3

LEININGER • *UNIX Developer's Tool Kit*, 0-07-911646-9

LOCKHART • *OSF DCE: Guide to Developing Distributed Applications*, 0-07-911481-4

RANADE, ZAMIR • *C++Primer for C Programmers*, 0-07-051487-9

SANCHEZ, CANTON • *Graphics Programming Solutions*, 0-07-911464-4

SANCHEZ, CANTON • *High Resolution Video Graphics*, 0-07-911646-9

SANCHEZ, CANTON • *PC Programmer's Handbook*, 0-07-054948-6

WALKER, SCHWALLER • *CPI-C Programming in C: An Application Developer's Guide to APPC*, 0-07-911733-3

WIGGINS • *The Internet for Everyone: A Guide for Users and Providers*, 0-07-067019-8

OS/2 Connectivity and Networking

A Guide to Communications Manager/2

John E. Johnston

McGraw-Hill, Inc.

New York San Francisco Washington, D.C. Auckland Bogotá
Caracas Lisbon London Madrid Mexico City Milan
Montreal New Delhi San Juan Singapore
Sydney Tokyo Toronto

Library of Congress Cataloging-in-Publication Data

Johnston, John E.
OS/2 connectivity and networking : a guide to communications Manager/2 John E. Johnston.
p. cm.
Includes index.
ISBN 0-07-032696-7
1. Operating systems (Computers) 2. OS/2 (Computer file) 3. Local area networks (Computer networks) I. Title.
QA76.76.063J64 1994
004.6'16—dc20 94-10369
CIP

1 2 3 4 5 6 7 8 9 0 DOH/DOH 9 0 9 8 7 6 5 4

ISBN 0-07-032696-7

The sponsoring editor for this book was Jerry Papke, the editing supervisor was Joseph Bertuna, and the production supervisor was Donald F. Schmidt. It was set in Century Schoolbook by McGraw-Hill's Professional Book Group composition unit.

Printed and bound by R. R. Donnelley & Sons Company.

Contents

Acknowledgments

This book is dedicated to Monica for all her patience and understanding during its writing. I could never have done it without you. Thank you, Meghann, Paul, and Daniel, who gave up a countless number of Sundays with Daddy at the park. Thank you, Jay, for sticking with me through thick and thin.

Preface

This book is about *interoperability*. When networks first began infiltrating the corporate walls, it was not uncommon for dual networks to be established, one for the SNA mainframe traffic and one for the networked personal computers. This duality also applied to printers. The end-users could have at their desks a mainframe terminal, a mainframe printer, a personal computer, and a personal computer printer. That does not leave much desk space for working. The multiple-terminal and -printer solution to corporate users' information needs is not sufficient or practical. Corporate information users demand seamless access to all the systems within the organization, whether it is a mainframe, a minicomputer, or a PC. These same users also demand systems that are easy to learn and master. OS/2 and CM/2 were designed to meet these requirements.

Information technology professionals now have the hardware and software components available to banish the dual networks once and for all. This book describes the *universal workstation and printer* concept. With this concept, a single OS/2 workstation accesses multiple hardware and software platforms. OS/2 has been christened "the integration platform." The design of the OS/2 operating system, its print subsystem, and Communications Manager/2 makes OS/2 the perfect platform for accessing multiple, disparate systems concurrently. Together, we will see how OS/2 and CM/2 can be used to connect to an SNA mainframe, a DEC/VAX, and a Novell NetWare local area network.

This book delves much further than just the concept layer. This book is packed with technical meat. It is filled with how-to solutions for today's real-world problems. There are many step-by-step examples on configuring OS/2 and CM/2 to access multiple systems concurrently.

OS/2 has proved itself as a stable platform for mission critical applications. There has been a considerable amount of discussion lately about which PC operating system will dominate the 1990s and beyond. OS/2 has found its place in the corporate world and will continue to play a major role in the future of data processing. CM/2 in conjunction with OS/2 provides an incredible amount of flexibility for network administrators. OS/2 with CM/2 truly fulfills the role of integration platform, as it was designed to do.

Interoperability between disparate hardware and software platforms is a difficult goal to attain, even with products like OS/2 and CM/2 that were designed to provide cross-platform connectivity. Each hardware and software component has its own intricacies that must be accommodated. It is relatively easy to configure OS/2 and CM/2 to provide host access via a Token Ring network. It is much more difficult to provide host access via an Ethernet network while also connecting to a Novell network and providing access to a DEC/VAX system. This book will show you how to achieve reliable interoperability between these systems. All the quirks of these systems will be discussed in detail so that you will know how to connect to multiple disparate systems. You will also learn how the components that provide interoperability work together to allow the universal workstation and printer concept to become a reality.

Who Should Read This Book

OS/2 Connectivity and Networking is an intermediate- to advanced-level book designed to meet the needs of three specific professional groups:

- Network administrators
- Data processing managers
- Mainframe system programmers

The network administrator will learn how to configure OS/2, NTS/2, and CM/2 to provide concurrent access to multiple systems. The many sample configurations illustrated in the book can be used as a guide to implementing cross-platform connectivity at your site. Chapter 1 covers mainframe communication basics. This chapter is designed for network administrators who have little or no exposure to the mainframe world. This mainframe overview describes all the most common mainframe connectivity options. The history of local-area network, to mainframe connectivity is also discussed. The sample LAN to mainframe connectivity scenarios explain, in detail, how to configure the mainframe in order to provide reliable connectivity. Chapter 1 provides a firm knowledge base for the OS/2 to SNA chapters that follow.

The network administrator will also learn about the bridging and routing requirements for OS/2 interoperability. We will discuss the bridging requirements for establishing an Ethernet to SNA host connection. The inner workings of bridging and routing will also be discussed in detail. We will learn how and when to use transparent bridging, source routing bridging, and source routing transparency. We will see how the spanning tree algorithm can allow us to introduce multiple redundant paths in an Ethernet environment for enhanced reliability. We will learn how to control spanning tree to suit our needs, rather than letting it go on its own to make the critical bridge blocking decisions.

Data processing managers will learn the basic concepts behind cross-platform connectivity. This foundation will enable these managers to make intelligent and informed decisions on the connectivity issues facing their organizations. The book explains methods for cutting cost while maintaining data and network integrity. Data processing managers can also use this book as a template for their disaster recovery planning. Chapter 8 shows the reader, step by step, how to configure an OS/2-CM/2 gateway to the mainframe. This is a complicated procedure, and in most shops this is a once-and-done installation. What happens if 2 years from now the gateway hard drive crashes and no one remembers how to configure it? You can use the step-by-step procedures as a guide to reestablish your critical network components.

Data processing managers can also use the information in this book to keep abreast of the latest trends in interoperability. Perhaps you already have a network installed with host and local-area network connectivity. Technology advances daily. Is your connectivity method already outdated? This book provides state-of-the-art interoperability methods for the most common hardware and software platforms in use in corporations today.

Mainframe systems programmers who wish to expand their horizons by entering the communications arena will truly enjoy this book. These professionals will, of course, skip right over Chapt. 1 on SNA basics. Systems programmers will appreciate the correlations between the mainframe connectivity parameters and how they relate to the LAN world. The hand shaking between the various platforms will become crystal-clear. Mainframe systems programmers are typically called upon to fix problems on systems that they have had little or no exposure to. Not only are they called upon to correct problems when given little or no background, but also they are expected to correct these problems quickly. Life as a systems programmer can be very demanding. This book will help you to understand how and why interoperability can be achieved. With a strong understanding of the components involved in cross-platform interconnectivity, you can be in a much better position when things break. Also Chap. 18 outlines all the support avenues available for OS/2, CM/2, and Novell.

How This Book Is Organized

OS/2 Connectivity and Networking introduces you to CM/2 and provides a cookbook approach to implementing cross-platform connectivity. Several step-by-step procedures are provided that show you how to implement the real-world connectivity scenarios.

The book is divided into four parts:

Part 1 3270 Hardware Configurations

Part 2 3270 Connectivity

Part 3 NetWare Connectivity

Part 4 DEC/VAX Connectivity

Part 1 3270 Hardware Configurations

This part of the book deals with the physical connectivity options available for host to local area network communications.

Chapter 1, Mainframe Connectivity Basics, describes how the mainframe talks to terminals and printers. The hardware and software components are described in detail. This chapter is very useful to PC network administrators. The mainframe connectivity concepts are explained, using many illustrations, so that SNA and its related components can be easily understood. This chapter also delves into one of the most useful components in the mainframe to local-area network connectivity, the downstream physical unit. Many of the connection scenarios illustrated in this book use the downstream PU host connectivity component. We will see how VTAM and the network control program work in conjunction to provide access to mainframe resources.

Chapter 2, 3174 TIC Connection, explains how a 3174 control unit can be used to connect a mainframe to a Token Ring local area network. This connectivity option can be extremely cost-effective in organizations where a Token Ring network is already established. The 3174 TIC option also allows the organization to utilize the full 16Mbits/s bandwidth available with Token Ring. We will look at the hardware components that are required to implement a TIC in a 3174. The memory requirements of these hardware components will also be illustrated. An actual 3174 microcode customization process will be explained in detail. If you have never configured a 3174 to support a TIC, an example is worth a thousand manuals. The sample customization was used in a real network and can help you to see how the different customization options relate to the overall connectivity scenario.

Chapter 3, 3725 TIC Connection, explains how a 3725 communications controller can be used to connect a mainframe to a Token Ring local area network. If you are planning to use a 3725 to connect your host to a Token Ring, make sure you read this chapter. The 3725 may not be your best option! The hardware components required for the TIC installation are described in detail. We will also look at a sample network control program (NCP) generation for the TIC implementation. We will also learn what changes are required in VTAM, the host communications software, in order to communicate with the 3725's TIC.

Chapter 4, 3745 TIC Connection, explains how a 3745 communications controller can be used to connect a mainframe to a Token Ring local area network. As with the 3725, we will explore the hardware and software components required to implement a TIC in an IBM 3745 communications controller. We will look at the NCP and VTAM modifications.

Chapter 5, The 3172 Interconnect Controller, focuses on how a 3172 control unit can be used to connect a mainframe to an Ethernet local area network. The 3172 host connectivity could well be the most cost-effective solution to your host to LAN connectivity needs.

Chapter 6, Bridges and Routers, offers a detailed explanation of what bridges and routers are and how they can be used to connect Token Ring LANs to Ethernet LANs. It also explains how routers can be used to improve the performance of the entire network. SNA traffic imposes special requirements for bridges and routers. Make sure you are aware of these requirements before you purchase one of these devices. This chapter alone could save you thousands of dollars. When you finish this chapter, you will know how bridges and routers work. We will look at transparent bridging, the spanning tree algorithm, source route bridging, and source route transparency. You will learn how to control multiple redundant paths in your network. You will also learn when a router should be used instead of a bridge. This one issue requires a firm understanding of today's networking abilities and components. The information in this chapter will help you to design a robust and reliable network.

Part 2 3270 Connectivity

Together, we will explore mainframe to LAN communications using several different connectivity methods. You will understand the difference between these host connection methods and will be able to determine the best host connectivity option for your individual application. The traditional method for providing host connectivity includes the implementation of a Token Ring network. We will explore this method, but we will also learn how to provide the same functionality by using an Ethernet network, for far fewer dollars.

This part of the book is filled with step-by-step configuration guides for OS/2, CM/2, NTS/2, and the host. Part 2 will help you establish your host to LAN connectivity in the most cost-effective and time-effective manner.

Chapter 7, OS/2 and APPN, discusses how CM/2 uses the Advanced Peer-to-Peer Networking (APPN) architecture to communicate with mainframe networks. A review of the APPN components is provided, and a sample APPC application is illustrated. In this chapter we will learn why IBM developed APPN. As we will see, APPN is poised as a major player in the interoperability world.

Chapter 8, Using an OS/2 Workstation as a Gateway to the Host, shows the reader how to set up and configure an OS/2 workstation as a mainframe gateway. This gateway PC can then be used by hundreds of other OS/2 workstations to access the mainframe. This chapter is extremely useful because there is very little documentation available on this subject, and the documentation that is available is inaccurate. This chapter also shows you how to implement a gateway on a Token Ring network and provide access to the mainframe via this gateway to Ethernet-connected clients, all without a bridge or a router. This is accomplished by installing two NIC adapters in the gateway PC: one Token Ring NIC and one Ethernet NIC. Then the components of CM/2 and NTS/2 are configured to allow this cross-topology connectivity to occur. The step-by-step guides provided in this chapter can also be modified and used as documentation for your network. Nothing is better for network documentation than a step-by-step configuration guide.

Chapter 9, Token Ring PU Emulation—Configuring CM/2, tells you how to configure CM/2 to access the mainframe as a physical unit (PU) from a Token Ring LAN. PU access to the host is the most flexible and trouble-free method to obtain mainframe connectivity. The manuals that come with CM/2 are very vague in this area. This chapter uses a simple-to-follow cookbook approach to implement this function. In the example in this chapter, a workstation is configured to emulate the host PU session and provides 15 terminal sessions and one printer session.

Chapter 10, Ethernet PU Emulation—Configuring CM/2 shows the reader how to configure CM/2 to access the mainframe as a PU from an Ethernet LAN. PU access to the host is the most flexible and trouble-free method to obtain mainframe connectivity. In order for Ethernet PU emulation connectivity to occur, special bridge and/or routing technologies must be established. We will look at these bridging requirements and will examine ways to implement the bridging in a cost-effective manner.

Chapter 11, Communications Manager/2 3270 Printer Support, contains an overview on how mainframe print is routed through the mainframe network components. Next, you are shown how OS/2 and CM/2 can be used to intercept mainframe print and route it to local PC printers. Routing print through a network is one of the most troublesome tasks performed by the network administrator. A clear understanding of the components involved in host printing and the networking components involved in routing this print through the network will help you to design a more trouble-free network printing system.

Part 3 NetWare Connectivity

In this section of the book, we will delve into OS/2 to LAN connectivity options. It is a simple matter to provide LAN connectivity to an OS/2 workstation. Obtaining coexistence, (concurrent LAN and host access via the same NIC adapter) is a little trickier. You will learn the concepts behind the most common coexistence methods. We will examine the LANSUP, ODINSUP, and the ODI2NDI network protocol drivers. These drivers are the heart of CM/2 and Novell coexistence. Which driver is right for your application? That all depends upon your configuration. We will then go a step further and learn how to implement these coexistence methods by performing actual CM/2 and NTS/2 configurations. We will also explore the NetWare OS/2 Requester product. This product, if implemented correctly, can help you implement the universal workstation and printer solution at your site.

Chapter 12, Communications Manager/2 and NetWare Coexistence, explains what coexistence is, the benefits of coexistence, and the methods that can be used to obtain coexistence. This material is extremely useful because obtaining coexistence is very difficult and is not documented very well. The mechanics of coexistence will be explored in great detail in this chapter. You will learn how and why the different coexistence drivers are used to provide cross-platform connectivity.

Chapter 13, Implementing CM/2, NTS/2, and NetWare Coexistence, gives the reader a step-by-step procedure for implementing coexistence between Novell, OS/2, and CM/2 host connectivity. No other published document explains, in this great detail, how to attain CM/2 and NetWare coexistence.

Chapter 14, Using the NetWare OS/2 Requester, is very useful. The OS/2 Requester is a product that allows OS/2 PCs to access Novell networks. This chapter explains some of the utilities and options available with this software component. There are some tricks to making DOS applications work effectively under Requester. This chapter explains all these nuances. We will learn about global and local NetWare log-ins and how these two components can be integrated into your network. We will also take a look at several of the tools provided with NetWare Requester.

Chapter 15, Printing through a Novell Network, explains the components available with the Novell print system. Ways to exploit this print system by using OS/2 and CM/2 are highlighted. Printing is difficult in a network environment. This chapter helps the reader overcome most of the common problems. We will also look at ways to troubleshoot your network printing system.

Part 4 DEC/VAX Connectivity

For those of you who need to connect to a DEC/VAX system, Part 4 is included on DEC/VAX connectivity. You will learn how to use an OS/2 workstation to provide concurrent access to a DEC/VAX system.

Chapter 16, DEC VT220 Emulation, shows you how to implement Terminal Emulation Services (TES) from InterConnections, Inc., to access a DEC/VAX from an OS/2 workstation. This product provides a very flexible and reliable method for accessing a DEC/VAX system.

Chapter 17, DEC Print Support, explains how to use Network Print Services (NPS) from InterConnections to route DEC print through a Novell network. This product uses the services of IPX to route DEC print. This enables you to utilize your current NetWare printing subsystem for your DEC/VAX printed output.

Chapter 18, OS/2 and Novell Support Avenues, will look at OS/2 support options. There are several support options available to you. Some of these options can be very expensive, while others are relatively inexpensive. The pros and cons of each support option are explained. When a network experiences problems, your corporation suffers and you are expected to correct the problems with blinding speed. This chapter will show you where to find the best support for your particular problem. You will learn the intricacies of these support avenues, allowing you to get the information you need in a timely manner.

Appendix A describes some of the tools provided with the OS/2 and CM/2 that can make the job of the network administrator a little easier.

Appendix B addresses some of the most common problems and questions that new network designers and administrators face when implementing a multiprotocol network. Questions pertaining to NetWare, OS/2, host access, and many other topics are covered in this appendix. Make sure you look through this section because it could save you countless hours of investigation.

The Glossary covers common mainframe and networking terms.

Communications Manager/2 Overview

Communications Manager/2 contains a wealth of enhancements above and beyond the Extended Services product. This is a partial list of these enhancements:

- The configuration panels have been completely redesigned using Presentation Manager windows.

- APPN End Node (EN) and Network Node (NN) support is now available with CM/2. If you are designing an APPN network, CM/2 can help you get there.
- X.25 support is now provided.
- First Failure Support Technology/2 (FFST/2) is included with CM/2. FFST/2 detects communications errors and collects and displays diagnostic information to help solve problems.
- The LAN Adapter and Protocol Support (LAPS) function of the old Extended Services product has been split into a separate product. This product is Network Transport Services/2 (NTS/2). NTS/2 is required if you plan to connect your OS/2 workstations to a local area network.
- Support for multiple-PU access. This allows an OS/2-CM/2 workstation to connect to as many as three mainframes concurrently.
- CM/2 now includes support for Integrated Services Digital Network (ISDN) Basic Rate Interface (BRI).

John E. Johnston

Part

1

3270 Hardware Configurations

One of the most common uses of OS/2 and CM/2 is to provide host access via a local area network (LAN). Before we delve into the actual mechanics of configuring OS/2, NTS/2, and CM/2, we must have a firm understanding of the physical connectivity options in the mainframe. The physical connectivity must be established before we proceed.

Part 1 deals with these mainframe connectivity options. We begin with an overview of the mainframe connectivity components, including VTAM, NCP, and SNA. We take a look at the history of mainframe to LAN connectivity options including the use of 3270 emulation adapters, distributed function terminals and physical unit gateways, and common host to Token Ring connectivity options. If you are a seasoned mainframe user, you can probably skim right through Chap. 1, Mainframe Connectivity Basics.

Next we take a closer look at the implementation considerations for the various connection methods. We examine the use of the 3174 control unit as a link to Token Ring networks. Then we consider the use of the 3725 and 3745 front-end processors. For those who wish to travel the Ethernet road to connectivity, we explore the IBM 3172 control unit.

We conclude Part 1 with a discussion of bridges and routers. These devices play a critical role in large internetworks, and a little planning in this area can save you a lot of time and money in the future. If you plan to combine Ethernet and Token Ring networks, you should pay particular attention to Chap. 6. Not all routers support the routing of SNA traffic between these topologies.

Chapter

1

Mainframe Connectivity Basics

Before we can jump into the world of OS/2-CM/2 host connectivity, we must have a firm understanding of the basics of mainframe communications. This chapter will review the basic mainframe communication components and will describe some of the more common connectivity options. The mainframe communications components and connectivity options are far too numerous to describe in this book, so only the most common options and the components that relate to CM/2 connectivity will be presented.

We begin with an overview of the major host connectivity components, such as the logical unit (LU) and the physical unit (PU). Next we look at the difference between the control unit terminal (CUT) and the distributed-function terminal (DFT). The roles that the CUTs and DFTs played in the early local-area network (LAN) gateway products will also be illustrated. We will continue with a look at the mainframe software components that provide connectivity. The functions of the virtual telecommunication access method (VTAM) and the network control program (NCP) will be discussed in detail. The history of mainframe-to-LAN connectivity will be explored in this chapter. We will look at DFT gateways and the spectrum of PU emulator gateways. We will round out the chapter with a section on how CM/2 can emulate the various Systems Network Architecture (SNA) components to provide host connectivity.

This chapter is designed for people with little or no exposure to mainframes. If you already have a strong SNA background, you may skip this chapter, with the exception of the discussion of the downstream PU (DSPU). Many of the CM/2 host connectivity options illustrated in this book build upon the DSPU host connectivity function. A clear understanding of the principles behind the downstream PU concept will help you on your journey to CM/2 to mainframe connectivity.

SNA Network Components

Most IBM and plug compatible mainframes use the IBM Systems Network Architecture (SNA) to provide connectivity between devices and programs running on the mainframe system. SNA is not a software product. It is a set of rules that are followed in the building of hardware and software components. Complying with this architecture allows these components to communicate with each other. SNA defines rules for several communications devices, such as terminals and terminal control units.

SNA also defines rules for communicating over telephone lines. This remote communication is performed by using a special host communications controller. IBM recently announced the Advanced Peer to Peer Networking (APPN) architecture. SNA is a very difficult (and expensive) protocol to implement over wide-area networks. APPN promises to reduce the expense and complexity of routing SNA traffic. We will take a closer look at the components and capabilities of APPN in a later chapter.

Physical units

A physical unit is an SNA component that controls other SNA devices. For example, a terminal control unit is a PU that manages many SNA terminals and printers. This type of PU is known as a PU type 2 or PU2. Figure 1.1 illustrates a typical host connecting to a PU with multiple terminals.

There are several other types of PUs. A PU type 5 is a host computer, and a PU type 4 is a front-end processor (FEP) communications controller. We will talk more about FEPs later in the chapter.

We will see that many of the current LAN-to-mainframe gateway products, including CM/2, provide host access by emulating the terminal control unit PU. This type of emulation allows a single gateway to support hundreds of mainframe sessions.

Logical units

One of the main components of any SNA network is the logical unit. An LU is an SNA software component that allows an end-user to access the SNA network.

There are several types of SNA LUs. An LU can be a terminal, a printer, or an application program. All terminal emulation programs, including the CM/2 3270 terminal emulation feature, emulate LUs.

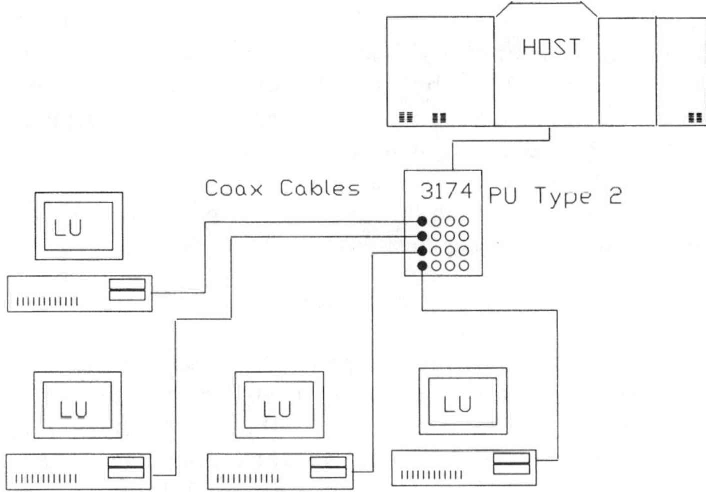

Figure 1.1 Typical host PU-LU configuration.

Most of these emulation programs can emulate both the terminal LU and the printer LU.

A special LU used by the Advanced Program to Program Communications (APPC) architecture is known as LU6.2. APPC provides a method for two programs to communicate directly with each other by using SNA as the transmission protocol. The beauty of APPC is that the two programs that are communicating with each other can be on different hardware and software platforms. For example, an APPC application can be written to pass records from a mainframe to an OS/2 personal computer attached to a local-area network. APPC provides a set of verbs that are common across all hardware and software platforms. Samples of these verbs are the SEND and CONFIRMED verbs. An LU6.2 program running on a DEC/VAX can ship a record to an LU6.2 program running on an IBM host using the SEND verb. When the IBM program receives the record, it can issue the CONFIRMED verb to let the DEC program know that the record was successfully received. APPC is already being used extensively in organizations where disparate computer systems must pass data between each other.

Control unit terminal

A control unit terminal (CUT) is connected to a terminal control unit and uses the control unit to process its keystrokes. This type of terminal can support only one host session at a time.

The CUT is a function of the control unit (3174) not the terminal device. When a 3174 control unit is configured, the terminal type is defined as either CUT or DFT.

Distributed-function terminal

A distributed-function terminal (DFT) is connected to a terminal control unit that does not require the control unit to manage its keystrokes. A given DFT can support up to five concurrent host sessions.

The DFT is a function of the control unit, not the terminal device. Most of the newer terminal emulation programs emulate DFTs. There are some gateway products that emulate a DFT to provide five host sessions to five different users on the network.

LU emulators

When personal computers (PCs) began infiltrating corporate data centers, products were developed which allowed these PCs to be connected to the mainframe SNA networks. To connect to the mainframe, a 3270 adapter card is placed in the PC and a coaxial connection is made between the adapter and a 3174 control unit. Figure 1.2 illustrates a typical PC to mainframe connection using a 3270 adapter.

Software is run on the PC which emulates the LU function. The combination of this hardware and software allows the PC to look just like a dumb terminal to the SNA network. Most LU emulation software supports both CUT and DFT devices.

VTAM

VTAM stands for *Virtual Telecommunications Access Method.* VTAM is a software product that runs continuously on the mainframe computer. VTAM controls all the LUs and PUs connected to the host. When a user logs on to a mainframe application, the following things happen:

- The user types in the log-on request at a terminal. That terminal already has an LU associated with it. We will talk more about this LU to terminal association later.
- The log-on request goes to VTAM. VTAM interrogates the request and checks its validity.
- VTAM then tells the application that an LU at a certain address wants to log on.
- The application then initiates a VTAM bind request to the LU. In the bind request, the application tells the LU what types of communications parameters the LU must be capable of in order to perform the connection. For example, the LU may be able to display 132 columns of data on the screen at one time. This is called a *model 5 terminal.* If the application supports model 5 terminals, this will be reflected in the bind process.
- VTAM passes the bind request from the application to the LU.

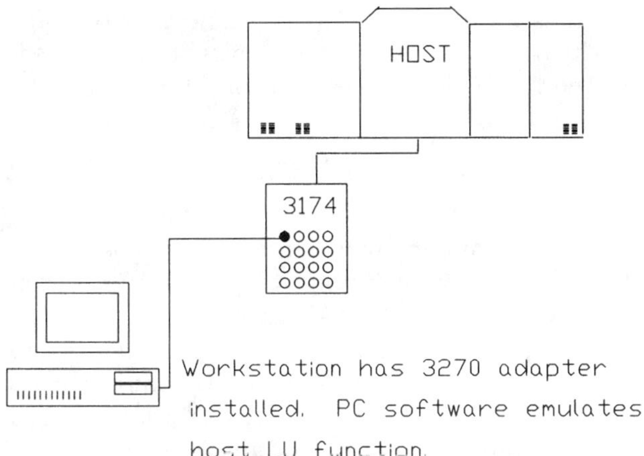

Figure 1.2 LU emulator connection.

- The LU looks at the bind request; and if the parameters are acceptable, the LU will accept the bind. At times the LU may reject the bind. This can happen if the application requires a model 5 display and the LU supports only a model 2 display.

VTAM has now established a session between an application program and an LU, as illustrated in Fig. 1.3. When the user logs out of the application, the LU will be available for another session.

You can think of VTAM as an old-time telephone operator sitting at a switchboard. Joe, the end-user, rings Sarah, the operator (VTAM), and tells her that he wants to talk to the Police Department (host appli-

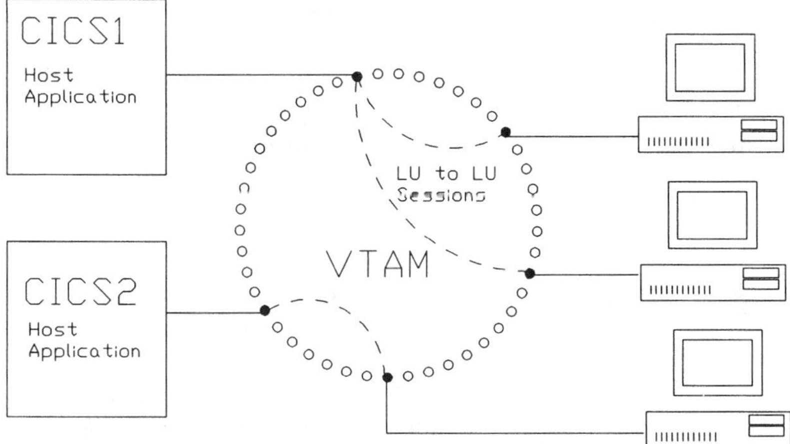

Figure 1.3 VTAM LU-to-LU sessions.

cation). Sarah (VTAM) rings the Police Department and says that Joe wants to talk to them. The police tell Sarah that they will talk to Joe if he will speak English (the bind). Joe agrees, and Sarah connects the two lines (LU-to-LU session).

VTAM configuration parameters

The mainframe systems programmer must define all the host's PUs and LUs to VTAM. This is done by modifying a VTAM configuration file, which, at most sites, is named SYS1.VTAMLST.

There are many configuration and tuning parameters in SYS1.VTAMLST. We will concentrate on the PU and LU definitions. As you recall, PUs control LUs. For example, the 3174 terminal control unit is a PU that controls multiple terminals and printers (LUs). Figure 1.4 shows an actual VTAM definition for a 3174 control unit.

Let's go through the main components of the PU and LU definitions illustrated in Fig. 1.4.

The first line tells VTAM that we are defining a *local* device named PUA60. Operators use the name PUA60 to control the device. They can manually activate and deactivate the entire device by using VTAM operator commands against the PUA60 name.

The second line defines the PU. The name A01A60 is associated with the PU. This can be any unique eight-character name. Most shops develop naming standards for all VTAM LU and PU names. The CUADDR parameter specifies the multiple virtual systems (MVS) address of the physical device. This device address is created by the MVS IOCP and MVSP system generation processes. The rest of the PU

```
PUA60 VBUILD TYPE=LOCAL
A01A60    PU    CUADDR=A60,
          DLOGMOD=M2SDLCQ,
          MAXBFRU=4,
          USSTAB=USSSNA,
          MODETAB=AMODETAB
A60002    LU LOCADDR=2
A60003    LU LOCADDR=3
          .
          .
          .
A60021    LU LOCADDR=21,DLOGMOD=S3270,SSCPFM=USSSCS
          .
          .
          .
```

Figure 1.4 PU and LU VTAM definitions.

definition parameters are used to specify tuning and default bind options.

The seventh line in Fig. 1.4 is a terminal LU definition. The name A60002 is assigned to the LU. The operator can use this name to activate, deactivate, and monitor the individual LU. The LOCADDR parameter specifies the 3174 port address assigned to this LU. The first port always starts with LOCADDR 2.

The last LU definition, A60021, is a printer LU definition. The methods used to define printers, terminals, and PUs vary from shop to shop. You should become familiar with your shop's standards before you add or modify VTAM parameters.

Network control program

The network control program (NCP) is a set of programs that run on the front-end processor (FEP) such as the 3725 or 3745. The NCP in conjunction with the FEP allows a user at one location to access resources running at another host computer. Figure 1.5 illustrates a typical 3745 NCP communicating with a remote site. Users at host 1 can access applications running on host 2, and users on host 2 can access applications running on host 1.

The FEP and NCP can also be used to provide access to the host resources to remote users without a central processing unit (CPU). This is done by using remote terminal control units, as illustrated in Fig. 1.6. A leased telephone line is established between the front-end processor and the remote location. The remote control unit is installed

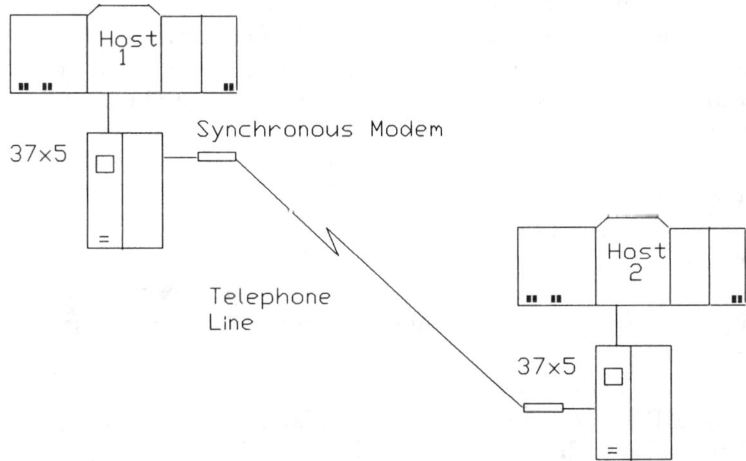

Figure 1.5 Connecting two hosts via 37x5 controllers.

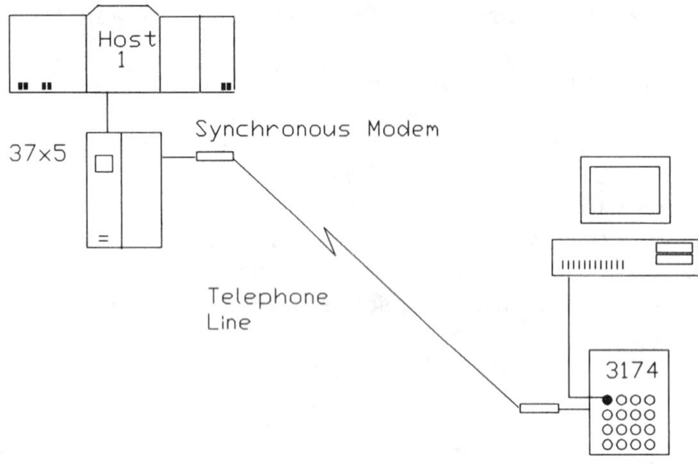

Figure 1.6 Accessing a remote site by a 37x5 controller and remote 3174.

at the remote site, and the telephone line is connected to it. Terminals are then connected to the remote control unit. The NCP, using the services of the front-end processor, will allow remote users to access the mainframe applications.

Mainframe to LAN Connectivity

As the evolution of the PC and local-area networks continued, products started appearing on the market which would allow LAN-attached workstations to access the mainframe without the need for a coaxial cable attachment to a 3174. These devices are known as *3270 gateways.* Two types of gateways are commonly used today: distributed-function terminal gateways and PU emulator gateways. The primary difference between the two types of gateways lies in the number of concurrent mainframe sessions they support. The distributed-function terminal (DFT) gateway can support only up to five concurrent sessions while the PU emulator gateway can support hundreds of concurrent host sessions.

The actual gateway is a PC connected to the host by using one of several methods discussed later in this chapter. The PC is also connected to the LAN by the appropriate network interface card (NIC) adapter. The client workstations run LU emulator software that communicates with the gateway PC software.

Most 3270 gateway products support both types of gateway connections, i.e., the DFT gateway and the PU emulator. Most gateway software packages also include the LU emulation software that must be run on the client workstations.

Distributed-function terminal gateways

A distributed-function terminal gateway allows users on the LAN to access the mainframe via a 3174 terminal control unit. The DFT gateway PC is connected to the LAN by the appropriate NIC adapter. The gateway PC also contains a 3270 coaxial adapter card. A coaxial cable is run from the 3174 control unit to the coaxial adapter on the gateway PC, as illustrated in Fig. 1.7. The software running on the gateway PC emulates a 3270 DFT and supports up to five concurrent host sessions.

The advantages of the DFT gateway are that

- The DFT gateway is simple to implement.
- The hardware costs are minimal.

The obvious disadvantages to the DFT gateway is the restriction to five concurrent mainframe sessions.

PU emulator gateways

Some 3270 gateways emulate a host terminal control unit, such as the 3174 shown in Fig. 1.1. These PU-emulating gateways can be connected to the mainframe in two ways: via a Token Ring network and via a 37x5 communications controller. The operation and functionality of these two types of gateways are almost identical.

Some of the newer PU-emulating gateways also support a method to emulate a mainframe PU while being attached to an Ethernet local-area network. This type of configuration requires the use of a special control unit such as the IBM 3172. The IBM 3172 connects Ethernet (or

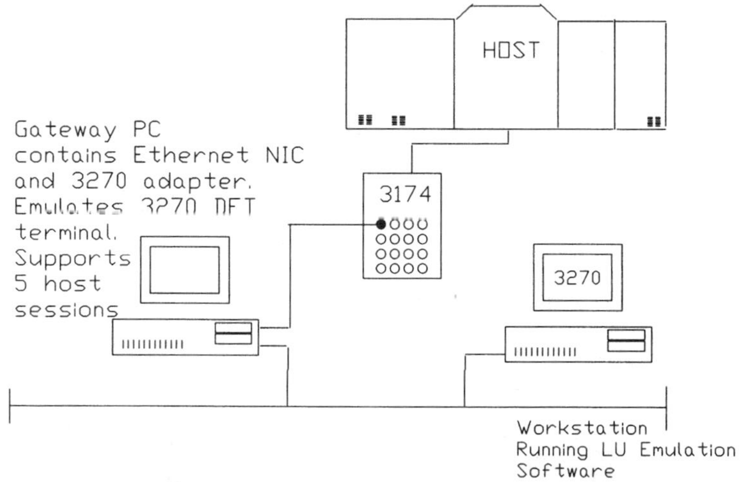

Figure 1.7 3270 DFT gateway.

Token Ring) networks directly to the mainframe in the same manner as the 3174 can connect a Token Ring network to a mainframe. Chapter 5 is dedicated to the IBM 3172 control unit and its functions.

37x5 connected PU emulator gateways

Connecting a PU emulator gateway to a 37x5 controller requires a synchronous adapter in the gateway PC and a pair of synchronous modems, as illustrated in Fig. 1.8.

The gateway PC runs software that emulates the SNA PU function and appears to the host as a remote 3174 control unit. Software is run on the client workstations on the LAN which emulate the host LU function. These LU emulators communicate with the gateway PU emulator to send and receive data from the mainframe.

The advantages of the 37x5 connected PU emulator gateway are as follows:

- The 37x5 connected PU emulator gateways support up to 128 concurrent host sessions.
- The host can be at a remote location, and communications between the modems can utilize a leased telephone line.
- The host can also be at the same location as the gateway, by using a null modem setup between the gateway and the front-end processor.
- Speeds of up to 64 kbits can be supported.

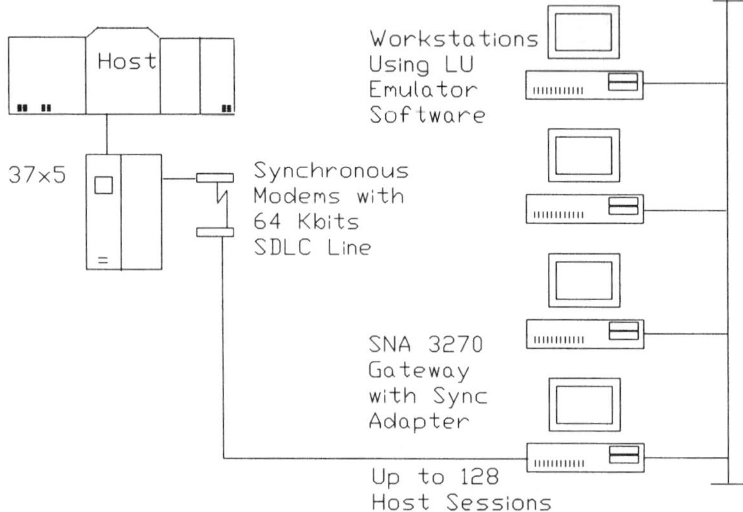

Figure 1.8 PU emulator 3270 gateway.

The disadvantages of the 37x5 connected PU emulator include these.

- It requires an expensive 37x5 control unit.
- It requires expensive synchronous modems.
- It requires an expensive synchronous adapter in the PC.

Token Ring connected PU emulator gateway

Connecting a PU-emulating 3270 gateway to a host via a Token Ring network involves a downstream physical unit (DSPU). The gateway PC emulates a local 3174 control unit and can support up to 128 concurrent host sessions. DSPUs are described later in this chapter. Figure 1.9 shows a 3270 gateway accessing the host as a DSPU.

The advantages of the Token Ring connected PU emulator gateways are that

- They support up to 128 concurrent host sessions.
- The speeds are as fast as or faster than those of terminals attached to local 3174 control units.
- The Token Ring connection provides very stable host access.

The disadvantages of the Token Ring connected PU emulator gateway are that

- They require either a 3174 or 37x5 control unit.
- They require a Token Ring network.

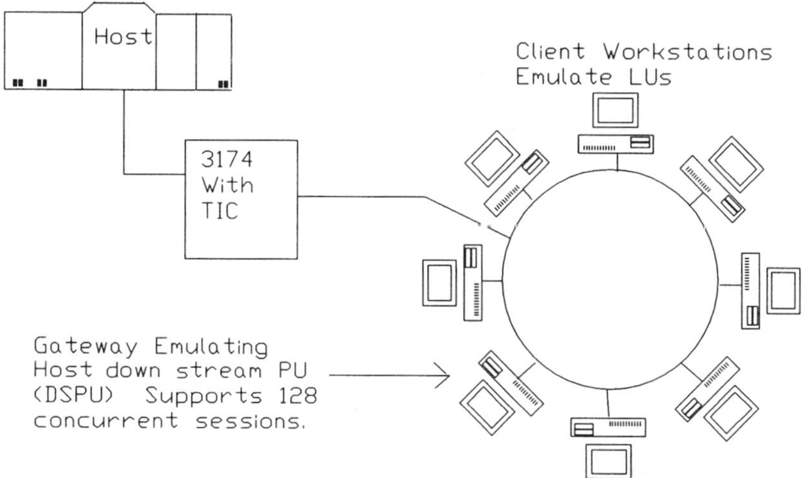

Figure 1.9 Accessing a host via a 3174 TIC connection.

Downstream physical unit

In an environment where the host connection is made by using a Token Ring network, the downstream physical unit method is used by both OS/2-CM/2 physical unit emulation and standard DOS PU emulation 3270 gateways. This is a very fast and reliable method for providing host access to LAN users. The DSPU method requires the installation of a Token Ring interface coupler (TIC) in a 3174, 3725, or 3745 control unit.

When a TIC is installed in a 3174 or 37x5 control unit, a group of downstream physical units are defined which are controlled by the TIC. These DSPUs are a critical component of mainframe to OS/2-CM/2 connectivity. The concept of downstream PUs is a little difficult to grasp initially. Let's take a look at how these DSPUs are used and configured to support OS/2 PU emulation.

The 3174 illustrated in Fig. 1.10 has an MVS address of 0A60. This address is specified in the MVSCP and IOCP configurations. The Token Ring address of the TIC is 400020101A60. This is specified in the 3174 customization, question number 900. This address must be unique within the Token Ring network. The address specified for the TIC is a *locally administered address* (LAA). Before we delve further into DSPUs, a clear understanding of locally administered addressing is required.

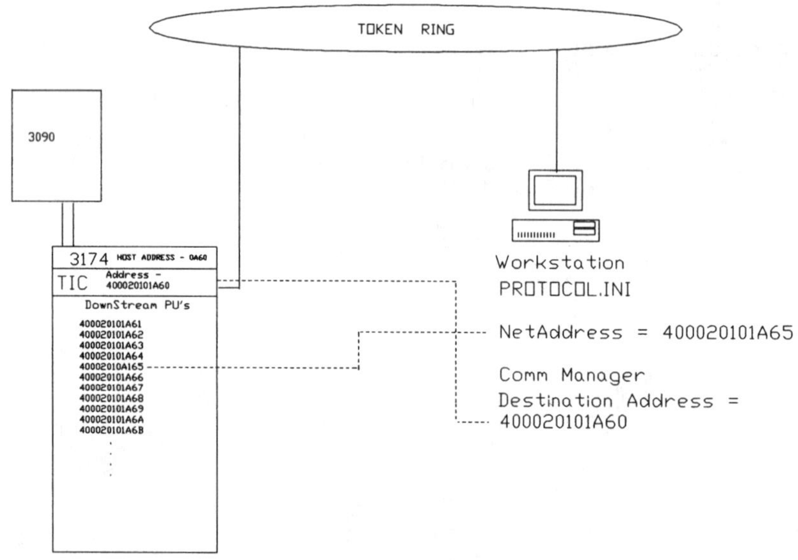

Figure 1.10 OS/2 workstation accessing a host as a PU.

Locally administered address

When you purchase an NIC adapter for your PC, the manufacturer assigns a unique, preset address. This address is "burned into" the chips. This manufacturer-set address is called a *universal address.* This address is used by the network to return packets to the correct PC. Although many network administrators use the universal address in their networks, methods exist to change this universal address. We will see later in this chapter that we must change the universal address of the NIC adapter in order to allow a CM/2 workstation to emulate a host PU by using the DSPU connectivity method.

You can change the address that the NIC presents to the network by specifying a locally administered address. Several methods can be used to set the LAA of a workstation. Communications Manager/2 uses the NetAddress statement in the PROTOCOL.INI file to set the LAA. Figure 1.11 illustrates how the LAA is set to 400020101A65 for an OS/2 workstation. The PROTOCOL.INI file is built by using the Network Transport Services/2 (NTS/2) configuration screens.

Each shop should develop standards for the assignment of LAAs. These standards should make the name meaningful for the network administrator. Refer to Fig. 1.12 for a sample LAA standard.

> **Suggestion** If you are already using locally administered addressing, you can configure your 3174 to use these addresses as its DSPUs. Thus you will not need to modify your current addressing scheme.

```
[PROT_MAN]
    DRIVERNAME = PROTMAN$

[IBMLXCFG]
 LANDD_nif=LANDD.NIF
 IBMTOK_nif=IBMTOK.NIF


[LANDD_nif]
    DRIVERNAME = LANDD$
    BINDINGS    = IBMTOK_nif
    Links       = 41
    Users       =  4
    Max_Saps    =  4
    NetAddress = "T400020101A65"

[IBMTOK_nif]
    DRIVERNAME = IBMTOK$
```

Figure 1.11 Setting the LAA for an OS/2 workstation.

Sample LAA Naming Convention

This sample LAA naming convention is a modified version of the convention in the "IBM Installation Guidelines for the IBM Token-Ring network Products", publication number GG24-3291-01. The LAA addresses conform to the following format:

4000 a bb cc ddd

Where 4000 is fixed

a = The station type
1 = 37xx gateway
2 = 3174 local gateway
3 = PC downstream
4 = 3174 03R/13R or 53R/63R DSPU

bb = Subarea number of VTAM

cc = Ring Number

ddd = Host Address

Figure 1.12 Sample LAA naming convection.

Making the TIC connection

When a TIC is installed on a 3174 or a 37x5 controller, the Token Ring addresses of the TIC's associated DSPUs are specified. For the 3174 controller this is done on customization question 940: ring address assignment. In Fig. 1.10 the first DSPU defined to the 3174 is Token Ring address 400020101A61.

To connect to the TIC and gain access to the host, we must *become* this DSPU. To become this DSPU in an OS/2-CM/2 workstation, simply code the DSPU address as our locally administered address during the Communications Manager/2 configuration. This will build the appropriate NetAddress statement in the PROTOCOL.INI file. We also must tell Communications Manager/2 that our destination address is the address of the TIC, in this case 400020101A60. The configuration of Communications Manager/2 will be covered in detail in later chapters of this book.

DOS 3270 gateway software can use this same DSPU method for becoming a downstream PU. The way in which the LAA is set is different for each PU emulation gateway package.

From the TIC to the host

How does it all tie together? When the 3174 is generated in MVS, a contiguous range of addresses must be configured in the host. These addresses will be used by the DSPUs. See Fig. 1.13. The host addresses are displayed in the lower left-hand corner.

In the example illustrated in Fig. 1.13, the actual 3174 is a channel attached to the host at address 0A60. Addresses 0A61 to 0A6B are generated for the DSPUs. These addresses are created by the MVS IOCP and MVSCP processes.

When the 3174 is configured, a set of DSPUs is defined. In the example illustrated in Fig. 1.13, these addresses are 400020101A61 to 400020101A6B. The first DSPU defined in the 3174 (address 40020101A61) will use the first host address after the actual 3174 address. So the DSPU at Token Ring address 400020101A61 will use host address 0A61. The DSPU at address 400020101A62 will use host address 0A62, and so on. See Chap. 2 for a more detailed explanation of the 3174 microcode configuration.

Figure 1.13 also shows the VTAM configurations for the actual 3174 controller and two of the downstream PUs. Notice how the CUADDR parameter relates to the host address.

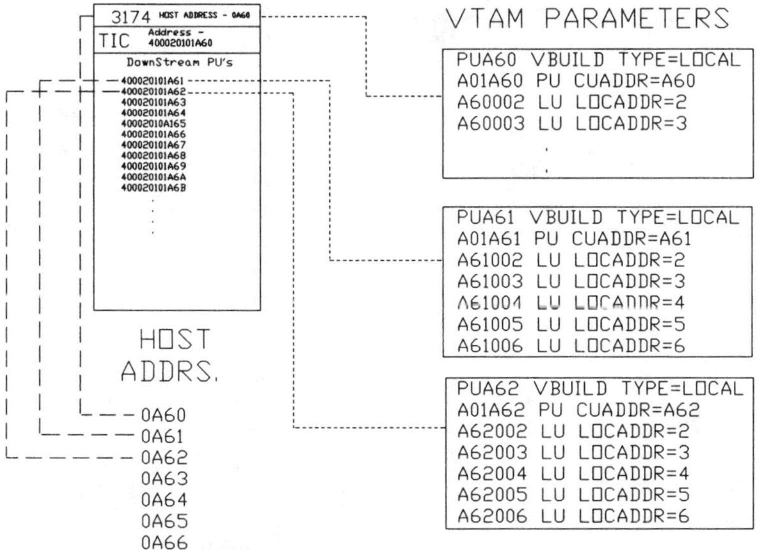

Figure 1.13 3174 TIC addressing technique.

The DSPU method for connecting to the mainframe on a Token Ring network can be used for both DOS and OS/2 gateways and for PU emulation on individual OS/2 workstations.

OS/2 SNA Components

OS/2 and Communications Manager/2 were designed to connect into SNA networks. Communications Manager/2 can present itself to the SNA network as either an LU (or multiple LUs) or a PU emulation gateway. CM/2 can also be configured as both a PU emulator gateway and multiple LU emulators within one personal computer. This type of configuration is a very reliable and flexible host connectivity option. All these options will be discussed in later chapters. Sample CM/2 and NTS/2 configurations will be provided for each of the major host connectivity options.

CM/2 LU emulation using a 3270 adapter

When Communications Manager/2 is configured as an LU or multiple LUs, the workstation must be connected to a PU. There are two ways to accomplish this. The simpler method is to install a 3270 emulation card in the workstation and to connect the card to a 3174 control unit (PU), as shown in Fig. 1.14. This type of connection works in the same manner as a dumb terminal connected to a host. You can define up to five host sessions (LUs) by using this method, if the terminal is defined as a DFT device. The user can switch between these sessions to access multiple-host applications concurrently.

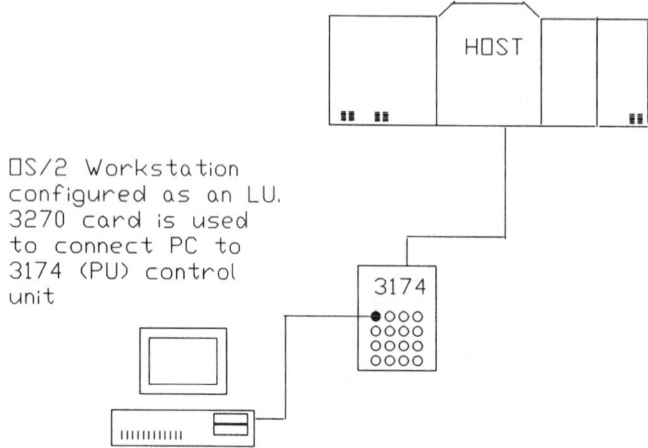

Figure 1.14 OS/2 accessing host as an LU by using a 3270 adapter.

CM/2 LU emulation using a 3270 gateway

Communications Manager/2 can also be configured as an LU or multiple LUs; but rather than using a 3270 adapter to connect to a 3174 control unit, it can access the host via a 3270 gateway.

In this scenario one OS/2 workstation is configured as the gateway (PU emulator), and that workstation can support up to 128 concurrent host connections. The workstations are configured as LUs and access the host via the 3270 gateway, as shown in Fig. 1.15. The actual communications configurations for this function will be illustrated in a later chapter.

The physical connection to the mainframe can be performed in several ways. Figure 1.15 illustrates a synchronous data link control (SDLC) connection via a front-end processor. The connection could also be made by using a 37x5 or 3174 TIC as illustrated in Fig. 1.16. The Token Ring 3270 connections will be discussed in detail in later chapters.

CM/2 PU-emulating workstation

In the example above, an OS/2 workstation is configured as a 3270 gateway. To perform this gateway function. Communications Manager/2 is configured to emulate the SNA PU (terminal control unit) function. Multiple client workstations are configured to emulate the LU function and access the host via the gateway PC.

Communications Manager/2 can also be configured to allow a single workstation access to the host by using this same PU emulation

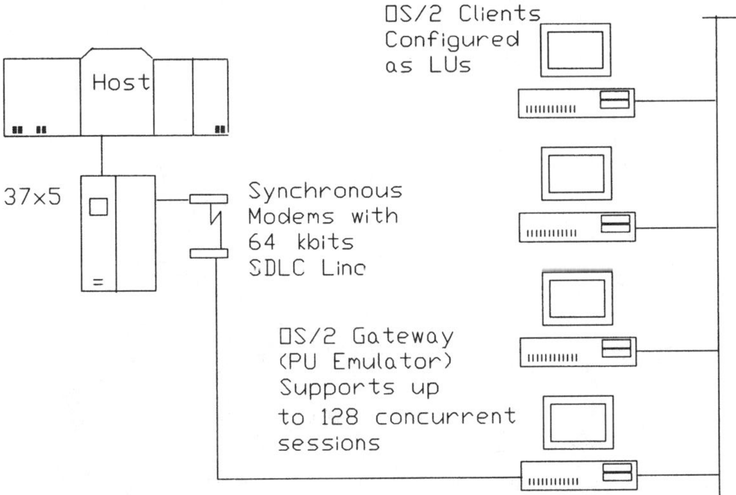

Figure 1.15 PU emulator 3270 gateway.

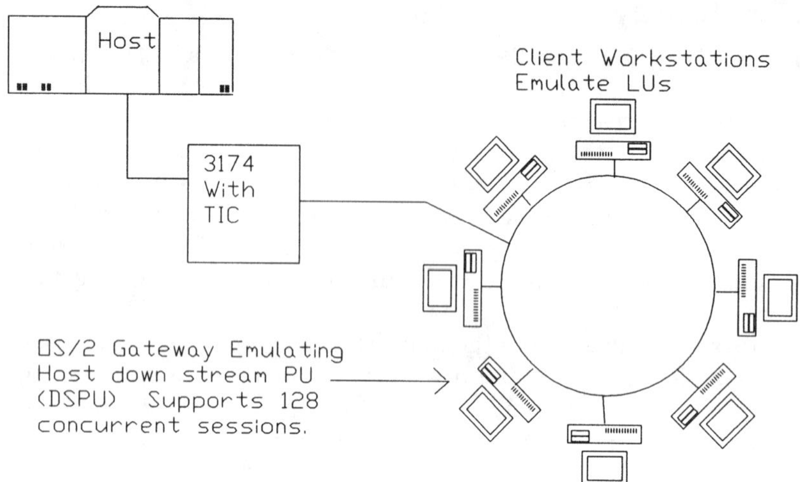

Figure 1.16 PU emulator gateway: accessing host via a 3174 TIC connection.

method. The only difference between this type of PU emulation and the gateway PU emulation is that there are no client workstations. The PC that is performing the PU emulation also performs the LU emulation. Figure 1.17 illustrates this configuration.

The user at the PU-emulating workstation can have up to five concurrent host sessions. The advantage of this type of configuration is that each user accesses the host by using a separate VTAM PU definition. This makes the VTAM configuration and troubleshooting much simpler.

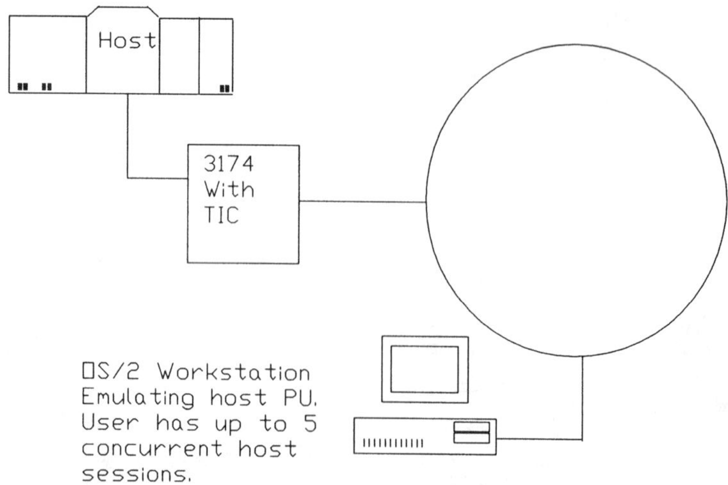

Figure 1.17 OS/2 PU-emulating workstation: accessing host via a 3174 TIC connection.

Conclusion

The world of SNA and its related components is very complex, and we have only begun to scratch the surface in this chapter. CM/2 was designed to work hand in hand with SNA and the new SNA routing architecture APPN. This built-in SNA support makes the implementation of CM/2 to host connectivity much simpler and much more reliable. As APPN evolves, you can be sure that OS/2 CM/2, and NTS/2 will play crucial roles in wide-area network connectivity.

Now that we have an understanding of the basic components of SNA and mainframe connectivity options, let's look more closely at the hardware that allows us to interconnect LANs with mainframe systems.

Chapter

2

3174 TIC Connection

The IBM 3174 control unit is a machine that was originally designed to control the access of multiple dumb terminals to the mainframe computer. Coaxial cables were used to connect these dumb terminals to the 3174. The 3174 would control the passing of data between the terminals and the applications running on the mainframe. When the Token Ring network evolved, the 3174 was upgraded to allow the Token Ring to connect to mainframe via the 3174. Using the 3174 communications controller to access a mainframe via a Token Ring network is very stable and reliable. This stability can be attributed to the facts that it has been around for quite a number of years and IBM developed both the 3174 and the Token Ring concept. Many sites already have 3174 control units installed for their terminals. When this is the case, using the 3174 to connect to the Token Ring network can be a very cost-effective solution. The 3174 supports both 4- and 16-Mbits/s Token Ring networks. The 3174 LAN connection supports only Token Ring networks. If you need to connect an Ethernet LAN to a mainframe, you must choose another connection method, such as the 3172 control unit. We will discuss the 3172 in Chap. 5.

The physical connection between the local-area network and the 3174 control unit requires several components. First, the 3174 control unit must be channel-attached to the mainframe. This provides the connection between the mainframe and the 3174. The mainframe operating system must be configured to recognize the 3174. In shops that use the MVS host operating system, this configuration is performed by using a combination of the Input/Output Configuration Program (IOCP) and the MVS Configuration Program (MVSCP). The IOCP configuration is used by the hardware control units, and the

MVSCP configuration is used by the host operating system components to access the various host peripheral devices.

To connect the 3174 controller to the Token Ring LAN, a Token Ring interface coupler (TIC) must be installed in the 3174. The 3174 TIC can be configured for either 4 or 16 Mbits/s Token Ring speeds.

Figure 2.1 illustrates a typical Token Ring environment using a Synoptics Token Ring concentrator. The 3174 is channel-attached to the mainframe by using standard mainframe bus and tag cables. In most installations, this channel connection is performed by the hardware vendor's systems engineer. The TIC in the 3174 is connected to a Token Ring module in the Synoptics concentrator. The LAN connection could also be made to a Token Ring multistation access unit (MAU) rather than to the Synoptics box. Other workstations and file servers that are connected to the Token Ring module, as illustrated in Fig. 2.1, are also part of the same Token Ring network.

Let's take a closer look at the components involved in the connection of the 3174 to the Token Ring LAN. Connecting the 3174 to a Token Ring LAN requires planning in the following areas:

3174 Model types

3174 Microcode levels

3174 Memory requirements

3174 Customization

IOCP/MVSCP configuration

VTAM definitions

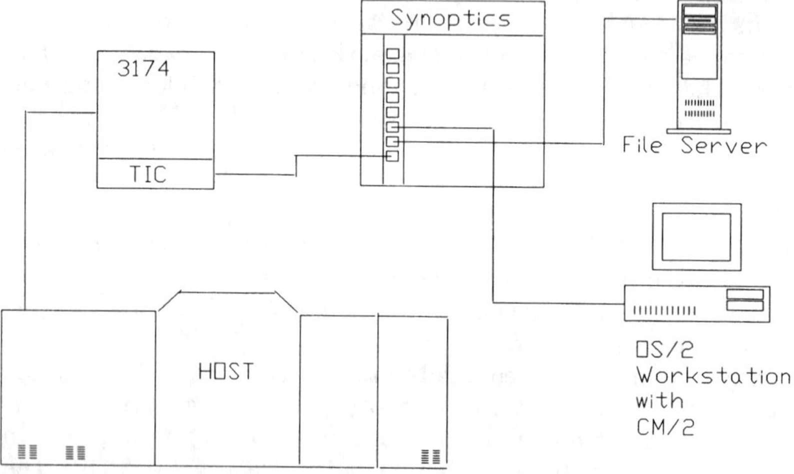

Figure 2.1 3174 connected to Synoptics Token Ring concentrator.

3174 Hardware Requirements

The 3174 TIC feature has several hardware requirements. Careful planning in this area will save you many headaches in the future.

Suggestion IBM published an excellent book on the 3174 Token Ring requirements, *Installation Guidelines for the IBM Token Ring Network Products,* order number GG24–3291–01.

Supported 3174 model types

There are many different 3174 model types. The 3174 TIC feature can be installed on several different models of both the local and remote 3174 control units. For local control units, the 1L and 11L models are supported. There are two major differences between them: capacity and performance. As with any computer device, the more speed and capacity you want, the more money it is going to cost you. Model 11L will allow you to configure more downstream PUs (DSPUs) than model 1L. Model 1L will support up to 140 DSPUs while the 11L can support up to 250 DSPUs. Model 11L will also provide better performance than the 1L model.

For remote-control units, the 1R/11R, 51R/61R, 2R/12R, and 52R/62R are supported.

3174 Microcode requirements

The 3174 controller utilizes microcode to control its internal operations. This microcode comes in several different versions, known as *configuration support levels.* The 3174 TIC feature requires either 3174 configuration support B or configuration support S. The configuration support that you need depends upon your requirements. To upgrade a 3174 to support a Token Ring network, you must order a hardware upgrade. This hardware upgrade is known as a *feature code.* You can order the TIC and the associated microcode by ordering one of two 3174 feature codes. These feature codes are numbers 3026 and 3044. The microcode that you need for your site depends upon the requirements of your LAN connection.

The 3174 feature code 3026 includes the following items:

- A Token Ring interface coupler that will support both 4 and 16 Mbits/s Token Ring speeds
- 3174 Microcode configuration support S
- An 8-ft cable to attach the TIC to a MAU

The 3174 feature code 3044 includes the following:

- A Token Ring interface coupler that will support both the 4 and 16 Mbits/s Token Ring speeds

- 3174 Microcode configuration support B or S
- An 8-ft cable to attach the TIC to a MAU

Suggestion Feature number 3044 with configuration support B will give better performance than using configuration support S.

3174 Memory requirements

The 3174 can be installed with many different storage amounts. The amount of storage required for the 3174 with the TIC feature depends upon the number of DSPUs to be defined in the 3174 customization. Additional 3174 features, such as the asynchronous emulation adapter (AEA), will also increase the 3174 memory requirements.

Suggestion IBM published a document entitled *Configuration Support B Storage Requirements.* This document shows how much storage is required for each 3174 feature. This document is available from your IBM systems engineer.

Figure 2.2 illustrates the storage requirements for a local 3174 with configuration supports B and S. (A local 3174 is simply a 3174 that is channel-attached to a mainframe.) These storage estimates do not include the storage required for other features that you may have installed on your 3174 control unit.

Figure 2.3 illustrates the storage requirements for a remote 3174 with configuration supports B and S. (A remote 3174 control unit is a 3174 that is attached to a remote mainframe by telephone lines.) These storage estimates do not include the storage required for other features that you may have installed on your 3174 control unit.

There is no easy way to tell if you are overloading the memory capacity of your 3174. When the memory is overcommitted, certain functions will cease. It is far better to install more memory than required than to risk running short of memory. The extra memory can always be used for future expansion.

Configuration Support S		Configuration Support B	
0 - 28 DSPUs	0.5 Mbyte	0 - 72 DSPUs	0.5 Mbyte
29 - 72 DSPUs	1.0 Mbyte	73 - 140 DSPUs	1.0 Mbyte
73 - 116 DSPUs	1.5 Mbytes	141 - 250 DSPUs	1.5 Mbytes
117 - 140 DSPUs	2.0 Mbytes		

Figure 2.2 Local 3174 memory requirements.

Configuration Support S		Configuration Support B	
0 - 72 DSPUs	0.5 Mbyte	0 - 28 DSPUs	0.5 Mbyte
73 - 140 DSPUs	1.0 Mbyte	29 - 72 DSPUs	1.0 Mbyte
		73 - 116 DSPUs	1.5 Mbytes
		117 - 140 DSPUs	2.0 Mbytes
		141 - 200 DSPUs	2.5 Mbytes
		201 - 250 DSPUs	3.0 Mbytes

Figure 2.3 Remote 3174 memory requirements.

3174 Customization Example

Before you can use a 3174 control unit, the unit must be configured. During this configuration process you tell the control unit what types of options are installed and what host address the 3174 may use. The remainder of this section will illustrate the customization required to implement a TIC and its associated DSPUs in a local 3174 control unit.

The following sample 3174 customization was performed on a local 3174 model 11L with configuration support B. The controller was channel-attached to an IBM mainframe at address A60. When configuring a 3174 control unit, you will be prompted to answer many questions. Each question has a question number associated with it. The 3174 customization planning sheets, which are provided with the manuals that come with your 3174, list these question by number. The 3174 manual explains these questions and their options in great detail. If you have never configured a 3174 control unit, you should thoroughly read the 3174 manuals before attempting the customization process. Only the questions which pertain to the 3174 TIC installation are illustrated in the example.

Question 100: 3174 Model designation

Answer: 11L

Explanation: This is the model type of the 3174. In this example, we are customizing a 3174 model 11L.

Question 101: Host attachment

Answer: 5

Explanation: The 5 specifies a local SNA controller.

Question 104: Control unit address

Answer: 60

Explanation: This is the hardware address of the 3174 control unit. This number must match the UNITADD parameter on the CNTLUNIT IOCP macro.

Question 105: Upper-limit address

Answer: 6F

Explanation: This is the address of the last DSPU to be defined in this control unit. In this example we are defining 15 DSPUs. The actual 3174 control unit will be using address 60, so we add 15 to 60 which equals 6F.

Question 900: Token Ring network address for the gateway

Answer: 4000 2010 1A60 04

Explanation: The value we enter in question 900 sets the locally administered address of the TIC. The convention used to assign this address is totally at the discretion of the user. Figure 2.4 illustrates a convention provided by IBM publication GG24–3291–01, *Installation Guidelines for the IBM Token Ring Network Products.*

In the answer to question 900, the ddd portion of the naming convention was modified to specify the host address number of the 3174 containing the TIC.

Question 905: Ring error monitoring (REM)

Answer: 1

Explanation: REM is a function of the Token Ring which allows the controller to accept error reports. This information is forwarded to NetView. A 1 enables the REM option and a 0 disables the function.

Question 908: Link subsystem name

Answer: TIC00A60

```
4000 a bb cc ddd

Where 4000 is fixed,

a is the station type
     1 = 37xx gateway address
     2 = 3174 local gateway

bb is the subarea number of VTAM or the NCP

cc is the ring number

ddd is a serial number
```

Figure 2.4 LAA naming convention.

Explanation: When alerts are sent to NetView, these characters identify the source of the errors.

Question 911: Ring speed

Answer: 1

Explanation: 0=4 Mbits/s with normal Token Ring release

1=16 Mbits/s with normal Token Ring release

2=16 Mbits/s with early Token Ring release

Please keep in mind that all devices on your token ring must be set to the same speed.

Question 940: Ring address assignment menu

Answer:

S	Ring address	SAP	T
60	4000 2010 1A60 04		
61	4000 2010 1A61 04	0	
62	4000 2010 1A62 04	0	
63	4000 2010 1A63 04	0	
64	4000 2010 1A64 04	0	
65	4000 2010 1A65 04	0	
66	4000 2010 1A66 04	0	
67	4000 2010 1A67 04	0	
68	4000 2010 1A68 04	0	
69	4000 2010 1A69 04	0	
6A	4000 2010 1A6A 04	0	
6B	4000 2010 1A6B 04	0	
6C	4000 2010 1A6C 04	0	
6D	4000 2010 1A6D 04	0	
6E	4000 2010 1A6E 04	0	
6F	4000 2010 1A6F 04	0	

Explanation: S is the range of host addresses which were previously defined with questions 104 and 105. The ring address is the 12-digit Token Ring address of each DSPU. The first row is the address of the TIC, and SAP is the service access point of the Token Ring devices. In SNA environments SAP is usually 04. Also T is the type of PU communication. A 0 should be specified for CM/2 PU emulation and CM/2 gateway access.

Question 941: Ring transmission definition

Answer:

S	Ring address	SAP	F	W
60	4000 2010 1A60 04			
61	4000 2010 1A61 04	2	4	
62	4000 2010 1A62 04	2	4	
63	4000 2010 1A63 04	2	4	

64	4000 2010 1A64 04	2	4
65	4000 2010 1A65 04	2	4
66	4000 2010 1A66 04	2	4
67	4000 2010 1A67 04	2	4
68	4000 2010 1A68 04	2	4
69	4000 2010 1A69 04	2	4
6A	4000 2010 1A6A 04	2	4
6B	4000 2010 1A6B 04	2	4
6C	4000 2010 1A6C 04	2	4
6D	4000 2010 1A6D 04	2	4
6E	4000 2010 1A6E 04	2	4
6F	4000 2010 1A6F 04	2	4

Explanation: The only columns that can be changed on this panel are the F and W columns. The value of W is always 2 and should not be modified. The default value for F is based upon your previous answers. There is no need to modify any of the values on this panel.

IOCP and MVSCP Definitions

Defining the 3174 and its associated DSPUs to a mainframe running the MVS operating system requires the customization of two configuration files. These configuration files are known as the Input/Output Configuration Program (IOCP) and the MVS Configuration Program (MVSCP). These configuration programs are used to tell both the hardware and the software components what types of peripheral devices are connected to the host. These configuration files consist of various macros such as the IODEVICE and CNTLUNIT macros. The IOCP and MVSCP definition macros can be combined into a single configuration file which is used for both the IOCP and MVSCP generation processes. The macro illustrations in this chapter contain all the parameters necessary to combine the two configuration files.

There are a few intricacies that must be followed in defining the 3174 and its DSPU to the host in order to prevent errors and achieve maximum performance.

Because of the special addressing requirements of the TIC, the 3174 must be defined to the host with an address ending with a 0, for example, A20.

Suggestion Each DSPU requires a separate host address. If you are planning to use many DSPUs or wish to expand the number of DSPUs in the future, you must make sure that a large, contiguous address range is available.

```
CNTLUNIT  PATH=(0A),SHARED=YB,PROTOCOL=D,
          UNIT=3791L,UNITADD=((60,16)),CUNUMBR=A60
```

Figure 2.5 MVS IOCP definition for a 3174.

The first configuration macro we must code is the CNTLUNIT macro. A CNTLUNIT macro must be defined for each control unit that is accessible by the mainframe. Several parameters are required on the CNTLUNIT macro which define the characteristics of the control unit and define how the 3174 is connected to the host.

Figure 2.5 is a sample CNTLUNIT macro for a locally attached 3174 control unit. The 3174 illustrated in Fig. 2.5 is attached to the host channel 0A as defined in the PATH=(0A) parameter. The SHARED=YB parameter specifies how some of the internal control blocks are accessed by the operating system. The value YB provides the best performance for 3174 TICs. The PROTOCOL and UNIT parameters should always be coded as shown in the illustration. The UNITADD=((60,16)) parameter tells the host that we are defining a TIC at address 60 with 15 DSPUs at addresses 61 to 6F. The CUNUMBR parameter specifies a unique address that the host uses to match the CNTLUNIT with the IODEVICE macros.

The next configuration macro we must define is the IODEVICE macro. Figure 2.6 illustrates a sample 3174 IODEVICE macro with 16 DSPUs.

Once the IOCP and MVS/CP definition files have been updated, special configuration programs must be run. These configuration programs use the definition files as input and create load modules for output. The system must be restarted to pick up the new configurations. The host system's programmer usually performs these generation processes. The entire process has been oversimplified in this discussion and should be attempted only by a trained professional. Mistakes in the generation process could cause the system's initial program load (IPL) to fail.

```
IODEVICE  ADDRESS=(A60,16),
          UNIT=3791L,STADET=N,
          CUNUMBR=A60
```

Figure 2.6 MVS IOCP definition for a 3174.

VTAM Definitions

Let's step back and see what we have defined so far. We have defined a locally attached 3174 model 11L control unit with the TIC feature. The 3174 is connected to the host at address A60. We have defined 15 DSPUs in the 3174 customization and in the IOCP and MVSCP configurations. The DSPUs will use host addresses A61 to A6F.

Now we must define the 3174 control unit and its DSPUs to VTAM. VTAM requires a VBUILD statement and a PU definition for each DSPU to be used. A VBUILD and PU definition for the native 3174 ports is also required. And LU statements are required for each PU definition. For more information on PUs and LUs refer to Chap. 1. Figure 2.7 illustrates a sample VTAM definition for the 3174 connected to the host at address A60.

We define the DSPUs in the same manner as we did for the local 3174 controller. Figure 2.8 illustrates the VTAM definition for the first DSPU. Notice that the DSPU uses host address A61 as defined in the CUADDR parameter. The additional 14 DSPUs would be defined using addresses (CUADDRs) A62 through A6F.

Once you have your 3174 and its associated DSPUs installed, defined to the host, and defined to VTAM, you are ready to configure Communication Manager/2 to access the host. There are several ways to do this by using the DSPU methodology.

Each CM/2 workstation can use a single DSPU to access the mainframe as a PU. This host connectivity is very stable and provides a great deal of flexibility for the network administrator. By having each user access the host as a PU, the network administrator can modify the host VTAM parameters for a given user, and these changes will affect only that user. Some of the VTAM changes that can be made involve the number of terminal and printer sessions defined for the user. The terminal types can also be modified to allow the user to utilize various

```
LSNA1A60  VBUILD   TYPE= LOCAL
PUA60     PU       CUADDR=A60,
                   DLOGMOD=M2SDLCQ,
                   MAXBFRU=4,
                   USSTAB=USSSNA,
                   MODETAB=AMODETAB
A6000002  LU       LOCADDR=2
A6000003  LU       LOCADDR=3
A6000004  LU       LOCADDR=4
                   .
                   .
                   .
A6000063           LOCADDR=63
```

Figure 2.7 VTAM definition for a 3174.

```
LSNA1A61   VBUILD    TYPE= LOCAL
PUA61      PU        CUADDR=A61,
                     DLOGMOD=M2SDLCQ,
                     MAXBFRU=4,
                     USSTAB=USSSNA,
                     MODETAB=AMODETAB
A6100002   LU        LOCADDR=2
A6100003   LU        LOCADDR=3
A6100004   LU        LOCADDR=4
A6100005   LU        LOCADDR=5
A6100006   LU        LOCADDR=6
```

Figure 2.8 VTAM definition for a 3174 DSPU.

3270 terminal types. For example, a 3270 model 5 device will display data 132 characters wide, while a 3270 model 2 will display only 80 columns of data. It is very common for a single CM/2 user to have one 3270 model 2 definition, one 3270 model 5 definition, and perhaps one 3270 model 4 definition. Chapters 9 and 10 show you how to configure a CM/2 workstation to access the host via a 3174 DSPU.

The DSPUs to the 3174 can also be used by a CM/2 gateway. The CM/2 gateway machine would be defined as a PU to the mainframe, and client CM/2 users would access the mainframe as LUs to the gateway PC. Chapter 8 will show you, step by step, how to implement the CM/2 host gateway function.

The 3174's DSPUs can also be used by other gateway products, such as the Netware SAA gateway or the RUMBA gateway.

Conclusion

The IBM 3174 is a very versatile networking component. It can control local and remote mainframe terminals and printers. An adapter known as the asynchronous emulation adapter (AEA) can be installed into a 3174 control unit which provides access to an ASCII host, such as a DEC/VAX. The AEA allows the end-user to access the mainframe resources on one session and access the DEC/VAX on another session. A hot key allows the user to switch back and forth. The installation of a TIC on the 3174 allows the mainframe to be connected to a Token Ring local-area network supporting both 4 and 16 Mbits/s Token Ring speeds. Yes, the 3174 is quite a versatile component.

Chapter

3

3725 TIC Connection

In this chapter we will discuss using the IBM 3725 communications controller to connect a Token Ring local-area network to a mainframe. Before we delve into the specifics of implementing the host-to-LAN connection, let's take a look at the history of the 3725.

The IBM 3725 controller is a front-end processor (FEP). The 3725 was initially designed to support remote 3270 mainframe users. These remote users could be connected to the 3725 in two ways. First, a special remote terminal control unit could be installed at the remote site. Dumb terminals are connected to the remote 3174 by coaxial cables. A leased telephone line then connects the remote 3174 to the 3725 front-end processor. The remote user could then access all the mainframe applications running on the host, just as if they were locally attached.

Second, the 3725 could be used to connect two mainframes together. This option requires that both sites have a front-end processor. The two FEPs are connected by a leased telephone line. With this type of configuration, all users can access the mainframe applications on both local and remote CPUs.

When IBM developed the Token Ring network, IBM saw the need to provide a connection mechanism between the mainframe and the Token Ring LAN. The front-end processor was chosen as the connection vehicle. The physical connection between the 3725 and the mainframe requires the installation of a Token Ring interface coupler (TIC) in the 3725 communications controller.

> **Suggestion** A word of caution. The 3725 TIC supports only 4 Mbits/s Token Ring speeds. If you require 16 Mbits/s speeds, you must use either the 3174 control unit with the TIC feature or the 3745 communications control unit with the TIC feature.

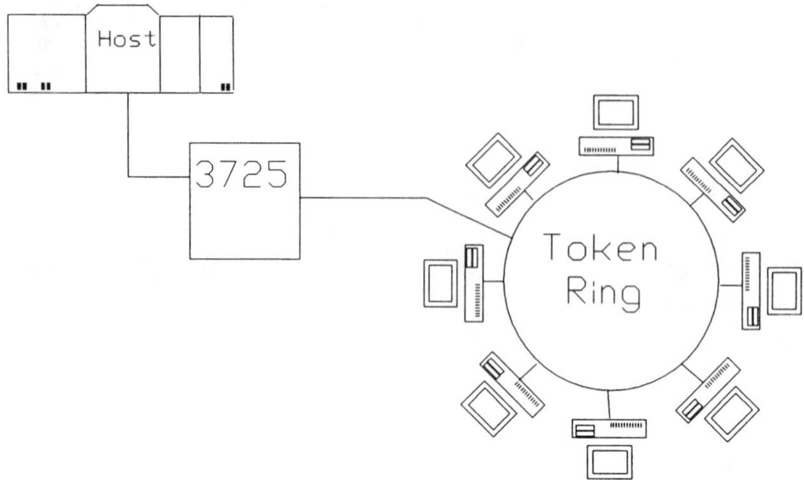

Figure 3.1 3725 Host to Token Ring connection.

Figure 3.1 illustrates a simple 3725 host-to-Token Ring network connection. The connection between the 3725 and the mainframe is made by using standard mainframe bus and tag cables. To connect the 3275 to the Token Ring LAN, a cable is run from the TIC to the Token Ring multistation access unit (MAU). If you are using a wiring concentrator, the cable is run from the 3725's TIC to a Token Ring card in the concentrator.

3725 Hardware Requirements

Installing a TIC in a 3725 requires the installation of several other 3725 hardware components. One of the main components of the 3725 is the line attachment base (LAB). There are several different types of LABs that can be installed in the 3725. The installation of the TIC requires a LAB type C in the 3725. The LAB type C is commonly referred to as a LAB-C. The IBM part number for the LAB-C feature is 4774.

When you order the LAB-C component, several items are included. The first component is known as the Token Ring network attachment subsystem (TRSS). The TRSS is comprised of a Token Ring multiplexer (TRM) and up to four Token Ring interface couplers. The TRM is used to control the various TICs that are installed with the feature.

3725 Microcode level requirements

The 3275 uses special software known as microcode to control its internal functions. This microcode is shipped with the 3725. The IBM systems engineer usually installs this microcode for the customer.

The microcode release levels are administered by using what are known as engineering change (EC) levels. As engineering changes are made to the microcode, the EC level of the microcode is increased. The 3725 communications controller must be running microcode EC level 873055 or higher in order to use the Token Ring network attachment subsystem. If your 3725 is not at this level, you should contact your IBM representative to have the new microcode loaded in your 3725 prior to installation of the TIC.

3725 Software Requirements

The 3725 requires a software product known as the Network Control Program (NCP). The NCP software consists of an assembler to which you feed special macros which define your Token Ring connection and other communications lines. The 3725 uses the NCP software to control the various lines and TIC connections established within the 3725. Items such as line speeds and priority are defined in the NCP.

In order to connect the 3725 to a Token Ring network, you must have NCP version 4 release 2 or higher.

NCP customization

After installing the TIC in the 3725, you must modify the NCP to tell the 3725 about the TIC. To perform the NCP modification, you must insert several NCP macro definitions into the NCP configuration file. The NCP uses a function known as the NCP Token Ring network interface (NTRI) to access the Token Ring network. We will discuss the macro modifications and additions that must be made to generate the NTRI support for the Token Ring interface.

The NCP OPTIONS macro

The first macro that must be modified is the OPTIONS macro. The NEWDEFN=YES parameter must be added to the NCP OPTIONS macro. Figure 3.2 illustrates how the OPTIONS macro should look with the NEWDEFN parameter added. Your OPTIONS macro may differ from the example, depending upon the configuration of your current 3725 controller.

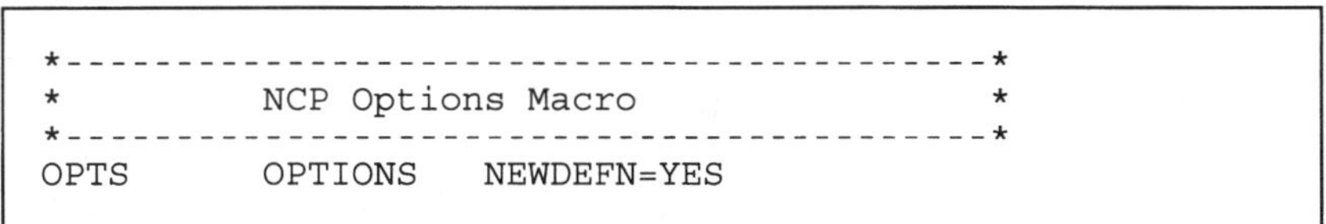

```
*-------------------------------------------*
*          NCP Options Macro                *
*-------------------------------------------*
OPTS       OPTIONS   NEWDEFN=YES
```

Figure 3.2 NCP OPTIONS macro definition.

The NCP BUILD macro

The next NCP macro that must be modified is the BUILD macro. Figure 3.3 is a sample NCP BUILD macro which includes the parameters required for the Token Ring network. Let's look at each of the parameters of the BUILD macro, shown in Fig. 3.3.

The LOCALTO parameter specifies the time-out value for the local Token Ring link. The default value of 1.5 should be satisfactory for most installations.

The MXRLINE parameter reflects the number of TICs installed. For the 3725 this number can be from 1 to 8. This number must match the number of physical line definitions coded in the NCP. We will discuss the physical line definitions later in this section.

The MXVLINE parameter defines the number of PUs that can connect to the 3725. This number must match the number of logical line definitions plus the number of lines generated by the Autogen utility. We will discuss the logical line definitions and the Autogen process later in this section.

The REMOTTO parameter defines the time-out value for the Token Ring link which is accessed via a bridge. The default value of 1.5 should be sufficient for most installations.

The NCP LUDRPOOL macro

The LUDRPOOL macro must be modified to reflect the number of concurrently active LUs. You should estimate the number of LUs that will be accessing the system from the Token Ring network and increase the NUMTYP2 parameter of the LUDRPOOL macro by this amount. Figure 3.4 is a sample LUDRPOOL macro.

Defining the TIC to the NCP

Now we must define the TIC(s) to the NCP. This is accomplished by using a combination of the GROUP, LINE, PU, and LU macros. Figure

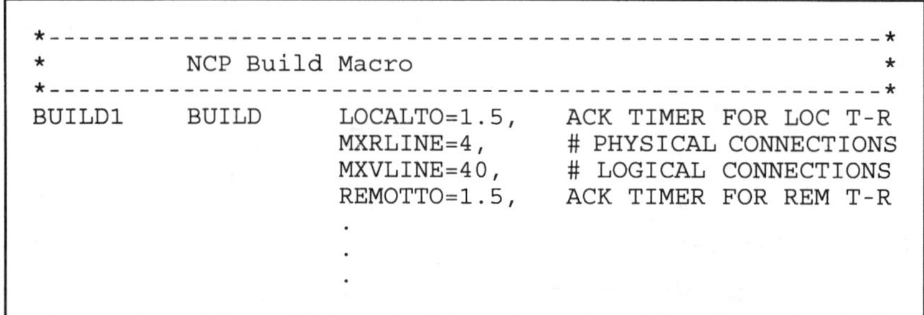

```
*-----------------------------------------------------*
*          NCP Build Macro                            *
*-----------------------------------------------------*
BUILD1    BUILD    LOCALTO=1.5,    ACK TIMER FOR LOC T-R
                   MXRLINE=4,      # PHYSICAL CONNECTIONS
                   MXVLINE=40,     # LOGICAL CONNECTIONS
                   REMOTTO=1.5,    ACK TIMER FOR REM T-R
                   .
                   .
                   .
```

Figure 3.3 NCP BUILD macro definition.

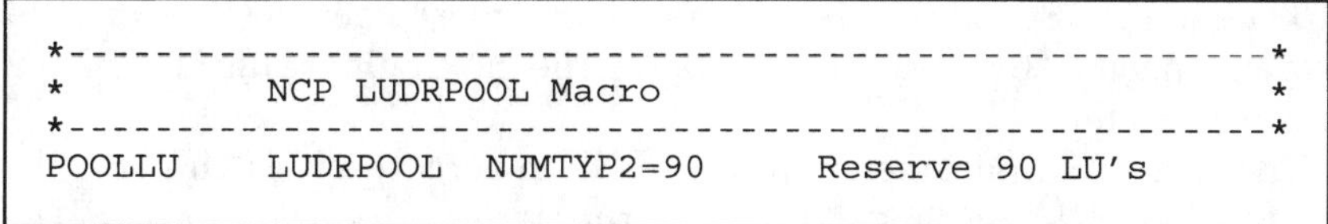

```
*------------------------------------------------------------*
*         NCP LUDRPOOL Macro                                 *
*------------------------------------------------------------*
POOLLU    LUDRPOOL  NUMTYP2=90      Reserve 90 LU's
```

Figure 3.4 NCP LUDRPOOL macro definition.

```
*------------------------------------------------------------*
*         NCP TIC DEFINITION                                 *
*------------------------------------------------------------*
TIC1GRP   GROUP     ECLTYPE=PHYSICAL

TIC1LIN   LINE      ADDRESS=(80,FULL),
                    PORTADD=0,
                    LOCADD=400001220000,
                    RCVBUFC=4095,
                    MAXTSL=1108

TIC1PU    PU

TIC1LU    LU        ISTATUS=INACTIVE
```

Figure 3.5 Sample NCP TIC definition.

3.5 illustrates a sample NCP TIC definition. Let's look more closely at the TIC definition.

Each TIC being defined must have a GROUP macro with the parameter ECLTYPE=PHYSICAL. This tells the NCP that you are defining a physical device (the TIC) attached to the 3725.

The next macro in the TIC definition is the LINE macro. The ADDRESS=(80,FULL) parameter tells the NCP that the TIC resides in the 3725 physical location 80. The values for this address can be 80–83, 112–115, 144–147, 176–179, 208–211, 240–243. The address you choose depends upon the physical configuration of your 3725.

The PORTADD parameter of the LINE macro can be a value in the range of 0 to 99. This number is used to connect the physical line and logical line definitions. The same value you specify for PORTADD should also be coded for the PHYPORT parameter on the logical line definition.

The LOCADD parameter of the LINE macro sets the LAA of the TIC. The LOCADD must follow the convention

4000abbbbbbb

where a is any number from 0 to 7 and b is any number from 0 to 9.

The RCVBUFC parameter of the LINE macro specifies the receive buffer capacity. IBM recommends using the maximum value of 4095 for this parameter.

The MAXTSL parameter of the LINE macro specifies the size, in bytes, of an SNA message known as the *path information unit* (PIU). For the best performance, 1108 should be specified.

Defining the DSPUs to the NCP

Each DSPU must be defined by using a LINE macro and PU macro. These macros must be coded beneath a GROUP macro with the ECLTYPE=LOGICAL parameter coded. The NCP generation process provides a method to automatically define your logical DSPU LINE and PU definitions. This process is known as Autogen. Figure 3.6 illustrates the definition of 10 DSPUs using the Autogen process.

The Autogen parameter of the GROUP macro tells the NCP compiler to generate 10 LINE and PU definitions for our DSPUs.

The CALL=INOUT parameter allows both dial-in and dial-out access to the host. This parameter is not applicable to the TIC, but it must be coded anyway.

The PHYPORT=0 parameter tells the NCP which TIC will support the DSPUs being defined. This value must match the PORTADD parameter for the physical definition of the TIC to be used.

Generating the NCP

After making all the required modifications to the NCP configuration file, you must run the NCP generation process to build the NCP load module. Examine the output of this generation closely, looking for errors and warning messages.

The last step in the NCP modification process is the loading of the new NCP into the 3725's memory. This is done by using the VTAM VARY ACT command.

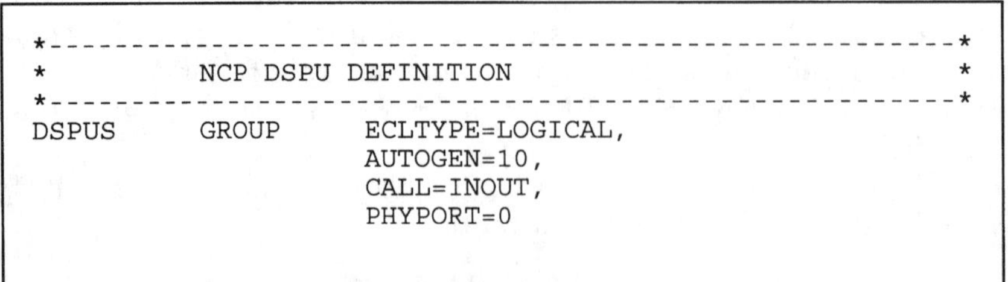

```
*-------------------------------------------------------*
*          NCP DSPU DEFINITION                           *
*-------------------------------------------------------*
DSPUS      GROUP      ECLTYPE=LOGICAL,
                      AUTOGEN=10,
                      CALL=INOUT,
                      PHYPORT=0
```

Figure 3.6 Using the NCP Autogen process.

VTAM definitions

After you have generated and loaded the NCP, you must define the DSPUs to VTAM. These definitions provide a means for the 3725 to communicate with the host communications program, VTAM. The 3725 accesses the DSPUs as switched PUs, and the definition of these DSPUs is very similar to that of SDLC switched PUs. Figure 3.7 is a sample definition of a 3725 DSPU.

The most important parameters in the VTAM definitions for DSPU connectivity are the DIALNO and GRPNUM parameters. The DIALNO parameter in the PATH statement tells the NCP how to find the DSPU. The format of the address is

```
DIALNO=xxyy4000abbccddd
```

where xx is the port number of the TIC (this number is defined by the PORTADD parameter) and yy is the service access point (SAP) of the workstation. For CM/2 devices, the SAP should always be 04. The remainder of the digits are the LAA of the DSPU. When we configure the CM/2 workstations, we will use this address in one of the configu-

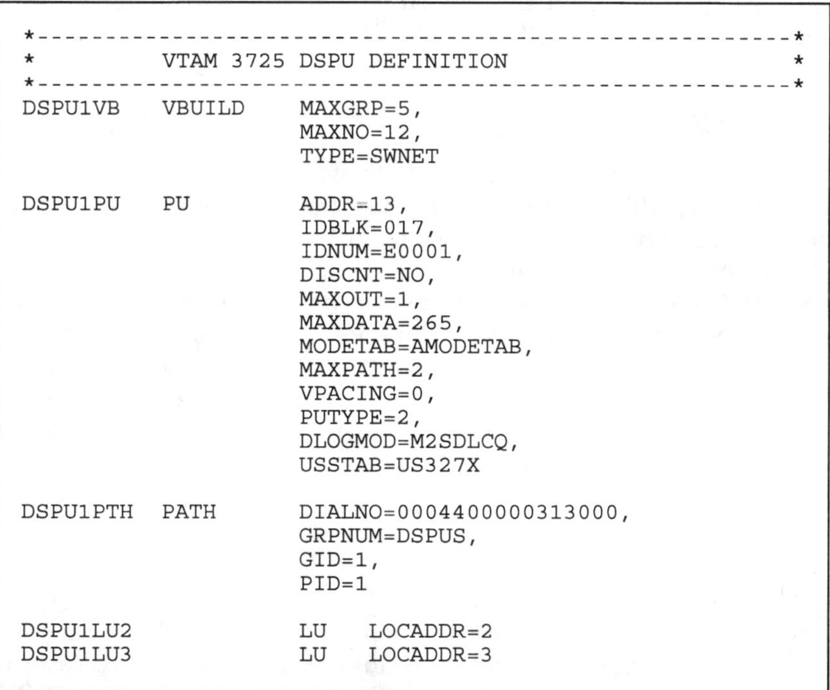

```
*------------------------------------------------------*
*          VTAM 3725 DSPU DEFINITION                   *
*------------------------------------------------------*
DSPU1VB    VBUILD    MAXGRP=5,
                     MAXNO=12,
                     TYPE=SWNET

DSPU1PU    PU        ADDR=13,
                     IDBLK=017,
                     IDNUM=E0001,
                     DISCNT=NO,
                     MAXOUT=1,
                     MAXDATA=265,
                     MODETAB=AMODETAB,
                     MAXPATH=2,
                     VPACING=0,
                     PUTYPE=2,
                     DLOGMOD=M2SDLCQ,
                     USSTAB=US327X

DSPU1PTH   PATH      DIALNO=0004400000313000,
                     GRPNUM=DSPUS,
                     GID=1,
                     PID=1

DSPU1LU2             LU    LOCADDR=2
DSPU1LU3             LU    LOCADDR=3
```

Figure 3.7 VTAM definition of a 3725 DSPU.

ration screens to access the host. IBM recommends the following format be followed for DSPU addressing:

4000 a bb cc ddd

where 4000 is fixed and

a = station type

1 = 37xx gateway

2 = 3174 local gateway

3 = PC type DSPU

4 = 3174 remote DSPU

5 = etc.

bb = subarea number of NCP or VTAM

cc = Token Ring number

ddd = serial number

The GRPNUM=DSPUS parameter tells the NCP where to find the GROUP definition for the DSPUs. The value for GRPNUM must match the name coded on the GROUP ECLTYPE=LOGICAL for the DSPUs.

The 3174 TIC versus the 3725 TIC

If you already have a 3725 and a 3174 installed in your shop, you may be wondering which box you should use for your LAN-to-mainframe connection. There are a couple of factors that you should investigate to help you make that decision. First, a TIC for the 3174 is less expensive than a TIC for the 3725. Second, keep in mind that the 3725 TIC can support only the 4 Mbits/s Token Ring speed networks. If you have a 16 Mbits/s Token Ring network, or plan to upgrade a 4 to a 16 Mbits/s Token Ring in the future, perhaps a 3725 TIC is not the wisest choice. The newer 3745 front-end processor can support both 4 and 16 Mbits/s Token Ring speeds. Chapter 4 covers the 3745 communications controller.

Conclusion

Now that you have all the hardware in place for your Token Ring-to-host connection, you are ready to configure CM/2. There are several ways you can configure CM/2 to access your host by using the DSPU methodology.

Each CM/2 workstation can use a single DSPU to access the mainframe as a PU. This host connectivity is very stable and provides a great deal of flexibility for the network administrator. By having each user access the host as a PU, the network administrator can modify the host VTAM parameters for a given user and these changes will affect only that user. Some of the VTAM changes that can be made concern the number of terminal and printer sessions defined for the user. The terminal types can also be modified to allow the user to utilize various 3270 terminal types. For example, a 3270 model 5 device will display data 132 characters wide, while a 3270 model 2 will display only 80 columns of data. It is very common for a single CM/2 user to have one 3270 model 2 definition, one 3270 model 5 definition, and perhaps one 3270 model 4 definition. Chapters 9 and 10 show you how to configure a CM/2 workstation to access the host via a 3725 DSPU.

The DSPUs to the 3725 can also be used by a CM/2 gateway. The CM/2 gateway machine would be defined as a PU to the mainframe, and client CM/2 users would access the mainframe as LUs to the gateway PC. Chapter 8 will show you, step by step, how to implement the CM/2 host gateway function.

The 3725's DSPUs can also be used by other gateway products, such as the Netware SAA gateway or the RUMBA gateway.

Chapter

4

3745 TIC Connection

In this chapter we will discuss using the IBM 3745 communications controller to connect a Token Ring local-area network to a mainframe.

The IBM 3745 communications controller, also known as a front-end processor (FEP), was designed for the large IBM mainframe shop that has many remote communications requirements. The IBM 3745 is a much more robust front-end processor than the older 3725 FEP. As with the 3725, the 3745 can be used to attach remote sites to the mainframe by leased and dial-up telephone lines. Again, just as with the 3725, the IBM 3745 can be used to connect two mainframes. When two mainframes are tied together by two front-end processors, the users connected to each of the mainframes can access the applications on the other (remote) mainframe, just as if those applications were running locally. Of course, the local applications would have a better performance response time.

The IBM 3745 communications controller can also be used to connect a Token Ring LAN to a mainframe. One of the primary differences between the Token Ring connections of the 3725 and the 3745 is that the 3745 supports 16 Mbits/s Token Ring speeds. The 3725 only supports 4 Mbits/s Token Ring speeds. To physically connect the 3745 to a mainframe requires the installation of a Token Ring interface coupler (TIC) in the 3745 communications controller.

Figure 4.1 illustrates a simple 3745 host to Token Ring network connection.

3745 Hardware Requirements

Installing a TIC in a 3745 communications controller requires planning in several areas, both in hardware and in software components.

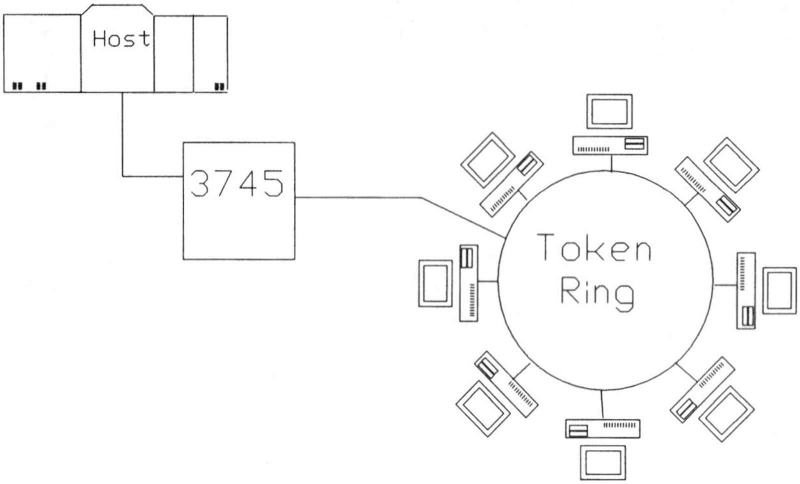

Figure 4.1 3745 Host-to-Token Ring connection.

First, let's take a look at the hardware features that are required to connect a 3745 to a Token Ring LAN.

The 3745 uses a Token Ring network attachment subsystem (TRSS) to connect to the Token Ring LAN. The TRSS comprises one to four Token Ring adapters (TRAs). Each TRA has two Token Ring interface couplers (TICs).

Before you order the TRA(s) for your network, you must determine the speed at which your Token Ring network is to run. If your network will be running at 4 Mbits/s, you should order a TRA type 1, feature code 4760. If your Token Ring network will be running at 16 Mbits/s speeds, you should order a TRA type 2, feature number 4770.

> **Suggestion** Your 3745 must have the TRA option installed in order to support the TIC installation. The feature code for the 3745 TRA option is 9763. Your 3745 can be upgraded to include this option if it is not currently installed.

3745 Software Requirements

The 3745 requires a software product known as the Network Control Program (NCP). The NCP software consists of an assembler to which you feed special macros that define your Token Ring connection and other communications lines. The 3745 uses the NCP software to control the various lines and TIC connections established within the 3745. Items such as line speeds and priority are defined in the NCP.

The TRA1 running at 4 Mbits/s Token Ring speeds requires one of the following NCP release levels:

NCP V5R1, NCP V5R2, NCP V5R2.1, NCP V5R3

The TRA2 running at 16 Mbits/s Token Ring speeds requires NCP V5R2.1 or higher.

NCP customization

After installing the TIC and its associated hardware components in the 3745, you must modify the NCP to tell the 3745 about the TIC. To perform the NCP modification, you must insert several NCP macro definitions into the NCP configuration file. Other macro definitions that are already defined in the NCP configuration will require some minor changes to provide support for the TIC feature. The NCP uses a function known as the NCP Token Ring network interface (NTRI) to access the Token Ring network. We will look at how the NCP macros must be added and modified to generate the NTRI support.

The NCP OPTIONS macro

The first macro that must be modified is the OPTIONS macro. The NEWDEFN=YES parameter must be specified on the OPTIONS macro. Figure 4.2 shows how the OPTIONS macro should look.

The NCP BUILD macro

The next NCP macro that must be modified is the BUILD macro. Figure 4.3 is a sample NCP BUILD macro which includes the parameters required for the Token Ring network. Let's look at each of the parameters of the BUILD macro shown in Fig. 4.3.

The LOCALTO parameter specifies the time-out value for the local Token Ring link. The default value of 1.5 should be satisfactory for most installations.

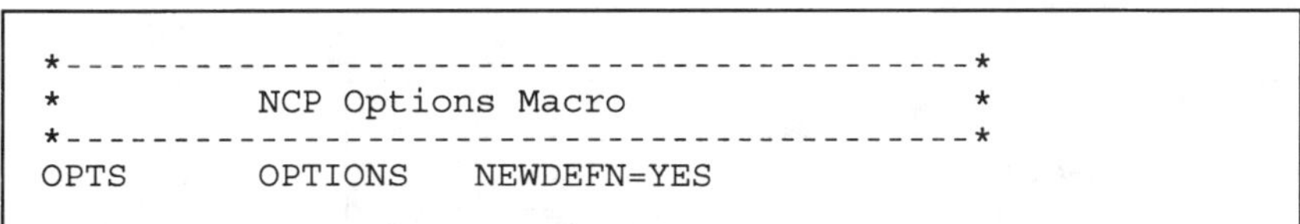

```
*-----------------------------------------*
*         NCP Options Macro               *
*-----------------------------------------*
OPTS      OPTIONS   NEWDEFN=YES
```

Figure 4.2 NCP OPTIONS macro definition.

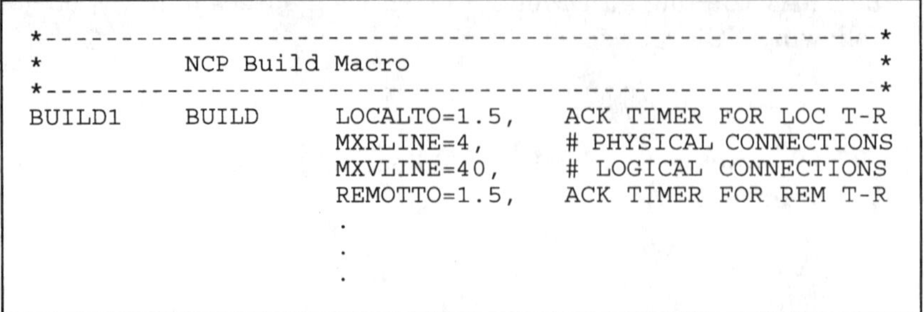

```
*-----------------------------------------------------*
*           NCP Build Macro                           *
*-----------------------------------------------------*
BUILD1      BUILD       LOCALTO=1.5,      ACK TIMER FOR LOC T-R
                        MXRLINE=4,        # PHYSICAL CONNECTIONS
                        MXVLINE=40,       # LOGICAL CONNECTIONS
                        REMOTTO=1.5,      ACK TIMER FOR REM T-R
                        .
                        .
                        .
```

Figure 4.3 NCP BUILD macro definition.

The MXRLINE parameter reflects the number of TICs installed. For the 3745 this number can be from 1 to 8. This number must match the number of physical line definitions coded in the NCP. We will discuss the physical line definitions later in this section.

The MXVLINE parameter defines the number of PUs that can connect to the 3745. This number must match the number of logical line definitions plus the number of lines generated by the Autogen utility. We will discuss the logical line definitions and the Autogen process later in this section.

The REMOTTO parameter defines the time-out value for the Token Ring link which is accessed via a bridge. The default value of 1.5 should be sufficient for most installations.

The NCP LUDRPOOL macro

The LUDRPOOL macro must be modified to reflect the number of concurrently active LUs. You should estimate the number of LUs that will be accessing the system from the Token Ring network and increase the NUMTYP2 parameter of the LUDRPOOL macro by this amount. Figure 4.4 shows a sample LUDRPOOL macro.

Defining the TIC to the NCP

Now we must define the TIC(s) to the NCP. This is accomplished by using a combination of the GROUP, LINE, PU, and LU macros. Figure

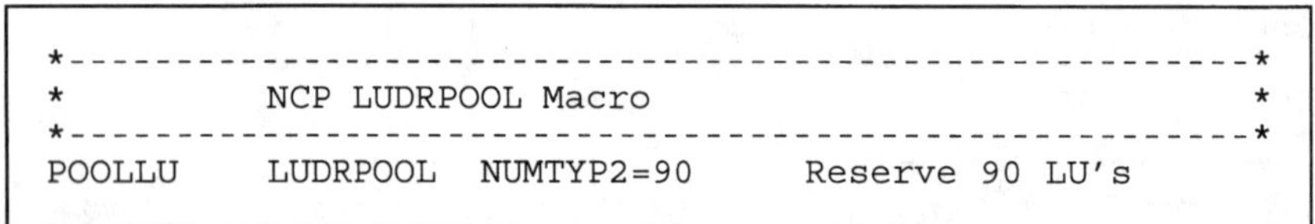

```
*-----------------------------------------------------*
*           NCP LUDRPOOL Macro                        *
*-----------------------------------------------------*
POOLLU      LUDRPOOL   NUMTYP2=90       Reserve 90 LU's
```

Figure 4.4 NCP LUDRPOOL macro definition.

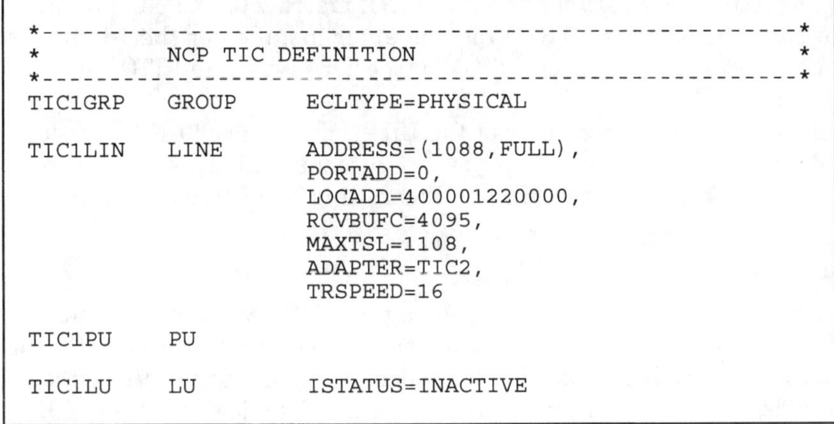

```
*---------------------------------------------------------------*
*          NCP TIC DEFINITION                                   *
*---------------------------------------------------------------*
TIC1GRP    GROUP      ECLTYPE=PHYSICAL

TIC1LIN    LINE       ADDRESS=(1088,FULL),
                      PORTADD=0,
                      LOCADD=400001220000,
                      RCVBUFC=4095,
                      MAXTSL=1108,
                      ADAPTER=TIC2,
                      TRSPEED=16

TIC1PU     PU

TIC1LU     LU         ISTATUS=INACTIVE
```

Figure 4.5 Sample NCP TIC definition.

4.5 illustrates a sample NCP TIC definition. Let's look more closely at the TIC definition.

Each TIC being defined must have a GROUP macro with the parameter ECLTYPE=PHYSICAL. This tells the NCP that we are defining a physical device (the TIC) attached to the 3745.

The next macro in the TIC definition is the LINE macro. The ADDRESS=(1088,FULL) parameter tells the NCP that the TIC resides in the 3745 physical location 1088. The values for this address can be 1088 to 1095. The address you choose depends upon the physical configuration of your 3745.

The PORTADD parameter of the LINE macro can be a value in the range from 0 to 99. This number is used to connect the physical line and logical line definitions. The same value you specify for PORTADD should also be coded for the PHYPORT parameter on the logical line definition.

The LOCADD parameter of the LINE macro sets the LAA of the TIC. The LOCADD must follow the convention

4000abbbbbbb

where a is any number from 0 to 7 and b is any number from 0 to 9.

The RCVBUFC parameter of the LINE macro specifies the receive buffer capacity. IBM recommends using the maximum value of 4095 for this parameter.

The MAXTSL parameter of the LINE macro specifies the size, in bytes, of an SNA frame known as the path information unit (PIU). For best performance, 1108 should be specified.

The ADAPTER parameter of the LINE macro tells the NCP whether we have the 4 Mbits/s TRA type 1 adapter installed or the 16 Mbits/s TRA type 2 adapter. Specify TIC1 for the TRA type 1 and TIC2 for TRA type 2.

The TRSPEED parameter of the LINE macro specifies the speed of the Token Ring network that you are attaching to. This value can be either 4 or 16, for 4 or 16 Mbits/s Token Ring speeds, respectively.

Defining the DSPUs to the NCP

Each DSPU must be defined by using a LINE macro and PU macro. These macros must be coded beneath a GROUP macro with the ECLTYPE=LOGICAL parameter coded. The NCP generation process provides a method to automatically define your logical DSPU LINE and PU definitions. This process is known as Autogen. Figure 4.6 illustrates the definition of 10 DSPUs by using the Autogen process.

The Autogen parameter of the GROUP macro tells the NCP compiler to generate 10 LINE and PU definitions for our DSPUs.

The CALL=INOUT parameter allows both dial-in and dial-out access to the host. This parameter is not applicable for the TIC, but it must be coded.

The PHYPORT=0 parameter tells the NCP which TIC will support the DSPUs being defined. This value must match the PORTADD parameter for the physical definition of the TIC to be used.

Generating the NCP

After making all the required modifications to the NCP configuration file, you must run the NCP generation process to build the NCP load module. Examine the output of this generation closely, looking for errors and warning messages.

The last step in the NCP modification process is the loading of the new NCP into the 3745's memory. This is accomplished by using the VTAM VARY ACT command.

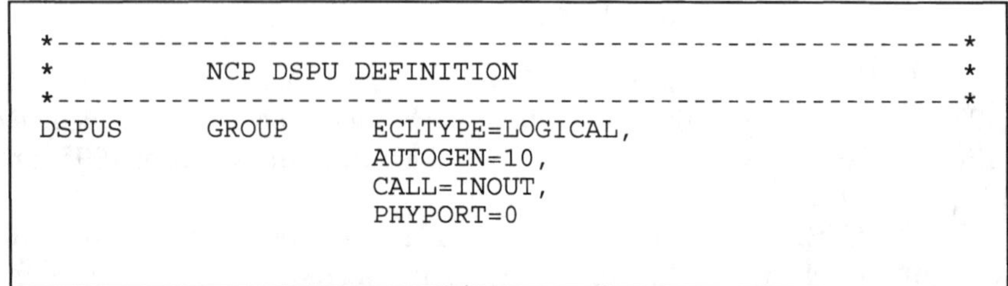

```
*-----------------------------------------------------------*
*          NCP DSPU DEFINITION                              *
*-----------------------------------------------------------*
DSPUS      GROUP      ECLTYPE=LOGICAL,
                      AUTOGEN=10,
                      CALL=INOUT,
                      PHYPORT=0
```

Figure 4.6 Using the NCP Autogen process.

VTAM definitions

After you have generated and loaded the NCP, you must define the DSPUs to VTAM. These definitions are required because they provide a means for the 3745 to communicate with the host communications program, VTAM. The 3745 accesses the DSPUs as switched PUs, and the definition of these DSPUs is very similar to that of SDLC switched PUs. Figure 4.7 is a sample definition of a DSPU.

The most important parameters in the VTAM definitions for DSPU connectivity are the DIALNO and GRPNUM parameters. The DIALNO parameter in the PATH statement tells the NCP how to find the DSPU. The format of the address is

DIALNO=xxyy4000abbccddd

where xx is the port number of the TIC (this number is defined by the PORTADD parameter) and yy is the service access point (SAP) of the workstation. For CM/2 devices, the SAP should always be 04.

The remainder of the digits are the LAA of the DSPU. When we configure the CM/2 workstations, we will use this address to access the

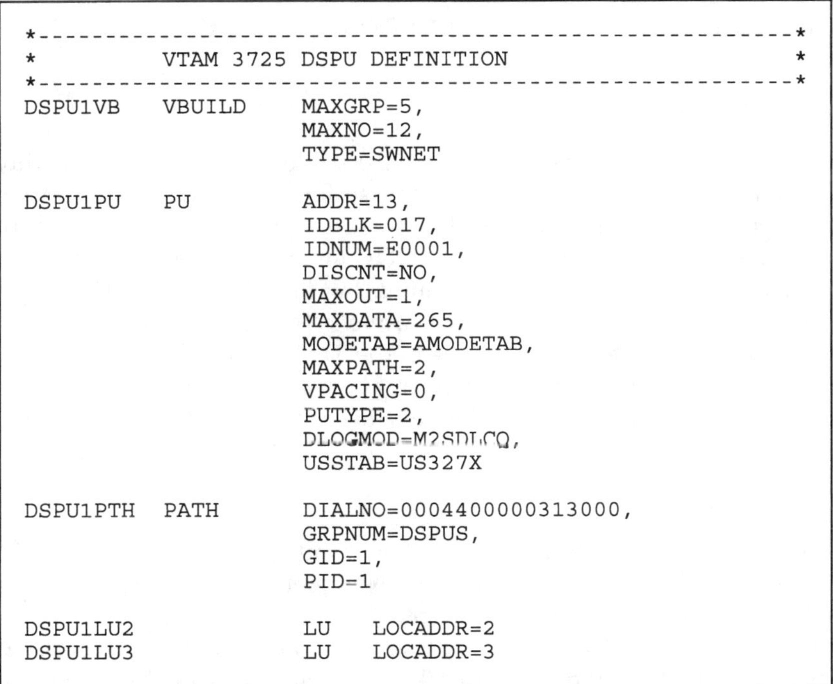

```
*-----------------------------------------------------*
*          VTAM 3725 DSPU DEFINITION                  *
*-----------------------------------------------------*
DSPU1VB    VBUILD     MAXGRP=5,
                      MAXNO=12,
                      TYPE=SWNET

DSPU1PU    PU         ADDR=13,
                      IDBLK=017,
                      IDNUM=E0001,
                      DISCNT=NO,
                      MAXOUT=1,
                      MAXDATA=265,
                      MODETAB=AMODETAB,
                      MAXPATH=2,
                      VPACING=0,
                      PUTYPE=2,
                      DLOGMOD=M2SDLCQ,
                      USSTAB=US327X

DSPU1PTH   PATH       DIALNO=0004400000313000,
                      GRPNUM=DSPUS,
                      GID=1,
                      PID=1

DSPU1LU2              LU   LOCADDR=2
DSPU1LU3              LU   LOCADDR=3
```

Figure 4.7 VTAM definition of a 3745 DSPU.

host. IBM recommends the following format be followed for DSPU addressing:

4000 a bb cc ddd

where 4000 is fixed and

a = station type

1 = 37xx gateway

2 = 3174 local gateway

3 = PC type DSPU

4 = 3174 remote DSPU

5 = etc.

bb = subarea number of NCP or VTAM

cc = Token Ring number

ddd = serial number

The GRPNUM=DSPUS parameter tells the NCP where to find the GROUP definition for the DSPUs. The value for GRPNUM must match the name coded on the GROUP ECLTYPE=LOGICAL for the DSPUs.

The 3174 TIC Versus the 3745 TIC

If you already have a 3745 and a 3174 installed in your shop, you may be wondering which box you should use for your LAN-to-mainframe connection. There are a couple of factors that you should investigate to help you with that decision. First, a TIC for the 3174 is less expensive than a TIC for the 3745. Keep in mind that both the 3174 TIC and the 3745 TIC support both 4 and 16 Mbits/s Token Ring speeds. Many shops will purchase both TICs, one in the 3745 and one in the 3174. The 3745 is used as the primary Token Ring connection. If a hardware error occurs, the 3174 TIC is enabled to take over the work of the failing TIC.

The 3745 TIC Versus the 3725 TIC

The 3725 is an older box, and it supports only Token Ring speeds of 4 Mbits/s. New enhancements for the NCP software that runs on the 3725 are no longer made. IBM implements these NCP enhancements only for the 3745. If you are in the position of deciding between utilizing a 3725 and a 3745, you must keep the above two points in mind. While the 3725 is substantially cheaper than the 3745 (you can obtain the 3725 only on the used market), its lack of functionality and the 4 Mbits/s Token Ring restriction may make the 3725 a poor choice for your application.

Conclusion

Now that you have all the hardware in place for your Token Ring-to-host connection, you are ready to configure CM/2. There are several ways you can configure CM/2 to access your host by using the DSPU methodology.

Each CM/2 workstation can use a single DSPU to access the mainframe as a PU. This host connectivity is very stable and provides a great deal of flexibility for the network administrator. By having each user access the host as a PU, the network administrator can modify the host VTAM parameters for a given user and these changes will affect only that user. Some of the VTAM changes that can be made concern the number of terminal and printer sessions defined for the user. The terminal types can also be modified to allow the user to utilize various 3270 terminal types. For example, a 3270 model 5 device will display data 132 characters wide, while a 3270 model 2 will display only 80 columns of data. It is very common for a single CM/2 user to have one 3270 model 2 definition, one 3270 model 5 definition, and perhaps one 3270 model 4 definition. Chapters 9 and 10 show you how to configure a CM/2 workstation to access the host via a 3725 DSPU.

The DSPUs to the 3745 can also be used by a CM/2 gateway. The CM/2 gateway machine would be defined as a PU to the mainframe, and client CM/2 users would access the mainframe as LUs to the gateway PC. Chapter 8 will show you, step by step, how to implement the CM/2 host gateway function.

The 3745's DSPUs can also be used by other gateway products, such as the Netware SAA gateway or the RUMBA gateway.

Chapter

5

IBM 3172 Interconnect Controller

Providing host access to workstations connected to local area networks is one of the first goals that large corporations set when integrating LANs into the corporate mainstream. Many sites fall into the trap of implementing Token Ring LANs, just to make the host connectivity simpler and more reliable.

Token Ring network components, including NIC adapters and concentrator cards, are much more expensive than comparable Ethernet adapters. In many instances Token Ring networking components are two or three times more expensive than comparable Ethernet networking components. Implementing large Token Ring networks just to make host access simpler is a costly decision. There are some valid reasons for implementing Token Ring networks. Token Ring, by its design, can provide more consistent response times under high-volume loads. At the time of this writing, Token Ring networks can attain a capacity of 16 Mbits/s while Ethernet is still at the 10 Mbits/s bandwidth. However, network component designers are currently working on 100 Mbits/s Ethernet devices, and these devices should be available in the very near future.

Rather than implementing corporatewide Token Ring networks, many companies have chosen to install a small Token Ring network to access the host resources and then implement bridges and routers to link to corporatewide Ethernet segments. While this type of network can be less expensive than pure Token Ring networks, the added cost and complexity of the routers and bridges can, in certain configurations, all but negate this cost savings. If your organization already owns a state-of-the-art router, or has plans to purchase a router for a wide-area network (WAN) configuration, then this type of mixed-topology network may be a good choice. The case for the mixed-topology solution can be made even stronger if your organization already has a 3174 controller or a 3725 or 3745 front-end processor in which a Token Ring interface adapter can be installed to provide the Token Ring to mainframe connectivity. If you are planning to implement a mixed-topology network using OS/2-CM/2 workstations, please read Chap. 6, Bridges and Routers. There are some special considerations related to bridging that must be addressed in order to make a mixed-topology network operate correctly.

Many organizations are opting to implement pure Ethernet networks. The IBM 3172 Interconnect Controller simplifies and stabilizes the mainframe connection to Ethernet networks. Large Ethernet networks can access host resources directly by using the 3172, without the need for an intermediate Token Ring local-area network. The cost and complexity of the network can be greatly reduced by using the 3172 Interconnect Controller.

The Hardware

The IBM 3172 Interconnect Controller is a hardware device that allows workstations attached to Ethernet or Token Ring LANs to access IBM mainframes. The 3172 operates in much the same manner as a 3174 or 37x5 controller with a TIC attachment. Downstream PUs are defined to the 3172 and VTAM. The workstations then access the host as one of these DSPUs. Each LAN adapter in the 3172 can support up to 256 DSPUs. The actual 3172 is a microchannel 80386 or 80486 based machine.

Host connection

Access to IBM mainframes is accomplished in one of three ways: via a T1 teleprocessing adapter, a parallel-channel adapter, or an ESCON channel adapter.

Figure 5.1 illustrates a 3172 Interconnect Controller accessing a host using a parallel-channel adapter. The parallel-channel adapter and the ESCON channel adapters operate in the same manner, except that the ESCON adapter supports ESCON, the new IBM channel architecture which uses fiber optics to transfer data. The channel adapter is a card which is installed in the 3172. Channel cables are then connected from the adapter to the mainframe.

The T1 adapter allows you to connect the 3172 to a remote host via a T1 telephone link. This configuration provides a method to establish a wide-area link to remote mainframe resources.

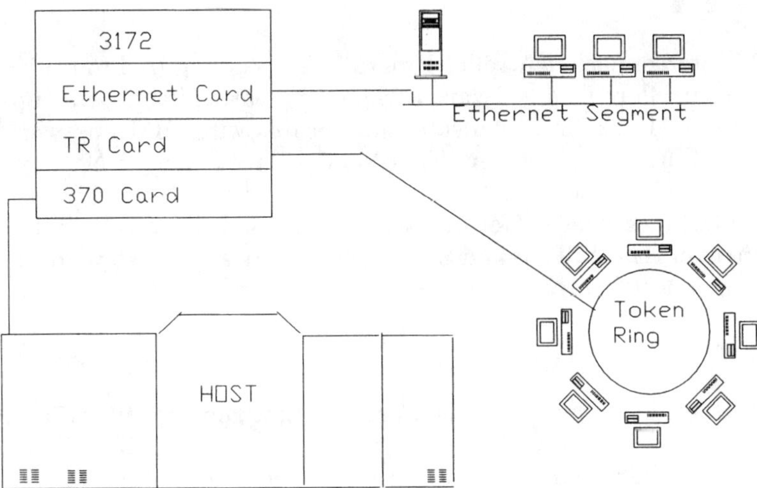

Figure 5.1 3172 interconnect controller.

LAN connection

The 3172 supports Ethernet, Token Ring, and FDDI local-area network connections. Each of these LAN types requires the installation of the appropriate LAN adapter card in the 3172. A maximum of four LAN adapter cards can be installed in the 3172. You can mix LAN adapter types; e.g., you can install one Token Ring adapter and three Ethernet adapters in a single 3172 controller.

Ethernet connection

To provide an Ethernet to host connection using a 3172, you must install an Ethernet adapter in the 3172 controller, as well as one of the host adapters discussed previously. The Ethernet adapter supports the IEEE 802.3 protocol as well as the Ethernet version 2 protocol.

Token Ring connection

The 3172 Token Ring adapter conforms to the 802.5 architecture and supports both 4 and 16 Mbits/s Token Ring data rates.

FDDI adapter

The 3172 model 3 controller supports the attachment to an FDDI network by using the 3172 FDDI adapter. The 3172 supports a maximum of one FDDI adapter per unit. The 3172 model 3 with the TCP/IP off-load product is required for FDDI support. The TCP/IP off-load facility is discussed later in this chapter.

3172 Software

The 3172 Interconnect Controller Program (ICP) is required to utilize the 3172 controller. This software controls the various adapters supported by the 3172. The ICP also communicates with IBM's network management program, NetView. This NetView link allows a NetView operator to initialize the 3172 from a NetView console. The 3172 also forwards alert messages to NetView when error conditions occur on the 3172 controller. The TCP/IP and SNA protocols are supported with the 3172 Interconnect Controller Program.

TCP/IP off-load

The TCP/IP off-load application is a product that runs on the 3172 in place of the Interconnect Controller Program. The TCP/IP off-load application is an OS/2-based program that off-loads some of the TCP/IP processing from the host, onto the 3172. FDDI, Token Ring, and Ethernet LANs are supported with the TCP/IP off-load product; however, only the TCP/IP protocol is supported. Since TCP/IP is the only protocol supported, you must run the host TCP/IP product in order to access host resources using the TCP/IP off-load product.

3172 Operator Facility/2

The 3172 Operator Facility/2 is a software product that assists users in installing, monitoring, and controlling the 3172 Interconnect Controller. This program can monitor up to sixteen 3172 controllers.

Host Software

The 3172 controller requires that VTAM version 3.4, or higher, run in the host. VTAM is a communications package that controls the downstream PUs associated with the 3172. You should also make sure that your VTAM software is at a relatively current maintenance level. This precaution could help to prevent problems during your implementation phase.

CM/2 Configuration Requirements

The CM/2 configuration for host access using a 3172 controller is accomplished in the same manner as a 3174 or 37x5 host connection. As with the 3174 and 37x5 connections, host access can be accomplished in two ways: each workstation can access the host as a PU, or a gateway PC can be established.

To access the host as a PU, the CM/2 workstation simply assumes the address of one of the DSPUs defined to the 3172. This is done by setting the CM/2 workstation's LAA to match one of the 3172's DSPU addresses. If you choose to implement the DSPU method for each CM/2 workstation, you should follow the 3174 or 37x5 CM/2 configuration examples in this book.

You can also use the CM/2 gateway function to connect workstations to the host via a 3172 controller. The CM/2 gateway function allows one CM/2 workstation to act as a control unit to the client CM/2 workstations. The gateway PC accesses the host as a PU, using one of the 3172's DSPUs. The client workstations then act as LUs to the gateway PC. See Chap. 8 on the CM/2 gateway function. You can follow the example in Chap. 8 if you wish to implement the gateway host access method using the 3172.

Conclusion

The IBM 3172 Interconnect Controller is the perfect solution to providing host to Ethernet LAN connectivity. Using the 3172, an organization can implement campuswide Ethernet workstations and can realize a substantial cost savings. Companies are no longer required to install small Token Ring networks just to provide host access. The components within the 3172 controller are quite impressive. The 3172 host module was used by the IBM LANRES product. LANRES allows Netware local-area networks to use mainframe disk drive for LAN data. Ethernet will probably become even more dominant when the 100 Mbits/s Ethernet components hit the market. The 3172 will help network designers take full advantage of the Ethernet network.

Chapter

6

Bridges and Routers

Many corporate MIS departments are facing the challenge of integrating SNA traffic with departmental or corporatewide local-area networks. When LANs first began infiltrating the corporate walls, dual networks were constructed, one for SNA traffic and one for LAN traffic. It was not uncommon for a user to have both a mainframe terminal and a LAN-connected PC at his or her desk. I visited one site where the poor users had four separate terminals at the station with four separate printers, each supporting a different system using separate network cabling systems. The days of the dual-network infrastructures are gone. A single wire connected at the end-user's workstation should be able to provide access to every hardware platform in the corporation, be it a mainframe, a minicomputer, or a file server.

For a single wire to support multiple hardware and software platforms, a network must be developed that supports the different protocols used by these various systems. A protocol is simply a set of rules that computers follow to communicate with each other. Different computers use different protocols. The design and deployment of this multiprotocol network are an extremely complicated undertaking. Not only must you support all the current hardware platforms and the communications protocols they utilize, but also you must be prepared to easily expand the network to support new hardware, software, and the protocols that these components utilize.

When a network grows with the addition of new users, the traffic on the network increases accordingly. To increase the capacity of the network, bridges and routers are used to split the network into multiple segments. Bridges and routers are also used to extend the network to remote sites.

Choosing a router or bridge is a very important step in the design of your network. The bridge or router must be capable of supporting all the current and planned communications protocols. Now think about this. How can you be expected to plan for the routing of communications protocols that have not even been developed yet? This is what makes the bridge and routing infrastructure so important and so complex.

In this chapter we will discuss some of the basic concepts that are used to extend networks. We will also explore the methods required to interconnect different topologies such as Ethernet and Token Ring. We will emphasize the components required to support both SNA and today's standard LAN protocols.

The first part of this chapter will lay the groundwork with the internal operations of bridges and routers. This material is very important to new network designers and administrators. If you do not fully understand what makes these devices work, you will have a very difficult time trying to make a purchasing decision.

Bridge Overview

Rather than simply jumping in and explaining what a bridge is, let's look at bridges from a different angle. Why were bridges invented in the first place? When LANs first came on the scene, they were usually small Ethernet LANs with a relatively small number of workstations and file servers connected to them. The LAN was primarily used to share printers and files between the users. Figure 6.1 illustrates one of these simple Ethernet LAN configurations.

The traffic on the Ethernet LAN begins to increase as more and more users are added to the LAN. Sooner or later, as the traffic continues to increase, the bandwidth of the little Ethernet LAN is overcommitted. Figure 6.2 illustrates an expanding Ethernet LAN. This overcommitment of the Ethernet bandwidth causes everything on the LAN to slow down.

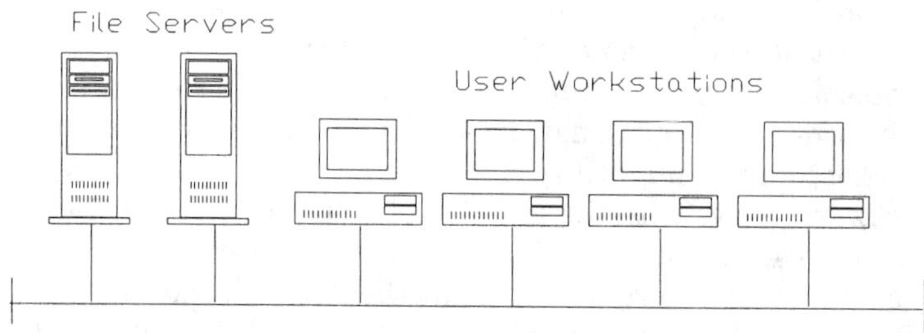

Figure 6.1 Typical small Ethernet LAN.

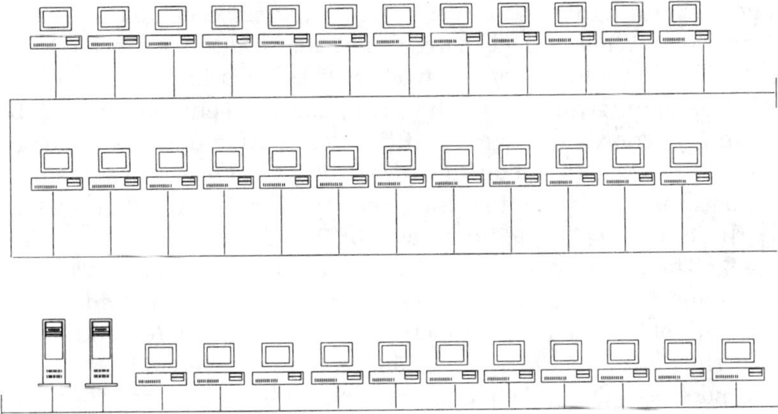

Figure 6.2 Expanding Ethernet LAN.

Bridges were developed to relieve the performance problems associated with overcommitted LAN bandwidth. Figure 6.3 shows how the same overcommitted LAN could be broken into two segments by using a bridge. All the workstations on the left-hand side of the bridge can communicate with each other and with the file server on that same segment, and none of that traffic will cross over the bridge to the right-hand segment. If a user on the left-hand side of the bridge needs to access the file server on the right-hand side, the bridge will forward those packets. As you can see, the bridging function can greatly reduce the traffic on a LAN, if it is configured properly.

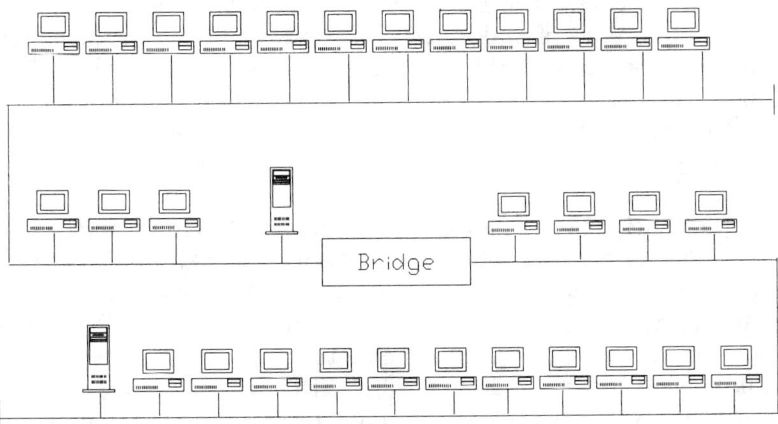

Figure 6.3 Segmented Ethernet LAN using a bridge.

Bridges maintain internal tables with the addresses of all the devices on the network. When a packet arrives at the bridge, the bridge looks at the destination address of the packet. If the destination address is on the same side (segment) of the bridge as the sending device, the bridge simply ignores the packet. If the destination address is on the other side of the bridge, the bridge forwards it to the other segment.

One very important point to remember about bridges is that they look at only the hardware or *media access control* (MAC) address to make their packet-forwarding decisions. Every device on the network must have a unique MAC address. NIC vendors "burn in" unique addresses into each adapter that is manufactured. This preset MAC address is known as the *universal address*. The address can be overridden by using software such as NTS/2. When a network address is overridden, the address is known as a locally administered address, or LAA.

Every packet on the network contains MAC addresses. Each packet contains a source MAC address and a destination MAC address. As the name implies, the source address is the address of the sending device, and the destination address is the address of the device where the packet is destined to be delivered.

Router Overview

In the bridge overview, we learned that bridges maintain tables of MAC addresses of the nodes on a LAN. The bridges uses these tables to determine whether the individual packets should be forwarded or not. Routers use a different method for making the packet-forwarding decisions. Routers do not look at the addresses of individual nodes; rather, routers look at network addresses. This is a very important point as this is the main difference between bridges and routers. Once again, bridges make packet-forwarding decisions based on tables of MAC addresses, while routers make packet-forwarding decisions based on tables of network addresses. In a way, the router has a simpler job to perform. Rather than having to keep track of all the node addresses, it only has to deal with network addresses. In a typical internetwork, there are far fewer network addresses than node addresses.

The next logical question is, Where does the router get the network address information? This information must be stored in the individual packets. Some protocols contain the network address field (such as IPX), while other protocols (such as SNA) do not. Protocols that contain the network address are known as *routable* protocols. We will discuss these routable protocols later in this chapter.

A router can also be viewed as a bridge with brains. A bridge can only make decisions based on the destination address of the packets. This is a yes/no decision; either the packet is forwarded to another segment, or it is ignored. A router can delve further into each packet and make many more decisions before forwarding or ignoring the packet. For example, a router can allow the network administrator to control which protocols are allowed on the network by not passing certain protocols through the router.

In large networks with multiple paths to certain devices, the network administrator can program the router to forward packets along the fastest path or via the cheapest path.

Routers are also very good security devices, especially in wide-area networks (WANs). The router can be configured to allow only certain devices to access the network from the WAN link.

Routers can also boost performance on wide-area links. Some network operating systems, such as Novell, issue many packets to all users. These packets, known as *broadcast packets,* are simply "I am here" packets. Novell file servers and print servers generate these packets several times a minute to tell the other network users that they exist. These broadcast messages do not usually cause any problems on a full 10-Mbits Ethernet local-area network, but on a wide-area link, these broadcast packets can seriously degrade the overall throughput and performance of the link. A router can be used to limit the number of "I am here" broadcast packets that are allowed to flow through the wide-area link. The router can be configured to pass these broadcast packets only once every 5 min rather than several times a minute.

Suggestion If you are planning to access Internet via your network, you must install a router in order to gain access.

Routable Protocols, Bridgeable Protocols, and Routing Protocols

Before we go any further, we should clear up a few terms. *Routable protocols,* as mentioned above, are protocols that contain routing information. This routing information comprises several different fields. Later in this chapter we will look at how these routing fields are used by routers to route packets throughout a network.

There are some protocols, such as NETBIOS, that cannot be routed. These protocols cannot be routed because they do not contain the fields in the packets for the routing information. Many people call these nonroutable protocols *bridgeable protocols.* This is really a misnomer, since all protocols can be bridged, even protocols that have routing information included in their packets.

Routing protocols are special protocols that are used by routers to communicate with each other. The routing information protocol (RIP) is one of these routing protocols.

Routing and Bridging Methods

Different network topologies use different routing methods. Token Ring networks use source routing to connect bridges and routers together, while most Ethernet networks use translational bridging. A new routing method, source routing transparency (SRT), is quickly becoming the preferred routing technique. SRT acts as a source routing bridge for source routing packets and as a translational bridge for other packets.

Let us take a look at some of the most common bridging and routing methods. A clear understanding in this area will help you to design more robust and reliable networks.

Transparent bridging

Most Ethernet networks use transparent bridging to communicate between routers and bridges. Transparent bridging is a completely different bridging method from source routing.

Figure 6.4 shows a typical Ethernet network consisting of four Ethernet segments and two bridges. If WS1 wishes to send a packet to WS4, the following actions are taken by the transparent bridging technique:

- The packet goes to bridge A via slot 1.
- Bridge A updates its internal table to reflect that WS1 can be accessed from slot 1.
- Bridge A examines its internal tables to see if it has an entry for WS4 (the destination address).

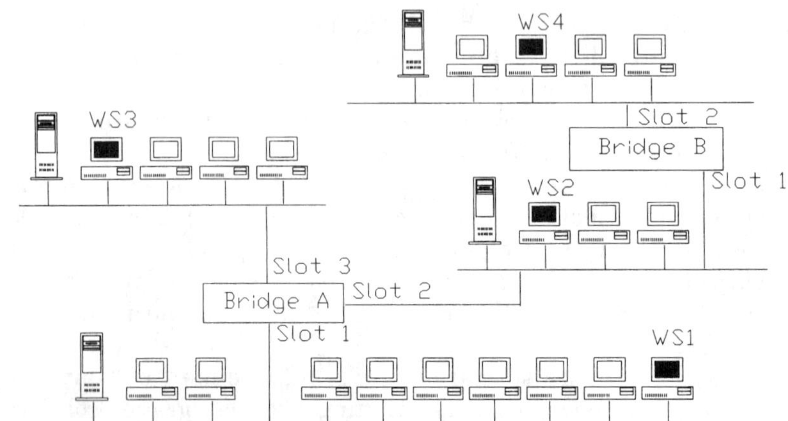

Figure 6.4 Transparent bridging.

- If Bridge A does not have an entry for WS4, it will forward the packet on all its ports, except the receiving port. So in this example bridge A will send the packet out through slot 2 and slot 3.
- Bridge B receives the packet. Bridge B updates its internal table to reflect that WS1 can be accessed via slot 1.
- Bridge B looks in its table to see if it has an entry for WS4, then forwards the packet through slot 2.

As you can see, these bridges are constantly learning about which devices are connected to the various segments of the network. As time goes on and the bridges learn more and more about the network, the performance of the forwarding process is enhanced. In our example, if WS4 returns a packet to WS1, the bridges already know which slots to forward the packet to by accessing the information in their internal tables.

Two important concepts were discussed in the above transparent bridging example. When a bridge receives a packet and it does not have a matching entry in its tables for the destination address, the bridge decides to forward the packet to each of its ports. This is known as *flooding*.

When the bridge does find a match for the destination address in its tables and it sends the packet to only one port, this process is known as *forwarding*.

Spanning tree

Things get a little more complicated when we introduce alternate paths in the transparent bridge network. Figure 6.5 illustrates an Ethernet network which contains multiple paths. Transparent bridging cannot tolerate multiple paths. Let's use an example to explain why.

In Fig. 6.5 we have a nice little network setup that has redundant links between the various segments. If we lose any single path in this network, we will have alternate path(s) to keep the traffic moving.

WS1 sends a packet destined for WS2. The following things happen (keep up now):

- The packet is sent to bridge A.
- Bridge A does not have an entry for WS2 in its tables, so bridge A floods the packet to all its ports (except, of course, the port from which the packet originated).
- Bridge B receives the packet, and it also floods the packet to all its ports since it has no match in its tables.
- Bridge D receives two packets, one from bridge A and one from bridge B. This may seem like a bad problem, and it is, but it is the least of our worries.

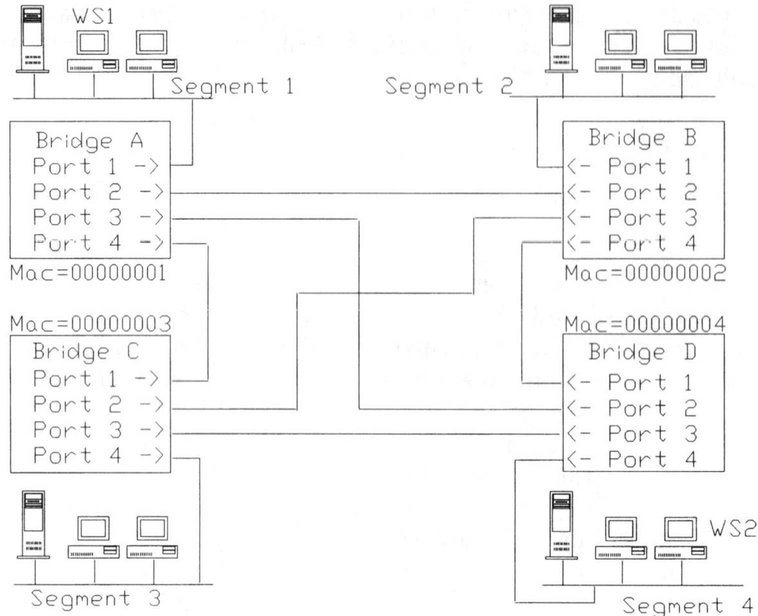

Figure 6.5 Redundant link network.

- Bridge C receives the packet from bridge A, and like the others, it floods the packet to all its ports.
- Now bridge C receives the packet from bridge B. Bridge C still does not have a match in its tables for WS2, so it once again floods the packet to all its ports.
- Now bridge A (the guy who started all this in the first place) receives the packet from bridge C. Bridge A, once again, floods.
- Now things are really out of hand. We have multiple copies of the packet being propagated and passed all around the network. This storm will eventually bring the network down.

The *spanning tree* was designed to stop this problem. Let's look again at Fig. 6.5 and see how the spanning tree operates. The first thing that happens when spanning tree is enabled is that a root bridge is designated. The bridges, all of which must have spanning tree enabled, talk to one another to decide which bridge will be the root. Two factors are used to determine the root bridge: priority and the bridge's MAC address. In Fig. 6.5 all the bridges have the same priority, so the choice of the root is based solely on the MAC address. The bridge with the lowest MAC address will be the root.

In order for spanning tree to keep the storms from occurring as described above, some of the bridge ports must be blocked. This blocking ensures that there are no redundant paths in the network. The bridge that is designated as the root cannot block any of its ports.

Now that the bridges have all decided that bridge A is going to be the root, they start deciding which ports must be blocked. The paths with the shortest path cost to the root remain enabled. Sounds complicated, doesn't it? Let's try to simplify it. When bridges are configured, a cost is given to each port. For our example let's assume that all the path costs are the same, 100.

Bridge A cannot block any of its ports since it is the root, so bridge A is out of the picture for now.

Bridge B must now decide which of its ports are to be blocked. Remember, only the least-cost path to the root remains enabled. Bridge B can get to the root from port 2 at a cost of 100. Bridge B can also get to bridge A via port 3 to bridge C then to bridge A at a cost of 200. Do you follow me so far? Bridge B can also get to A via port 4 to bridge D to bridge C then to A for a cost of 300. So bridge B blocks ports 3 and 4.

Bridge C, using the same type of method, would block ports 2 and 3.

Bridge D will block ports 1 and 3.

Logically our network will look like Fig. 6.6. This could present a problem for us. What if most of our traffic occurs between segments 2 and 4? The traffic between these two segments, in this scenario, must always go through bridge A. There are two ways to change this. First, we could use priorities to make bridge B always be the root. If bridge B is the root, it cannot block its port to segment 4. Second, we could adjust the priorities on bridge D's ports 2 and 3. We could set these priorities up in such a manner that bridge D would always find that port 1 is its least-cost path to bridge A.

There is a lot of planning that must be done when you are designing multiple paths in your network. Mistakes in this area could make your network performance suffer.

So why even design multiple paths if they are going to be blocked anyway? If one of the active paths in the network fails, the blocked ports will be unblocked. When this happens, the entire root discovery and port blocking mechanisms are reinitiated. So the alternate paths are still useful when paths are disabled.

Source routing

IBM uses source routing for communicating between routers and bridges. Source routing uses the discovery process to find the path(s) from one device to another. The source (sending) device transmits a dis-

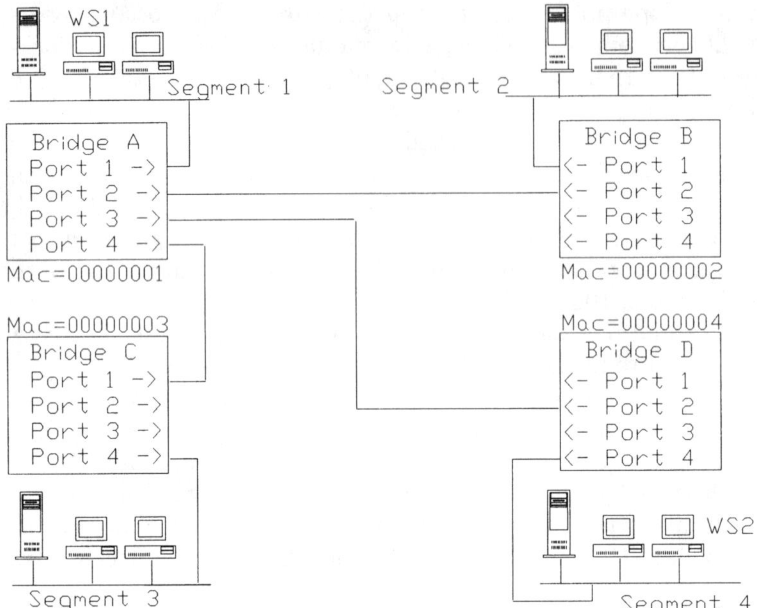

Figure 6.6 Logical network after spanning tree port blocking.

covery frame on the network with the destination address of the device it is trying to communicate with. This discovery frame is routed through all the bridges and routers on the network. As the frame passes through each router, the address of that router is stored in the packet. When the destination device receives each of these discovery frames, it sends them back to the sender. The discovery frame gets back to the sender by using the routing information that is now stored in the packet. When the sending device receives the discovery frame(s), it will choose the best route and send the data packets.

Figure 6.7 illustrates how the source routing discovery function works. The source device in Fig. 6.7 wishes to send data to the destination device with address 1001. The source device sends a discovery frame to device 1001. One of the discovery frames goes from the source device, through bridge C, to device 1001. This information is stored in the discovery packet. The other discovery frame travels from the source device, through bridge A, through bridge B, and on to device 1001. When the sending device receives these two discovery frames, with the routing information complete, it will choose the path through bridge C.

Let's delve a little deeper into source routing, and we will discover how it can actually improve the performance of a network by overcoming some of the shortcomings of the spanning tree algorithm. Figure 6.8 illustrates a more complicated Token Ring network. Source routing will

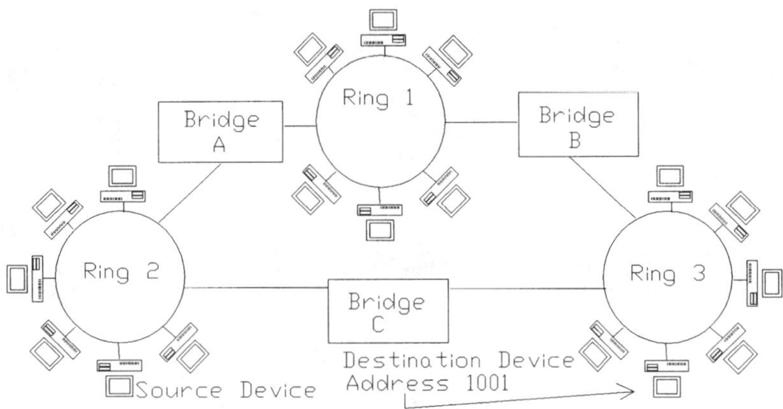

Discovery Frame 1 = Bridge C -> 1001
Discovery Frame 2 = Bridge A -> Bridge B -> 1001

Figure 6.7 Source routing discovery process.

designate a root bridge, in much the same manner as spanning tree. In this example, bridge A is the root bridge.

Source routing also goes through a similar blocking technique as spanning tree. These blocked paths, however, are not exactly blocked. The source routing bridges (or bridge ports) can be in one of two states: an all-routes bridge or a single-route bridge. Rather than blocking a bridge, source routing turns that bridge into an all-routes bridge.

Let's take a look at how these all-routes and single-route bridges work to prevent storms and boost network performance. In Fig. 6.8, WS1 needs to find WS2. So WS1 sends out what is known as a *single-route broadcast* to WS2. The packet goes to bridge A. All the bridge ports on bridge A are single-route bridges, so the packet is sent out on ports 2, 3, and 4 of bridge A.

Bridge B receives the packet from bridge A. Ports 3 and 4 of bridge B are set to all-routes bridges. Because of this, the single-route broadcast packet is not forwarded on these ports.

So, all-routes bridges cannot forward single-route broadcast messages.

The same scenario happens on bridge C.

Because of this blocking of the packet by the all-routes bridges, WS2 receives only one packet. Now things get complicated. WS2 sends an all-routes broadcast back to WS1. Now all the bridges get a crack at the packet. The packet goes from bridge D to bridge B, then on to bridge A. The packet also goes from bridge D to bridge C to bridge A. The packet also goes from bridge D to bridge A. Now WS1 receives many packets back from WS2.

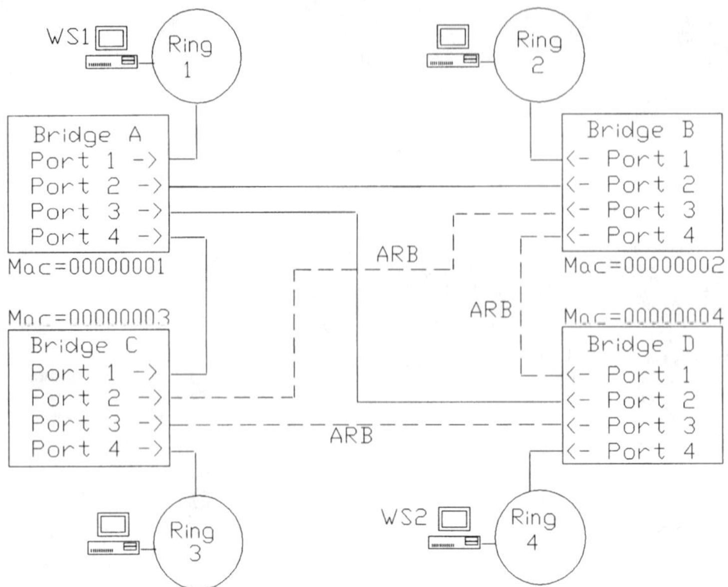

Figure 6.8 All-routes and single-route bridges.

WS1 will use the routing information in the first packet it receives for all future communications to WS2. This may not be the shortest path. It appears that the best route from WS2 to WS1 is from bridge D to bridge A. In this example, let's assume that this path is extremely busy. When WS1 received the multiple packets from the all-routes broadcast from WS2, the path from bridge D to bridge B to bridge A got back first.

WS1 will then use specific routed frames to communicate with WS2. This specific routed frame contains the following routing information to get to WS2:

Bridge A to bridge B to bridge D to ring 4

As you can see (you do see, don't you?), source routing can utilize the paths that would otherwise be blocked by the spanning tree algorithm. This can help improve the overall performance and capacity of a given network.

Connecting source routing and transparent bridging networks

Source routing is fine if your network consists only of Token Ring networks, and transparent bridging is fine if your network consists only of Ethernet segments. Matters become a little more complicated when source routing networks and transparent bridging networks need to communicate with each other.

One method of connecting these two different networks is to use a specialized bridge which translates the routing information between the two bridging methods. The IBM 8209 and the CrossComm ILAN products provide this functionality.

Source routing transparency (SRT) provides another method to connect source routing and transparent bridging networks. With SRT, the individual packets are interrogated and translated between the source routing and transparent bridging techniques.

CM/2 and source routing transparency

There are certain CM/2 LAN-to-host connectivity scenarios that require special attention when bridges and routers are implemented. The complication occurs only in mixed Ethernet and Token Ring environments where the DSPU method is used to access the host. Figure 6.9 illustrates this type of scenario.

Suggestion When accessing the host, as a DSPU of a 3174 or 37x5 TIC, from an Ethernet workstation, you must connect the Ethernet to the Token Ring with a bridge or router that supports SRT.

There are several bridges and routers, which support SRT, that can be used to allow Ethernet workstations to access the host via Token

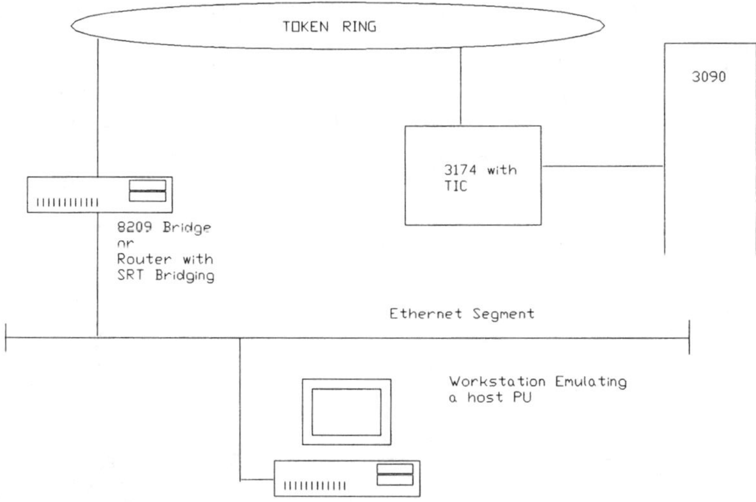

Figure 6.9 Ethernet workstation accessing host as a PU.

Ring DSPUs. The following products support the routing of SNA between Ethernet and Token Ring networks:

IBM 8209 bridge

CrossComm ILAN bridge

CISCO router

SRT is quickly becoming an accepted standard, and many router vendors are currently developing SRT support for their products.

If you have a connectivity scenario as shown in Fig. 6.9, with mixed Ethernet and Token Ring networks, you can configure CM/2 in a manner where SRT, and the complexity associated with it, is not required. To accomplish this, you must implement the CM/2 gateway function. Figure 6.10 illustrates a typical CM/2 gateway configuration in a mixed Token Ring and Ethernet environment.

There are advantages and disadvantages to implementing the CM/2 gateway for host access. One of the biggest advantages is the elimination of the need for a bridge or router. The connectivity scenario shown in Fig. 6.10 does not require a bridge or router for host access. A bridge or router would be required if the user needed to access other resources on the Token Ring network, such as a Novell file server. However, this bridge or router would not require the SRT functionality.

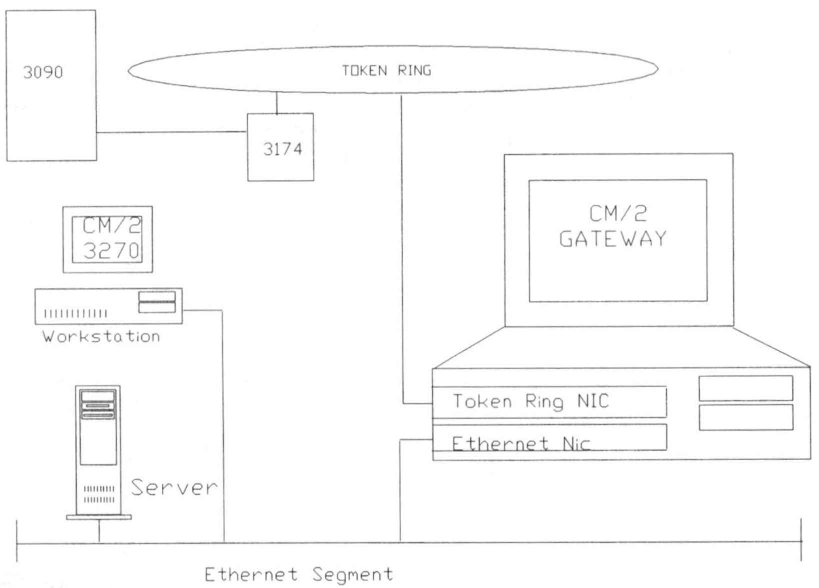

Figure 6.10 Using a CM/2 gateway.

The IBM 8209

The IBM 8209, as mentioned earlier, can be used to solve the SNA routing problems associated with the connectivity scenario illustrated in Fig. 6.9. The IBM 8209 has been around for a long time and is a very stable product. One of the problems with the 8209 is that it has only two ports, one for Ethernet and one for Token Ring.

The CrossComm ILAN

The ILAN bridge can also solve SNA routing problems. One of the advantages of the ILAN is its multiple network connection ports.

CISCO router

CISCO has been a pioneer in the SNA routing arena. The current CISCO routers support SRT.

WellFleet routers

The WellFleet routers announced support for SRT in upcoming releases of their router software.

Netware routers

Novell provides router software bundled with Netware. These routers only process the IPX/SPX protocol. There are two types of Netware routers: internal and external. Netware routers are extremely cost-effective for Netware-only installations where multiple-protocol support is not required. CM/2 host access can be provided in a network using Netware routers if the CM/2 gateway function is used to provide the 3270 connection.

Internal Netware routers are implemented by installing two or more NICs in a file server as illustrated in Fig. 6.11. The drivers of these NICs are loaded by using the Netware LOAD command. The logical networks are connected by using the Netware BIND command.

External Netware routers are implemented by installing two or more NICs in a dedicated PC. The Netware ROUTE.EXE program is configured by using the ROUTEGEN.EXE program. The output of the ROUTEGEN process is a customized ROUTE.EXE program; this is run on the dedicated router PC.

Note Novell recently announced a multiple-protocol router NLM which supports source routing. The NLM will allow SNA traffic to be bridged along with IPX/SPX traffic on Token Ring LANs.

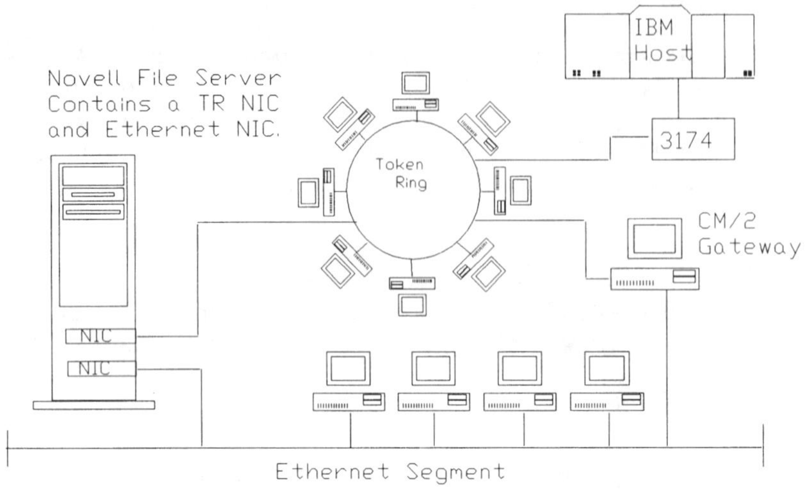

Figure 6.11 Netware internal router.

Netware TCP/IP router

Novell also provides a method to integrate its IPX/SPX protocol-based networks with TCP/IP networks. To accomplish this, Netware 3.x provides the TCPIP NLM. This NLM allows the Novell 3.x file server to act as a TCP/IP router.

Router selection

There are many other router and bridge vendors. The router or bridge is one of the most important network components you will implement. Care should be taken in the selection of a bridge or router vendor. The following points should be addressed when you select a bridge or router for your network:

- Does the bridge or router support wide-area links (WANs)?
- Does the bridge or router support SRT?
- Does the bridge or router support all the protocols you plan to use on your network?
- How many ports does the bridge or router support?
- Does the vendor keep up with new technologies, such as FDDI and ATM?

Suggestion You should not mix routers from different vendors in the same local-area network. In many cases, the routers talk to each other using proprietary codes. If a mix of different vendors' routers is implemented, the routers might not be able to communicate with each other.

Multiprotocol network routing and bridging considerations

There are two basic types of communications protocols, as seen from a bridging or routing perspective: routable protocols and bridgeable protocols. The difference between the two is the presence, or lack of, routing information fields in the packets. Protocols which have routing information fields can be routed, while all other protocols can only be bridged.

Knowing whether the protocols used in your network are routable or bridgeable is an important factor in designing your network. For example, if you are planning to design an internetwork with multiple connecting paths, using routable protocols would make the most sense. Using routable protocols in this instance would allow the routers to determine and use the alternate paths when the primary path is disabled. Bridges cannot perform this function.

> **Suggestion** A good rule of thumb for protocol selection: If you have a choice between a routable protocol and a bridgeable protocol, choose the routable protocol.

Figure 6.12 illustrates some of the bridgeable and routable network protocols.

A bridge or a router?

This question is asked time and time again by network designers and administrators, and it is not easy to answer. Let's look at the features that a router provides above and beyond those provided by bridges:

- A router can be used to decrease the amount of broadcast packets sent over a wide-area link. This fact alone is extremely important. WAN links are slow enough as they are. Any reduction in traffic on these links helps the WAN performance tremendously.
- A router can be used as a security device. Let's say that you have a dedicated server for the payroll department. Only users from one of your Ethernet LANs should be able to access this server. A router can

Bridgable Protocols	Routable Protocols
SNA	TCP/IP
NetBios	XNS
DEC/LAT	DEC/NET
	IPX

Figure 6.12 Bridgeable and routable protocols.

be configured to keep all nodes, except the ones you designate, from accessing the server.

- A router is required if you wish to access Internet.
- A router can act as a bridge for nonroutable protocols.
- Most router vendors keep up with technology and continuously provide support for the new protocols.

Money is another factor. A router will always cost more than a bridge, sometimes a substantial amount more. You must make sure that your organization will realize benefits from the extra expenditure.

Conclusion

This chapter was by no means a thorough guide to designing a network by using bridges and routers. The goal of the chapter was to discuss the fundamentals of bridging and routing. Today's multiprotocol and multitopology networks are very complex data highways. Routers and bridges help keep these data highways less congested. The design of SNA requires that the network designer pay special attention to its bridging requirements. We saw several methods, including the 8209 bridge and the SRT bridging protocol, that help us with our SNA routing troubles.

Part

2

3270 Connectivity

Part 2 will guide you through the complexities involved in establishing your mainframe connectivity. We will begin with an overview of APPN and APPC architectures and discuss how OS/2 and CM/2 are positioned to take advantage of these architectures and protocols.

Next we will see how to configure a CM/2 workstation as a gateway machine. This single gateway machine can provide host access for hundreds of users with very little mainframe overhead. The sample gateway scenario that is illustrated also shows you how to use a CM/2 gateway machine to allow Ethernet users to access your host via a Token Ring connection. This scenario does not require the implementation of a complex router or bridge. The gateway machine handles all the Ethernet-to-Token Ring translation for us. We will also look at implicit and explicit LU definitions and how they can be used together.

Next we will see how a Token Ring workstation can be configured to emulate a host PU to access the mainframe. PU emulation is one of the most stable methods for host connectivity. We will see how PU emulation provides the network administrator with an incredible amount of flexibility in configuring host connectivity.

Host PU emulation can also be performed on Ethernet workstations. This option is a little more complicated than Token Ring PU emulation because it could require the use of a router or SNA bridge. We will learn when a router is required and will see a step-by-step configuration for Ethernet PU emulation.

Providing print support has always been difficult in networked environments. Chapter 11 deals strictly with host printing via OS/2 workstations. We will learn the concepts behind host printing. We will follow a print job from the host, to the network, to OS/2, and then down to the printer. We will explore the configurations for each of these printing components.

Chapter

7

CM/2 and APPN

APPN Overview

Advanced Peer to Peer Networking (APPN) is IBM's new networking architecture. APPN is intended to help large host-based SNA sites migrate to a true peer-to-peer based networking scheme. As of today, the direction and future of APPN are not quite clear. Many corporations are questioning the benefits of APPN, while other vendors are marching along with other peer-to-peer solutions.

Why APPN?

A shift from proprietary architectures to open systems has been in progress over the last few years. SNA has long been IBM's proprietary architecture for mainframe network traffic. As the shift to open architectures continues, network component designers are trying to make SNA fit into this open architecture. These designers are trying such things as encapsulating SNA into TCP/IP packets. This type of solution provides the flexible routing properties of TCP/IP for SNA traffic. TCP/IP fails with SNA traffic in the reliability area. The error checking and recovery are not as stringent with TCP/IP as with native SNA.

IBM recognized the need to provide a more flexible routing technique for SNA traffic on today's multiprotocol networks. The goal was to provide more routing flexibility for SNA traffic while maintaining the reliability of native SNA. APPN was designed to meet these goals.

The Future of APPN

So, what does APPN mean to you today? APPN is still in its early stages and is experiencing growing pains. There are some strong benefits associated with the APPN architecture. Routing SNA traffic over a wide-area network is a complicated task. SNA is very timing-dependent, and because of this, routing becomes more complicated. APPN promises to alleviate these routing problems. Another strength of APPN is its automatic reconfiguration process. As new APPN nodes are added to the network, the routing tables of all the network nodes are automatically synchronized. APPN also provides a method to establish multiple links between nodes. This can help to reroute traffic in the event of a network node failure. APPN networks will not require major conversions in large SNA-based networks. This fact alone will help to ensure the success of the architecture.

APPN still has a long road to travel. The APPN network node specifications are still an IBM proprietary architecture. CISCO Systems, a router vendor, at one time began developing an open architecture which performs many of the same functions as APPN. The goal was to combine the functions of APPN with TCP/IP. CISCO has since retreated from this endeavor. While APPN promises to solve many of the real-world problems facing large SNA-based corporate data centers, the competition for the networking architecture of the future is still open.

APPC Versus APPN

Many people seem to think that Advanced Program to Program Communications (APPC) and APPN are one in the same. They are not.

APPN is a networking architecture. APPN is comprised of several hardware and software components, which we will discuss later in this chapter, that allow remote sites to communicate with each other.

APPC is a protocol that allows two programs to talk to each other and pass data back and forth. APPC transaction programs can use APPN as the network which provides the physical connection between the two programs. The beauty of APPC is that programs on different hardware and software platforms can communicate with each other.

Sample APPC Application

To visualize the difference between APPC and APPN, let us look at a sample APPC application and then see how an APPN network could be used with this application.

This sample application deals with a hospital's need to share real-time information. As patients are admitted to the hospital, information about these patients is keyed into a mainframe-based system. This mainframe system generates a record for each patient which is placed into a database. The hospital also has a radiology system which is run on a DEC/VAX system.

The physician orders an x-ray on a patient. The nurse calls radiology and sets up a time for the procedure. The radiology clerk then looks up the patient on the mainframe system and rekeys the patient's name, address, insurance information, etc., into the radiology system. This information is used to track the procedure and to bill the insurance company.

An APPC application was written to automate the rekeying of data into the radiology system. This application consists of two separate programs: a CICS transaction running on the mainframe and a process running on the DEC/VAX. The physical connection between the mainframe and the DEC is made via an SNA gateway. This gateway is comprised of a special hardware box that looks like a PU to the host. Software is run on the DEC side that allows the DEC to access the gateway box as a DECNET line.

The mainframe CICS transaction scans the database once every couple of minutes, looking for new records added to the patient database. When a new record is found, the mainframe program issues an APPC ALLOCATE verb to logically connect to the DEC APPC process. The DEC program sends a confirmation that the allocation was successful. Next the mainframe CICS program copies the data from the database into a buffer in memory and issues the APPC SEND_DATA verb. The data are then sent from the CICS program to the DEC program. When the DEC program receives the data, it then issues the CONFIRM verb to acknowledge receipt of the data. Next the DEC program converts the data from EBCDIC to ASCII and uses these data to update the radiology database.

Now when a radiology procedure is ordered, the radiology personnel simply key in the patient's name and all the patient's data are available.

How does APPN fit into this scenario? If the DEC/VAX supported APPN, APPN could be used in place of the SNA gateway box to provide the physical connectivity between the two machines. APPN can be viewed as the network, while APPC can be viewed as a protocol that is routed through this network.

APPN Components

Before we delve into the components of APPN, let's look at the standard SNA approach to remote connectivity. Figure 7.1 illustrates a typical host to remote site connection. The host site uses a 37x5 front-end processor which runs a special communications package known as the Network Control Program (NCP). The NCP talks with VTAM, the

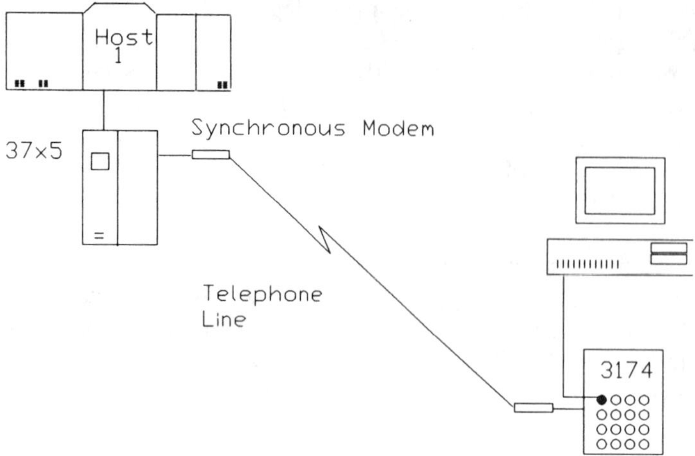

Figure 7.1 Accessing a remote site via a 37x5 controller and remote 3174.

mainframe communications software. A telephone line is connected to the front-end processor via a synchronous modem. On the other end of the phone line, at the remote site, another synchronous modem connects the telephone line to a 3174 terminal control unit. Terminals are then connected to this 3174 control unit, and the users can then access the applications running on the remote mainframe.

Let's see how an APPN network can be established to provide this same type of connectivity. Figure 7.2 illustrates a simple APPN network configuration.

APPN network nodes

Notice in Fig. 7.2 that the 37x5 and the remote 3174 control unit are replaced with APPN network nodes. An APPN network node (NN) is the heart of the APPN architecture. The network node is used to perform the routing function in the network. One of the beauties of APPN is the ability of the network nodes to automatically reconfigure themselves as the APPN network grows. When a new network node is added to the APPN network, the other network nodes in the system automatically update their routing tables to include this new node.

Another benefit of APPN is the ability to route SNA traffic, over a wide-area network, without the use of an expensive front-end processor. This does not mean that front-end processors will be obsolete. Front-end processors will be able to participate in APPN networks as network nodes. Smaller sites that do not have large mainframes can participate in APPN networks without the need for the front-end

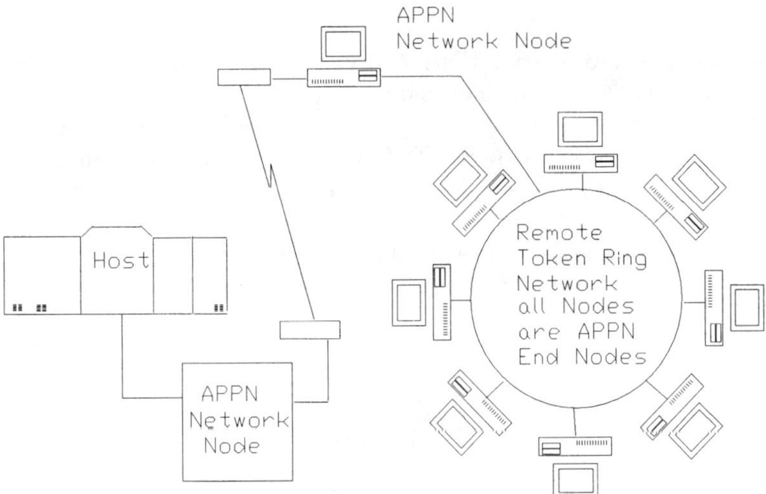

Figure 7.2 Simple APPN connection.

processor. These smaller sites can use other devices in place of the front-end processor to provide the network node function.

These devices include the AS/400, the RS/6000, the 6611 router, the 3174 control unit, and an OS/2 workstation.

APPN end nodes

We return to the example illustrated in Fig. 7.2. The remote Token Ring network is comprised of several nodes and an APPN network node. The nodes are running OS/2 and CM/2 and are defined as APPN end nodes (ENs). The APPN end node uses the services of the APPN network nodes to attach to the remote mainframe. The end nodes can then access all the host applications.

IBM recently published the APPN end node specifications. This will allow other hardware vendors to participate in the APPN architecture. Theoretically, any hardware device that implements the APPN end node specifications can participate in an APPN network and access host-based SNA applications.

APPN low entry nodes

APPN low entry nodes (LENs) are a special type of End Node. The LEN can access the APPN network, but the LEN must be predefined to a network node.

Conclusion

We learned in Chap. 6 that SNA has some very stringent bridging requirements. These requirements do not lend themselves to the common wide-area networking technologies in place today. The alternative was to implement very expensive SNA wide-area links using front-end processors. APPN promises to be the SNA routing savior. We can utilize the features of APPN to design wide-area networks that can pass SNA traffic just as well as the front-end processors can. Better yet, APPN can run over a multiprotocol network. We get the best of both worlds.

Chapter

8

CM/2 Workstation as Gateway to the Host

CM/2 provides a method to use a single workstation as a gateway to the host. This functionality can be used as the sole host access mechanism for your network nodes. At times, implementing a CM/2 gateway is a sound decision. However, depending upon your topology and your mainframe access needs, the gateway may not be your best choice for accessing host resources.

The goal of this chapter is to show you what a gateway is and when you should use the gateway feature. We will also discuss how to configure CM/2 to implement the gateway function, and we will learn how to configure the client workstations so as to access the mainframe via the gateway. We will discuss implicit and explicit LU definitions, the use of LU pools, and 3270 printer definitions. The VTAM definitions and how they relate to the CM/2 configurations will be discussed. We will look at some of the methods that can be used to diagnose and troubleshoot problems with the gateway.

What Is a CM/2 Gateway?

As you recall from Chap. 1, a gateway is a PC running special software that emulates a mainframe physical unit (PU). The mainframe PU is a device that controls the operation of multiple host terminals. Client PCs run special software that communicates with the software on the gateway PC.

How does CM/2 fit into this picture? CM/2 can be configured as both a gateway and a client PC. In a local-area network environment, the

CM/2 gateway PC is configured to access the host as a downstream PU (DSPU). For a detailed description of the DSPU, please refer to Chap. 1. The CM/2 gateway emulates a host PU and can support up to 254 client workstations. We will look, in detail, at the steps required to configure CM/2 so as to emulate the host PU function.

The client workstations also run CM/2. The client's CM/2 software is configured in a manner where it communicates with the CM/2 gateway PC. These client workstations emulate mainframe logical units (LUs). Each client workstation can have different types of host LUs defined to it. For example, one client workstation could have two model 2 terminal sessions and one printer session. Another client could have one model 2 terminal, one model 4 terminal, one model 5 terminal, and one printer session. The different LU types defined on the client can be configured in any manner you wish.

When Should You Use the CM/2 Gateway Function?

The best scenario for utilizing a CM/2 gateway is in mixed-topology environments. Many organizations implement a small Token Ring network in order to provide mainframe access. Then, because of cost or other reasons, multiple Ethernet LANs are implemented at the end-user's stations. Figure 8.1 illustrates a typical network with a mixture of Token Ring and Ethernet. The host is connected to the Token Ring via a TIC in a 3174 control unit. The client workstations and servers

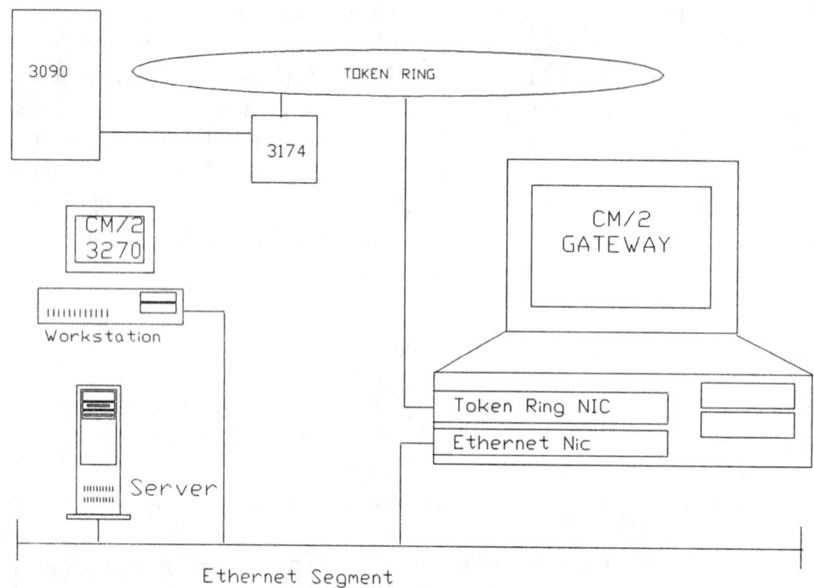

Figure 8.1 A CM/2 gateway configuration.

are attached to an Ethernet segment. The CM/2 gateway fits perfectly in this environment. Let's see why.

In a mixed-topology environment, such as Token Ring and Ethernet, two NIC adapters are installed in the CM/2 gateway PC, one for Ethernet and one for Token Ring, as shown in Fig. 8.1. The Token Ring NIC is configured, using CM/2 and NTS/2, to become a downstream PU to a 3174, 3725, or 3745 host controller. The mechanics for configuring this type of function will be fully explained in this chapter. The Ethernet NIC is attached to one of the Ethernet segments. Notice that there are no routers or bridges in the network shown in Fig. 8.1. When CM/2 is configured correctly, the client workstations will be able to access the host without the need for a router or bridge. The gateway provides the packet translations for us. When CM/2 and NTS/2 are configured on the gateway, as we will see, you tell CM/2 that the gateway PC is the link between the Token Ring network and the Ethernet network. Client workstations can reside on both the Token Ring network and the Ethernet network. Client workstations from both topologies will be able to access the host using the services of the gateway.

You may be asking yourself, Why would I want a configuration like this? There is one decisive reason—cost. Accessing the mainframe from a network is fairly inexpensive, and very reliable, if you are using a Token Ring network and a TIC in a 3174 control unit. It is much cheaper than a 3172 Ethernet controller. Ethernet NICs and associated network equipment, such as intelligent wiring hubs, are about half as expensive as comparable Token Ring equipment. So, if you have several hundred or perhaps thousands of client workstations on your LAN, the cost savings of using Ethernet NICs is quite substantial.

When Not to Use the CM/2 Gateway Feature

The gateway could be used in a pure Token Ring environment or a pure Ethernet environment, but this may not be the most effective method for providing host access to your users. The CM/2 gateway emulates a host PU and supports many client workstations. If there is a problem with the gateway PC, all the client workstations lose their host sessions. CM/2 can also be configured to emulate both a host PU and its associated LUs using the same workstation. In other words, each CM/2 workstation could be its own gateway to the mainframe, supporting only the LUs that it has defined to itself. There are several advantages to this option. If the user has a problem with his or her PC, no other users on the network, or on the mainframe, are affected. This method for providing host access can also perform better than the gateway feature since the traffic is not required to pass through a separate gateway PC. The network is also less complex, since one less component is required. Finally, mainframe configuration and troubleshooting become much simpler. For example, if a gateway user wished to change one of her or his terminal sessions from a model 2 terminal to a model 5 terminal, the entire gateway and all its associated clients would be disrupted. If that user were performing its own PU function, only that workstation would be affected by the change.

There is a drawback to allowing each workstation to act as its own gateway to the mainframe: More mainframe resources are required. This increase in mainframe resources is primarily in the number of DSPUs defined within the mainframe. This may or may not be a problem, depending on your environment. If you are using a 3174 controller to provide your DSPUs, it can support about 200 DSPUs. Refer to Chap. 2 to see how the number of DSPUs that the 3174 can support is dependent upon the amount of memory installed in the control unit and the number of other features that are installed. If a 3745 provides your DSPUs, you have no problem. The 3745 supports many thousands of DSPUs.

When CM/2 users perform their own gateway functions but my network has a mixed topology

If you have a Token Ring network to provide host access and use an Ethernet network to reach your users, you may still be able to get away without a gateway. This type of configuration requires the use of a specialized bridge or router that supports source routing transparency. Chapter 10, Ethernet PU Emulation—Configuring CM/2, and Chap. 6, Bridges and Routers, explain how you can accomplish this goal.

CM/2 Gateway Hardware Requirements

The remainder of this chapter will concentrate on using the CM/2 gateway function in a mixed Token Ring and Ethernet environment. We will look at some sample CM/2 gateway and client configurations. These sample configurations can be slightly modified to service pure Ethernet or pure Token Ring networks.

The actual gateway PC should consist of at least a 386 processor with 8 Mbytes of memory. You could probably get away with using 6 Mbytes of memory, but performance could suffer. The gateway PC must also contain both a Token Ring and an Ethernet NIC. Before you jump into the CM/2 configuration, you should check your network connections to make sure they are operational.

Implicit and Explicit LU Definitions

The CM/2 gateway feature allows you to choose either implicit or explicit LU definitions. Implicit LUs are a pool of host sessions (LUs) that are used on a first-come, first-served basis by the client workstations. For example, if you have 100 LUs defined to the gateway, these LUs will be used by the first 100 clients. The 101st client will be denied access until one of the implicit LUs is freed by another client.

Explicit LU definitions are "hard-assigned" to individual clients. For example, LUs numbered 2, 3, and 4 can be used only by client 1; LUs 5, 6, 7, and 8 are assigned to client 2; and so on.

There are advantages and disadvantages to both options. The implicit LU definitions are much simpler to define; however, the user will always get a different host address when she or he logs on to the mainframe. This may present security problems at your site. If all the implicit LUs are in use, some users will not be able to access the host until other users log off. You should also check your host application software for terminal address restrictions. Some CICS programs build profiles for individual users based on their terminal addresses. If the user had a different terminal session address each time he or she logged on, this would cause a problem for the CICS application.

Explicit LUs guarantee that the user will always access the host using the same host (VTAM) address. Explicit LUs are more difficult to define, and if the user is not logged on, their LU(s) cannot be used by other clients. There are advantages and disadvantages to explicit LU definitions. The end-user always gets the same host terminal address, so host applications and security are not issues.

The disadvantage of explicit LU definitions is that if the user who is assigned to a specific LU is not signed on, no other user on the network can utilize that address. This could be a problem if you are running short of host terminal addresses.

Configuring CM/2 on the Gateway PC

Before you begin the configuration of CM/2 for the gateway feature, you must install OS/2, CM/2, and NTS/2 on the gateway PC. You should also make sure that the appropriate NICs are installed on the gateway and that the network connections are operational.

Okay, let's get started.

Step 1 Double-click on the CM/2 icon.

Step 2 Double-click on the Communications Manager setup icon.

Step 3 Click on Setup on the initial screen.

Step 4 Enter a configuration name and description on the Open Configuration screen, as illustrated in Fig. 8.2, then click on OK.

Step 5 You will be asked if this is a new configuration. Click on Yes.

Step 6 You will be asked if this configuration is for this workstation. Click on Yes.

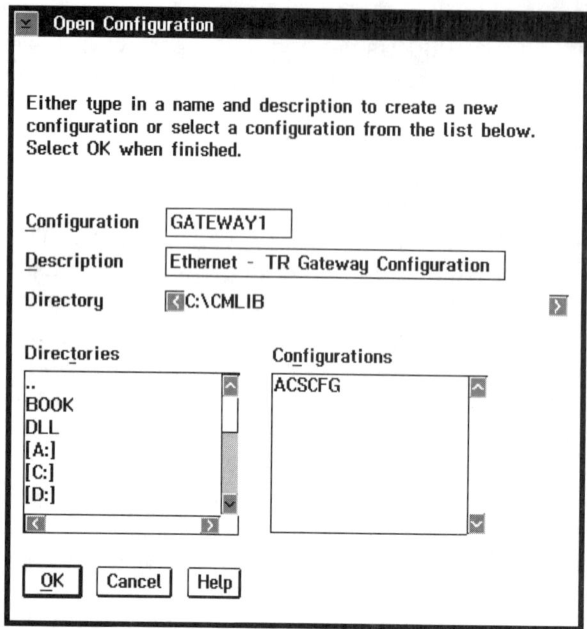

Figure 8.2 Name the configuration file. [*Reprinted by permission from IBM's OS/2 2.0, Copyright (1988, 1992) International Business Machines Corporation.*]

Step 7 The Communications Manager Configuration screen will be displayed (see Fig. 8.3). Click on Gateway, then click on Configure.

Step 8 The screen shown in Fig. 8.4 will be displayed. Click on SNA local node characteristics, then click on Configure. Figure 8.5 will be illustrated.

Step 9 Enter your network ID in the first field. This name can be any eight characters you choose. The name is used for problem notification only.

Next you must enter the local node name. This name should match the VTAM PU definition for the gateway. In our example we choose LSNA1A71. This is the name of the member in SYS1.VTAMLST that defines the PU definition for the gateway. We will discuss the mainframe (VTAM) definition a little later.

Next you should enter the local node ID. The first 3 bytes of this field will be filled in for you with 05D. You should enter 00000 in the next field if you are accessing a local host.

In the Local node alias name field, you should enter the same name you placed in the Local node name field.
Click on OK.

Step 10 You should now be returned to the Communications Manager Profile List Sheet screen, as illustrated in Fig. 8.6. Notice the checkmark in front of the SNA local node characteristics entry. This means that this section has been configured.

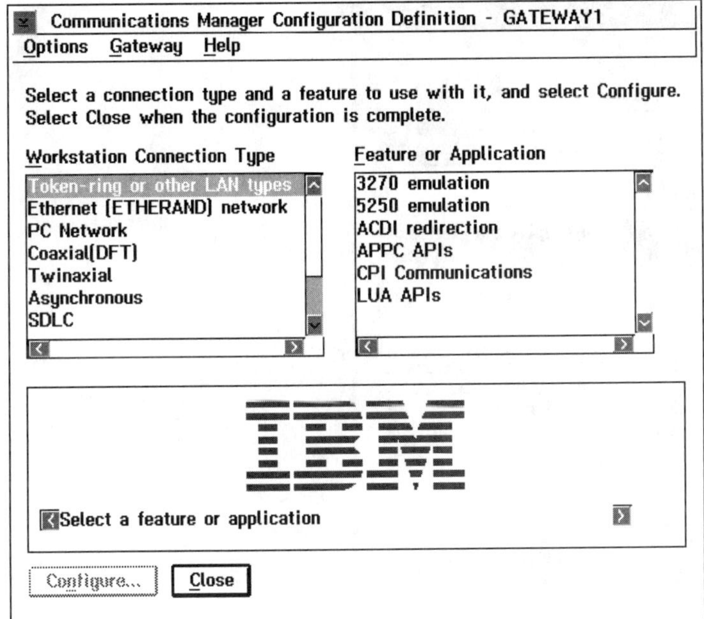

Figure 8.3 Select the gateway option. [*Reprinted by permission from IBM's OS/2 2.0, Copyright (1988, 1992) International Business Machines Corporation.*]

Click on Gateway—Host and host LU pools, then click on Configure. The panel shown in Fig. 8.7 will be displayed.

Step 11 Click on Links. Figure 8.8 should be displayed. Make sure that Token Ring or other LAN type is displayed in the DLC type field, then click on Configure. Figure 8.9 should be displayed.

Step 12 In Fig. 8.9 we must change the Maximum number of link stations field from 4 to 255. If you leave this value set to 4, only 4 host sessions will be active at any given time.

Enter the network ID name in the C&SM LAN ID field. To keep things simple, you should use the same name you specified in Fig. 8.5.

Click on OK.

Step 13 You will be returned to the panel illustrated in Fig. 8.8. Notice that the Create button is now highlighted. Click on Create, and Fig. 8.10 will be displayed.

Step 14 The only field that you need to enter in Fig. 8.10 is the LAN destination address. This is an extremely important field. You must enter the Token Ring address of your TIC in this field. This address is specified in the 3174 or 37x5 configuration. In this example, the TIC address is 400020101A60.

After you enter the LAN destination address, click on OK. Figure 8.11 will now be displayed. Click on Close, and Fig. 8.12 will be displayed.

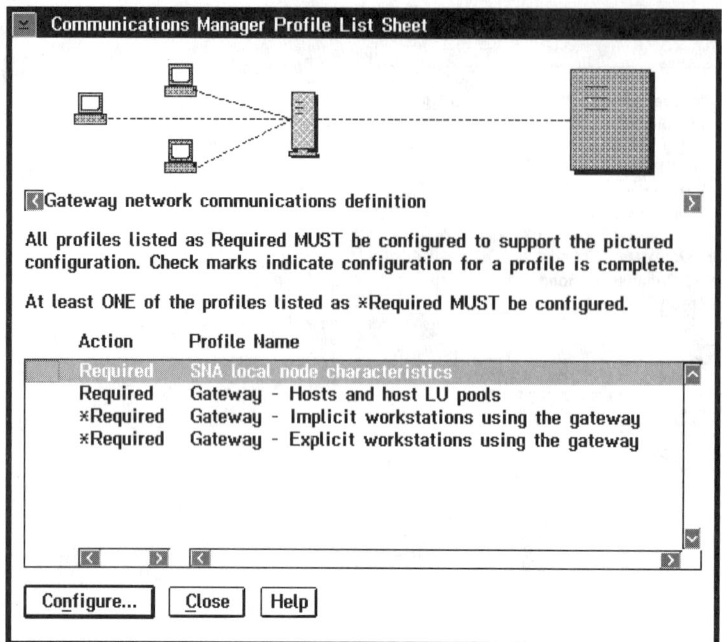

Figure 8.4 Select SNA local node characteristics. [*Reprinted by permission from IBM's OS/2 2.0, Copyright (1988, 1992) International Business Machines Corporation.*]

Local Node Characteristics

Required values

Network ID TOKENRBB

Local node name LSNA1A71

Node type

End node

Network node

Additional values

Local node ID (hex) 05D 00000

Local node alias name LSNA1A71

Optional comment

Activate Attach Manager at start up

OK Cancel Help

Figure 8.5 Defining the local node characteristics. [*Reprinted by permission from IBM's OS/2 2.0, Copyright (1988, 1992) International Business Machines Corporation.*]

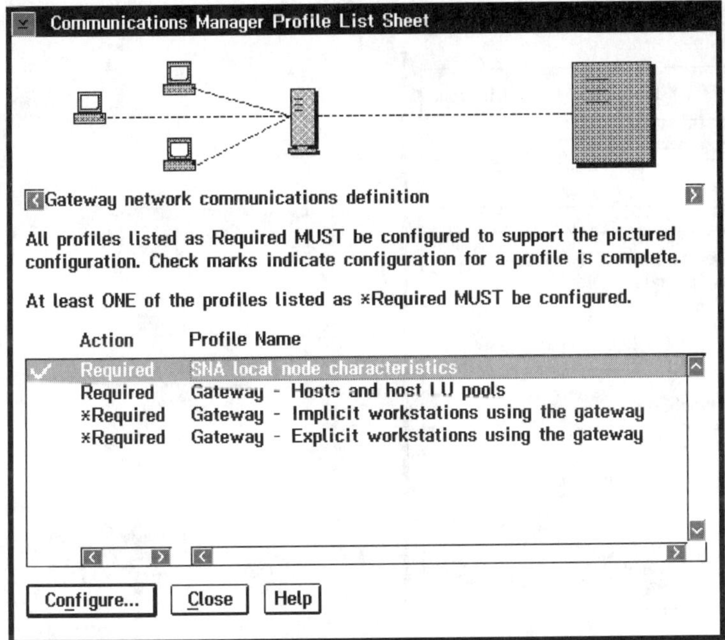

Figure 8.6 Select gateway hosts and LU pools. [*Reprinted by permission from IBM's OS/2 2.0, Copyright (1988, 1992) International Business Machines Corporation.*]

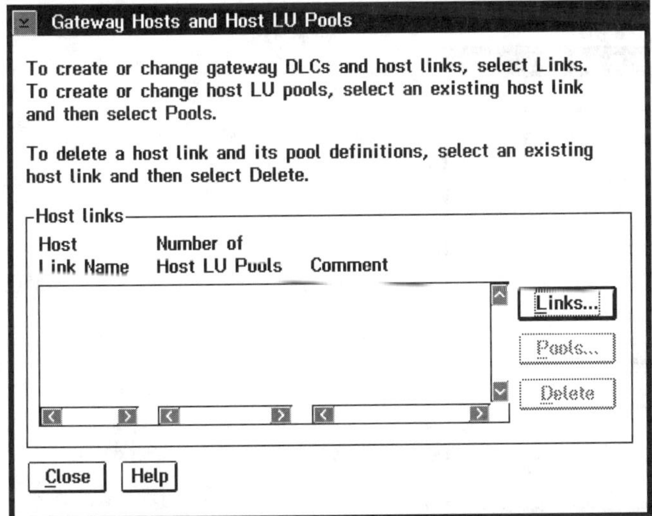

Figure 8.7 Creating the host link. [*Reprinted by permission from IBM's OS/2 2.0, Copyright (1988, 1992) International Business Machines Corporation.*]

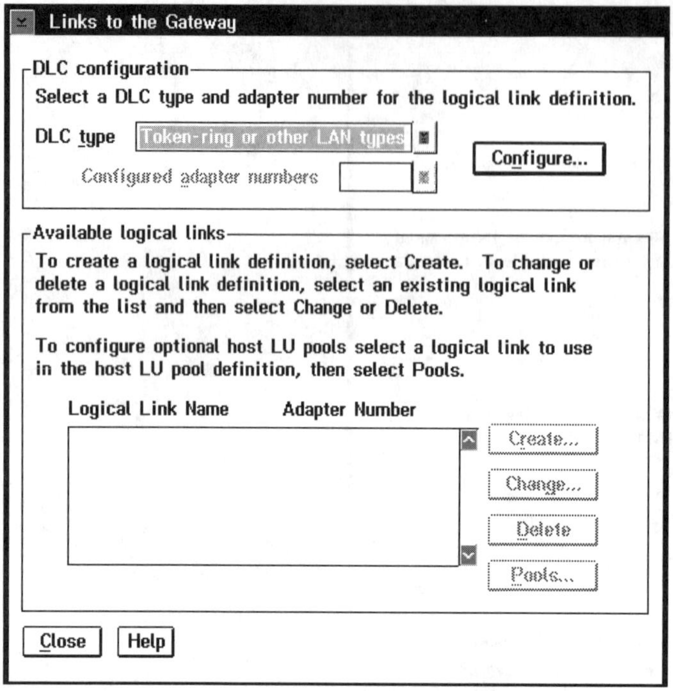

Links to the Gateway

DLC configuration

Select a DLC type and adapter number for the logical link definition.

DLC type Token-ring or other LAN types

Configured adapter numbers

Configure...

Available logical links

To create a logical link definition, select Create. To change or delete a logical link definition, select an existing logical link from the list and then select Change or Delete.

To configure optional host LU pools select a logical link to use in the host LU pool definition, then select Pools.

Logical Link Name Adapter Number

Create...

Change...

Delete

Pools...

Close Help

Figure 8.8 Linking to the host. [*Reprinted by permission from IBM's OS/2 2.0, Copyright (1988, 1992) International Business Machines Corporation.*]

Token Ring or Other LAN Types DLC Adapter Parameters

Adapter 0

Free unused links

Send alert for beaconing

Window count

Send window count 4 (1 - 8)

Receive window count 4 (1 - 8)

Maximum number of link stations 255 (1 - 255)

Maximum I-field size 1929 (265 - 16393)

Percent of incoming calls (%) 0 (0 - 100)

C&SM LAN ID TOKENRBB

Connection network name (optional) .

OK Delete Cancel Help

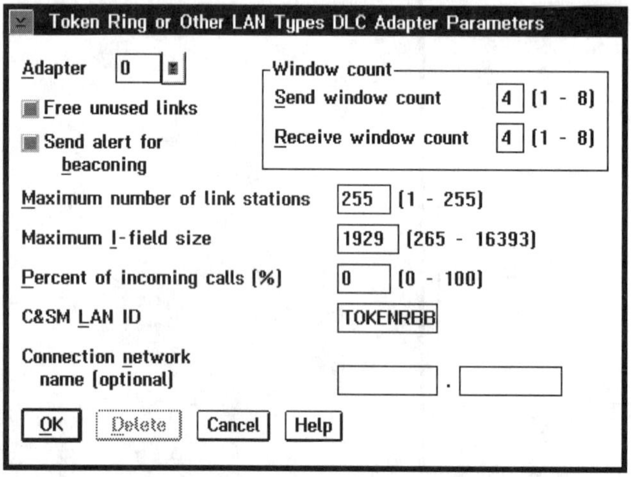

Figure 8.9 Defining the Token Ring adapter. [*Reprinted by permission from IBM's OS/2 2.0, Copyright (1988, 1992) International Business Machines Corporation.*]

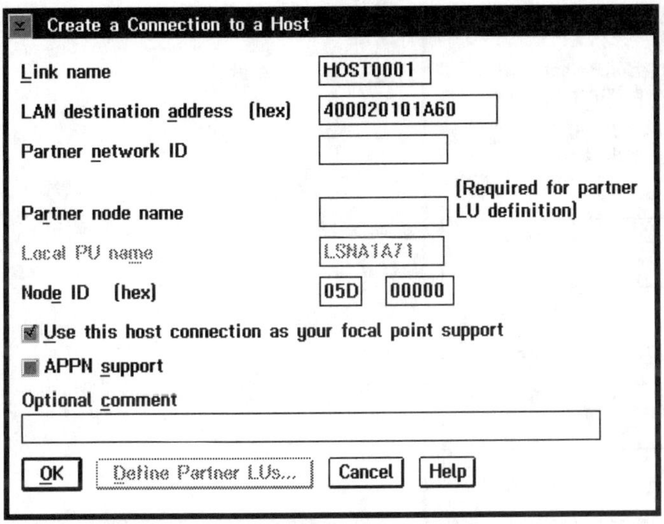

Create a Connection to a Host

Link name: HOST0001
LAN destination address (hex): 400020101A60
Partner network ID
Partner node name (Required for partner LU definition)
Local PU name: LSNA1A71
Node ID (hex): 05D 00000
Use this host connection as your focal point support
APPN support
Optional comment

OK | Define Partner LUs... | Cancel | Help

Figure 8.10 Entering the LAN destination address. [*Reprinted by permission from IBM's OS/2 2.0, Copyright (1988, 1992) International Business Machines Corporation.*]

Links to the Gateway

DLC configuration
Select a DLC type and adapter number for the logical link definition.
DLC type: Token-ring or other LAN types
Configured adapter numbers: 0
Configure...

Available logical links
To create a logical link definition, select Create. To change or delete a logical link definition, select an existing logical link from the list and then select Change or Delete.

To configure optional host LU pools select a logical link to use in the host LU pool definition, then select Pools.

Logical Link Name	Adapter Number
HOST0001	0

Create... | Change... | Delete | Pools...

Close | Help

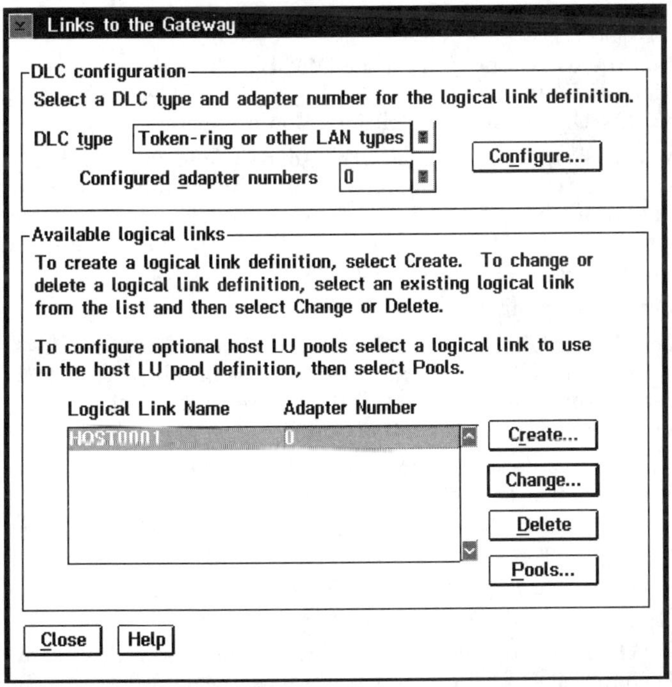

Figure 8.11 Close the gateway link configuration. [*Reprinted by permission from IBM's OS/2 2.0, Copyright (1988, 1992) International Business Machines Corporation.*]

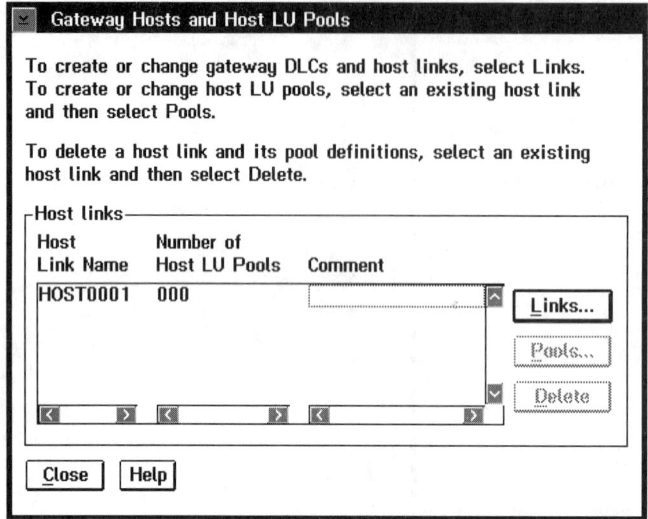

Figure 8.12 Define the Ethernet link. [*Reprinted by permission from IBM's OS/2 2.0, Copyright (1988, 1992) International Business Machines Corporation.*]

Step 15 Click on Links to bring up Fig. 8.13.

Step 16 Click on the box to the right of the DLC type field. You will see a selection list as illustrated in Fig. 8.14. Select Ethernet (ETHERAND) network, then click on Configure.

Step 17 Figure 8.15 should be displayed. The Adapter field should already have a 1 entered into it. You must change the maximum number of link stations from 4 to 255. You should enter the network name of your Ethernet segment in the C&SM LAN ID field. This is an eight-character name that is used for problem isolation.

Click on OK to bring up Fig. 8.16.

Step 18 Click on Close in Fig. 8.16, which will return you to the Gateway—Hosts and host LU pools screen. Click on Close in this panel, which will return you to Fig. 8.4. Notice that there is now a checkmark on the Hosts and host LU pools option.

Step 19 Now we are at a decision point. We must decide if we want to use implicit or explicit LU definitions. There is a section in the beginning of this chapter describing the pros and cons of both these LU definition methods.

If you wish to configure implicit LUs, you should skip to the "Defining Implicit LU Pools on the Gateway" section of this chapter.

We will choose explicit definitions for the remainder of this example. The implicit LU definition procedure will be described later in the chapter.

Click on Gateway—Explicit workstations using the gateway, then click on Configure.

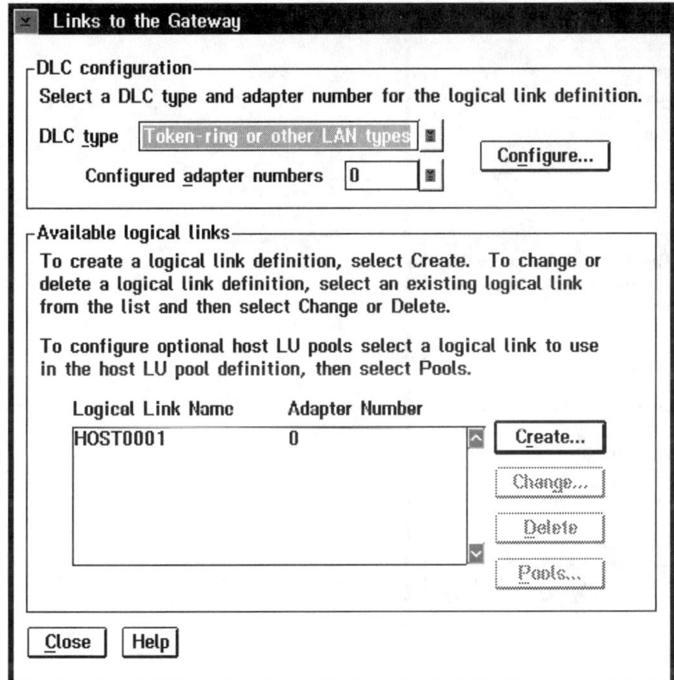

Figure 8.13 Selecting the DLC type. [*Reprinted by permission from IBM's OS/2 2.0, Copyright (1988, 1992) International Business Machines Corporation.*]

Step 20 Figure 8.17 should be displayed on your screen. Click on Links.

Step 21 Figure 8.18 should now be displayed. Notice that the DLC type field is set to Token Ring. Click on the box to the right of this field, and select Ethernet (ETHERAND) network.

Step 22 Click on Create to bring up Fig. 8.19. The Link name field should already have WKST0001 entered into it.

Now we must enter the LAN destination address field. This is a critical field, and care must be taken to ensure communications between the client and the gateway.

The destination address in Fig. 8.19 is the address of the client's NIC. Keep in mind that we are defining explicit LUs. We are about to tell the gateway how to determine which LUs a client workstation will use to access the host.

There are two types of NIC addresses: universal addresses and locally administered addresses (LAAs). The universal address is a unique number burned into the chips of the NIC. This address can be overridden by specifying an LAA. There are different methods for specifying the LAA, depending upon the NIC's application. With CM/2, the LAA is set by using the NTS/2 product. The setting of the LAA for the client workstations will be discussed a little

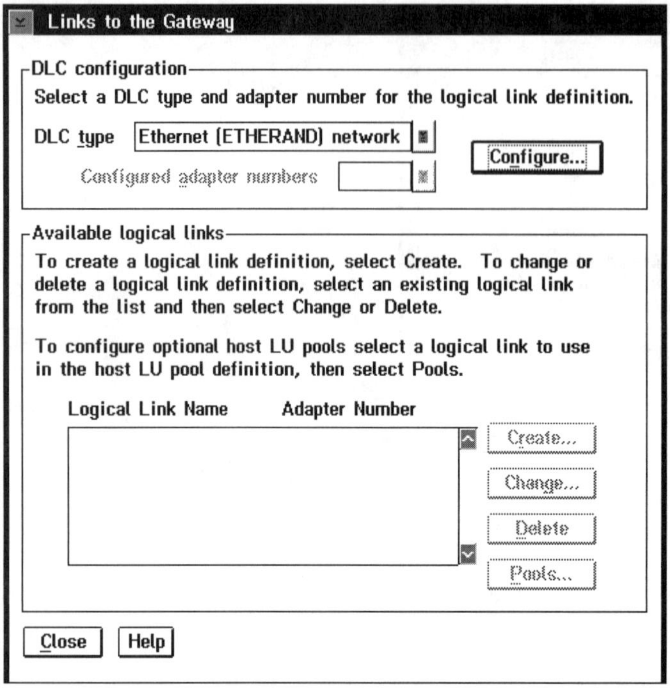

Links to the Gateway

DLC configuration

Select a DLC type and adapter number for the logical link definition.

DLC type Ethernet (ETHERAND) network

Configure...

Configured adapter numbers

Available logical links

To create a logical link definition, select Create. To change or delete a logical link definition, select an existing logical link from the list and then select Change or Delete.

To configure optional host LU pools select a logical link to use in the host LU pool definition, then select Pools.

Logical Link Name Adapter Number

Create... Change... Delete Pools...

Close Help

Figure 8.14 Configuring the Ethernet adapter. [*Reprinted by permission from IBM's OS/2 2.0, Copyright (1988, 1992) International Business Machines Corporation.*]

Ethernet (ETHERAND) Network DLC Adapter Parameters

Adapter 1

Free unused links

Window count

Send window count 4 (1 - 8)

Receive window count 4 (1 - 8)

Maximum number of link stations 255 (1 - 255)

Maximum I-field size 1417 (265 - 1417)

Percent of incoming calls (%) 0 (0 - 100)

C&SM LAN ID ETHER001

Connection network name (optional) .

OK Delete Cancel Help

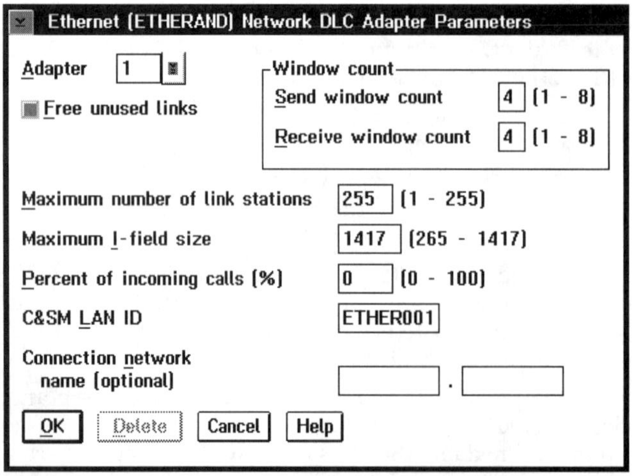

Figure 8.15 Selecting the Ethernet adapter parameters. [*Reprinted by permission from IBM's OS/2 2.0, Copyright (1988, 1992) International Business Machines Corporation.*]

Links to the Gateway

DLC configuration

Select a DLC type and adapter number for the logical link definition.

DLC type Ethernet (ETHERAND) network

Configured adapter numbers 1

Configure...

Available logical links

To create a logical link definition, select Create. To change or delete a logical link definition, select an existing logical link from the list and then select Change or Delete.

To configure optional host LU pools select a logical link to use in the host LU pool definition, then select Pools.

Logical Link Name Adapter Number

Create...

Change...

Delete

Pools...

Close Help

Figure 8.16 Completing the Ethernet link. [*Reprinted by permission from IBM's OS/2 2.0, Copyright (1988, 1992) International Business Machines Corporation.*]

Explicit Workstations Using the Gateway

To create or change gateway DLCs and workstation links, select Links. To create or change workstation LUs, select an existing workstation link and then select LUs.

To delete a workstation link and its LU definitions, select an existing workstation link and then select Delete.

Workstation links

Workstation Link Name	Number of Workstation LUs	Comment

Links...

LUs...

Delete

Close Help

Figure 8.17 Beginning the explicit workstation definition. [*Reprinted by permission from IBM's OS/2 2.0, Copyright (1988, 1992) International Business Machines Corporation.*]

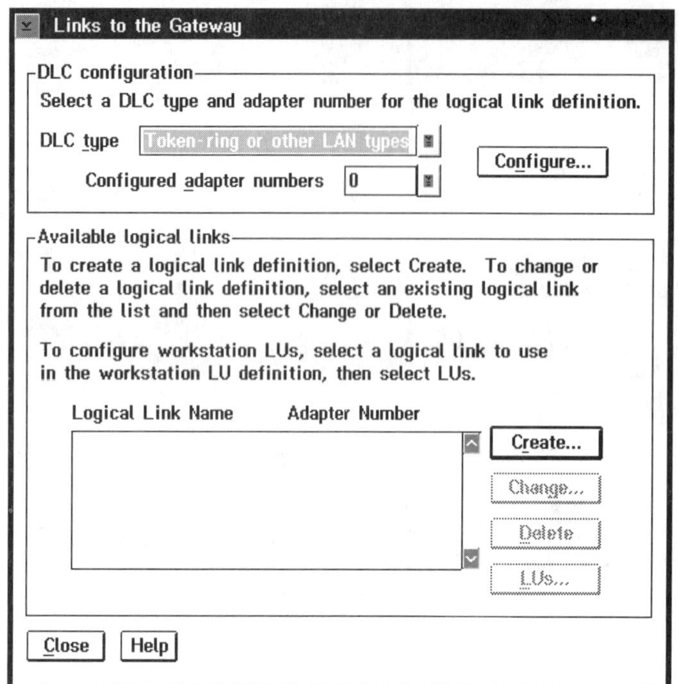

Figure 8.18 Select the ETHERAND DLC. [*Reprinted by permission from IBM's OS/2 2.0, Copyright (1988, 1992) International Business Machines Corporation.*]

Create a Connection to a Workstation

Link name WKST0001

LAN destination address (hex)

Note: The LAN destination address may need to be reversed.
See help windows for additional information.

Optional comment

OK Cancel Help

Figure 8.19 Enter the LAN destination address. [*Reprinted by permission from IBM's OS/2 2.0, Copyright (1988, 1992) International Business Machines Corporation.*]

later. All examples in this book use the LAA method rather than the NIC's universal address. Using LAAs allows the network administrator to swap NICs in the client workstations without reconfiguring the CM/2 gateway.

Back to our example. We are about to enter the LAA of the client NIC in the LAN destination address field in Fig. 8.19. The LAA of the client is 400001001064. Notice the comment in Fig. 8.19 which reads, "Note: The LAN destination address may need to be reversed." The procedure shown in Fig. 8.20 should be used to convert the client's NIC address to its bit-reversed image.

In our example the NIC address 400001001064 converts to 020080000826. This value should be placed in the LAN destination address field in Fig. 8.19.

Select OK after entering the bit-reversed LAN destination address.

Step 23 The panel shown in Fig. 8.18 should be displayed on your screen. A logical link name of WKST0001 should be in the lower box. Select LUs to bring up Fig. 8.21.

Step 24 Click on Create to display Fig. 8.22. This is where we connect the client workstation to a particular host (VTAM) address. Figure 8.23 illustrates the VTAM PU definition for the gateway.

Notice the first LU definition statement:

```
A7100002 LU LOCADDR=2
```

The A7100002 is the actual host (VTAM) address of the first LU defined to the gateway. This address should be entered into the LU name field in Fig. 8.22. These fields do not have to match in order for CM/2 to access the host; however, troubleshooting is much simpler when you have some method for correlating a workstation with a host LU address.

The first LU definition also states LOCADDR=2. This number should be entered into the Workstation NAU address and the Host NAU address fields. Figure 8.24 shows how your completed Workstation LU Definition screen should look.

Click on OK. Figure 8.25 should be displayed.

Step 25 Repeat step 24 to define the number of concurrent host sessions that the client workstation will have. In our example the second LU defined will use LU name A7100003 and NAU address 3. The next LU will use LU name A7100004 and NAU address 4, and so on through LU name A7100006. Figure 8.25 illustrates the completed Workstation Link Definition screen. Click on OK in Fig. 8.25.

Step 26 The CM/2 gateway definition is now completed. Click on Close on each screen until Fig. 8.26 is displayed. You must click on Yes to complete the gateway configuration. After you click on Yes, you will be prompted to insert certain CM/2 installation diskettes.

Address Bit Reversal Procedure

To determine the bit reversed NIC address, follow this procedure. For this example we will be reversing address 400001001064.

Step 1 Separate the address into two character fields:

40 00 01 00 10 64

Step 2 Reverse the positions of the characters in the two character sets:

04 00 10 00 01 46

Step 3 Use the following chart to bit reverse each number:

0 to 0
1 to 8
2 to 4
3 to C
4 to 2
5 to A
6 to 6
7 to E
8 to 1
9 to 9
A to 5
B to D
C to 3
D to B
E to 7
F to F

Using the above chart our example address 400001001064 converts to 020080000826

Figure 8.20 Address bit-reversal procedure.

Workstation Link Definition
Workstation link name WKST0001
Workstation LUs
LU Name
Workstation NAU Address
Host Link Name
Host NAU Address
Pool Name
Create...
Change...
Delete
Optional comment
OK
Help

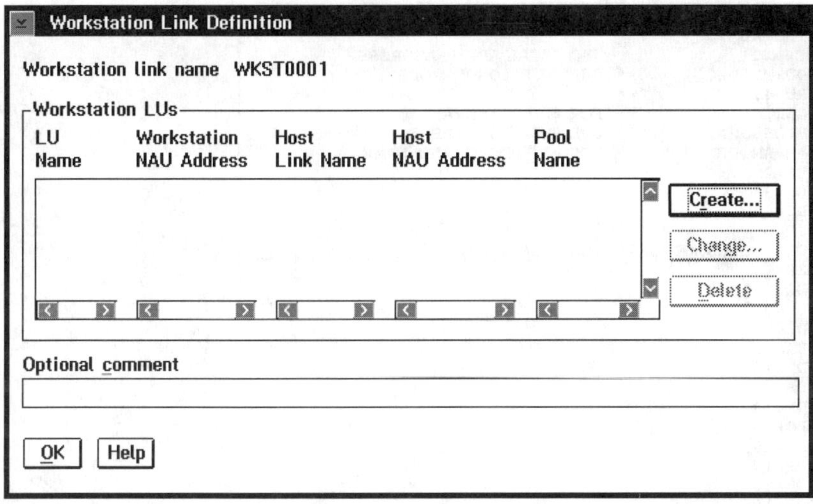

Figure 8.21 Defining the workstation link to the gateway. [*Reprinted by permission from IBM's OS/2 2.0, Copyright (1988, 1992) International Business Machines Corporation.*]

Workstation LU Definition
Host link name HOST0001
Workstation link name WKST0001
LU name
Workstation NAU address (001 - 254)
LU type
Pooled
Pool name
Dedicated
Host NAU address (001 - 254)
OK
Cancel
Help

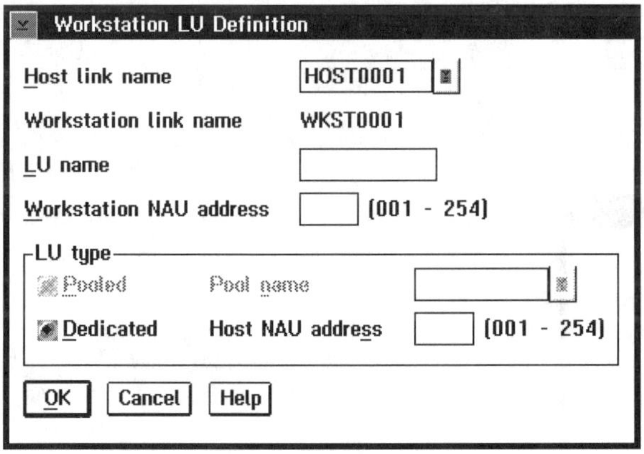

Figure 8.22 Entering the LU address. [*Reprinted by permission from IBM's OS/2 2.0, Copyright (1988, 1992) International Business Machines Corporation.*]

```
LSNA1A71 VBUILD TYPE=LOCAL
A01CA71  PU     CUADDR=A71,          ** PHYSICAL UNIT ADDRESS
                DLOGMOD=M2SDLCQ,     ** DEFAULT LOGON MODE ENTRY
                MAXBFRU=4,           **
                PACING=1,            ** FOR SNA GATEWAY
                USSTAB=USSSNA,       ** USE SNA USS TABLE
                MODETAB=AMODETAB     ** LOGON MODE TABLE NAME
A7100002 LU     LOCADDR=2
A7100003 LU     LOCADDR=3
A7100004 LU     LOCADDR=4
A7100005 LU     LOCADDR=5
A7100006 LU     LOCADDR=6,DLOGMOD=S3270,SSCPFM=USSSCS
A7100007 LU     LOCADDR=7
A7100008 LU     LOCADDR=8
A7100009 LU     LOCADDR=9
A7100010 LU     LOCADDR=10
A7100011 LU     LOCADDR=11
A7100012 LU     LOCADDR=12
A7100013 LU     LOCADDR=13
A7100014 LU     LOCADDR=14
A7100015 LU     LOCADDR=15
A7100016 LU     LOCADDR=16
A7100017 LU     LOCADDR=17
A7100018 LU     LOCADDR=18
A7100019 LU     LOCADDR=19
A7100020 LU     LOCADDR=20
A7100021 LU     LOCADDR=21
A7100022 LU     LOCADDR=22
A7100023 LU     LOCADDR=23
A7100024 LU     LOCADDR=24
A7100025 LU     LOCADDR=25
A7100026 LU     LOCADDR=26
A7100027 LU     LOCADDR=27
A7100028 LU     LOCADDR=28
```

Figure 8.23 Sample gateway VTAM definition.

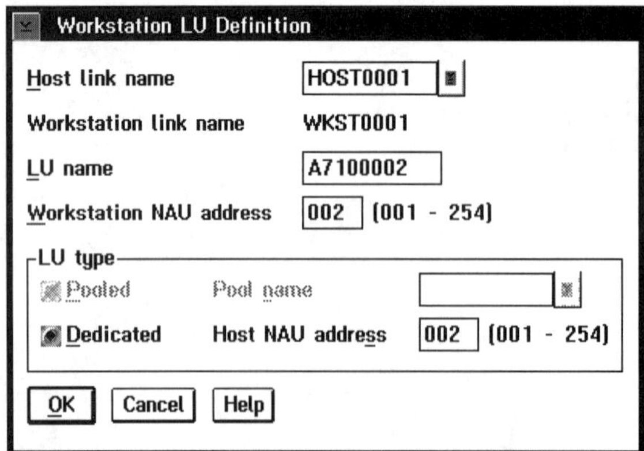

Figure 8.24 Enter the LU address and LU name. [*Reprinted by permission from IBM's OS/2 2.0, Copyright (1988, 1992) International Business Machines Corporation.*]

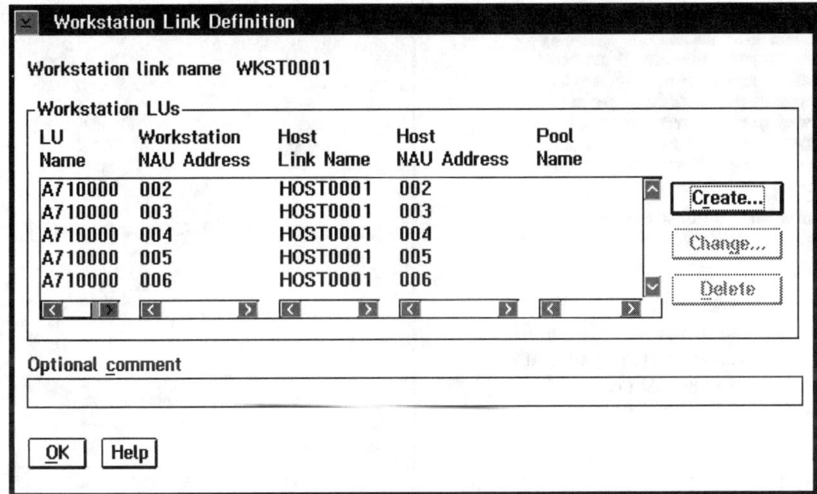

Figure 8.25 Completed workstation LU definition. [*Reprinted by permission from IBM's OS/2 2.0, Copyright (1988, 1992) International Business Machines Corporation.*]

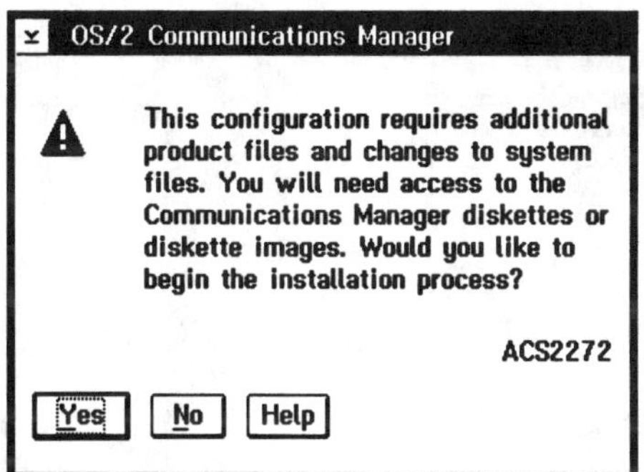

Figure 8.26 Installing additional CM/2 files. [*Reprinted by permission from IBM's OS/2 2.0, Copyright (1988, 1992) International Business Machines Corporation.*]

NTS/2 Gateway Configuration

Now we must configure NTS/2 to define our Token Ring and Ethernet NICs and the protocols they support. If you do not already have NTS/2 installed on the gateway PC, do this now.

To configure NTS/2 for the gateway configuration, follow this procedure.

Step 1 Open an OS/2 full-screen session. Change directories to C:\IBMCOM. If IBMCOM does not exist, then NTS/2 has not been installed.

Step 2 Enter LAPS at the OS/2 prompt. Figure 8.27 will be displayed.

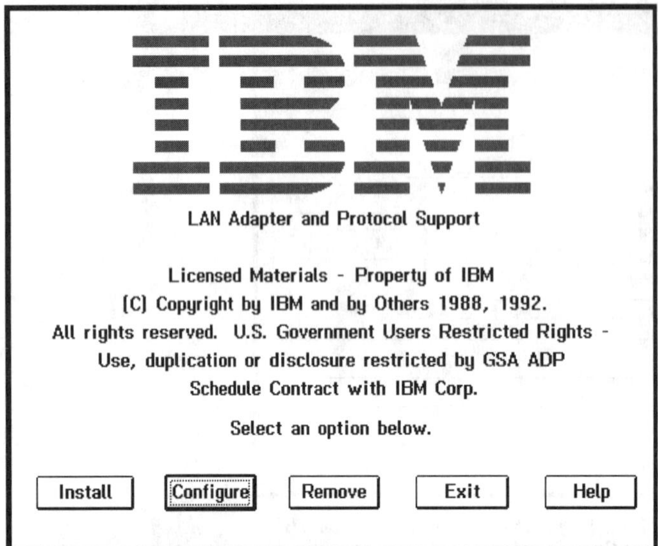

Figure 8.27 Initial LAPS screen. [*Reprinted by permission from IBM's OS/2 2.0, Copyright (1988, 1992) International Business Machines Corporation.*]

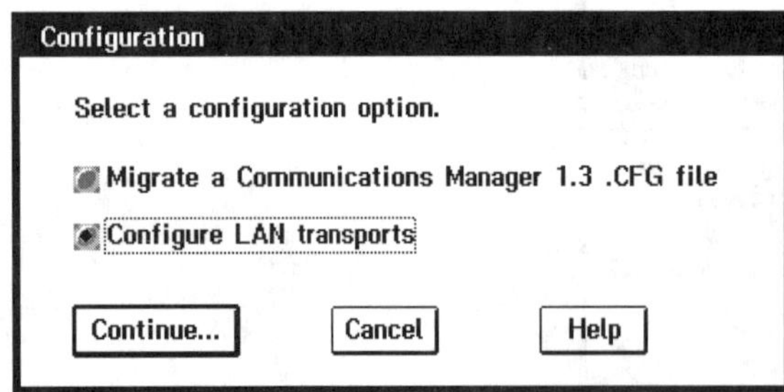

Figure 8.28 Select the configure option. [*Reprinted by permission from IBM's OS/2 2.0, Copyright (1988, 1992) International Business Machines Corporation.*]

Step 3 Click on Configure, and Fig. 8.28 will be displayed.

Step 4 Click on Configure LAN transports, then click on Continue. Figure 8.29 will be displayed.

Step 5 As you recall from the CM/2 configuration, there are two NIC adapters in the gateway PC. Adapter 0 is a Token Ring NIC, and adapter 1 is an Ethernet NIC. You must define these two NICs to NTS/2.

Browse through the network adapters section in Fig. 8.29, and select IBM Token Ring network adapters. If you have a Busmaster adapter installed, you should choose that entry. Click on the Add button, and the adapter entry should move down to the current configuration section.

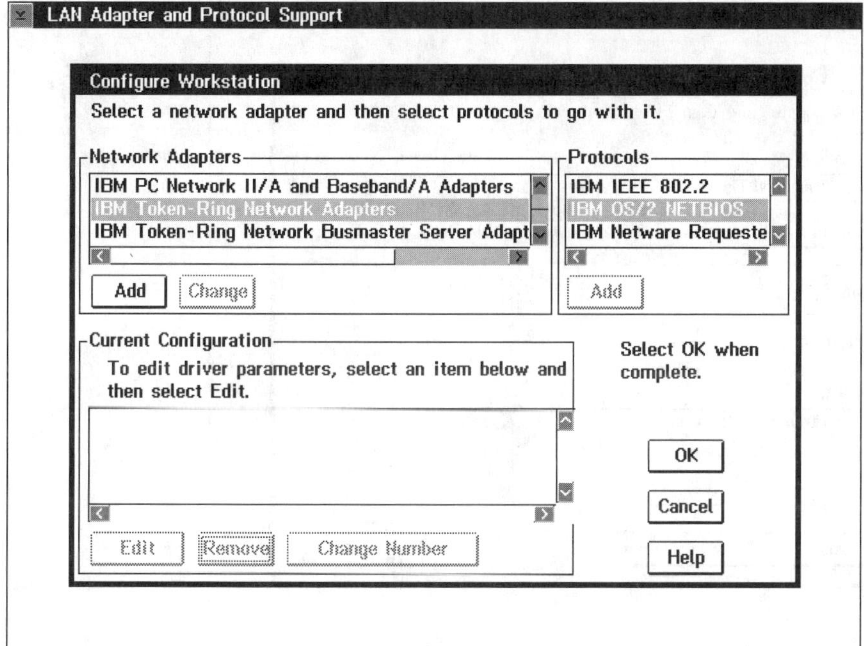

Figure 8.29 Select the Token Ring adapter. [*Reprinted by permission from IBM's OS/2 2.0, Copyright (1988, 1992) International Business Machines Corporation.*]

Step 6 In the protocols section, select IBM IEEE 802.2, the click on Add. The 802.2 protocol should move down to the current configuration section. Your screen should resemble Fig. 8.30.

Step 7 Click on the IBM IEEE 802.2 entry in the current configuration section of your screen, then click on Edit. Figure 8.31 should be displayed.

You are at another critical configuration screen for the gateway. The gateway is accessing the host, using the downstream PU (DSPU) method. As Chap. 1 described, to use the DSPU method, the gateway must *become* one of the DSPUs defined in the 3174 TIC or 37x5 TIC configuration.

Figure 8.32 illustrates the network configuration for which this gateway is being configured. A TIC installed in a 3174 is connected to a Token Ring. One of the DSPUs defined to the 3174 is 400020101A71. The Token Ring NIC in the CM/2 gateway will become this DSPU.

So, you must enter the address of the DSPU that you are going to use in the Network adapter address field in Fig. 8.31. This will set the LAA of the Token Ring NIC to the address of the DSPU defined in the TIC. The default parameters for the other fields in Fig. 8.31 will suffice.

Select OK after entering the network adapter address.

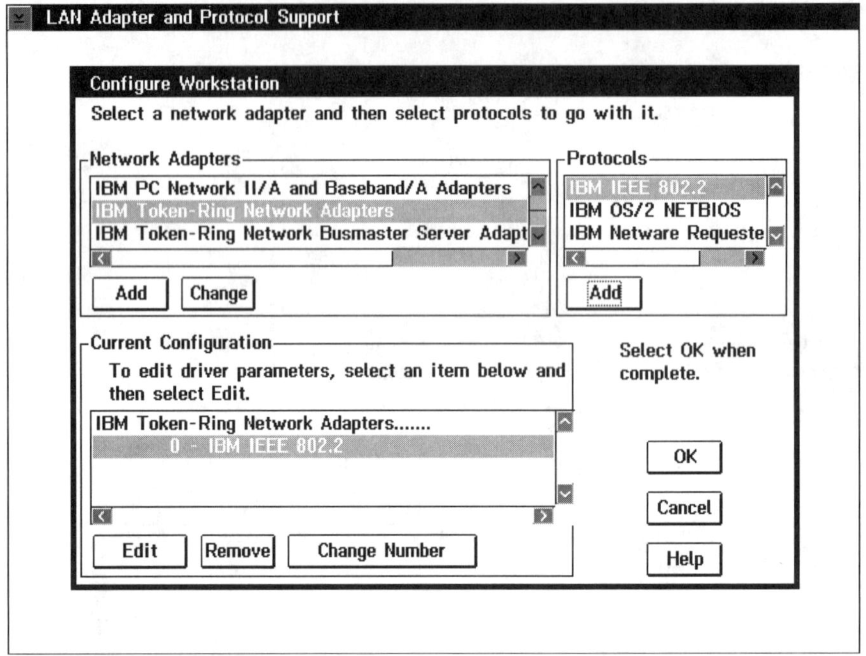

Figure 8.30 Select the IEEE 802.2 protocol. [*Reprinted by permission from IBM's OS/2 2.0, Copyright (1988, 1992) International Business Machines Corporation.*]

Parameters for IBM IEEE 802.2

Edit the parameters as needed. Except for parameters preceded by "*", changes affect all instances of the driver.

*Network adapter address	400020101A71
*Type of Ethernet driver support	I
*System key value	0
*Adapter open options	2000
*802 trace level	0
*Maximum link stations	8
*Maximum SAPs	3
*Maximum group SAPs	0
*Maximum number of users	3

OK Cancel Range Help

Figure 8.31 Enter the LAA. [*Reprinted by permission from IBM's OS/2 2.0, Copyright (1988, 1992) International Business Machines Corporation.*]

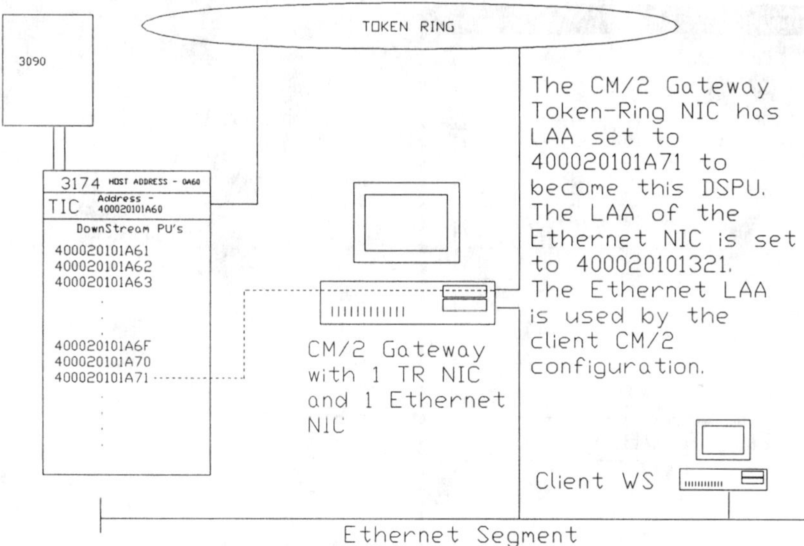

Figure 8.32 CM/2 gateway specifications.

Step 8 Click on the IBM Token Ring network adapters entry in the current configuration section, then click on Edit. Figure 8.33 will be displayed. Enter the same network adapter address that you specified in the previous step, then click on OK.

Step 9 In Fig. 8.34, browse through the list of NIC types in the network adapters section, and click on the type of Ethernet adapter you have installed in the gateway PC. For this example we will choose the 3Com 3C503 adapter. Click on Add to move the adapter to the current configuration section.

Step 10 Click on the IBM IEEE 802.2 protocol in the protocols section, then click on Add to move it to the current configuration section. Your screen should resemble Fig. 8.34.

Step 11 In the current configuration section, click on the IBM 802.2 entry beneath the Ethernet NIC adapter entry, then click on Edit. Figure 8.35 will be displayed.

Step 12 You must enter a locally administered address in the Network adapter address field, just as you did for the Token Ring protocol. The address you specify will be used when the client workstations are defined, so you should jot down this address. In this example, we choose 400020101321 for our Ethernet LAA. Click on OK to return to the LAPS panel.

Step 13 Click on the Ethernet adapter entry in the current configuration section, then click on Edit. Figure 8.36 will be displayed. Enter the same LAA as you did for the previous step, then click on OK.

Step 14 Click on OK to complete the configuration. When you see the ini-

Parameters for IBM Token-Ring Network Adapters

Edit the parameters as needed.

Early release	NO
Adapter Mode	PRIMARY
Network adapter address	400020101A71
Shared RAM address	
Maximum number of queued transmits	6
Number of receive buffers	2
Receive buffer size	256
Number of adapter transmit buffers	1
Transmit buffer size	

OK | Cancel | Range | Help

Figure 8.33 Entering the network adapter address. [*Reprinted by permission from IBM's OS/2 2.0, Copyright (1988, 1992) International Business Machines Corporation.*]

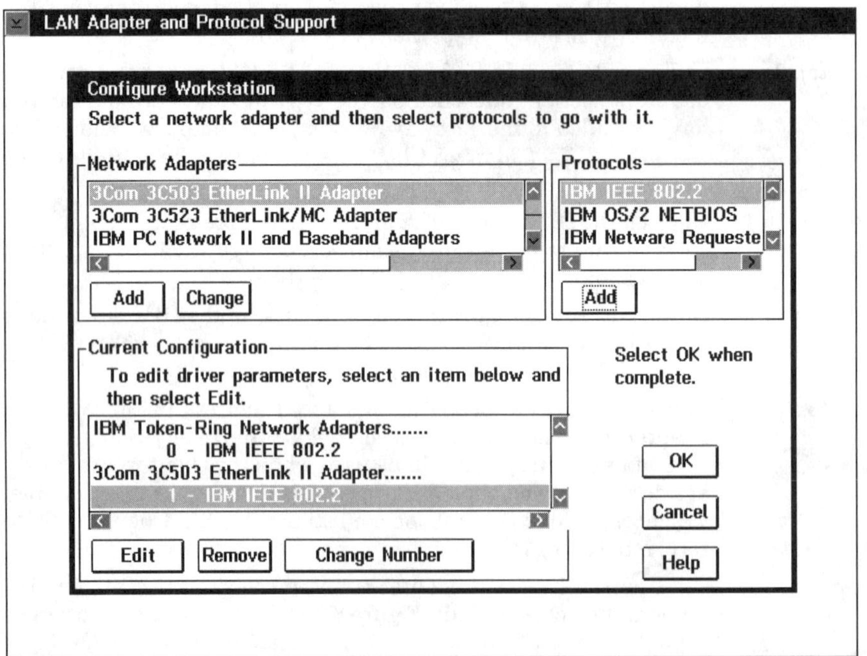

Figure 8.34 Configuring the Ethernet adapter. [*Reprinted by permission from IBM's OS/2 2.0, Copyright (1988, 1992) International Business Machines Corporation.*]

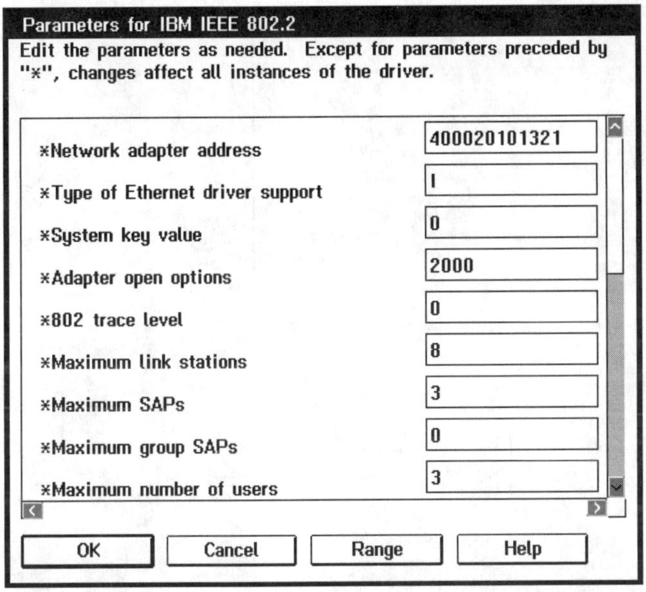

Parameters for IBM IEEE 802.2

Edit the parameters as needed. Except for parameters preceded by "*", changes affect all instances of the driver.

*Network adapter address	400020101321
*Type of Ethernet driver support	I
*System key value	0
*Adapter open options	2000
*802 trace level	0
*Maximum link stations	8
*Maximum SAPs	3
*Maximum group SAPs	0
*Maximum number of users	3

OK Cancel Range Help

Figure 8.35 Setting the LAA. [*Reprinted by permission from IBM's OS/2 2.0, Copyright (1988, 1992) International Business Machines Corporation.*]

Parameters for 3Com 3C503 EtherLink II Adapter

Edit the parameters as needed.

Network adapter address	400020101321
Interrupt level	3
I/O base address	300
Transceiver	ONBOARD
Maximum number of queued transmits	8
Number of adapter transmit buffers	2

OK Cancel Range Help

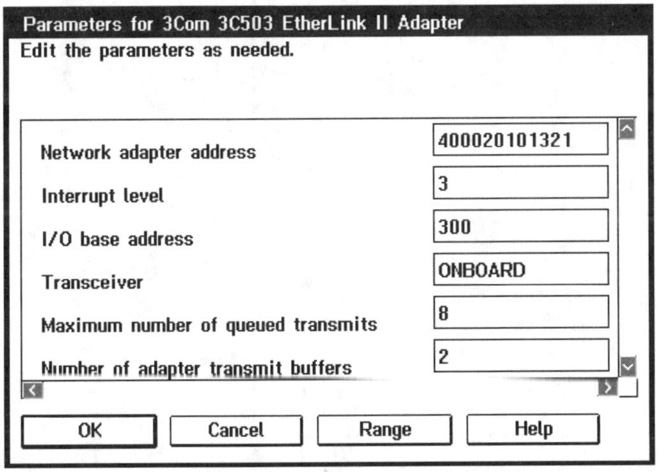

Figure 8.36 Setting the network adapter address. [*Reprinted by permission from IBM's OS/2 2.0, Copyright (1988, 1992) International Business Machines Corporation.*]

```
[PROT_MAN]

   DRIVERNAME = PROTMAN$

[IBMLXCFG]

   IBMTOK_nif = IBMTOK.nif
   LANDD_nif = LANDD.nif
   ELNKII_nif = ELNKII.nif

[LANDD_nif]

   DriverName = LANDD$
   Bindings = IBMTOK_nif,ELNKII_nif
   NETADDRESS = "400020101A71","400020101321"
   ETHERAND_TYPE = "I","I"
   SYSTEM_KEY = 0x0,0x0
   OPEN_OPTIONS = 0x2000,0x2000
   TRACE = 0x0,0x0
   LINKS = 8,8
   MAX_SAPS = 3,3
   MAX_G_SAPS = 0,0
   USERS = 3,3
   TI_TICK_G1 = 255,255
   T1_TICK_G1 = 15,15
   T2_TICK_G1 = 3,3
   TI_TICK_G2 = 255,255
   T1_TICK_G2 = 25,25
   T2_TICK_G2 = 10,10
   IPACKETS = 250,250
   UIPACKETS = 100,100
   MAXTRANSMITS = 6,6
   MINTRANSMITS = 2,2
   TCBS = 64,64
   GDTS = 30,30
   ELEMENTS = 800,800

[IBMTOK_nif]

   DriverName = IBMTOK$
   ADAPTER = "PRIMARY"
   NETADDRESS = "400020101A71"
   MAXTRANSMITS = 6
   RECVBUFS = 2
   RECVBUFSIZE = 256
   XMITBUFS = 1

[ELNKII_nif]

   DriverName = ELNKII$
   netaddress = "400020101321"
   interrupt = 3
   ioaddress = 0x300
   transceiver = "ONBOARD"
   maxtransmits = 8
   xmitbufs = 2
```

Figure 8.37 Sample PROTOCOL.INI file.

tial LAPS screen, click on Exit. The program will then tell you it is modifying CONFIG.SYS. Click on Continue.

Figure 8.37 is the C:\IBMCOM\PROTOCOL.INI file that was created by this exercise.

Step 15 Now you must make sure that the host (VTAM) definitions are in place for the gateway PU. The PU name for the gateway is

LSNA1A71, so you must create member SYS1.VTAMLST-(LSNA1A71) to define the gateway to VTAM.

Figure 8.23 is the PU/LU definition for this sample configuration. Please keep in mind that each shop defines PUs and LUs a little differently. You should follow the standards of your installation when modifying VTAM definitions.

Step 16 After defining the PU to VTAM, you must activate it. To do this, enter the following command through the mainframe system console:

```
V NET,ACT,ID=LSNA1A71
```

Step 17 You should now reboot your gateway PC and look closely for errors when Communications Manager starts.

Client Workstation CM/2 Configuration for Explicit LUs

Now that the gateway PC has been configured, we are ready to configure the client workstation. The client workstation should be connected to the same Ethernet segment that the gateway is attached to. The client can be on a different Ethernet segment than the gateway is installed on, if a bridge connects the two Ethernet segments. This bridge must be a true bridge. The Novell bridge (which is actually a router) will not suffice. If you have a router installed to connect the Ethernet segments in your LAN, you must enable bridging for these Ethernet segments.

If you have not already done so, install CM/2 and NTS/2 on the client PC.

This section describes how to configure a CM/2 client workstation to access the gateway using explicit LU definitions. We will see how to configure implicit LUs later in this chapter. We will configure this client PC to have four terminal sessions and one printer session. Let's get started.

Step 1 Double-click on the CM/2 icon.

Step 2 Double-click on the Communications Manager setup icon.

Step 3 Click on Setup on the initial screen.

Step 4 Enter a configuration name and description on the Open Configuration screen, then click on OK.

Step 5 You will be asked if this is a new configuration. Click on Yes.

Step 6 You will be asked if this configuration is for this workstation. Click on Yes.

Step 7 Figure 8.38 should be displayed on your screen. Select Ethernet (ETHERAND) network under the workstation connection type. Select 3270 emulation under the feature or application section. Click on Configure.

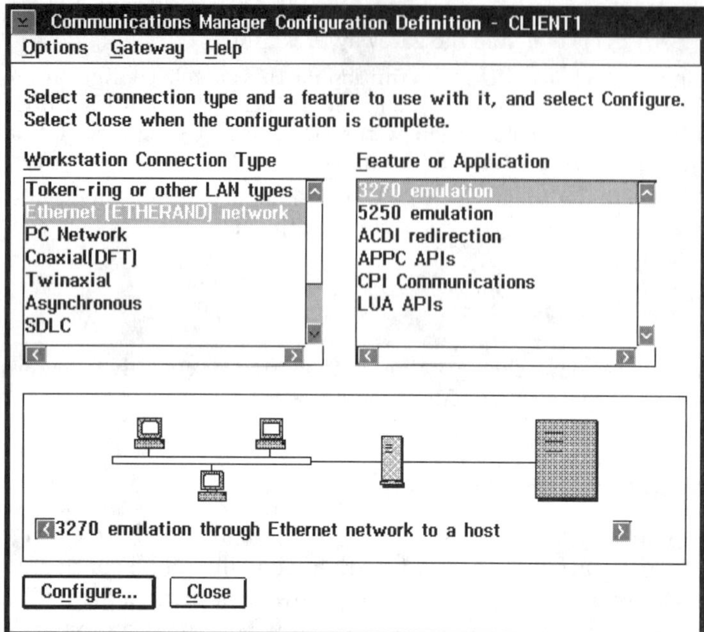

Figure 8.38 Defining and Ethernet client. [*Reprinted by permission from IBM's OS/2 2.0, Copyright (1988, 1992) International Business Machines Corporation.*]

Step 8 Figure 8.39 should be displayed. Enter the name of your Ethernet network in the Network ID field. This should match the name you placed in Fig. 8.15.

Enter WKST0001 in the Local node name field. The name you place in this field must match the link name entry in Fig. 8.19.

If you are accessing a local host, key in 00000 for the second part of the local node ID. The first part of this field should already contain 05D.

The LAN destination address is an important field. The client workstation (the one we are currently configuring) communicates directly with the Ethernet card in the gateway PC. In our example, we set the LAA of the gateway's Ethernet NIC to 400020101321. This was done when we configured NTS/2 using Figs. 8.35 and 8.36. Bit-reverse this address, using the procedure illustrated in Fig. 8.37, and key the result in the LAN destination address field. In this example the address 400020101321 translates to 02000408C884.

You are defining four terminal sessions and one printer session. You must enter the number of terminal sessions on the last field on Fig. 8.39. For this example, enter a 4, then click on Advanced.

Step 9 Figure 8.40 should be displayed. Click on 3270 emulation, then click on Configure. Figure 8.41 should be displayed.

Step 10 Click on File, then click on New. Figure 8.42 should be displayed.

3270 Emulation through Ethernet (ETHERAND) Network

Network ID ETHER001

Local node name WKST0001

Local node ID (hex) 05D 00000

LAN destination address (hex) 02000408C884

Number of terminal sessions 4

OK Advanced... Cancel Help

Figure 8.39 Setting the destination address. [*Reprinted by permission from IBM's OS/2 2.0, Copyright (1988, 1992) International Business Machines Corporation.*]

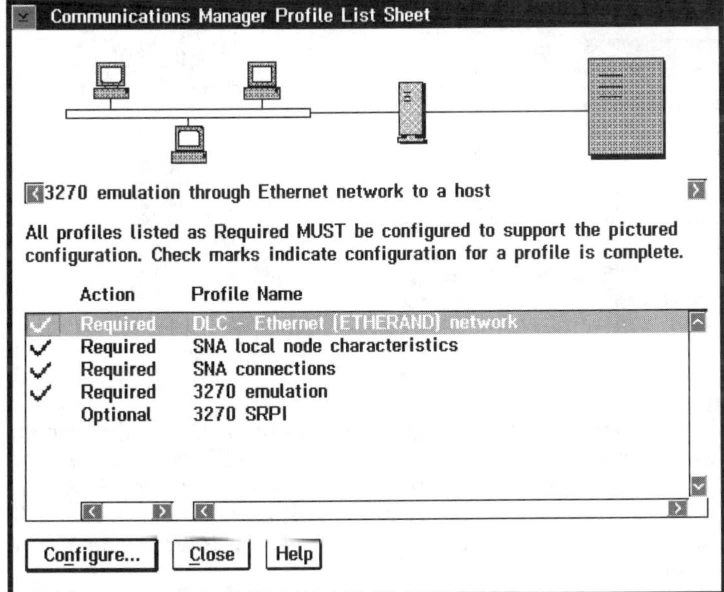

Figure 8.40 Select 3270 emulation. [*Reprinted by permission from IBM's OS/2 2.0, Copyright (1988, 1992) International Business Machines Corporation.*]

Step 11 Click on Logical printer, then click on OK.

Step 12 Figure 8.43 should be displayed. Notice that the short session name is already filled in for you. The only information you need to provide in this panel is the LU local/NAU address. The number you place in this field relates to the LOCADDR parameter in the

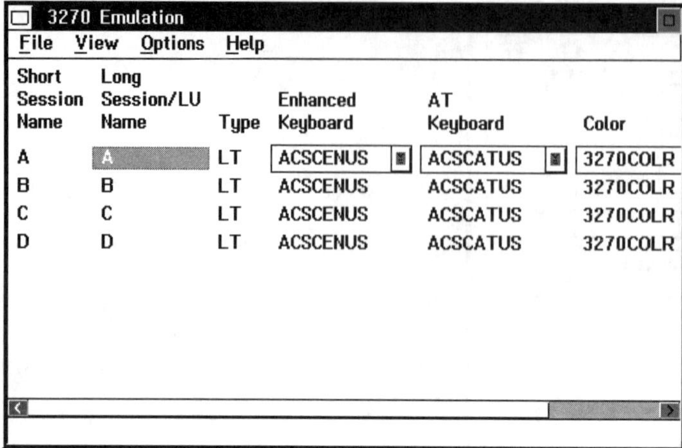

Figure 8.41 Viewing the 3270 sessions defined. [*Reprinted by permission from IBM's OS/2 2.0, Copyright (1988, 1992) International Business Machines Corporation.*]

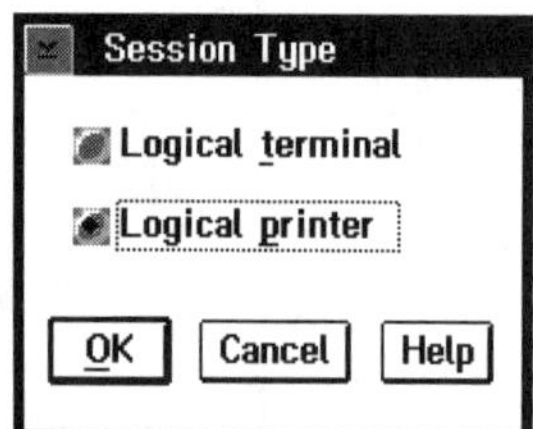

Figure 8.42 Adding a 3270 printer. [*Reprinted by permission from IBM's OS/2 2.0, Copyright (1988, 1992) International Business Machines Corporation.*]

VTAM configuration, as illustrated in Fig. 8.23. In this example we choose 6 as the LU address. Notice that in Fig. 8.23, LOCADDR 6 is defined differently from the other LUs. You must make sure that the number you specify in the LU address field in Fig. 8.43 corresponds to an LU address that defines a printer in your VTAM definition.

Click on Save as, to bring up Fig. 8.44.

Step 13 You must enter the long session/LU name in Fig. 8.44. For consistency reasons, enter the same name as defined in the short session name in Fig. 8.43. Click on OK.

Step 14 Close the 3270 emulation window by double-clicking on the upper left-hand corner. Close the remaining CM/2 setup windows by clicking on Close.

Step 15 You will be asked if you want to update the system files. You should allow the updates to occur.

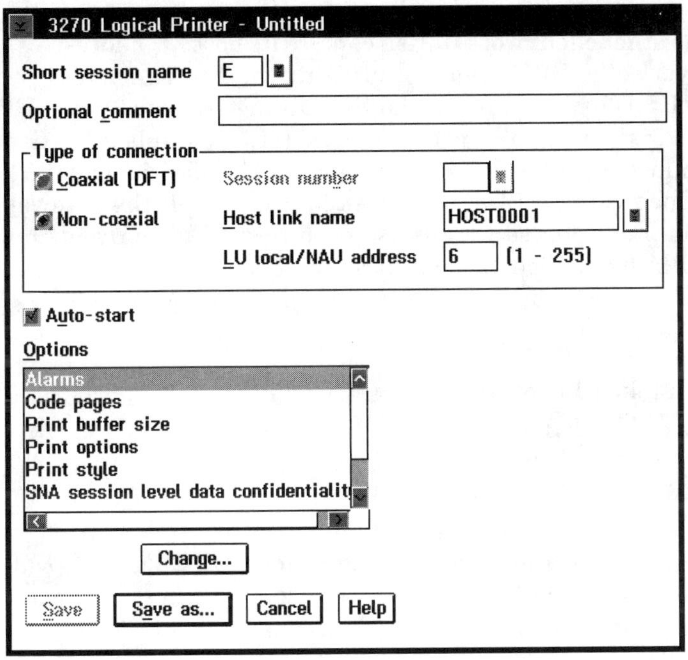

Figure 8.43 Entering the printer's LU address. [*Reprinted by permission from IBM's OS/2 2.0, Copyright (1988, 1992) International Business Machines Corporation.*]

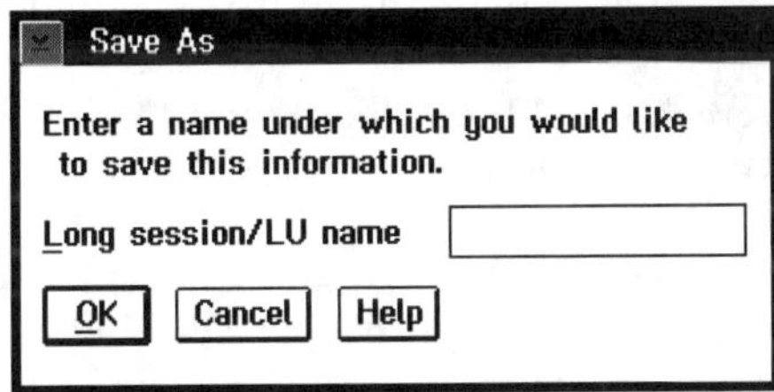

Figure 8.44 Entering the long session name for the printer. [*Reprinted by permission from IBM's OS/2 2.0, Copyright (1988, 1992) International Business Machines Corporation.*]

Step 16 You should reboot your system, then bring up CM/2. If all the components are defined properly, your host sessions should activate.

Defining Implicit LU Pools on the Gateway

So far we have been dealing with explicit LU definitions. We have configured the gateway so that the client workstation always uses the same host LU address. There are advantages and disadvantages to the explicit LU assignment method, as described earlier. One of the major disadvantages is that when a client workstation is not accessing the mainframe, no other client workstation can use its host LU address(es). This is not a very efficient method for utilizing the host resources.

With implicit LU definitions, we will be defining groups of host LUs that will be shared among all the client workstations. Implicit LU definitions are much simpler than the explicit LU definition method. When we defined explicit LUs, we were required to tell the gateway which NIC adapter address was to use each host LU. We avoid this complexity with the implicit LU definition method.

We will look at the steps required for the gateway CM/2 configuration to do the following:

- Define five implicit LU pools on the gateway PC:
  LUs 7 to 10 will be defined as pool_lu2.
  LUs 11 to 14 will be defined as pool_lu3.
  LUs 15 to 18 will be defined as pool_lu4.
  LUs 19 to 22 will be defined as pool_lu5.
- On the client workstation we will define four LUs. One LU will access the host via pool_lu2, another will access the host via pool—lu3, and so on through pool_lu5.

Let's get started by adding the implicit LU definitions to the gateway PC.

Step 1 Follow steps 1 through 18 from the "Configuring CM/2 on the Gateway PC" section earlier in this chapter, if you have not already done so.

Step 2 Your screen should look like Fig. 8.45, with the SNA local node characteristics and the Gateway—Hosts and host LU pools field already defined.

Click on Gateway—Hosts and host LU pools, then click on Configure, and Fig. 8.46 should be displayed.

Step 3 Click on the HOST0001 entry, then click on Pools. Figure 8.47 should be displayed.

Step 4 Click on Create in Fig. 8.47. This will bring up Fig. 8.48. Enter pool_lu2 as the pool name, then click on Create.

Step 5 Figure 8.49 should be displayed. Enter 7 as the start NAU address and 10 as the end NAU address, then press OK. This should return you to Fig. 8.48.

Step 6 Click on OK in Fig. 8.48. This will return you to Fig. 8.47.

Step 7 Repeat steps 4 through 6 until you define all four LU pools. When you are finished, you should return to a panel that looks like Fig. 8.50.

Step 8 Click on OK and Close on each panel, until you return to Fig. 8.45.

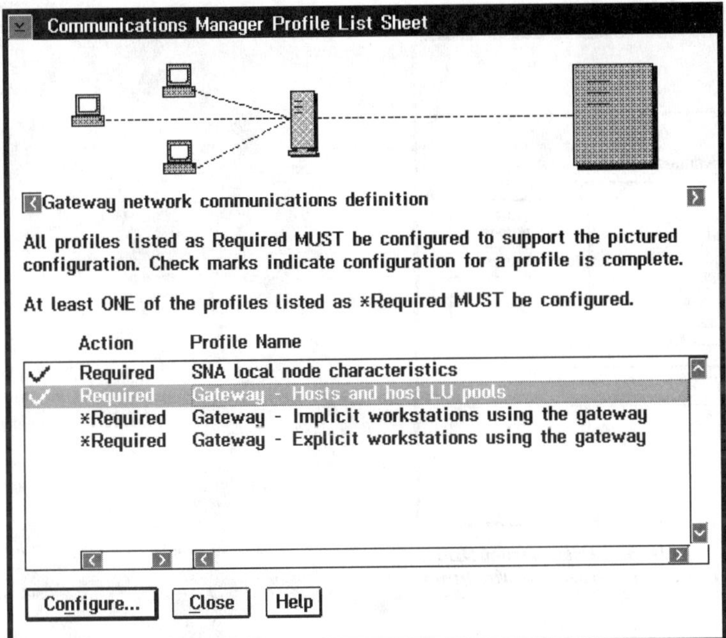

Figure 8.45 Preparing to define implicit LU pools. [*Reprinted by permission from IBM's OS/2 2.0, Copyright (1988, 1992) International Business Machines Corporation.*]

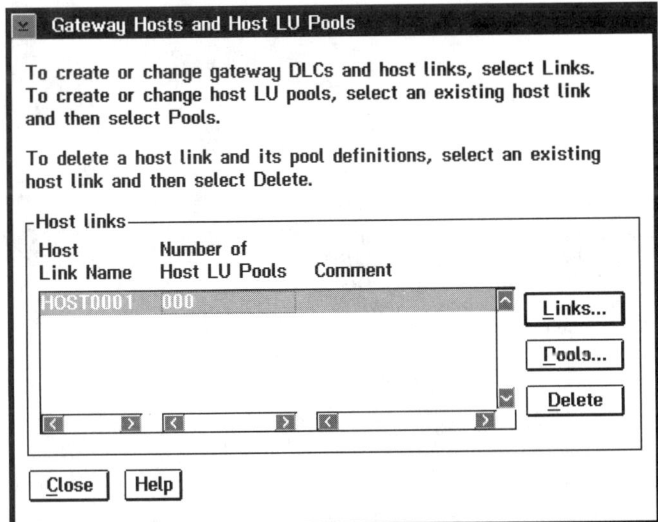

Figure 8.46 Modify the host link. [*Reprinted by permission from IBM's OS/2 2.0, Copyright (1988, 1992) International Business Machines Corporation.*]

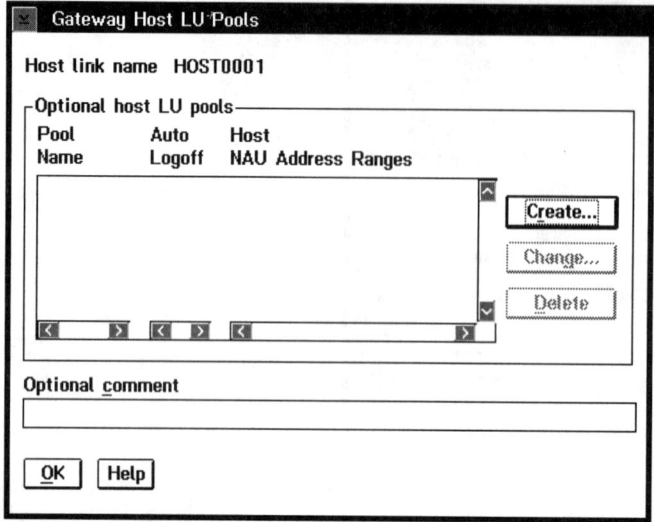

Figure 8.47 Create an LU pool. [*Reprinted by permission from IBM's OS/2 2.0, Copyright (1988, 1992) International Business Machines Corporation.*]

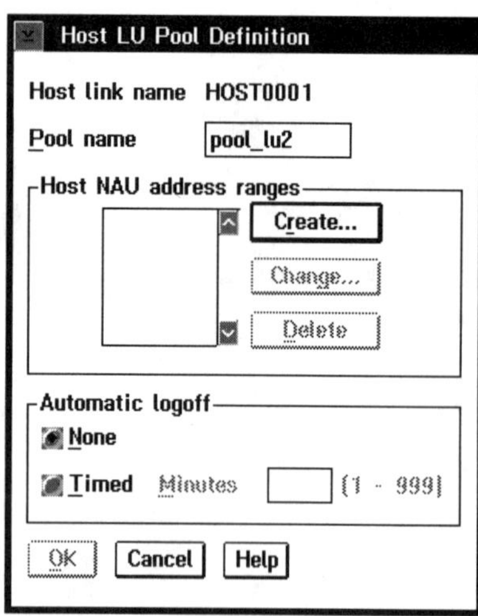

Figure 8.48 Enter the pool name. [*Reprinted by permission from IBM's OS/2 2.0, Copyright (1988, 1992) International Business Machines Corporation.*]

Host NAU Address Ranges

Start NAU address [7] (001 - 254)

End NAU address [10] (007 - 254)

OK Cancel Help

Figure 8.49 Enter the host LU range. [*Reprinted by permission from IBM's OS/2 2.0, Copyright (1988, 1992) International Business Machines Corporation.*]

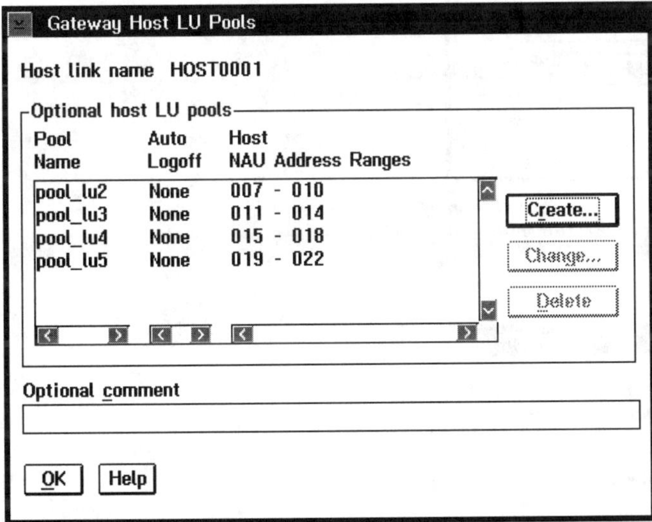

Figure 8.50 The completed LU pool screen. [*Reprinted by permission from IBM's OS/2 2.0, Copyright (1988, 1992) International Business Machines Corporation.*]

Step 9 From Fig. 8.45, click on Gateway—Implicit workstations using the gateway, then click on Configure.

Step 10 Figure 8.51 should be displayed. Select Ethernet (ETHERAND) network from the selection list, then click on Implicit LUs.

Step 11 Figure 8.52 should be displayed. Click on Create to bring up Fig. 8.53.

Step 12 The Host link name and Pool name fields in Fig. 8.53 should already be filled in for you with HOST0001 and pool_lu2, respectively. Enter 2 in the Workstation NAU address, then click on OK. This will return you to Fig. 8.52.

Step 13 Click on Create, and Fig. 8.53 will be redisplayed. Click on the arrow to the right of the Pool name field to bring up the selection

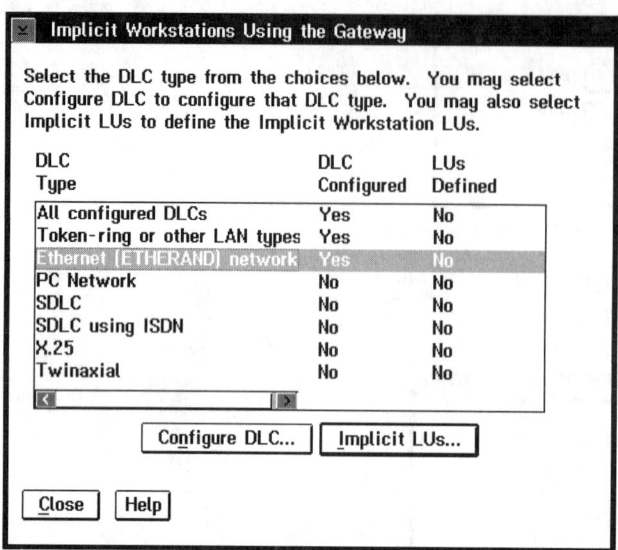

Figure 8.51 Modify the Ethernet link. [*Reprinted by permission from IBM's OS/2 2.0, Copyright (1988, 1992) International Business Machines Corporation.*]

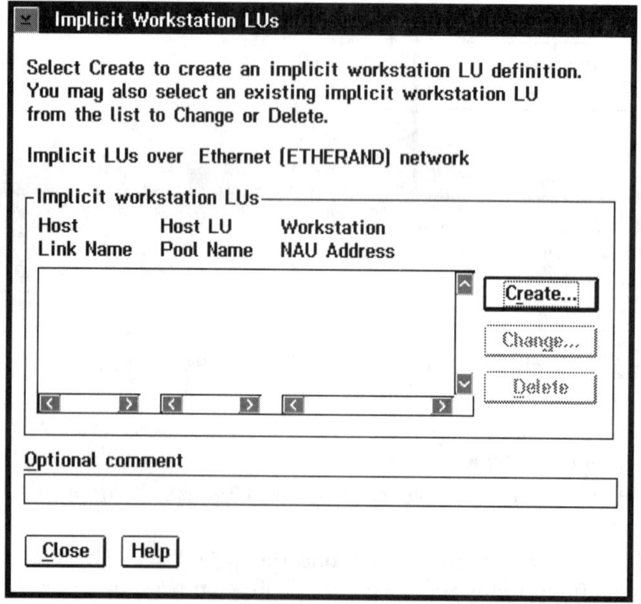

Figure 8.52 Creating the workstation-to-LU_pool correlation. [*Reprinted by permission from IBM's OS/2 2.0, Copyright (1988, 1992) International Business Machines Corporation.*]

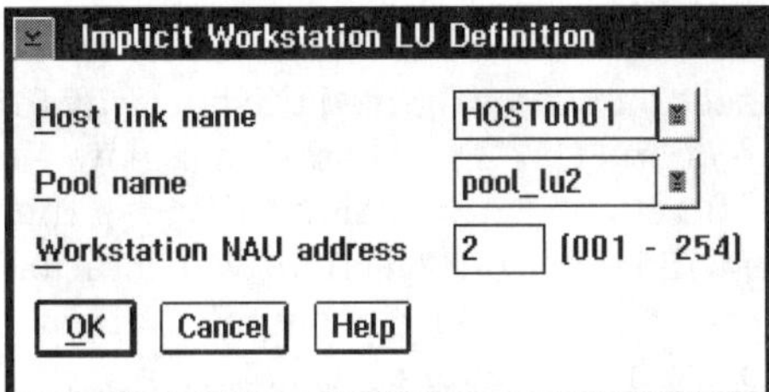

Figure 8.53 Assign a workstation LU number to the implicit pools. [*Reprinted by permission from IBM's OS/2 2.0, Copyright (1988, 1992) International Business Machines Corporation.*]

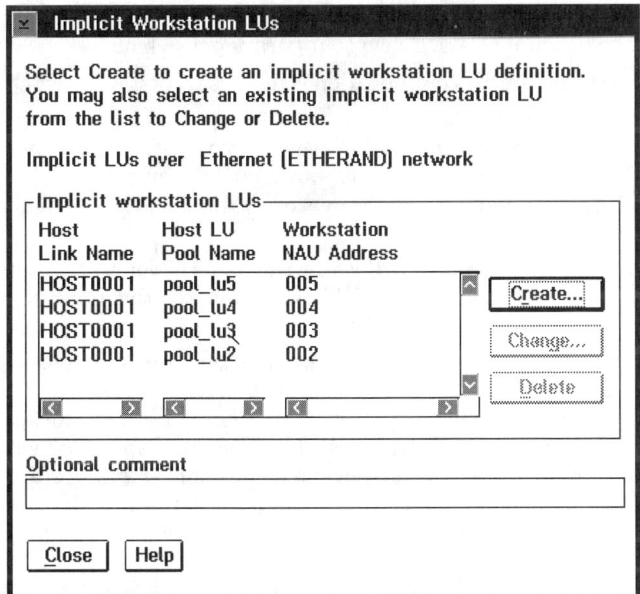

Figure 8.54 The completed workstation-to-LU-pool correlation. [*Reprinted by permission from IBM's OS/2 2.0, Copyright (1988, 1992) International Business Machines Corporation.*]

list. Select pool_lu3, then enter a 3 in the Workstation NAU address field.

Step 14 Repeat step 13 to add pool_lu4 and pool_lu5. Use Workstation NAU addresses 4 and 5 for these pools.

Step 15 When you are finished, your screen should look like Fig. 8.54.

Step 16 Click on Close in each panel until you back all the way out of the CM/2 setup program. You should now perform the "NTS/2 Gateway Configuration" section from earlier in this chapter, if you have not already done so.

Client Workstation CM/2 Configuration for Implicit LUs

In the previous section we configured the gateway to accept implicit LU log-ons from the client CM/2 workstations. Now we are ready to configure CM/2 on the client workstation to access the host via the CM/2 gateway PC. We will be defining a client workstation that has four host terminal sessions. This procedure assumes that you already have CM/2 and NTS/2 installed on the client workstation.

Step 1 Double-click on the CM/2 icon.

Step 2 Double-click on the Communications Manager setup icon.

Step 3 Click on Setup on the initial screen.

Step 4 Enter a configuration name and description on the Open Configuration screen, then click on OK.

Step 5 You will be asked if this is a new configuration. Click on Yes.

Step 6 You will be asked if this configuration is for this workstation. Click on Yes.

Step 7 Figure 8.38 should be displayed on your screen. Select Ethernet (ETHERAND) network under the workstation connection type. Select 3270 emulation under the feature or application section. Click on Configure.

Step 8 Figure 8.39 should be displayed. Enter the name of your Ethernet network in the Network ID field. This should match the name you placed in Fig. 8.15.

The name you enter for the Local node name field in Fig. 8.39 is used purely for troubleshooting measures. You can enter any eight characters that you wish in this field. There are monitoring screens in the gateway PC on which this name will appear when the client workstation is active. You should develop a naming standard for the local node names that will allow you to identify the client workstation by using this name. For this example I will simply key in my last name.

If you are accessing a local host, key in 00000 for the second part of the local node ID. The first part of this field should already contain 05D.

The LAN destination address is an important field. The client workstation (the one we are currently configuring) communicates directly with the Ethernet card in the gateway PC. In our example, we set the LAA of the gateway's Ethernet NIC to 400020101321. This was done when we configured NTS/2, using Figs. 8.35 and 8.36. We must bit-reverse this address, using the procedure illustrated in Fig. 8.37, and key the result in the LAN destination address field. In this example, the address 400020101321 translates to 02000408C884.

We are defining four terminal sessions. Enter the number of terminal sessions on the last field on Fig. 8.39. For this example, enter a 4, then click on OK.

Step 9 Close the remaining CM/2 setup windows by clicking on Close.

Step 10 You will be asked if you want to update the system files. You should allow the updates to occur.

Step 11 You should reboot your system, then bring up CM/2. If all the components are defined properly, your host sessions should activate.

A lot of things happened behind the scenes when we defined the implicit LU client workstation. If you are responsible for the administration and/or troubleshooting of your network, you need to know just what happened and why it worked.

As you recall, we established the following implicit LU pools on the gateway PC:

Pool name	LU address range	Client LU correlation
pool—lu2	7–10	2
pool—lu3	11–14	3
pool—lu4	15–18	4
pool—lu5	19–22	5

When we configured the client workstation, we defined four terminal sessions. The CM/2 setup program automatically assigns LU address 2 to the first (A) terminal session, 3 to the second (B) terminal session, 4 to the third (C) terminal session, and 5 to the fourth (D) terminal session.

When the client workstation shakes hands with the CM/2 gateway PC, the gateway PC will see that the client workstation is requesting four terminal sessions using LU addresses 2 to 5. For the first terminal session, the gateway will choose the first open LU from the pool_lu2 implicit LU pool. The LU is chosen from this pool because the client is trying to access the host using LU address 2. The second client terminal session has LU address 3 defined. The gateway will see the 3 and choose an open LU from the pool_lu3 implicit pool. This process continues through remaining terminal sessions.

Figure 8.55 illustrates how the implicit LU pools relate to the host (VTAM) definition. Any client workstation accessing the host using LU address 2 will connect to the host using a VTAM address in the range of A7100007 to A7100010. You can mix implicit and explicit LU definitions in your gateway.

Troubleshooting Gateway Problems

As we have seen, the CM/2 gateway and client configurations can be rather complex. And, of course, along with complexity come problems. CM/2 provides a multitude of tools to help you isolate and identify configuration and network problems.

```
LSNA1A71 VBUILD TYPE=LOCAL
A01CA71  PU     CUADDR=A71,          ** PHYSICAL UNIT ADDRESS
                DLOGMOD=M2SDLCQ,     ** DEFAULT LOGON MODE ENTRY
                MAXBFRU=4,           **
                PACING=1,            ** FOR SNA GATEWAY
                USSTAB=USSSNA,       ** USE SNA USS TABLE
                MODETAB=AMODETAB     ** LOGON MODE TABLE NAME
A7100002 LU     LOCADDR=2
A7100003 LU     LOCADDR=3
A7100004 LU     LOCADDR=4
A7100005 LU     LOCADDR=5
A7100006 LU     LOCADDR=6,DLOGMOD=S3270,SSCPFM=USSSCS

A7100007 LU     LOCADDR=7             pool_lu2
A7100008 LU     LOCADDR=8             pool_lu2
A7100009 LU     LOCADDR=9             pool_lu2
A7100010 LU     LOCADDR=10            pool_lu2

A7100011 LU     LOCADDR=11            pool_lu3
A7100012 LU     LOCADDR=12            pool_lu3
A7100013 LU     LOCADDR=13            pool_lu3
A7100014 LU     LOCADDR=14            pool_lu3

A7100015 LU     LOCADDR=15            pool_lu4
A7100016 LU     LOCADDR=16            pool_lu4
A7100017 LU     LOCADDR=17            pool_lu4
A7100018 LU     LOCADDR=18            pool_lu4

A7100019 LU     LOCADDR=19            pool_lu5
A7100020 LU     LOCADDR=20            pool_lu5
A7100021 LU     LOCADDR=21            pool_lu5
A7100022 LU     LOCADDR=22            pool_lu5

A7100023 LU     LOCADDR=23
A7100024 LU     LOCADDR=24
A7100025 LU     LOCADDR=25
A7100026 LU     LOCADDR=26
A7100027 LU     LOCADDR=27
A7100028 LU     LOCADDR=28
```

Figure 8.55 VTAM to implicit LU pool correlation.

It is recommended that you follow a logical approach when troubleshooting gateway problems, and, by all means, never change more than one thing at a time during troubleshooting.

Ensure NIC adapter initialization

The first step in debugging gateway problems is to make sure that your NIC adapter was properly initialized by CM/2. The simplest way to do this is to browse file

```
C:\IBMCOM\LANTRAN.LOG
```

Figure 8.56 illustrates a sample LANTRAN.LOG from the gateway PC configured in the previous examples. As you scan down Fig. 8.56, you

```
IBM OS/2 LANMSGDD [09/01/92] 2.01 is loaded and operational.
IBM OS/2 LAN Protocol Manager
IBM OS/2 LANDD [09/01/92] 2.01.3
IBM OS/2 LANDLLDD 2.01
IBM OS/2 LANDLLDD is loaded and operational.
IBM - IBM Token-Ring Network Driver, Version V.2.02
IBM OS/2 ODI2NDI v1.0 [09/01/92]
IBM OS/2 NETBEUI 2.01
IBM OS/2 NETBIOS 4.0
Adapter 0 has 95 NCBs, 40 sessions, and 21 names available to NETBIOS
applications.
NETBIOS 4.0 is loaded and operational.
IBM LANVDD is loaded and operational.
IBM OS/2 LAN Netbind
IBM Token-Ring adapter data rate is 16 mbps.
IBM LANDD is accessing IBM 802.5 LAN Interface.
Adapter 0 was initialized and opened successfully.
Adapter 0 is using node address 400020101A71.
IBM LANDD was successfully bound to MAC: IBMTOK_nif->VECTOR.
IBM LANDD is accessing IBM 802.3 LAN Interface.
Adapter 1 was initialized and opened successfully.
Adapter 1 is using node address 400020101321.  The Token-Ring format is
02000408C884.
IBM LANDD was successfully bound to MAC: ELNKII_nif.
ODI2NDI.OS2 was successfully bound to MAC VECTOR.
Adapter 0 is using node address 400020101A71.
```

Figure 8.56 LANTRAN.LOG file from the gateway PC.

will see that NIC adapter 0 (the Token Ring NIC) was successfully initialized and was assigned LAA 400020101A71.

Further down the LANTRAN.LOG file you will see that adapter 1 (the Ethernet adapter) was also successfully initialized using LAA 400020101321. The bit-reversed format of the address is also displayed for you.

You can also check the status of your NIC adapter(s) in another manner. Double-click on the CM/2 icon, then double-click on Subsystem management. Figure 8.57 should be displayed.

Double-click on the SNA subsystem line item, and Fig. 8.58 will be displayed. Double-click on the Data link controls line item, and Fig. 8.59 will be displayed. Figure 8.59 shows the status of the two NIC adapters in our gateway PC. Both of these adapters should be in active status.

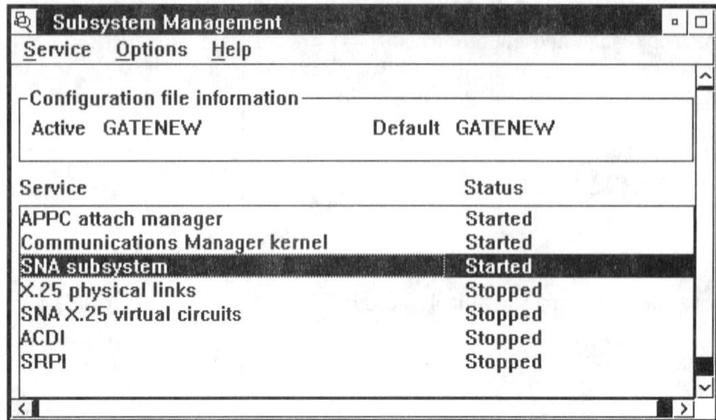

Figure 8.57 Checking the status of your gateway NIC adapters. [*Reprinted by permission from IBM's OS/2 2.0, Copyright (1988, 1992) International Business Machines Corporation.*]

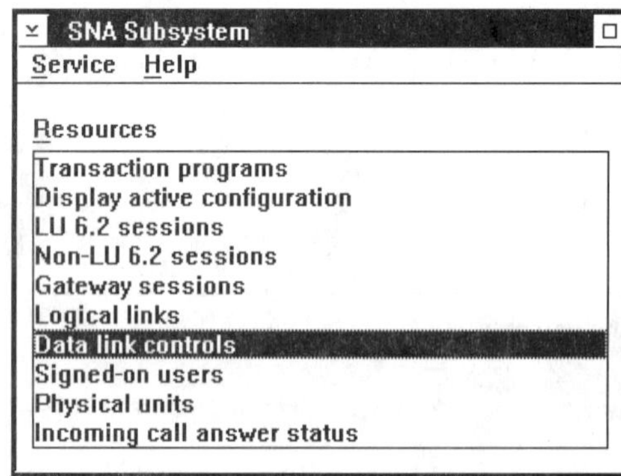

Figure 8.58 Select the data-link controls option. [*Reprinted by permission from IBM's OS/2 2.0, Copyright (1988, 1992) International Business Machines Corporation.*]

Monitoring gateway usage

From time to time you will need to know which users are currently accessing the gateway. CM/2 provides several utilities to give you this information. To see who is currently accessing your gateway, follow these steps:

Step 1 Double-click on the CM/2 icon.

Step 2 Double-click on the Subsystem management icon. Figure 8.58 should be displayed.

Step 3 Double-click on the Logical links line item. Figure 8.60 should be displayed on your screen.

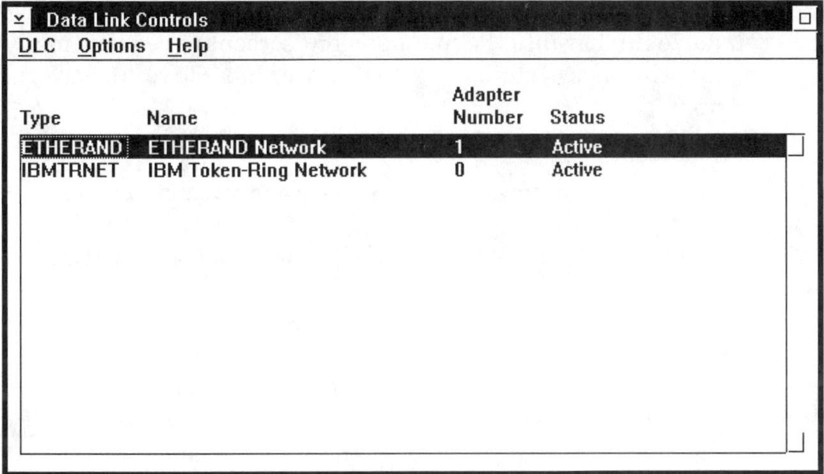

Figure 8.59 Displaying the status of the NIC adapters. [*Reprinted by permission from IBM's OS/2 2.0, Copyright (1988, 1992) International Business Machines Corporation.*]

Logical Links

Link Options Help

Link Name	Partner Network ID	Partner Name	Partner Type	Active Sessions	Link Status
@AAAAAAA	ETHER001	JOHNSTON	EN	11	Active
HOST0001			LEN	22	Active
WKST0001			Learn	0	Inactive

Figure 8.60 Monitoring the gateway logical links. [*Reprinted by permission from IBM's OS/2 2.0, Copyright (1988, 1992) International Business Machines Corporation.*]

Notice the two line items in Fig. 8.60. The second line item is telling you that the HOST0001 connection is active. This is the actual link to the mainframe.

The first line item in Fig. 8.60 tells you that partner name Johnston is active. Johnston is the name we placed in the Local node name field when we configured the client workstation for implicit LU access.

You can delve further into the management screens to see how many terminal and printer sessions each gateway user has active. To perform this operation:

Step 1 Double-click on the CM/2 icon.

Step 2 Double-click on the Subsystem management icon. Figure 8.58 should be displayed.

Step 3 Double-click on the Gateway sessions line item. Figure 8.61 will be displayed.

Notice that four host sessions are active in Fig. 8.61. To find out more about these sessions...

Step 4 Click on the Session title bar option, then click on Details. Figure 8.62 will be displayed.

Figure 8.62 provides you with a wealth of information. You can see the adapter number used on the client workstation, the LU local address specified on the client workstation, the pool name that was used for implicit LU access, and the actual host LU address assigned to the client.

There are many other monitoring and troubleshooting tools provided with CM/2. The best way to learn how to use these tools is to jump in and try them out. Be careful, though; some of the options on the panels can deactivate individual sessions or the entire gateway.

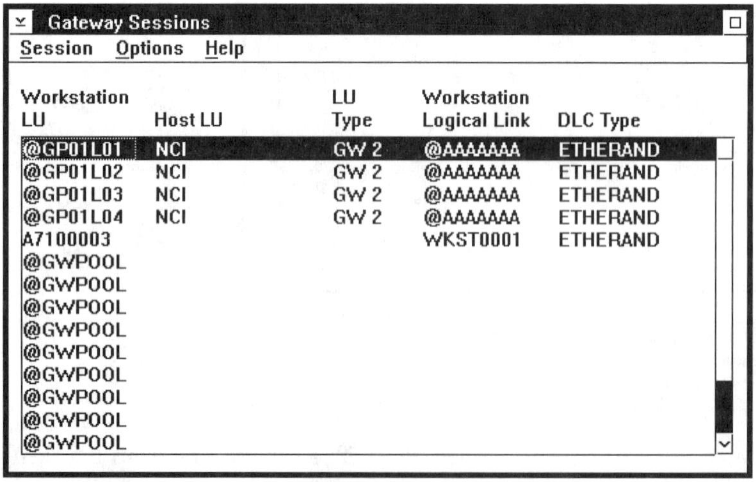

Gateway Sessions

Session Options Help

Workstation LU	Host LU	LU Type	Workstation Logical Link	DLC Type
@GP01L01	NCI	GW 2	@AAAAAAA	ETHERAND
@GP01L02	NCI	GW 2	@AAAAAAA	ETHERAND
@GP01L03	NCI	GW 2	@AAAAAAA	ETHERAND
@GP01L04	NCI	GW 2	@AAAAAAA	ETHERAND
A7100003			WKST0001	ETHERAND
@GWPOOL				
@GWPOOL				
@GWPOOL				
@GWPOOL				
@GWPOOL				
@GWPOOL				
@GWPOOL				
@GWPOOL				
@GWPOOL				

Figure 8.61 Monitoring the gateway sessions. [*Reprinted by permission from IBM's OS/2 2.0, Copyright (1988, 1992) International Business Machines Corporation.*]

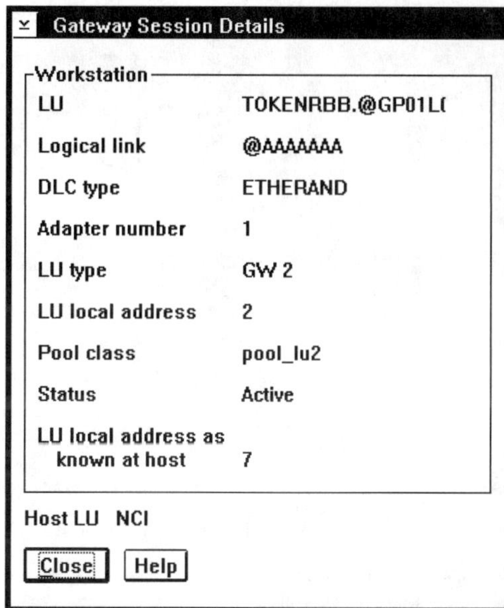

Figure 8.62 Displaying a gateway session's details. [*Reprinted by permission from IBM's OS/2 2.0, Copyright (1988, 1992) International Business Machines Corporation.*]

Conclusion

The CM/2 gateway feature can be a tremendous asset for organizations that wish to use a Token Ring network to provide host connectivity while implementing a campuswide Ethernet network for the end-users. The CM/2 gateway can be used as a vehicle to pass the SNA traffic between the Ethernet local-area network and the Token Ring network, as illustrated in the sample configuration in this chapter. Organizations that implement the gateway feature in this type of environment benefit in several areas. They retain the stability and reliability of the Token Ring to mainframe connectivity, while enjoying a cost savings by implementing Ethernet-attached workstations for most of the network. Most of these sites already have a 3174 or 37x5 controller which can be used to provide the host connectivity. This scenario also allows the organization to move SNA between topologies without the need for an expensive and complex bridge and/or routing system.

Chapter

9

Token Ring PU Emulation —Configuring CM/2

Perhaps the most common method for providing host connectivity to Token Ring local-area network users is the implementation of PU-emulating software. This type of connectivity is so popular because PU emulation is extremely flexible and at the same time very reliable. Using the PU emulation method, each individual CM/2 workstation emulates a mainframe terminal control unit. The CM/2 workstation also emulates the mainframe LU functions. The LU functions provide the terminal and printer functions. So the CM/2 workstation that accesses the host by using the PU emulation function actually performs as a small terminal control unit with its associated terminals and printers all combined into one box.

Each CM/2 client workstation has its own connection into VTAM, the mainframe communications program. Because of this, troubleshooting and host configuration are simpler and less disruptive to the entire network. For example, if a user decides to add another printer session to his or her CM/2 configuration, the following steps are required under the PU emulation host access method:

- The CM/2 software is configured to add the new printer session.
- The VTAM configuration file for that user is updated to reflect the new printer.
- The host operator recycles (inactivates, then reactivates) the VTAM definition for the user.
- CM/2 is recycled.

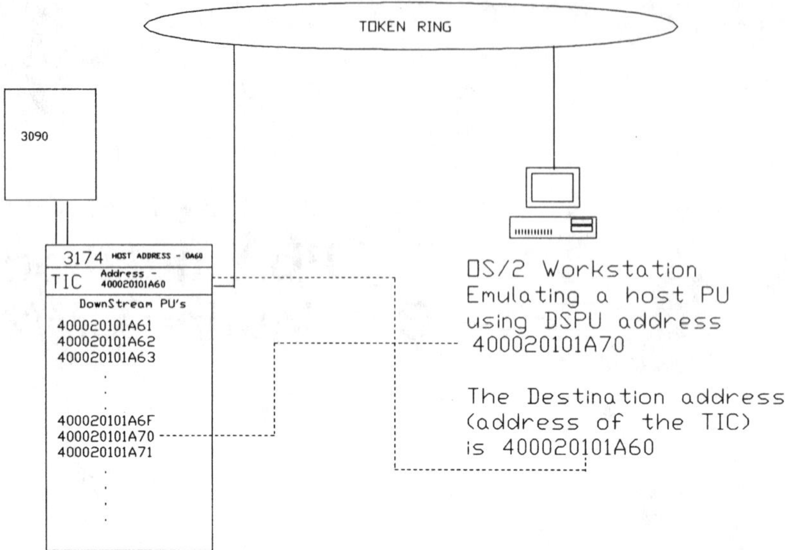

Figure 9.1 OS/2 workstation accessing a host as a PU.

That's all there is to it. If the user had been accessing the host through a gateway, the entire gateway connection to the host would require recycling. This process would need to be scheduled for off hours, otherwise every user accessing the mainframe through the gateway would be disrupted.

The goal of this chapter is to show you how to configure OS/2 and Communications Manager/2 to emulate an SNA PU on a Token Ring LAN. Figure 9.1 illustrates the type of host connection we will be configuring. An OS/2 workstation will be emulating a host PU. The workstation will support 15 terminal sessions and one printer session. The workstation will use the DSPU method for accessing the host through a 3174 control unit. This configuration would also work for a DSPU associated with a TIC installed on an IBM 3725 or 3745 host front-end processor.

Included in this chapter is a step-by-step configuration of Communications Manager/2. By following this step-by-step guide, you will have an operational CM/2 Token Ring PU-emulating workstation.

Prerequisites

Before we begin with the actual CM/2 PU emulation configuration, make sure that your network is set up properly to allow the host PU connectivity to occur.

First, you should already have OS/2 and Communication Manager/2 installed on the workstation you plan to use for the PU emulation.

When you install Communications Manager/2, you are given the option of simply loading the software or loading and customizing the software. You should just load the software without performing the customization (configuration). Don't worry if you already performed the customization, because we will be starting with a fresh configuration file at the beginning of the step-by-step configuration example.

This workstation must have a Token Ring NIC installed. The workstation used in this example had an IBM 16/4 NIC adapter. You should also have a connection into the Token Ring network. This connection can be either the standard IBM cabling into a Token Ring MAU or one of the newer, unshielded twisted pair (UTP) Token Ring connections into a wiring concentrator. It is advisable to test the Token Ring network connection prior to the CM/2 configuration exercise. One of the best ways to test the connection is to connect a workstation that is already working on the Token Ring to the cable to be tested. Testing the Token Ring connection prior to the Communications Manager/2 configuration could help if problems arise with the configuration.

You must also have LAPS installed on the workstation you are configuring. LAPS is part of the IBM NTS/2 product. As with the installation of the CM/2 software, you should choose to only install the software without performing the customization. Again, don't worry if you have already customized the LAPS-NTS/2 product, as we will be starting with a fresh configuration file.

You must have a TIC connection to the host on the same Token Ring network that the workstation is connected to. The TIC can reside on a different ring if the appropriate bridge or router configuration is present. The TIC can reside in a 3174 terminal control unit or a 3725 or 3745 communications front-end processor. Refer to Fig. 9.2 for an illustration of the minimum network requirements. The TIC must have at least one DSPU defined for our use. You will need to know the address of both the TIC and the associated DSPU. For more information on the TIC setup or DSPUs, refer to the earlier chapters.

Later in the chapter we will configure the host VTAM parameters. Don't worry if you do not have a strong VTAM knowledge base. We will be discussing the host VTAM requirements and how they relate to the local-area network in detail as we progress through the actual Communications Manager/2 configuration.

Communications Manager/2 Configuration

The best way to begin the configuration is to start with a fresh configuration file. So, let's get started.

Step 1 Double-click on the Communications Manager/2 icon. The panel displayed in Fig. 9.3 will be displayed.

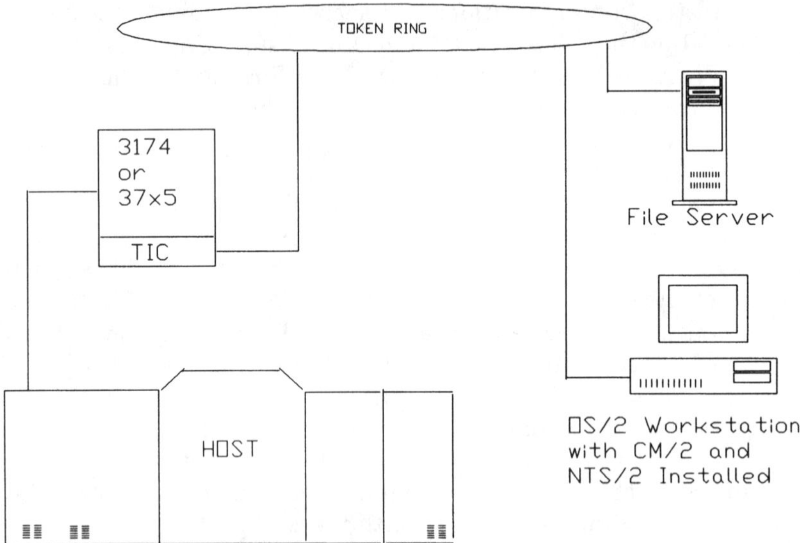

Figure 9.2 Minimum network requirements.

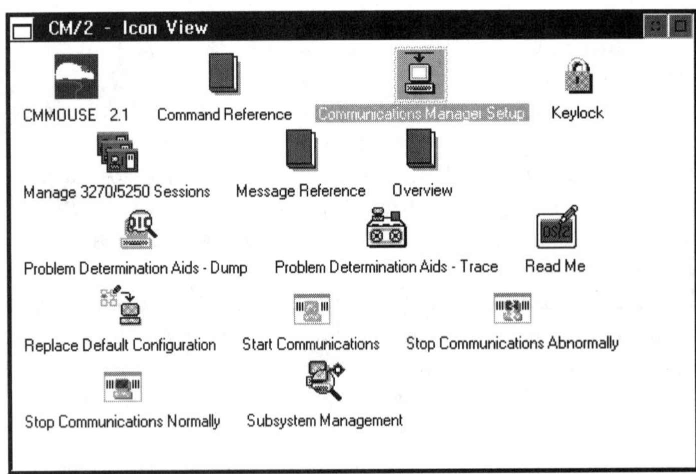

Figure 9.3 The CM/2 folder. [*Reprinted by permission from IBM's OS/2 2.0, Copyright (1988, 1992) International Business Machines Corporation.*]

Step 2 Double-click on the Communications Manager setup icon. The panel illustrated in Fig. 9.4 will be displayed.

Step 3 Click on OK to bring up the panel illustrated in Fig. 9.5.

Step 4 Select Setup, and Fig. 9.6 will be displayed.

Step 5 Type in a configuration name and a description. You should choose a meaningful name for your configuration. In the future you may

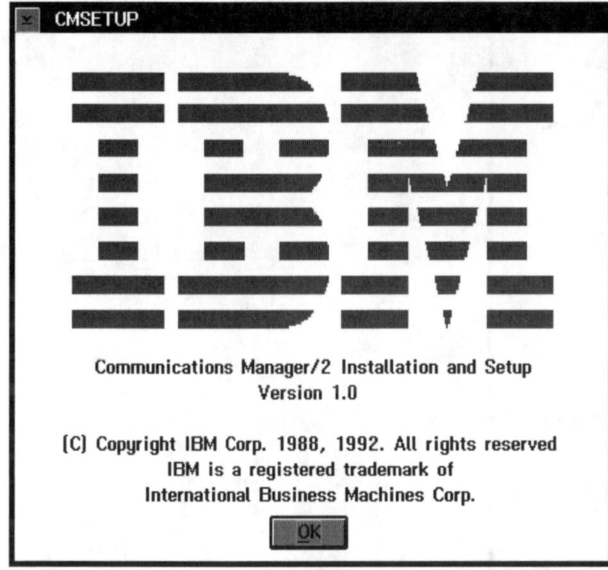

Figure 9.4 Initial CM/2 setup screen. [*Reprinted by permission from IBM's OS/2 2.0, Copyright (1988, 1992) International Business Machines Corporation.*]

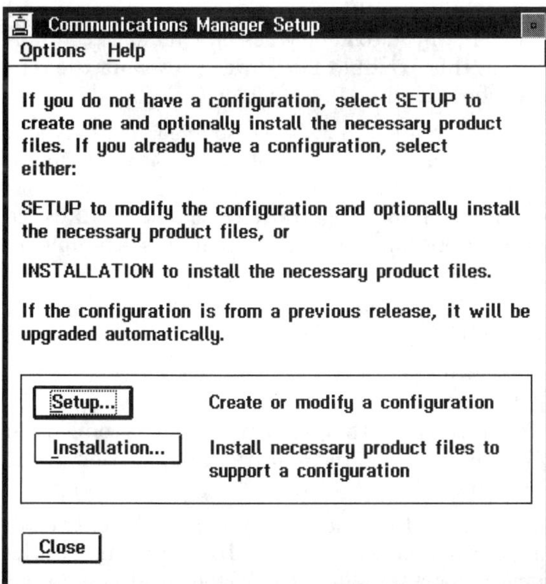

Figure 9.5 Entering the CM/2 setup utility. [*Reprinted by permission from IBM's OS/2 2.0, Copyright (1988, 1992) International Business Machines Corporation.*]

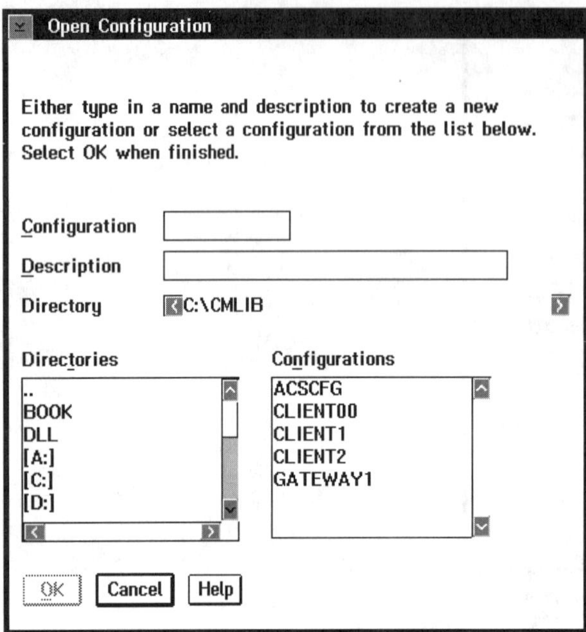

Figure 9.6 Starting a new CM/2 configuration file. [*Reprinted by permission from IBM's OS/2 2.0, Copyright (1988, 1992) International Business Machines Corporation.*]

have multiple configurations within the same workstation. A good naming standard will help you to keep track of what each configuration was used for. In this example TRPU was chosen for the configuration name, as shown in Fig. 9.7. Click on OK.

Step 6 The message illustrated in Fig. 9.8 will be displayed, asking you if this is a new configuration. In this example we will be creating a new configuration file. Do not attempt to modify an existing configuration file for this sample configuration. Doing so will cause your configuration screens and the screens in this example to become out of sync. Click on Yes.

Step 7 Next you will be asked if this configuration will be used for this workstation, as shown in Fig. 9.9. Click on Yes.

Step 8 The next panel, shown in Fig. 9.10, requires two pieces of information: the workstation connection type and the feature or application. Click on Token Ring or other LAN types as the connection type. Click on 3270 emulation as the feature or application. Click on Configure to continue.

Step 9 The panel shown in Fig. 9.11 will be displayed next. All entries in this panel must be completed. The network ID is the name of the SNA network that the workstation is connected to. If you do not know the name of your SNA network, any name will work. This

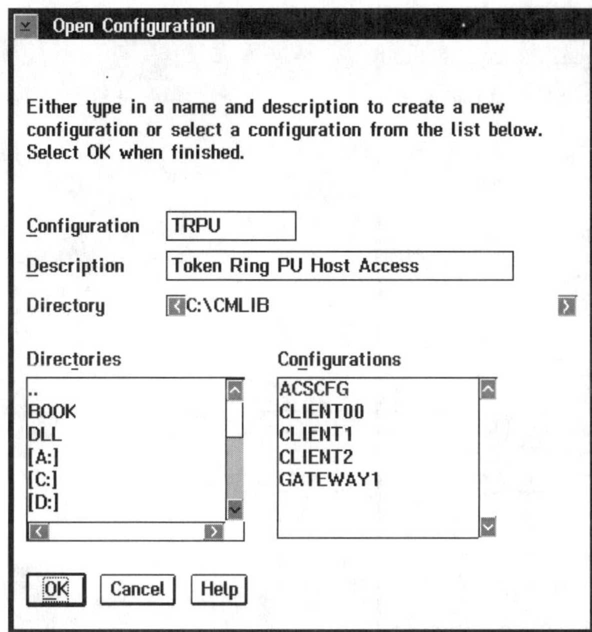

Figure 9.7 Naming the CM/2 configuration file. [*Reprinted by permission from IBM's OS/2 2.0, Copyright (1988, 1992) International Business Machines Corporation.*]

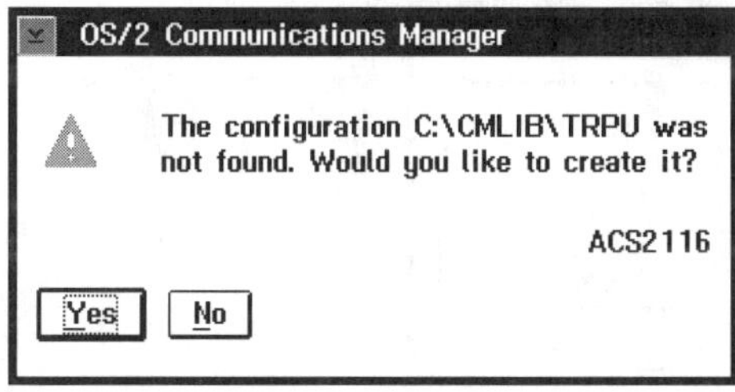

Figure 9.8 Confirming the creation of a new configuration file. [*Reprinted by permission from IBM's OS/2 2.0, Copyright (1988, 1992) International Business Machines Corporation.*]

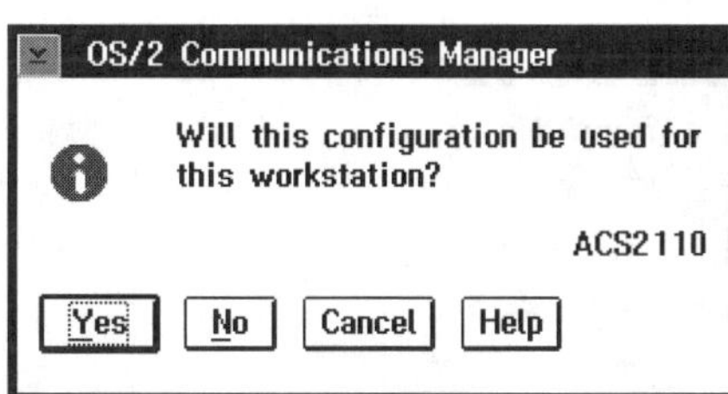

Figure 9.9 Confirming the use of the configuration file. [*Reprinted by permission from IBM's OS/2 2.0, Copyright (1988, 1992) International Business Machines Corporation.*]

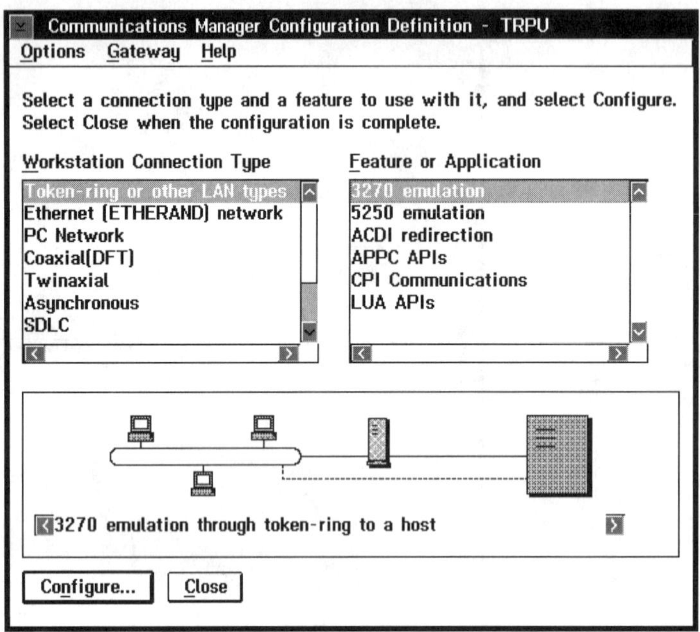

Figure 9.10 Entering the Token Ring 3270 configuration phase. [*Reprinted by permission from IBM's OS/2 2.0, Copyright (1988, 1992) International Business Machines Corporation.*]

3270 Emulation through Token-Ring

Network ID

Local node name

Local node ID (hex) 05D

LAN destination address (hex)

Number of terminal sessions 1

OK Advanced... Cancel Help

Figure 9.11 Entering the node characteristics. [*Reprinted by permission from IBM's OS/2 2.0, Copyright (1988, 1992) International Business Machines Corporation.*]

name is primarily used for problem notification. For the sake of completeness, ask your host systems programmer who is in charge of VTAM for the name of your host SNA network.

Step 10 The Local Node name field in Fig. 9.11 should be the member name of the VTAM configuration file that defines this PU. In this example, LSNA1A70 was chosen. This means that there must be a member named LSNA1A70 in SYS1.VTAMLST, the host VTAM definition library. Figure 9.12 shows the actual SYS1.VTAMLST (LSNA1A70) definition. Keeping this name the same as the host VTAM definition file makes troubleshooting and network documentation much simpler.

Step 11 The Local Node ID field in Fig. 9.11 is already partially filled in for you with the hexadecimal value 05D. If you are connecting to a local host, key in 00000 in the second portion of this field, as illustrated in Fig. 9.13. If you are connecting to a remote host, ask the host systems programmer in charge of the NCP at the remote mainframe site for the value of this field.

Step 12 The LAN destination address field, shown in Fig. 9.11, must contain the Token Ring address of the 3174 or 37x5 TIC that you are attempting to establish a connection with. This is a very important field. If this address is coded incorrectly, no communications can occur between the CM/2 workstation and the host. If you are connecting to a 3174 control unit, this address can be found in the

```
LSNA1A70 VBUILD TYPE=LOCAL
A01A70   PU     CUADDR=A70,
                 DLOGMOD=M2SDLCQ,
                 MAXBFRU=4,
                 PACING=1,
                 USSTAB=USSSNA,
                 MODETAB=AMODETAB
*                STATOPT='TR DSPU 400020101A70'
A7000002 LU      LOCADDR=2                   A Session
A7000003 LU      LOCADDR=3                   B Session
A7000004 LU      LOCADDR=4                   C Session
A7000005 LU      LOCADDR=5                   D Session
A7000006 LU      LOCADDR=6                   E Session
A7000007 LU      LOCADDR=7                   F Session
A7000008 LU      LOCADDR=8                   G Session
A7000009 LU      LOCADDR=9                   H Session
A7000010 LU      LOCADDR=10                  I Session
A7000011 LU      LOCADDR=11                  J Session
A7000012 LU      LOCADDR=12                  K Session
A7000013 LU      LOCADDR=13                  L Session
A7000014 LU      LOCADDR=14                  M Session
A7000015 LU      LOCADDR=15                  N Session
A7000016 LU      LOCADDR=16                  O Session
A7000017 LU      LOCADDR=17,DLOGMOD=S3270,SSCPFM=USSSCS
```

Figure 9.12 VTAM parameters for the PU.

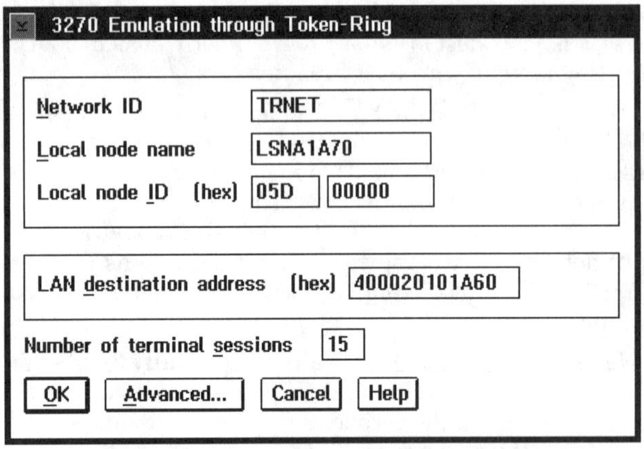

3270 Emulation through Token-Ring

Network ID TRNET

Local node name LSNA1A70

Local node ID (hex) 05D 00000

LAN destination address (hex) 400020101A60

Number of terminal sessions 15

OK Advanced... Cancel Help

Figure 9.13 Completed node characteristics configuration. [*Reprinted by permission from IBM's OS/2 2.0, Copyright (1988, 1992) International Business Machines Corporation.*]

3174's customization. This customization can be displayed or printed by using the functions of the 3174. If you are connecting to a TIC in a 3725 or 3745 front-end processor, this address can be found in the NCP definition file.

Step 13 Key in the number of terminal sessions you wish in the Number of terminal sessions field. This number does not include printer sessions. Communications Manager/2 supports up to a total of 16 terminal and printer sessions. In the example shown in Fig. 9.13, 15 terminal sessions were specified. One printer session will be configured later.

Step 14 Click on Advanced, and the panel shown in Fig. 9.14 will be displayed.

Step 15 Click on 3270 Emulation, then click on Configure. The panel illustrated in Fig. 9.15 will be displayed.

Step 16 Click on File, then click on New, and the screen shown in Fig. 9.16 will be displayed.

Step 17 Click on Logical printer, then click on OK to bring up the panel in Fig. 9.17.

Step 18 The only information you need to key into Fig. 9.17 is the LU local/NAU address field. This number is the LU number of the printer we are defining. We already have 15 terminal sessions defined (A through O). If you refer to the host PU definition in Fig. 9.12, you will notice that the LU addresses begin with address 2. So the A terminal session uses LU number 2, the B session uses LU number 3, and so on up to session O, which uses LU number 16. The printer we are defining should use the next available LU, which is 17.

Step 19 Click on Save as, and Fig. 9.18 will be displayed. Enter P as the long session/LU name, and click on OK.

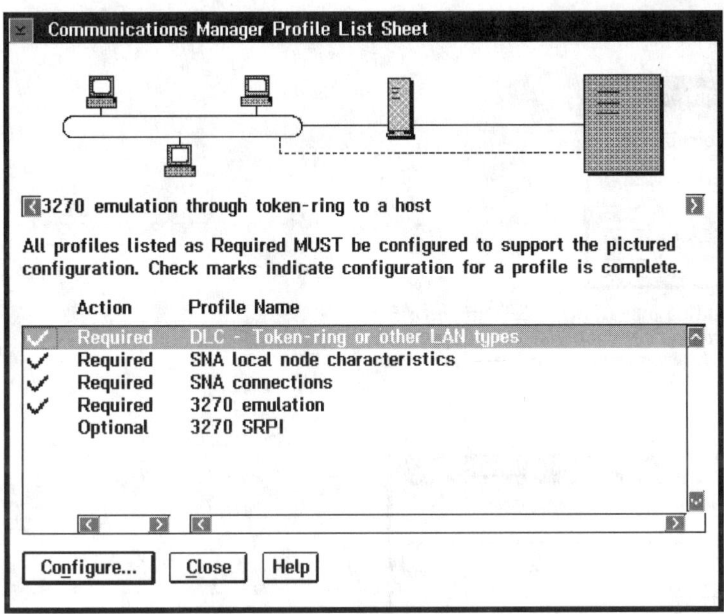

Figure 9.14 The advanced 3270 configuration panel. [*Reprinted by permission from IBM's OS/2 2.0, Copyright (1988, 1992) International Business Machines Corporation.*]

3270 Emulation

File View Options Help

Short Session Name	Long Session/LU Name	Type	Enhanced Keyboard	AT Keyboard	Color
A	A	LT	ACSCENUS	ACSCATUS	3270COLR
B	B	LT	ACSCENUS	ACSCATUS	3270COLR
C	C	LT	ACSCENUS	ACSCATUS	3270COLR
D	D	LT	ACSCENUS	ACSCATUS	3270COLR
E	E	LT	ACSCENUS	ACSCATUS	3270COLR
F	F	LT	ACSCENUS	ACSCATUS	3270COLR
G	G	LT	ACSCENUS	ACSCATUS	3270COLR
H	H	LT	ACSCENUS	ACSCATUS	3270COLR
I	I	LT	ACSCENUS	ACSCATUS	3270COLR
J	J	LT	ACSCENUS	ACSCATUS	3270COLR
K	K	LT	ACSCENUS	ACSCATUS	3270COLR
L	L	LT	ACSCENUS	ACSCATUS	3270COLR
M	M	LT	ACSCENUS	ACSCATUS	3270COLR
N	N	LT	ACSCENUS	ACSCATUS	3270COLR
O	O	LT	ACSCENUS	ACSCATUS	3270COLR

Figure 9.15 Viewing the 3270 session definitions. [*Reprinted by permission from IBM's OS/2 2.0, Copyright (1988, 1992) International Business Machines Corporation.*]

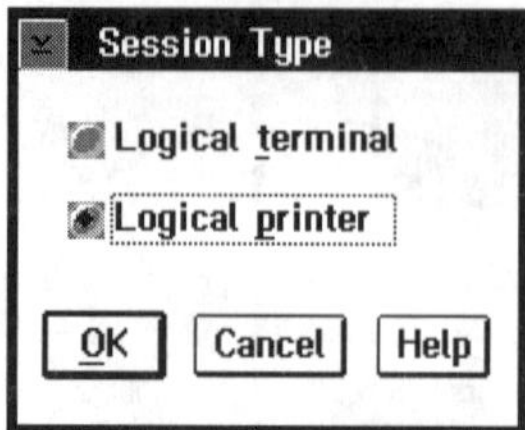

Figure 9.16 Adding a 3270 printer. [*Reprinted by permission from IBM's OS/2 2.0, Copyright (1988, 1992) International Business Machines Corporation.*]

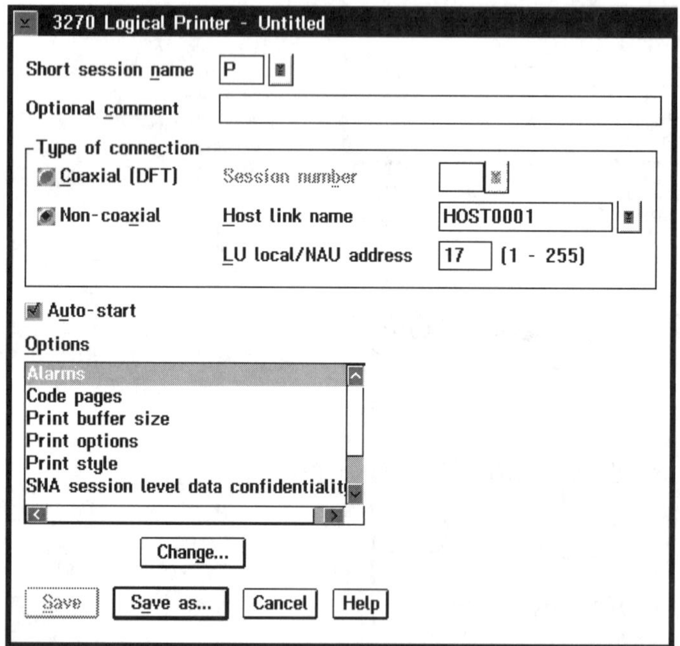

Figure 9.17 Assigning an LU to the printer. [*Reprinted by permission from IBM's OS/2 2.0, Copyright (1988, 1992) International Business Machines Corporation.*]

Save As

Enter a name under which you would like to save this information.

Long session/LU name P

OK Cancel Help

Figure 9.18 Naming the 3270 printer session. [*Reprinted by permission from IBM's OS/2 2.0, Copyright (1988, 1992) International Business Machines Corporation.*]

Step 20 The 3270 Emulation screen will be redisplayed. Close this by double-clicking on the upper left-hand corner.

Step 21 The Communications Manager Profile List Sheet screen will be redisplayed. Click on Close to close this window.

Step 22 The Communications Manager Configuration Definition screen will be redisplayed. Click on Close. At this time the configuration will be verified by the setup program. Figure 9.19 will be displayed during the verification process. If any errors occur, you will be asked if you wish to view the error log. All CM/2 configuration errors must be resolved before you continue to the next step in this example.

Step 23 If no errors occurred during the configuration verification process, you will be asked if you would like to update the system files, as illustrated in Fig. 9.20. Click on Yes.

Step 24 You should receive the Communication Manager Completion screen shown in Fig. 9.21. Click on OK.

Step 25 Close the Communication Manager setup. The actual Communications Manager/2 configuration is now complete. We are not finished yet. We must still define the LAN transport that we will be utilizing to access the network.

Step 26 Now we must configure LAPS. Open an OS/2 full-screen session. Enter CD\IBMCOM to switch to the correct directory. If the IBMCOM directory does not exist, it means that LAPS has not been installed on this workstation. If this is the case with the PC you are using, you should stop now and install the NTS/2 product. You

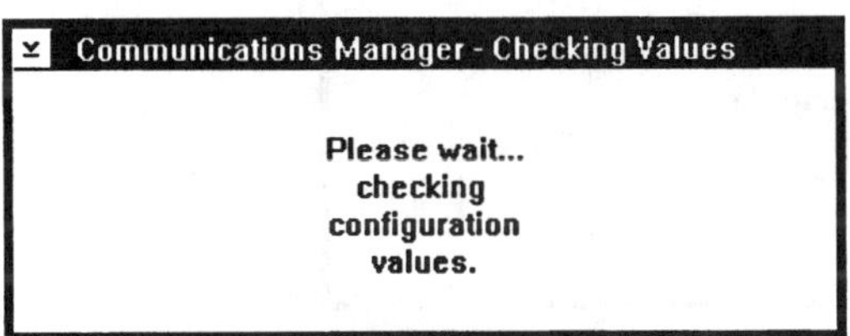

Figure 9.19 The verify process. [*Reprinted by permission from IBM's OS/2 2.0, Copyright (1988, 1992) International Business Machines Corporation.*]

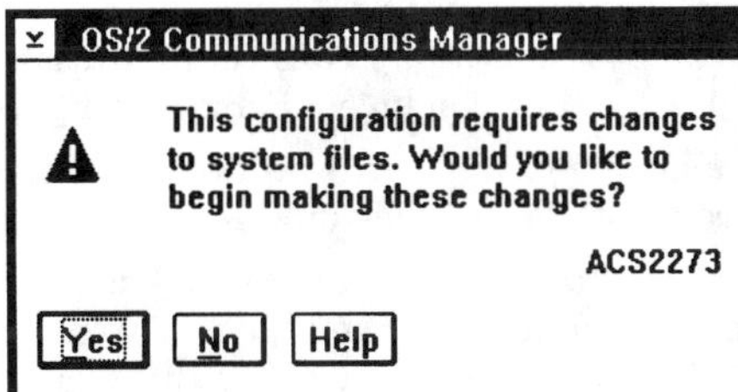

Figure 9.20 Completing the configuration. [*Reprinted by permission from IBM's OS/2 2.0, Copyright (1988, 1992) International Business Machines Corporation.*]

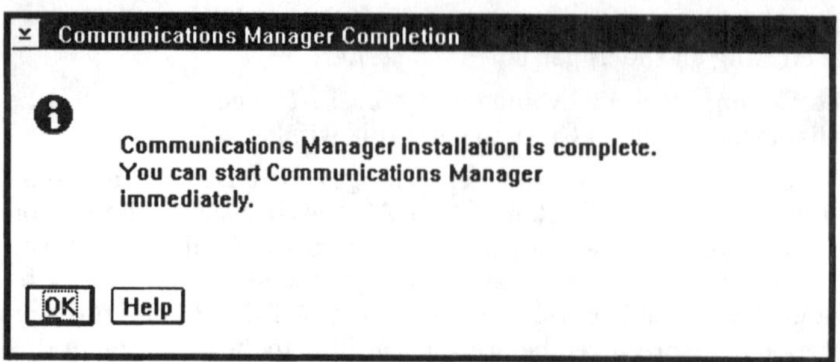

Figure 9.21 The completion message. [*Reprinted by permission from IBM's OS/2 2.0, Copyright (1988, 1992) International Business Machines Corporation.*]

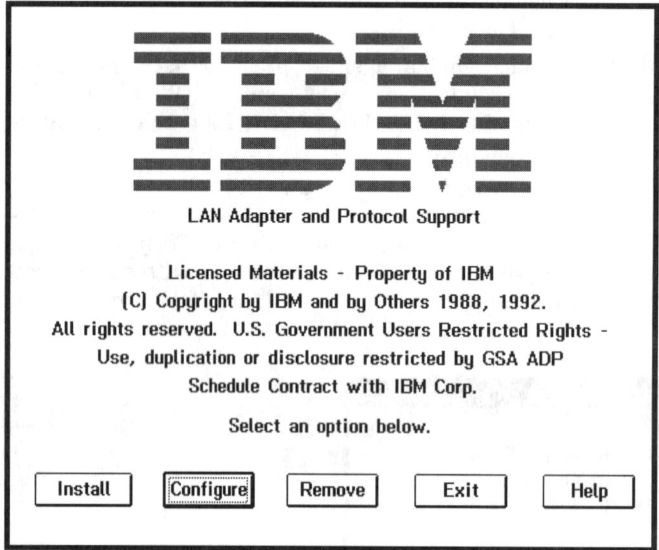

Figure 9.22 Entering the LAPS configuration utility. [*Reprinted by permission from IBM's OS/2 2.0, Copyright (1988, 1992) International Business Machines Corporation.*]

will not be able to implement CM/2 host connectivity via a local-area network without the NTS/2 product.

Enter LAPS to start the LAPS configuration program. The panel in Fig. 9.22 will be displayed. Select Configure.

Step 27 The panel in Fig. 9.23 will be displayed next. Select Configure LAN transports, then click on Continue.

Step 28 Figure 9.24 illustrates the next panel. Scroll through the network adapters list, and select the type of Token Ring adapter you have installed in your workstation. For this example, IBM Token Ring network adapters was chosen (Fig. 9.25). Click on Add, and the

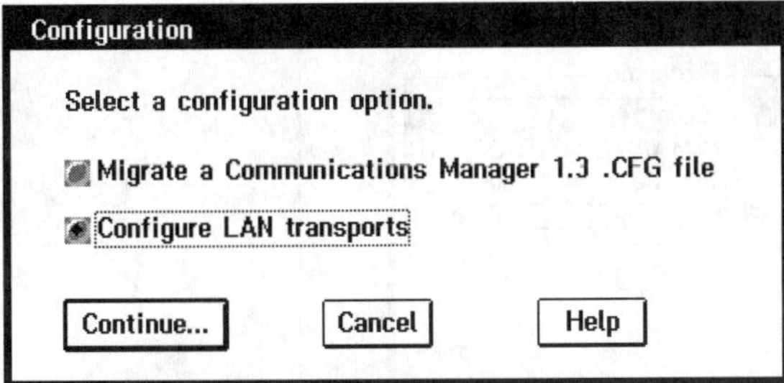

Figure 9.23 Selecting the LAPS configuration function.

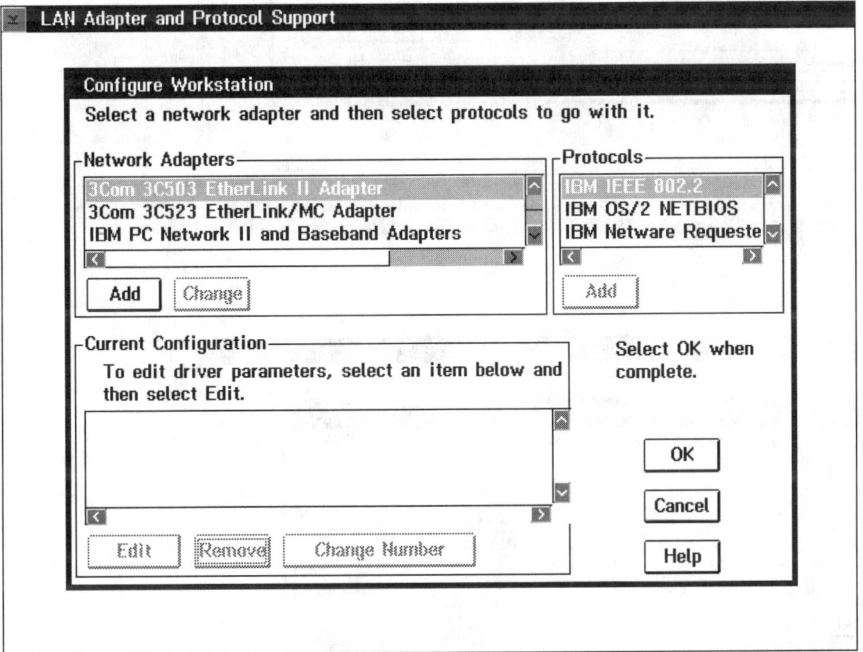

Figure 9.24 Selecting the NIC adapter to be modified. [*Reprinted by permission from IBM's OS/2 2.0, Copyright (1988, 1992) International Business Machines Corporation.*]

adapter you selected should move down to the current configuration area, as illustrated in Fig. 9.25.

Step 29 In the protocols list, click on IBM IEEE 802.2, then click on the Add button. The 802.2 protocol should move down to the current configuration area. If any of your applications require NETBIOS, you should do the same to add the IBM OS/2 NETBIOS protocol. Your screen should look like the panel in Fig. 9.26.

Step 30 Click on the IBM Token Ring network adapters in the current configuration area, then click on the Edit button.

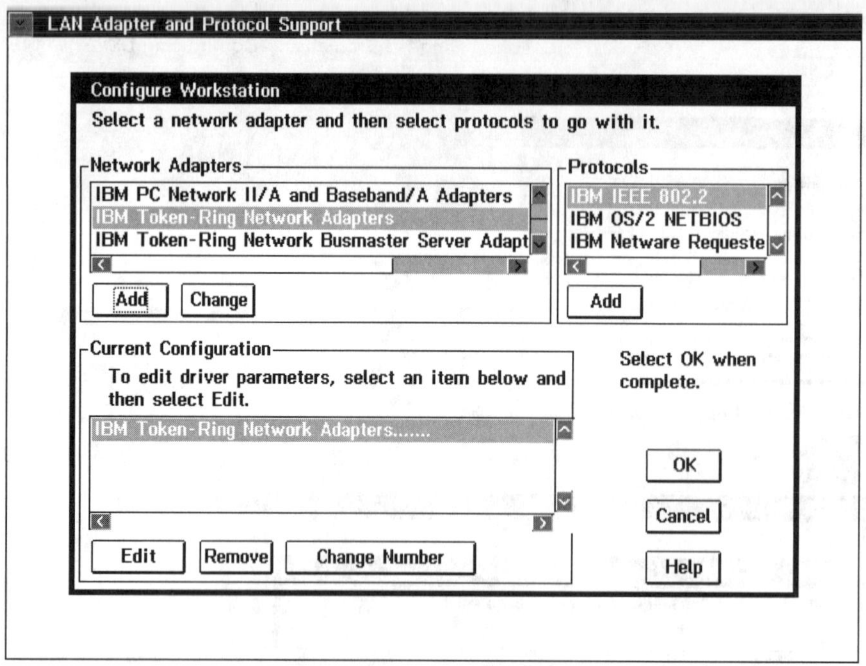

Figure 9.25 Adding the IEEE 802.2 protocol to the Token Ring NIC adapter. [*Reprinted by permission from IBM's OS/2 2.0, Copyright (1988, 1992) International Business Machines Corporation.*]

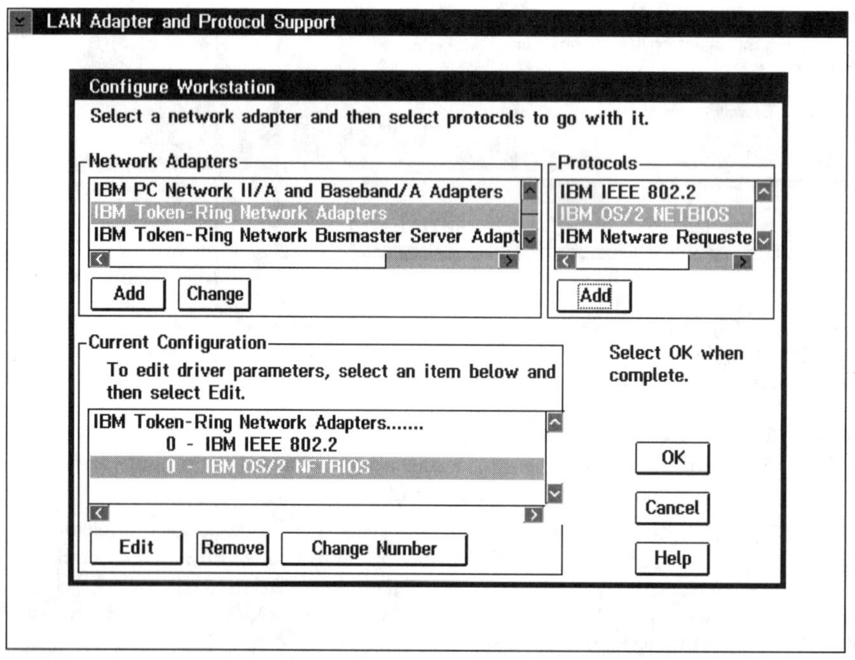

Figure 9.26 Adding the NETBIOS protocol to the Token Ring NIC adapter. [*Reprinted by permission from IBM's OS/2 2.0, Copyright (1988, 1992) International Business Machines Corporation.*]

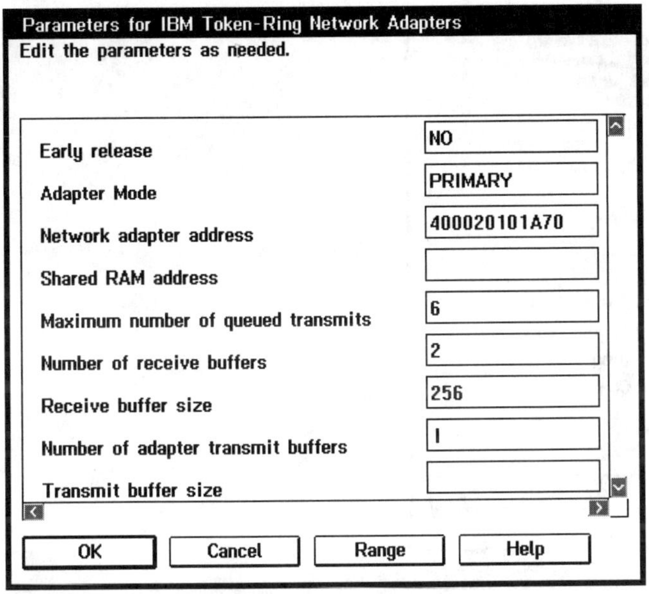

Parameters for IBM Token-Ring Network Adapters

Edit the parameters as needed.

Early release	NO
Adapter Mode	PRIMARY
Network adapter address	400020101A70
Shared RAM address	
Maximum number of queued transmits	6
Number of receive buffers	2
Receive buffer size	256
Number of adapter transmit buffers	1
Transmit buffer size	

OK Cancel Range Help

Figure 9.27 Entering the LAA. [*Reprinted by permission from IBM's OS/2 2.0, Copyright (1988, 1992) International Business Machines Corporation.*]

Step 31 This step is crucial for the downstream PU method. The panel illustrated in Fig. 9.27 will be displayed.

As you recall from Chap. 1, the DSPU host-to-LAN connectivity method requires that the workstation *become* the downstream PU defined in the 3174, 3725, or 3745 controller. To do this, we must override the universal address, which was burned into the NIC adapter by the NIC manufacturer, with a locally administered address. We specify a locally administered address by keying in a value in the Network adapter address field, as shown in Fig. 9.27. This address is the Token Ring address of one of the downstream PUs defined in the 3174 or 37x5. Make sure that the DSPU chosen is not being used by any other device in your network.

Step 32 Click on OK, and Fig. 9.28 will be displayed. Click on Exit.

Step 33 Figure 9.29 will ask you if you want to update CONFIG.SYS. Then select Continue.

Step 34 When the update is completed, exit the LAPS program.

Step 35 Now it is time to define your workstation to the VTAM software on the mainframe. VTAM has a configuration file which controls all the mainframe communication devices. In most shops the name of this file is SYS1.VTAMLST.

In the CM/2 configuration panel illustrated in Fig. 9.13, we chose LSNA1A70 as the local node name. This name must be defined to VTAM by placing a member named LSNA1A70 into SYS1.VTAMLST. A sample of this member is shown in Fig. 9.12.

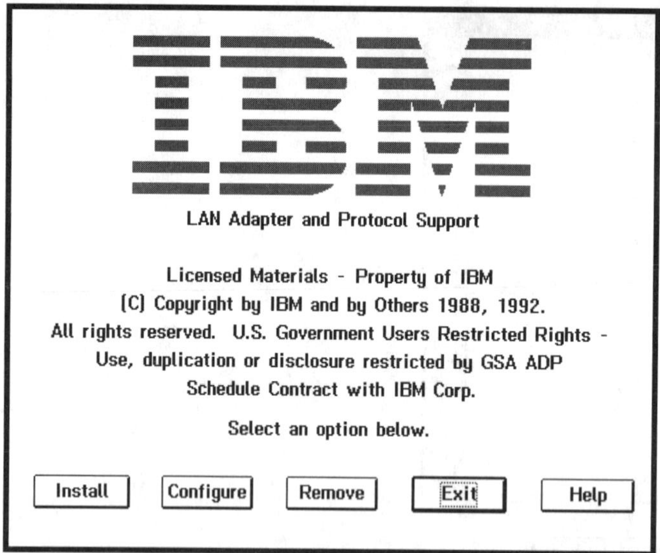

Figure 9.28 Exiting the LAPS utility. [*Reprinted by permission from IBM's OS/2 2.0, Copyright (1988, 1992) International Business Machines Corporation.*]

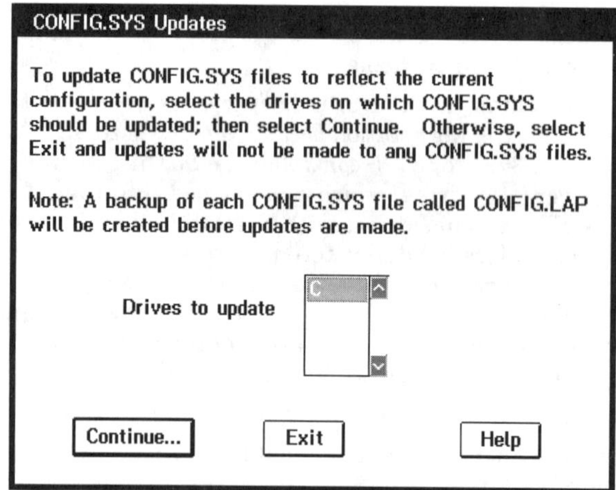

Figure 9.29 Confirming the updates to CONFIG.SYS. [*Reprinted by permission from IBM's OS/2 2.0, Copyright (1988, 1992) International Business Machines Corporation.*]

The first line of the LSNA1A70 member tells VTAM that we are defining a local resource.

The second line tells VTAM that we are defining a PU named A01A70. This PU uses MVS address A70. Refer to Chap. 1 for an explanation of how the PU, MVS address, and DSPU relate to each other.

The remaining lines tell VTAM that this PU controls 16 LUs named A7000002 through A7000017. Notice the LOCADDR parameter.

After this member is created in SYS1.VTAMLST, you need to activate the PU and its related LUs. Use the following VTAM command to do this:

```
V NET,ACT,ID=LSNA1A70,SCOPE=ALL
```

Step 36 Shut down and reboot your workstation. After your PC reboots, go into the Communications Manager/2 icon and double-click on the Start communications icon. If everything was configured correctly, your host sessions should come up!

Figure 9.30 is the CONFIG.SYS file that was created from the above example. Figure 9.31 is the IBMCOM\PROTOCOL.INI file created.

```
IFS=C:\OS2\HPFS.IFS /CACHE:64 /CRECL:4
DEVICE=C:\CMLIB\ROCSDD.SYS
DEVICE=C:\IBMCOM\PROTOCOL\LANPDD.OS2
DEVICE=C:\IBMCOM\PROTOCOL\LANVDD.OS2
PROTSHELL=C:\OS2\PMSHELL.EXE
SET USER_INI=C:\OS2\OS2.INI
SET SYSTEM_INI=C:\OS2\OS2SYS.INI
SET OS2_SHELL=C:\OS2\CMD.EXE
SET AUTOSTART=PROGRAMS,TASKLIST,FOLDERS
SET RUNWORKPLACE=C:\OS2\PMSHELL.EXE
SET COMSPEC=C:\OS2\CMD.EXE
LIBPATH=C:\IBMCOM\DLL;.;C:\OS2\DLL;C:\MUGLIB\DLL;C:\OS2\MDOS;C:\;
C:\OS2\APPS\DLL;C:\CMLIB\DLL;
SET
PATH=C:\OS2;C:\MUGLIB;C:\OS2\SYSTEM;C:\OS2\MDOS\WINOS2;C:\OS2\INS
TALL;C:\;C:\OS2\MDOS;C:\OS2\APPS;L:\OS2;P:\OS2;C:\CMLIB;
SET
DPATH=C:\IBMCOM;C:\OS2;C:\MUGLIB\DLL;C:\OS2\SYSTEM;C:\OS2\MDOS\WI
NOS2;C:\OS2\INSTALL;C:\;C:\OS2\BITMAP;C:\OS2\MDOS;C:\OS2\APPS;C:\
CMLIB;
SET PROMPT=$i[$p]
SET HELP=C:\OS2\HELP;C:\OS2\HELP\TUTORIAL;C:\CMLIB;
SET GLOSSARY=C:\OS2\HELP\GLOSS;
PRIORITY_DISK_IO=YES
FILES=20
DEVICE=C:\IBMCOM\LANMSGDD.OS2 /I:C:\IBMCOM
DEVICE=C:\IBMCOM\PROTMAN.OS2 /I:C:\IBMCOM
DEVICE=C:\IBMCOM\PROTOCOL\LANDD.OS2
DEVICE=C:\IBMCOM\PROTOCOL\LANDLLDD.OS2
DEVICE=C:\OS2\TESTCFG.SYS
DEVICE=C:\OS2\DOS.SYS
DEVICE=C:\OS2\PMDD.SYS
BUFFERS=30
IOPL=YES
DISKCACHE=384,LW
MAXWAIT=3
MEMMAN=SWAP,PROTECT
SWAPPATH=C:\OS2\SYSTEM 2048 4096
BREAK=OFF
THREADS=256
PRINTMONBUFSIZE=134,134,134
COUNTRY=001,C:\OS2\SYSTEM\COUNTRY.SYS
SET KEYS=ON
REM SET DELDIR=C:\DELETE,512;D:\DELETE,512;
BASEDEV=PRINT01.SYS
BASEDEV=IBM1FLPY.ADD
BASEDEV=IBM1S506.ADD
BASEDEV=OS2DASD.DMD
SET BOOKSHELF=C:\OS2\BOOK;C:\CMLIB\BOOK;
SET EPATH=C:\OS2\APPS
REM DEVICE=C:\OS2\APPS\SASYNCDA.SYS
PROTECTONLY=NO
SHELL=C:\OS2\MDOS\COMMAND.COM C:\OS2\MDOS /P
```

Figure 9.30 Sample CONFIG.SYS file.

```
FCBS=16,8
RMSIZE=640
DEVICE=C:\OS2\MDOS\VEMM.SYS
DEVICE=C:\OS2\MDOS\VMOUSE.SYS
DOS=LOW,NOUMB
DEVICE=C:\OS2\MDOS\VDPX.SYS
DEVICE=C:\OS2\MDOS\VXMS.SYS /UMB
DEVICE=C:\OS2\MDOS\VDPMI.SYS
DEVICE=C:\OS2\MDOS\VWIN.SYS
DEVICE=C:\OS2\MDOS\VCDROM.SYS
DEVINFO=SCR,VGA,C:\OS2\VIOTBL.DCP
SET VIDEO_DEVICES=VIO_VGA
SET VIO_VGA=DEVICE(BVHVGA,BVHSVGA)
DEVICE=C:\OS2\MDOS\VSVGA.SYS
DEVICE=C:\OS2\POINTDD.SYS
DEVICE=C:\OS2\MOUSE.SYS
DEVICE=C:\OS2\COM.SYS
DEVICE=C:\OS2\MDOS\VCOM.SYS
CODEPAGE=437,850
DEVINFO=KBD,US,C:\OS2\KEYBOARD.DCP

RUN=C:\OS2\EPW.EXE
RUN=C:\IBMCOM\PROTOCOL\LANDLL.EXE
RUN=C:\IBMCOM\PROTOCOL\NETBIND.EXE
RUN=C:\IBMCOM\LANMSGEX.EXE

DEVICE=C:\IBMCOM\PROTOCOL\NETBEUI.OS2
DEVICE=C:\IBMCOM\PROTOCOL\NETBIOS.OS2

DEVICE=C:\CMLIB\ACSLANDD.SYS
DEVICE=C:\CMLIB\CMKFMDE.SYS
DEVICE=C:\OS2\LOG.SYS
RUN=C:\OS2\SYSTEM\LOGDAEM.EXE
RUN=C:\OS2\EPWROUT.EXE 1
DEVICE=C:\IBMCOM\MACS\IBMTOK.OS2
```

Figure 9.30 Sample CONFIG.SYS file (*Continued*).

```
[PROT_MAN]

   DRIVERNAME = PROTMAN$

[IBMLXCFG]

   IBMTOK_nif = IBMTOK.nif
   LANDD_nif = LANDD.nif
   NETBEUI_nif = NETBEUI.nif

[LANDD_nif]

   DriverName = LANDD$
   Bindings = IBMTOK_nif
   ETHERAND_TYPE = "I"
   SYSTEM_KEY = 0x0
   OPEN_OPTIONS = 0x2000
   TRACE = 0x0
   LINKS = 8
   MAX_SAPS = 3
   MAX_G_SAPS = 0
   USERS = 3
   TI_TICK_G1 = 255
   T1_TICK_G1 = 15
   T2_TICK_G1 = 3
   TI_TICK_G2 = 255
   T1_TICK_G2 = 25
   T2_TICK_G2 = 10
   IPACKETS = 250
   UIPACKETS = 100
   MAXTRANSMITS = 6
   MINTRANSMITS = 2
   TCBS = 64
   GDTS = 30
   ELEMENTS = 800

[NETBEUI_nif]

   DriverName = netbeui$
   Bindings = IBMTOK_nif
   ETHERAND_TYPE = "I"
   USEADDRREV = "YES"
   OS2TRACEMASK = 0x0
   SESSIONS = 40
   NCBS = 95
   NAMES = 21
   SELECTORS = 5
   USEMAXDATAGRAM = "NO"
   ADAPTRATE = 1000
   WINDOWERRORS = 0
   MAXDATARCV = 4168
   TI = 30000
   T1 = 500
   T2 = 200
```

Figure 9.31 Sample PROTOCOL.INI file.

```
  MAXIN = 1
  MAXOUT = 1
  NETBIOSTIMEOUT = 500
  NETBIOSRETRIES = 8
  NAMECACHE = 0
  PIGGYBACKACKS = 1
  DATAGRAMPACKETS = 2
  PACKETS = 350
  LOOPPACKETS = 1
  PIPELINE = 5
  MAXTRANSMITS = 6
  MINTRANSMITS = 2
  DLCRETRIES = 5

IBMTOK_nif]

  DriverName = IBMTOK$
  ADAPTER = "PRIMARY"
  NETADDRESS = "400020101A70"
  MAXTRANSMITS = 6
  RECVBUFS = 2
  RECVBUFSIZE = 256
  XMITBUFS = 1
```

Figure 9.31 Sample PROTOCOL.INI file (*Continued*).

Conclusion

Token Ring PU emulation is perhaps the most stable and reliable method for providing mainframe access. Almost every gateway product on the market today supports the Token Ring downstream PU connectivity option. CM/2, with the services of OS/2 and NTS/2, takes full advantage of the capabilities of the DSPU.

Chapter

10

Ethernet PU Emulation —Configuring CM/2

So far we have talked about CM/2 host PU support only for the Token Ring environment. It is possible, with the right components and configuration, to allow an Ethernet workstation to access the host as a downstream PU. Before continuing, you should have a firm understanding of the concepts of CM/2 PU support.

The reason that PU emulation host connectivity is so popular is that PU emulation is both extremely flexible and very reliable. Using the PU emulation method, each individual CM/2 workstation emulates a mainframe terminal control unit. The CM/2 workstation also emulates the mainframe LU functions. The LU functions provide the terminal and printer functions. So the CM/2 workstation that accesses the host by using the PU emulation function actually performs as a small terminal control unit with its associated terminals and printers all combined into one box.

Each CM/2 client workstation has its own connection into VTAM, the mainframe communications software. Because each client workstation has its own VTAM connection, troubleshooting and host configuration are simpler and less disruptive to the entire network. For example, if the user decides to add another printer session to the CM/2 configuration, the following steps are required under the PU emulation host access method:

- The CM/2 software is configured to add the new printer session.
- The VTAM configuration file for that user is updated to reflect the new printer.

- The host operator recycles (inactivates, then reactivates) the VTAM definition for the user.
- CM/2 is recycled.

That's all there is to it. If the user had been accessing the host through a gateway, the entire gateway connection to the host would need to be recycled. This process would need to be scheduled for off hours, otherwise every user accessing the mainframe through the gateway would be disrupted.

PU emulation on an Ethernet segment has all the benefits of Token Ring PU emulation, as described in previous chapters. Ethernet PU emulation has an added benefit over Token Ring PU emulation—it can be less expensive. This cost savings is realized because of the price difference between Token Ring and Ethernet NIC adapters. Token Ring NIC adapters can cost up to 3 times the price of Ethernet adapters. Shops with hundreds or even thousands of workstations can attain quite a cost savings by using Ethernet rather than Token Ring.

Ethernet PU emulation can be accomplished by using one of two host connection scenarios, Ethernet host connections and Token Ring host connections. Each of these host connection methods has advantages and disadvantages. We will discuss both host connection types.

The actual configuration of the CM/2 workstation is the same regardless of the host connection method you choose to implement. These CM/2 configurations are the same for both types of host connections because they both use the downstream PU (DSPU) host connection mechanism. The DSPU host connection method allows the OS/2 workstation to become one of the PUs that is defined to a Token Ring TIC, an Ethernet 3172 controller, or other 3172 look-alike box such as the Memorex 1174 controller. The concept behind DSPU host access is described, in detail, in Chap. 1.

Ethernet PU Emulation Using an Ethernet Host Connection

Figure 10.1 illustrates an OS/2-CM/2 workstation accessing the host as a DSPU in a pure Ethernet environment. The physical connection between the host and the Ethernet LAN is made by an IBM 3172 Ethernet controller. The Memorex 1174 controller could also be used in place of the 3172.

There are several benefits to this type of configuration:

- Each workstation accesses the host as a separate PU. This gives the network administrator and the mainframe systems programmer a lot of flexibility when setting up and troubleshooting the host access.

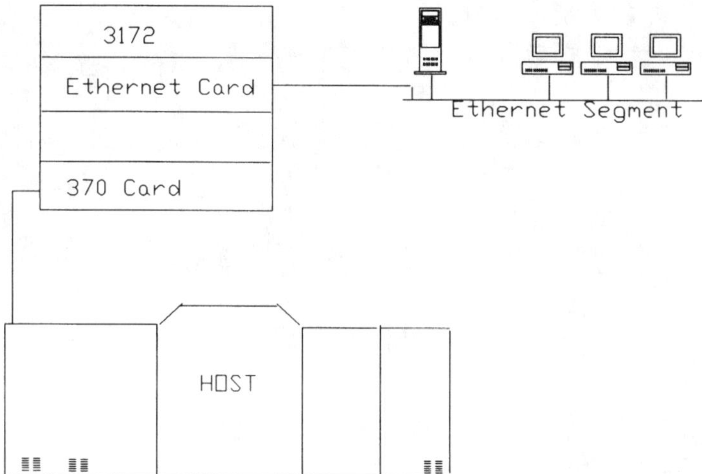

Figure 10.1 Ethernet PU emulation via an Ethernet host connection.

- The communications equipment, including NIC adapters and wiring concentrator cards, is less expensive than the Token Ring counterparts.
- A pure Ethernet environment does not require complex bridging and routing software.

Ethernet PU Emulation Using a Token Ring Host Connection

Ethernet PU emulation using a Token Ring host connection, as illustrated in Fig. 10.2, introduces another layer of complexity to the network. In order to have an Ethernet workstation participate in the downstream PU method via a Token Ring host connection, we must be able to pass SNA traffic from the Token Ring to the Ethernet segment. IBM saw the need for this functionality and developed the 8209 bridge.

The workstation shown in Fig. 10.2 is configured to access the host as a PU. A Token Ring connection is made to the host by a 3174 control unit which has a TIC installed. A 37x5 communications controller, with a TIC installed, could be used in place of the 3174. The SNA traffic is routed from the Token Ring to the Ethernet segment via an 8209 bridge.

Bridges and Routers

In a pure Token Ring environment, the TIC encapsulates the SNA traffic within Token Ring packets and places them on the network. An OS/2 workstation that is emulating a host PU receives these SNA Token Ring packets and uses these packets to reconstruct 3270 screens or

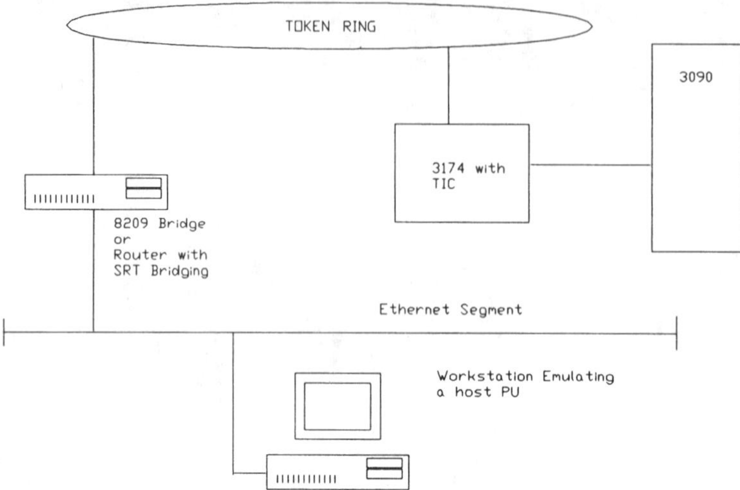

Figure 10.2 Ethernet PU emulation via Token Ring host connection.

print. The workstation sends SNA traffic back to the host in Token Ring packets. The TIC then breaks these packets down into native SNA packets and places them on the SNA network.

To emulate a PU on an Ethernet workstation by using a Token Ring host connection, as illustrated in Fig. 10.2, an additional translation step must occur. The TIC must still encapsulate the SNA traffic with Token Ring packets and place the data on the Token Ring network. Now the Token Ring encapsulated SNA traffic must be translated to the Ethernet frame type and forwarded to the proper Ethernet segment. A bridge or a router must be used to perform this forwarding function.

Not all bridges and routers support the transport of SNA traffic. SNA is a very difficult protocol to route because it is extremely timing-dependent. If the PU or LU emulator does not respond to the host within a certain time frame, VTAM will automatically reset the device. This reset will disrupt the terminal sessions at that workstation.

Another problem with bridging and routing SNA traffic from Token Ring to Ethernet is that there are no standards defined to perform the translation. IBM saw the need for Token Ring to Ethernet SNA bridging and developed its own standards with the 8209 bridge.

Several router vendors support the 8209 bridge function. The actual function is known as source routing transparency, or SRT. SRT acts as a source routing bridge when passing Token Ring frames and acts as a transparent bridge when passing Ethernet frames. If you are planning to implement Ethernet PU host access in a mixed Token Ring and Ethernet environment, make sure that your bridge or router supports

SRT. Of course, the other alternative is to implement the IBM 8209 bridge.

Chapter 6 includes a detailed explanation of bridges, routers, source routing, transparent bridging, and many other bridge and routing issues. You should have a strong understanding of these concepts before attempting to implement cross-topology CM/2 host access.

Configuring CM/2 to Provide Ethernet PU Support

The following procedure will guide you through a step-by-step OS/2-CM/2 configuration. The end result of this effort will be an OS/2 workstation on an Ethernet segment which will emulate a host PU. The workstation will support four host terminal sessions and one host printer session. This configuration will work with both the Token Ring host connection and the Ethernet host connection.

Prerequisites

Before we begin with the actual CM/2 PU emulation configuration, make sure that your network is set up properly to allow the host PU connectivity to occur.

First, you should already have OS/2 and Communications Manager/2 installed on the workstation you plan to use for the PU emulation. When you install Communications Manager/2, you are given the option of simply loading the software or loading and customizing the software. You should just load the software without performing the customization (configuration). Don't worry if you already performed the customization, because we will be starting with a fresh configuration file at the beginning of the step-by-step configuration example.

This workstation must have an Ethernet NIC installed. The workstation in this example used a 3COM 3C503 NIC adapter. You should also have a connection into the Ethernet network. This connection can be any type of Ethernet cabling. Many of the newer networks are using unshielded twisted pair (UTP) Ethernet connections into a wiring concentrator. It is advisable to test the Ethernet network connection prior to the CM/2 configuration exercise. One of the best ways to test the connection is to connect a workstation that is already working on Ethernet to the cable to be tested. Testing the Ethernet connection prior to the Communications Manager/2 configuration could help if problems arise with the configuration.

You must also have LAPS installed on the workstation you are configuring. LAPS is part of the IBM NTS/2 product. As with the installation of the CM/2 software, you should choose to only install the software without performing the customization. Again, don't worry if you have already customized the LAPS-NTS/2 product, as we will be starting with a fresh configuration file.

If you are planning to access the host via a Token Ring network, you must have a TIC connection to the host. The TIC can reside in a 3174 terminal control unit or a 3725 or a 3745 communications front-end processor. The TIC must have at least one DSPU defined for our use. You will need to know the address of both the TIC and the associated DSPU. For more information on the TIC setup or DSPUs, please refer to the earlier chapters. You must also have a bridge or router that supports SNA connecting the Token Ring network and the Ethernet segment.

If you are planning to access the host via a 3172-type Ethernet controller, you should already have the 3172 installed and tested (if possible) prior to implementing your first CM/2 PU-emulating workstation. This preparatory work will help with the troubleshooting efforts if problems arise.

Later in the chapter we will configure the host VTAM parameters. Don't worry if you do not have a strong VTAM knowledge base. We will be discussing the host VTAM requirements and how they relate to the local-area network in detail as we progress through the actual Communications Manager/2 configuration.

Communications Manager/2 configuration

The best way to begin the configuration is to start with a fresh configuration file. So, let's get started.

Step 1 Double-click on the Communications Manager/2 icon. The panel displayed in Fig. 10.3 will be displayed.

Step 2 Double-click on the Communications Manager setup icon.

Step 3 Click on OK to bring up the panel illustrated in Fig. 10.4.

Step 4 Select Setup and Fig. 10.5 will be displayed.

Step 5 Type in a configuration name and a description. For this example, ETPU was chosen for the configuration name. Click on OK.

Step 6 A message will be displayed asking you if this is a new configuration. Click on Yes.

Step 7 Next you will be asked if this configuration will be used for this workstation. Click on Yes.

Step 8 The next panel, shown in Fig. 10.6, requires two pieces of information: the workstation connection type and the feature or application. Click on Ethernet (ETHERAND) network as the connection type. Click on 3270 emulation as the feature or application. Click on Configure to continue.

Step 9 The panel shown in Fig. 10.7 will be displayed next. All entries in this panel must be completed. The network ID is the name of the

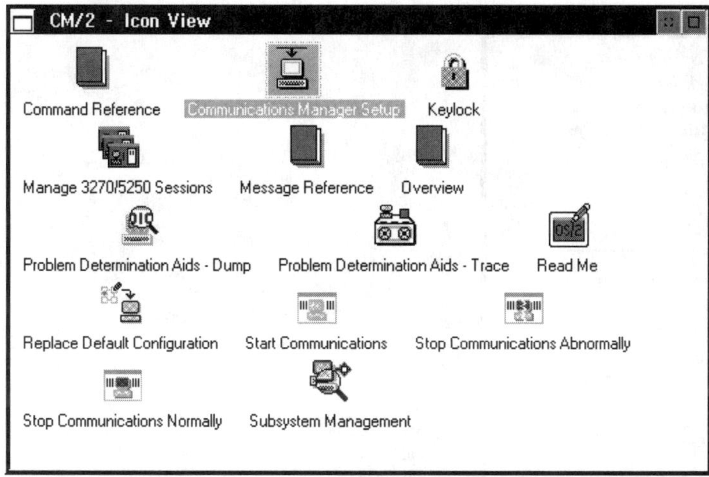

Figure 10.3 CM/2 folder contents. [*Reprinted by permission from IBM's OS/2 2.0, Copyright (1988, 1992) International Business Machines Corporation.*]

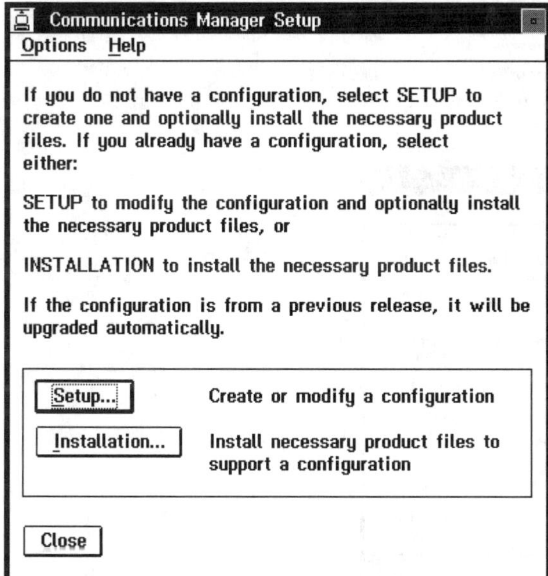

Figure 10.4 Entering the CM/2 setup utility. [*Reprinted by permission from IBM's OS/2 2.0, Copyright (1988, 1992) International Business Machines Corporation.*]

SNA network that the workstation is connected to. If you do not know the name of your SNA network, any name will work. This name is primarily used for problem notification. For completeness, ask your host systems programmer who is in charge of VTAM for the name of your host SNA network.

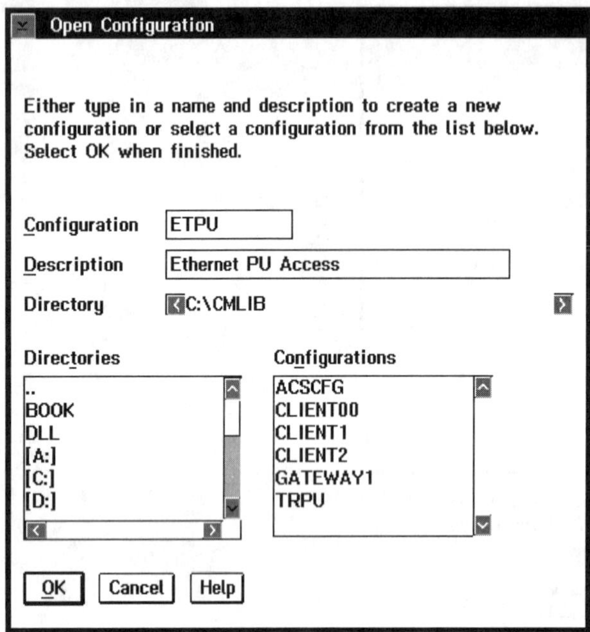

Figure 10.5 Naming the new CM/2 configuration file. [*Reprinted by permission from IBM's OS/2 2.0, Copyright (1988, 1992) International Business Machines Corporation.*]

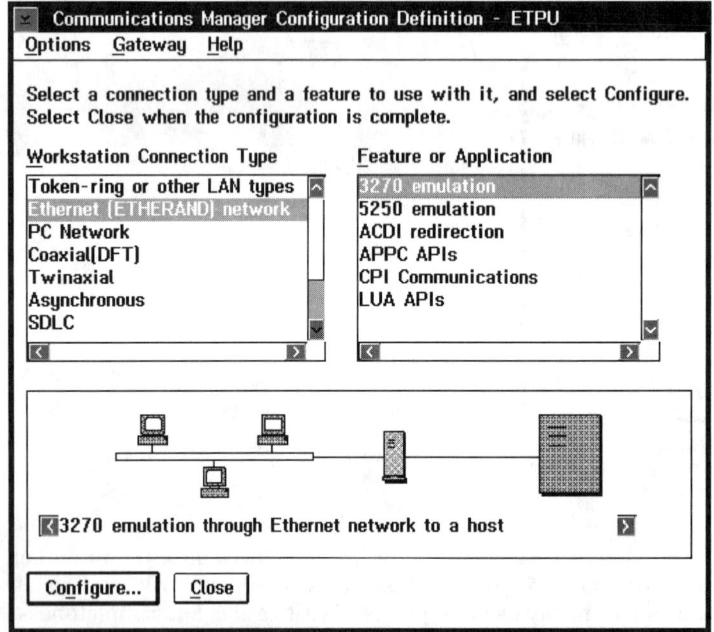

Figure 10.6 Selecting the Ethernet 3270 configuration option. [*Reprinted by permission from IBM's OS/2 2.0, Copyright (1988, 1992) International Business Machines Corporation.*]

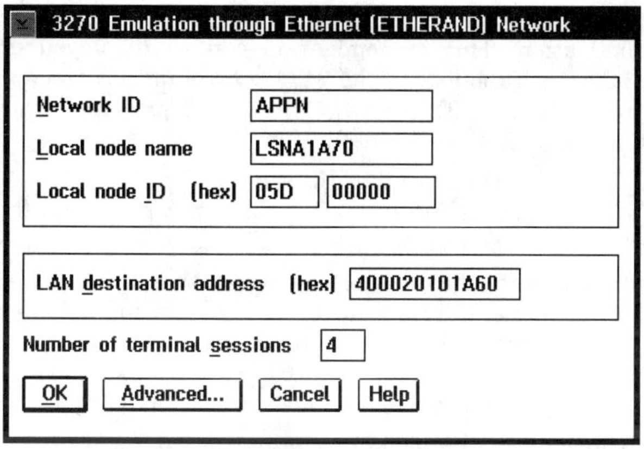

3270 Emulation through Ethernet (ETHERAND) Network

Network ID: APPN
Local node name: LSNA1A70
Local node ID (hex): 05D 00000

LAN destination address (hex): 400020101A60

Number of terminal sessions: 4

OK | Advanced... | Cancel | Help

Figure 10.7 Entering the local node parameters. [*Reprinted by permission from IBM's OS/2 2.0, Copyright (1988, 1992) International Business Machines Corporation.*]

Step 10 The Local node name field in Fig. 10.7 should match the member name of the VTAM configuration file that defines this PU. In this example, LSNA1A70 was chosen. This means that there must be a member named LSNA1A70 in SYS1.VTAMLST, the host VTAM definition library. Figure 10.8 is the actual SYS1.VTAMLST (LSNA1A70) definition. Keeping this name the same as the host VTAM definition file makes troubleshooting and network documentation much simpler.

Step 11 The Local node ID field in Fig. 10.7 will already be partially filled in for you with the hexadecimal value 05D. If you are connecting to a local host, key in 00000 in the second portion of this field. If you are connecting to a remote host, ask your host systems programmer in charge of the NCP at the remote mainframe site for the value of this field.

Step 12 The LAN destination address field, shown in Fig. 10.7, must contain the network address of the 3172, 3174, or 37x5 TIC that you are attempting to establish a connection with. This is a very important field. If this address is coded incorrectly, no communications can occur between the CM/2 workstation and the host. If you are

```
LSNA1A70 VBUILD TYPE=LOCAL
A01A70   PU     CUADDR=A70,
                 DLOGMOD=M2SDLCQ,
                 MAXBFRU=4,
                 PACING=1,
                 USSTAB=USSSNA,
                 MODETAB=AMODETAB
*                STATOPT='DSPU 400020101A70'
A7000002 LU      LOCADDR=2             A Session
A7000003 LU      LOCADDR=3             B Session
A7000004 LU      LOCADDR=4             C Session
A7000005 LU      LOCADDR=5             D Session
A7000006 LU      LOCADDR=6,DLOGMOD=S3270,SSCPFM=USSSCS
```

Figure 10.8 Sample VTAM PU definition.

connecting to a 3174 control unit, this address can be found in the 3174's customization. This customization can be displayed or printed by using the functions of the 3174 control unit. If you are connecting to a TIC in a 3725 or 3745 front-end processor, this address can be found in the NCP definition file.

If you are linking to a 3172, or other Ethernet controller, you may need to bit-reverse the LAN destination address. A procedure for performing this bit reversal is provided in Fig. 7.20.

Step 13 Key in the number of the terminal session you wish in the Number of terminal sessions field. This number does not include printer sessions. CM/2 supports up to a total of 16 terminal and printer sessions. In the example shown in Fig. 10.7, four terminal sessions were specified. One printer session will be configured later.

Step 14 Click on Advanced, and the panel shown in Fig. 10.9 will be displayed.

Step 15 Click on 3270 emulation, then click on Configure. The panel illustrated in Fig. 10.10 will be displayed.

Step 16 Click on File, then click on New and the screen shown in Fig. 10.11 will be displayed.

Step 17 Click on Logical printer, then click on OK to bring up the panel in Fig. 10.12.

Step 18 The only information you need to key into Fig. 10.12 is the LU local/NAU address field. This number is the LU number of the

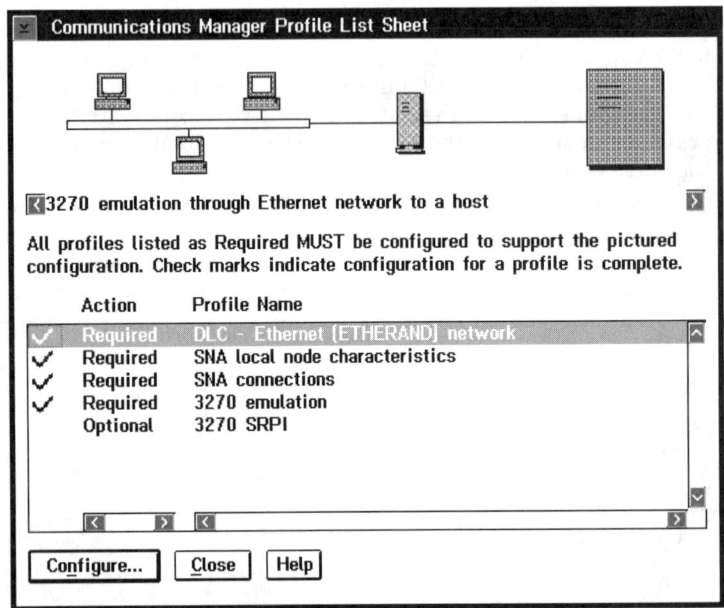

Figure 10.9 Accessing the CM/2 Advanced Configuration screen. [*Reprinted by permission from IBM's OS/2 2.0, Copyright (1988, 1992) International Business Machines Corporation.*]

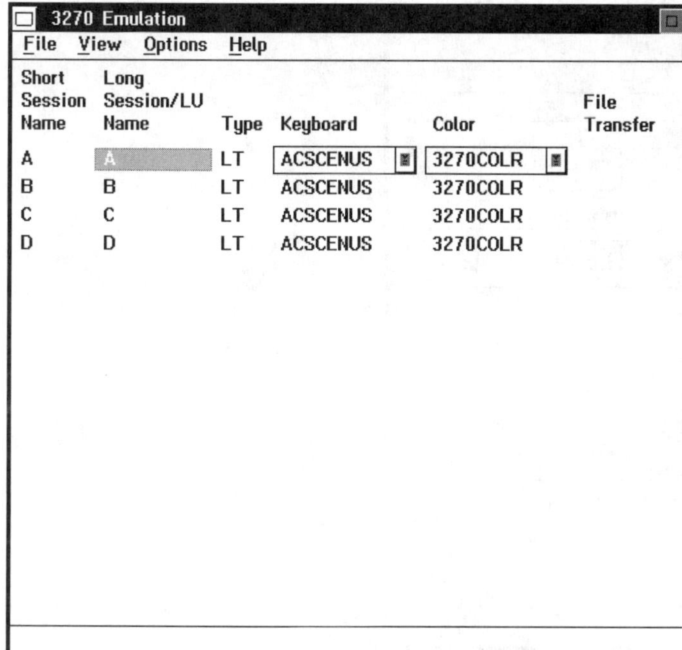

Figure 10.10 Viewing the 3270 emulation sessions. [*Reprinted by permission from IBM's OS/2 2.0, Copyright (1988, 1992) International Business Machines Corporation.*]

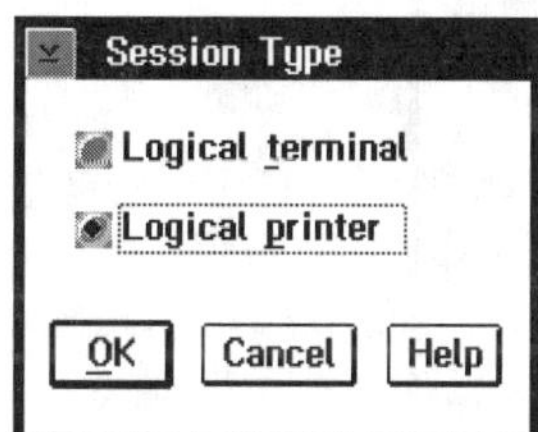

Figure 10.11 Adding a 3270 printer. [*Reprinted by permission from IBM's OS/2 2.0, Copyright (1988, 1992) International Business Machines Corporation.*]

printer we are defining. We already have four terminal sessions defined (A through D). If you refer to the host PU definition in Fig. 10.8, you will notice that the LU addresses begin with address 2. So the A terminal session uses LU number 2, the B session uses LU number 3, the C session uses LU number 4, and the D session uses LU number 5. The printer we are defining should use the next available LU, which is 6.

Step 19 Click on Save as, and Fig. 10.13 will be displayed. Enter E as the long session/LU name, and click on OK.

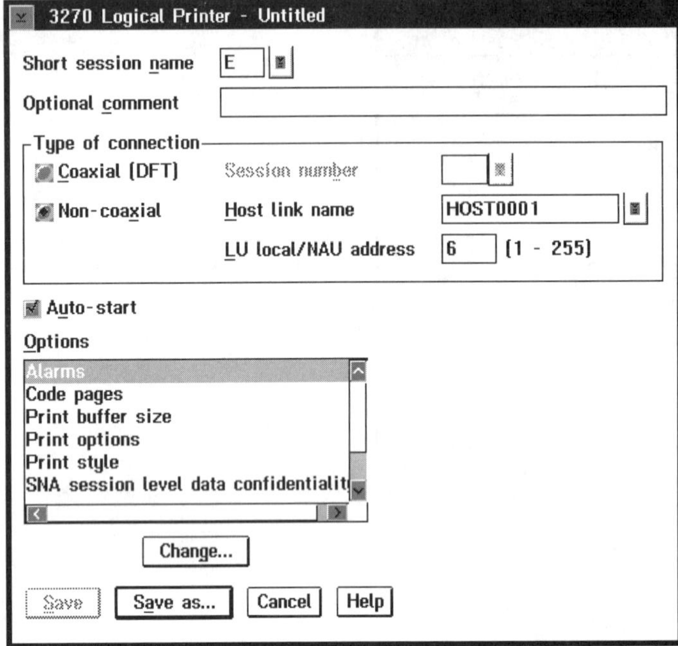

Figure 10.12 Assigning an LU to the printer session. [*Reprinted by permission from IBM's OS/2 2.0, Copyright (1988, 1992) International Business Machines Corporation.*]

Save As

Enter a name under which you would like to save this information.

Long session/LU name E

OK Cancel Help

Figure 10.13 Naming the printer session. [*Reprinted by permission from IBM's OS/2 2.0, Copyright (1988, 1992) International Business Machines Corporation.*]

Step 20 The 3270 emulation screen will be redisplayed. Close this by double-clicking on the upper left-hand corner.

Step 21 The Communications Manager Profile List Sheet screen will be redisplayed. Click on Close to close this window.

Step 22 The Communications Manager Configuration Definition screen will be redisplayed. Click on Close. At this time the configuration will be verified by the setup program.

Step 23 Next you will be asked if you would like to update the system files, as illustrated in Fig. 10.14. Click on Yes.

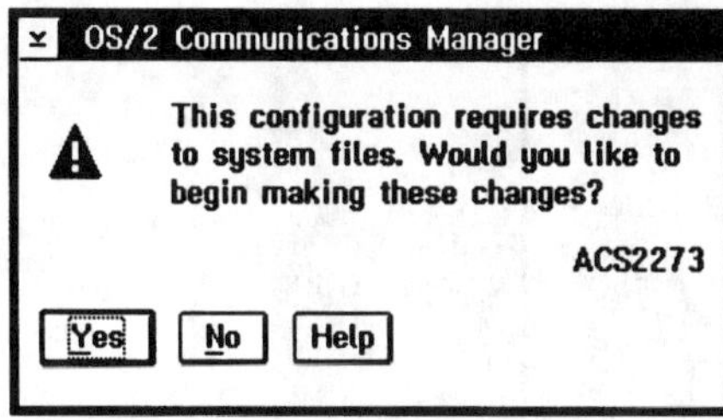

Figure 10.14 Confirming the system file changes. [*Reprinted by permission from IBM's OS/2 2.0, Copyright (1988, 1992) International Business Machines Corporation.*]

Step 24 You should receive the Communications Manager Completion screen. Click on OK.

Step 25 Close the Communications Manager setup.

Step 26 Now we must configure LAPS. Open an OS/2 full-screen session. Enter CD\IBMCOM to switch to the correct directory. If the IBMCOM directory does not exist, it means that LAPS has not been installed on this workstation. If this is the case with the PC you are using, stop now and install the NTS/2 product. You will not be able to implement CM/2 host connectivity via a local-area network without the NTS/2 product.

Enter LAPS to start the LAPS configuration program. The panel in Fig. 10.15 will be displayed. Select Configure.

Step 27 The panel in Fig. 10.16 will be displayed next. Select Configure LAN transports, then click on Continue.

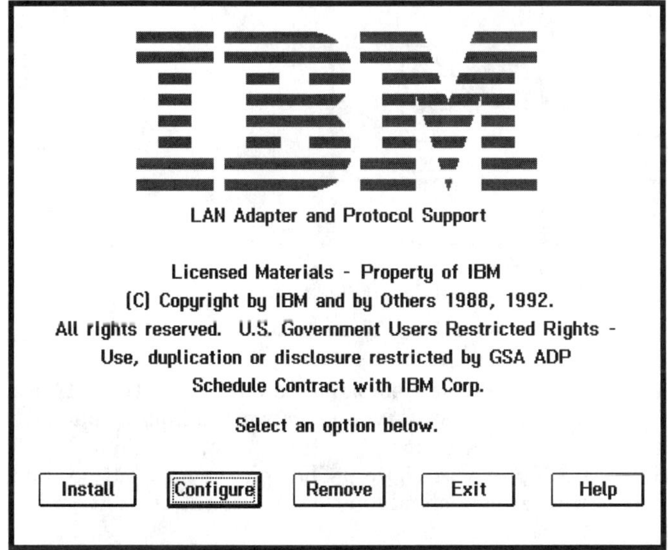

Figure 10.15 Initial LAPS configuration screen. [*Reprinted by permission from IBM's OS/2 2.0, Copyright (1988, 1992) International Business Machines Corporation.*]

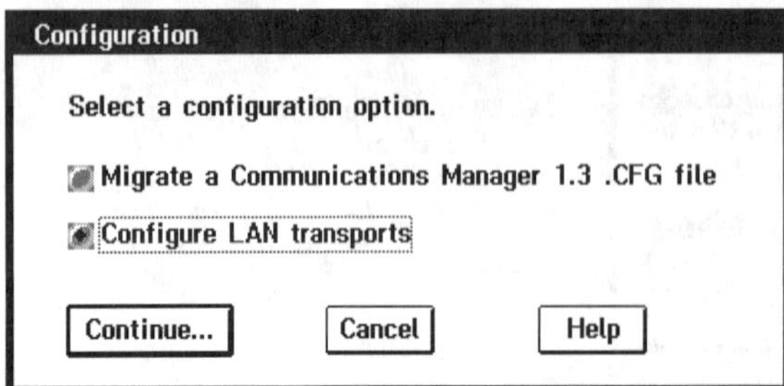

Figure 10.16 Selecting the LAPS configuration utility. [*Reprinted by permission from IBM's OS/2 2.0, Copyright (1988, 1992) International Business Machines Corporation.*]

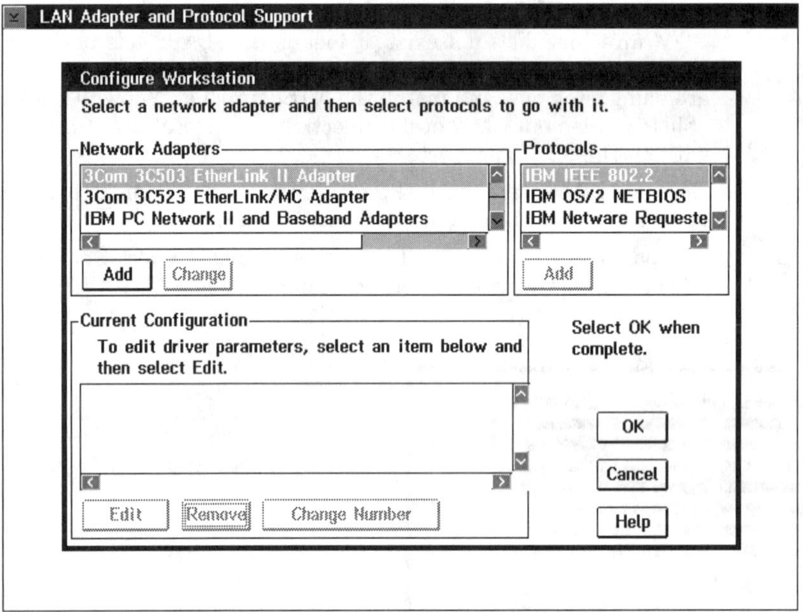

Figure 10.17 Adding the IEEE 802.2 protocol to the Ethernet adapter. [*Reprinted by permission from IBM's OS/2 2.0, Copyright (1988, 1992) International Business Machines Corporation.*]

Step 28 Figure 10.17 illustrates the next panel. Scroll through the network adapters list, and select the type of network adapter you have installed in your workstation. For this example, 3Com 3C503 EtherLink II Adapter was chosen. Click on the Add button, and the adapter you selected should move down to the current configuration area.

Step 29 In the protocols list click on IBM IEEE 802.2, then click on the Add button. The 802.2 protocol should move down to the current con-

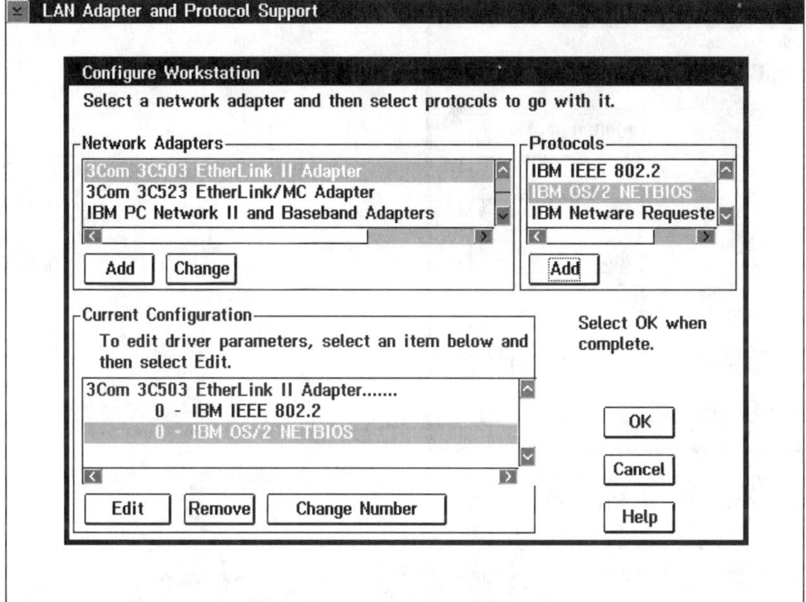

Figure 10.18 Adding the NETBIOS protocol to the Ethernet adapter. [*Reprinted by permission from IBM's OS/2 2.0, Copyright (1988, 1992) International Business Machines Corporation.*]

figuration area. If any of your applications require the use of NETBIOS, you should do the same to add the IBM OS/2 NETBIOS protocol. Your screen should look like the panel in Fig. 10.18.

Step 30 Click on the adapter you chose in the current configuration area, then click on the Edit button.

Step 31 This step is crucial for the downstream PU method. The panel illustrated in Fig. 10.19 will be displayed.

As you recall from Chap. 1, the DSPU host-to-LAN connectivity method requires that the workstation *become* the downstream PU defined in the 3174, 3725, or 3745 controller. To do this, we must override the universal address, which was burned into the NIC adapter by the NIC manufacturer, with a locally administered address. We specify a locally administered address by keying in a value in the Network adapter address field, as shown in Fig. 10.19. This address is the Token Ring address of one of the downstream PUs defined in the 3174 or 37x5. Make sure that the DSPU chosen is not being used by any other device in your network.

In this example we chose 40020101A70 as the locally administered address.

If you are linking to a 3172, or other Ethernet controller, you may need to bit-reverse the LAN destination address. A procedure for performing this bit reversal is provided in Fig. 7.20.

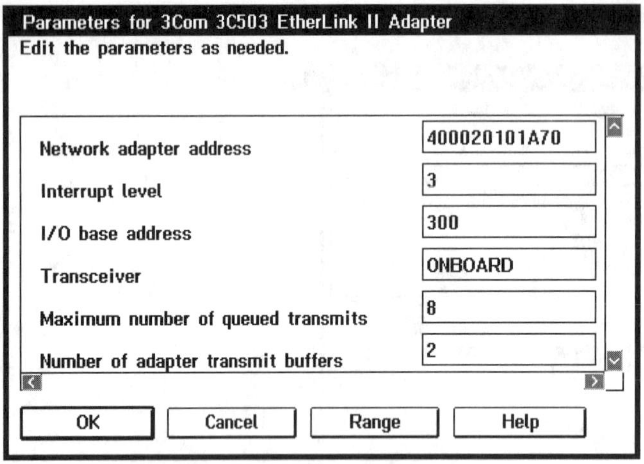

Parameters for 3Com 3C503 EtherLink II Adapter

Edit the parameters as needed.

Network adapter address	400020101A70
Interrupt level	3
I/O base address	300
Transceiver	ONBOARD
Maximum number of queued transmits	8
Number of adapter transmit buffers	2

OK Cancel Range Help

Figure 10.19 Assigning the LAA. [*Reprinted by permission from IBM's OS/2 2.0, Copyright (1988, 1992) International Business Machines Corporation.*]

IBM

LAN Adapter and Protocol Support

Licensed Materials - Property of IBM

(C) Copyright by IBM and by Others 1988, 1992.

All rights reserved. U.S. Government Users Restricted Rights - Use, duplication or disclosure restricted by GSA ADP Schedule Contract with IBM Corp.

Select an option below.

Install Configure Remove Exit Help

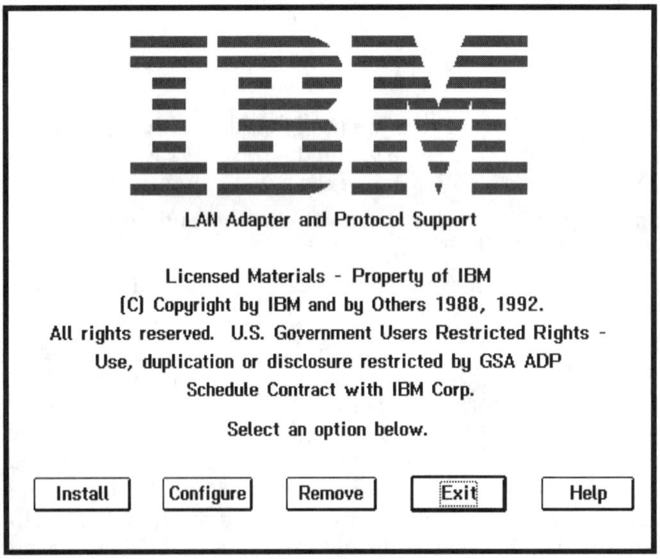

Figure 10.20 Exiting the LAPS utility. [*Reprinted by permission from IBM's OS/2 2.0, Copyright (1988, 1992) International Business Machines Corporation.*]

Step 32 Click on OK, and Fig. 10.20 will be displayed. Click on Exit.

Step 33 The next panel will ask you if you want to update CONFIG.SYS. Then select Continue.

Step 34 When the update is completed, exit the LAPS program.

Step 35 Now it is time to define your workstation to the VTAM software on the mainframe. VTAM has a configuration file which controls all the mainframe communications devices. In most shops the name of this file is SYS1.VTAMLST.

In the CM/2 configuration panel illustrated in Fig. 10.7, we chose LSNA1A70 as the local node name. This name must be defined to VTAM by placing a member named LSNA1A70 into SYS1.VTAMLST. A sample of this member is shown in Fig. 10.8.

The first line of the LSNA1A70 member tells VTAM that we are defining a local resource.

The second line tells VTAM that we are defining a PU named A01A70. This PU uses MVS address A70. Refer to Chap. 1 for an explanation of how the PU, MVS address, and DSPU relate to each other.

The remaining lines tell VTAM that this PU controls five LUs named A7000002 to A7000006. Notice the LOCADDR parameter.

After this member is created in SYS1.VTAMLST, you need to vary the PU and its related LUs active. Use the following VTAM command to do this:

```
V NET,ACT,ID=LSNA1A70,SCOPE=ALL
```

Step 36 Shut down and reboot your workstation. After your PC reboots, go into the Communications Manager/2 icon and double-click on the Start communications icon. If everything was configured correctly, your host sessions should come up!

Conclusion

More and more organizations are breaking the old traditional rules for mainframe connectivity. This is one of the reasons that IBM developed the APPN architecture. Organizations are pulling away from the traditional Token Ring mainframe access method and are opting for the less expensive Ethernet options. As we learned in this chapter, breaking the traditional connectivity mold must be performed with caution. SNA is not a friendly protocol to support in a multiprotocol network. The bridging requirements to allow Ethernet to participate in the downstream physical unit emulation must be met in order to provide a stable host access mechanism.

Chapter

11

Communications Manager/2 3270 Printer Support

More and more corporations are trying to migrate in the direction of the paperless office. While there are many advantages to this paperless office, such as instantaneous access to information, most organizations are still a long way from this ideal. This means that as we design our state-of-the-art, multiprotocol networks, we must still provide support for mainframe print. Providing terminal access to mainframe resources is a relatively simple task to perform. Providing 3270 printer support can be a little more difficult. The reason for the added difficulty in providing mainframe print support is that there are more hardware and software components involved in host printing systems. Another reason that providing mainframe print support on a local-area network is difficult is that we must make a PC printer look like a mainframe printer. This task alone does not appear to be overly difficult, until you look at all the different types of PC printers on the market today. It is not unusual for a single organization to have a dozen or more different types of printers installed on its local-area network. Our task is to make each of these printers capable of printing mainframe print data streams.

In this chapter we will look at all the hardware and software components required to provide mainframe printer support on a local-area network. We will also look at the specific resources available with OS/2 and CM/2 to make our goal of providing host VTAM printer support a reality.

CM/2 provides 3270 printer support for each type of host connection scenario explained in earlier chapters. The 3270 print support is identical no matter which host connectivity method you choose. Before we delve into the mechanics of CM/2 3270 print support, let's review the standard mainframe printer connectivity approach.

Standard 3270 Printer Connectivity

In the olden days, there was only one way to provide 3270 print support. A mainframe printer would be connected to a 3x74 terminal control unit via coaxial cable. Figure 11.1 illustrates this configuration.

The 3270 printers are defined to VTAM, a set of host programs that control 3270 terminals and printers, as LU type 1 or 3. CM/2 supports both LU types 1 and 3. Figure 11.2 illustrates a sample VTAM definition for a 3x74 control unit. The first seven lines in Fig. 11.2 define the con-

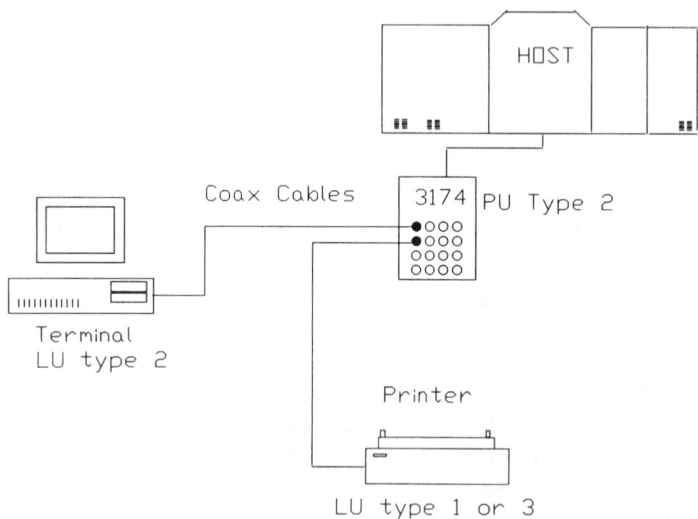

Figure 11.1 Typical host printer connection.

```
LSNA1A40 VBUILD TYPE=LOCAL
A01CA40  PU     CUADDR=A40,         ** PHYSICAL UNIT ADDRESS
                DLOGMOD=M2SDLCQ,   ** DEFAULT LOGON MODE ENTRY NAME
                MAXBFRU=4,          **
                USSTAB=USSSNA,      ** USE SNA USS TABLE
                MODETAB=AMODETAB    ** LOGON MODE TABLE NAME
*               STATOPT='3174 SNA CONTROLLER'
A4000002 LU     LOCADDR=2,DLOGMOD=M2SDLCQ
A4000003 LU     LOCADDR=3
A4000004 LU     LOCADDR=4,
                DLOGMOD=S3270,      ** DEFAULT LOG MODE ENTRY NAME
                SSCPFM=USSSCS       ** VTAM - SNA SCS PRINTER
                .
                .
                .
                .
```

Figure 11.2 VTAM definitions for terminals and printers.

trol unit to VTAM. The remaining lines define the LUs. The first two LU definitions define terminals at VTAM addresses A4000002 and A4000003. The last LU definition defines a printer at address A4000004.

Using standard 3270 printer connectivity, a print data stream is created by an application running on the host such as CICS or TSO. The mainframe application routes the print, using the services of VTAM, to the printer's LU address. VTAM then acts as a mail carrier and delivers the print to the host printer. VTAM also controls the error checking associated with the printing of the data stream. Chapter 1 contains an overview of how VTAM interacts between mainframe applications and terminals and printers.

There is another type of host printer. These printers are attached to the mainframe by a channel. Channel-attached printers do not use the services of VTAM to control their operation. These printers use a *job entry subsystem* (JES) to control their printing. Channel-attached printer support cannot be duplicated on a local-area network with the state of current technology. The remainder of this chapter deals only with the VTAM-controlled mainframe printer support.

CM/2 Printer Connectivity

There are many ways that an OS/2-CM/2 workstation can be connected to the host, including a coaxial connection to a 3x74 control unit, a Token Ring or Ethernet connection via a gateway, and Token Ring or Ethernet PU emulation. The CM/2 3270 printing and the host configuration parameters are exactly the same for every type of host configuration.

OS/2 Printing Components

Before we continue with our exploration of CM/2 host printing, we must have a thorough understanding of how the base OS/2 operating system handles printed output.

OS/2 is a true multitasking operating system, meaning that several applications can run concurrently. Without some type of operating system component to control printing, these concurrently running programs would each try to control the printer. This would result in interleaved print—a few lines from one program, then a few lines from the next program, and so on.

OS/2 uses a *spooling* mechanism to prevent this problem. When a program creates printed output, the output is placed in a special area on the hard drive called the *spool,* as illustrated in Fig. 11.3. When multiple applications are running concurrently on an OS/2 workstation, the printer output from each application is stored as a separate entity within the OS/2 spool data set. The OS/2 print driver reads the entities

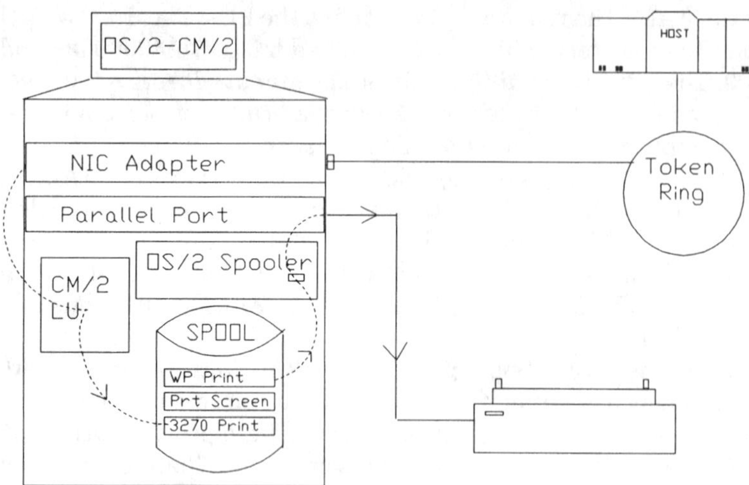

Figure 11.3 3270-OS/2 print routing.

in the spool and directs the data to the printer, one entity (or print job) at a time. The printer is connected to the OS/2 workstation by one of the parallel or COMM ports.

The method by which 3270 print is received on an OS/2-CM/2 workstation is a little different from the print generated by an application running on the workstation. To provide host print support, a 3270 printer is defined on the workstation by the CM/2 configuration utility. To the mainframe, this printer looks just like any other mainframe printer. The mainframe does not know and does not care that the printer is actually an OS/2 program that is emulating the mainframe printer device. The host applications will generate the print data stream, then VTAM will pass this data stream to the CM/2 printer emulation program. When CM/2 receives 3270 print from the host, CM/2 translates the data from EBCDIC to ASCII and then sends the print to the OS/2 spooling component. From the spool, the print job is treated just like any other OS/2 print job. The beauty of the OS/2 spooling mechanism is apparent. Print output can be stored and forwarded from multiple applications running concurrently on the OS/2 workstation. The spooling mechanism also accepts print data from applications running outside the OS/2 workstation, such as the mainframe print.

Implementing CM/2 Printer Support

The OS/2 printing components and the CM/2 3270 printer support work hand in hand to produce host print. Before you begin trying to implement CM/2 3270 printer support, make sure that the base OS/2 printing components are in working order. These components should be defined and thoroughly tested in order to make the 3270 printer implementation easier to troubleshoot. The first step in this process is the defining of a printer to the OS/2 operating system.

Defining an OS/2 printer

Defining a printer to OS/2 is relatively simple. Let's go through a step-by-step OS/2 printer definition:

Step 1 Double-click on the Templates icon. The panel in Fig. 11.4 will be displayed.

Step 2 Place the cursor on the Printer icon, then press and hold down the right mouse button. Drag the Printer icon to the desktop by moving the mouse.

Step 3 When you let go of the right button, Fig. 11.5 will be displayed. Type any name you wish in the Name field. This name is displayed on the

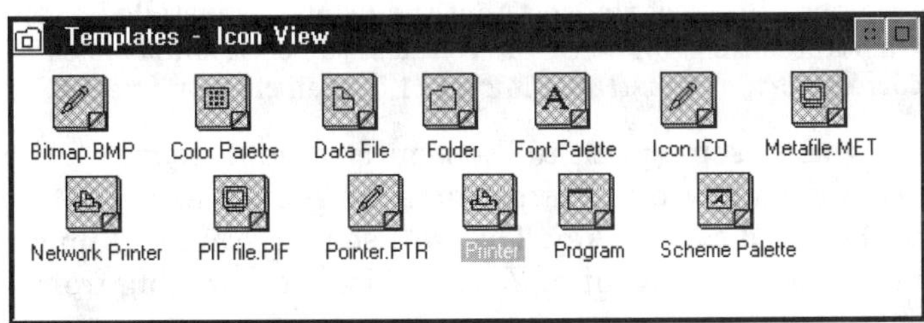

Figure 11.4 Selecting the OS/2 printer template.

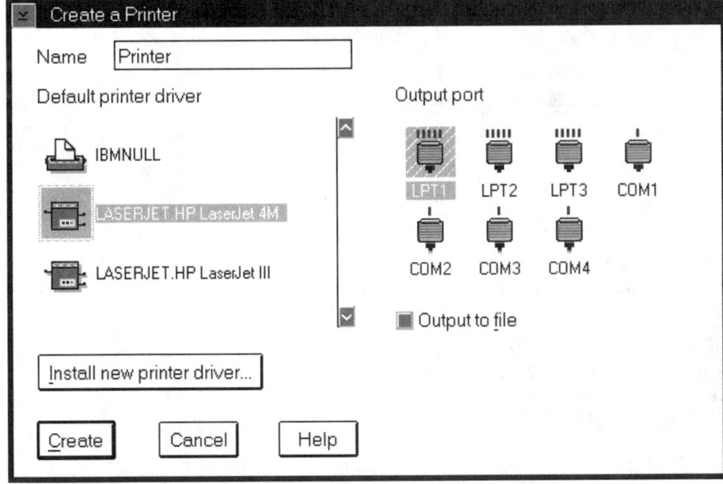

Figure 11.5 Naming the OS/2 printer.

OS/2 desktop and should be descriptive of the printer. OS/2 supports the definition of multiple printers. For example, you could have a LaserJet attached to the LPT1: port and a DeskJet attached to the LPT2: port. You should choose a name that correlates with the printer you are defining.

Step 4 There may or may not be a list of drivers displayed for you to choose from, depending upon how OS/2 was originally installed. If there is a list of drivers, scan the list and select the driver that matches your printer.

If there were no printers in your list, or if you cannot find the correct driver, you should click on Install new printer driver. The panel shown in Fig. 11.6 will be displayed. You may now scan this list and click on the appropriate driver. Next click on the Install button. Follow the prompts as the system asks you to insert the appropriate printer driver diskette that came with the OS/2.

If you are installing a third-party print driver, you should click on the Other OS/2 printer driver button and follow the prompts to load the driver.

Step 5 Now we need to select the port that the printer is installed on. In most instances this will be LPT1. To select the port, simply click on the correct port, as illustrated in Fig. 11.5, then click on Create.

You should now send some print to the printer to make sure all the OS/2 printing components are operating correctly. A simple way to test this is to press the Print Screen key. This will send a graphical image of your current screen to the printer. You can also test printing from a

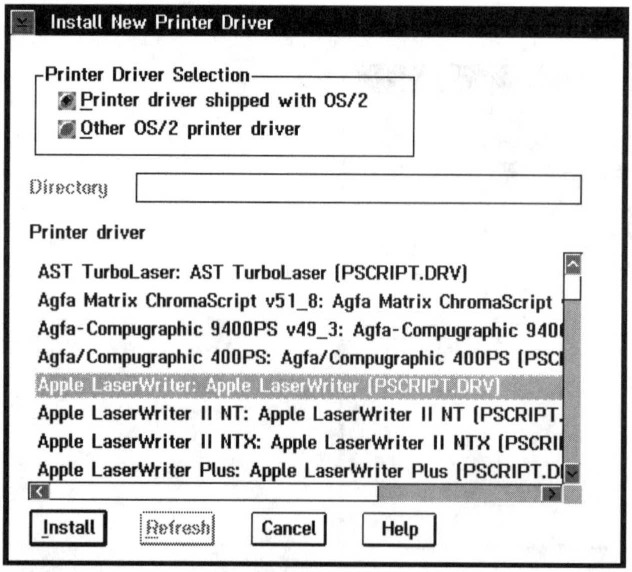

Figure 11.6 Selecting the OS/2 print driver.

DOS program. Before you try printing from a DOS application, make sure you have the following statement in your CONFIG.SYS file:

```
DEVICE=C:\OS2\MDOS\LPTDD.SYS
```

Another method to test the OS/2 print setup is to redirect a file to the printer. The following command can be issued from a DOS box to do this:

```
TYPE C:\CONFIG.SYS > LPT1
```

This command will cause the CONFIG.SYS file to be printed. If you are using a port other than LPT1 for your printer, specify that port in the TYPE command.

Configuring CM/2 for printer support

Now we are ready to add the 3270 printer support to our CM/2 workstation. The following procedure will guide you through a step-by-step example of adding a single 3270 printer session to a previously configured CM/2 system. The following items are assumed to have already been accomplished:

- OS/2 has been installed on your workstation.
- The OS/2 print components have been created and tested.
- CM/2 has been installed and configured for host access using any of the supported host configurations. Make sure that the terminal devices that you defined in CM/2 are working prior to testing the 3270 printing component. This will ensure that your host connectivity is installed and operating correctly.

Step 1 Double-click on the Communications Manager/2 icon.

Step 2 Double-click on the Communications Manager setup icon.

Step 3 Select Setup and Fig. 11.7 will be displayed.

Step 4 The name and description of your current configuration should be displayed. Click on OK.

Step 5 The panel illustrated in Fig. 11.8 will be displayed. In the workstation connection type list, select the type of host connection that you are using. For this example we are connected to an Ethernet network and access the host via a gateway. Next select 3270 emulation from the feature or application list, then click on Configure.

Step 6 The panel shown in Fig. 11.9 will be displayed next. Select 3270 emulation, then click on Configure. The screen shown in Fig. 11.10 will be displayed. This screen shows you all your 3270 terminal and printer definitions.

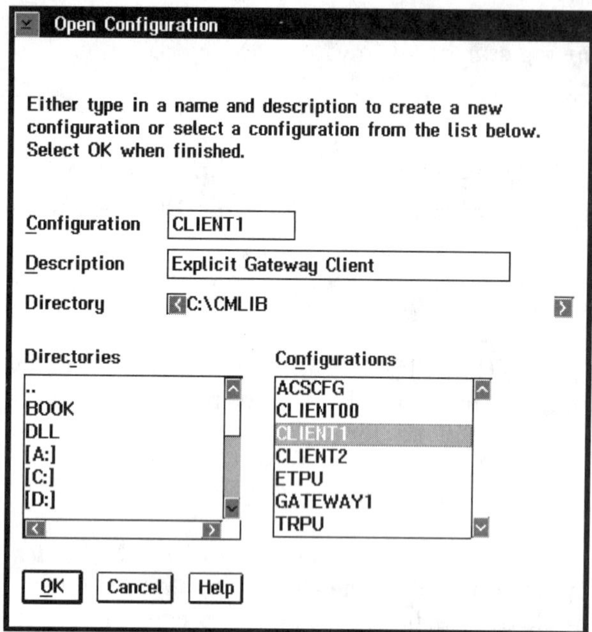

Figure 11.7 Opening your current CM/2 configuration file. [*Reprinted by permission from IBM's OS/2 2.0, Copyright (1988, 1992) International Business Machines Corporation.*]

Step 7 Click on File, then click on New, and the screen shown in Fig. 11.11 will be displayed.

Step 8 Click on Logical printer, then click on OK to bring up the panel in Fig. 11.12.

Step 9 The only information you need to key into Fig. 11.12 is the LU local/NAU address field. This is the LU number of the printer we are defining. Before we go any further, you must have a firm understanding of the mechanics of the LU/NAU (Network Accessible Unit) address field.

If you are accessing the host in PU emulation mode, the LU number that you place in this field will be the number of your last terminal session plus 1. For example, if you have four terminals defined, the A session would use LU address 2, the B session would use LU address 3, the C session would use address 4, and the D session would use address 5. So your new printer, session E, would use LU address 6.

If you are accessing the host via a gateway, as in this example, the LU address number must match the profile that is built on the gateway machine.

Step 10 Click on Save as, and Fig. 11.13 will be displayed. You must enter the long session name in this field. I usually use the same value in the long session name as in the short session name, as illustrated in Fig. 11.12. After entering the name, click on OK.

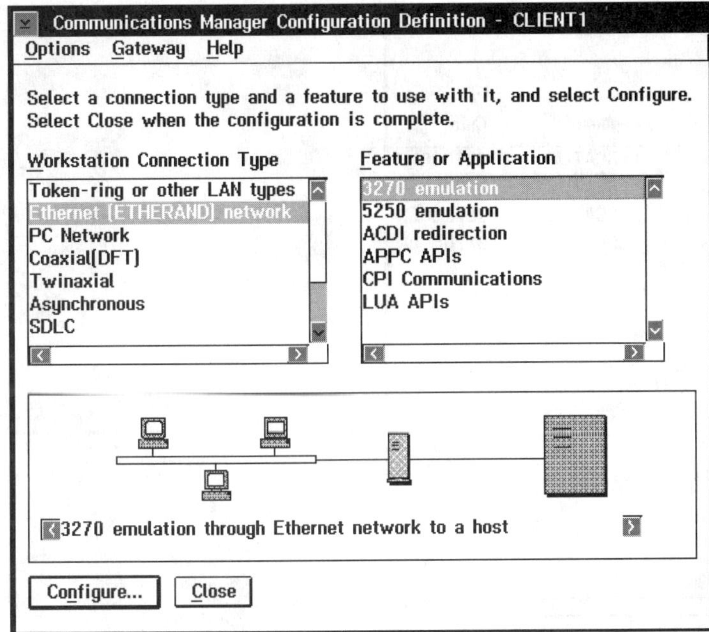

Figure 11.8 Enter the 3270 configuration option. [*Reprinted by permission from IBM's OS/2 2.0, Copyright (1988, 1992) International Business Machines Corporation.*]

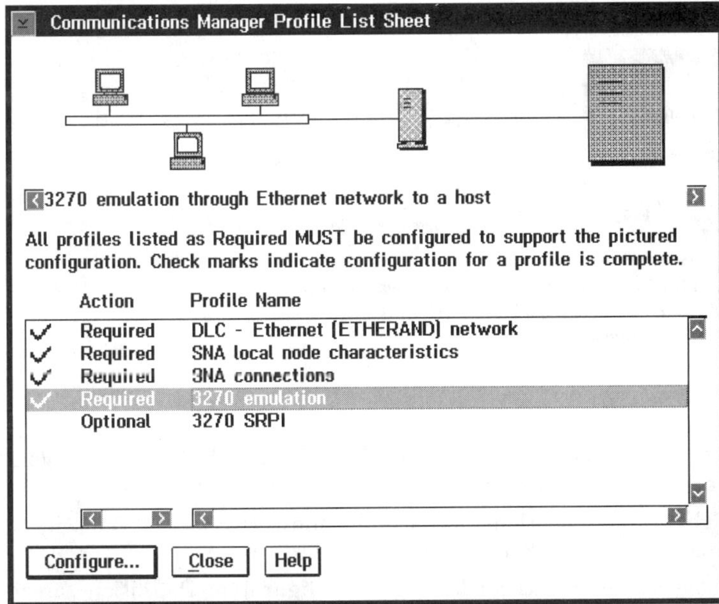

Figure 11.9 Selecting the 3270 emulation feature. [*Reprinted by permission from IBM's OS/2 2.0, Copyright (1988, 1992) International Business Machines Corporation.*]

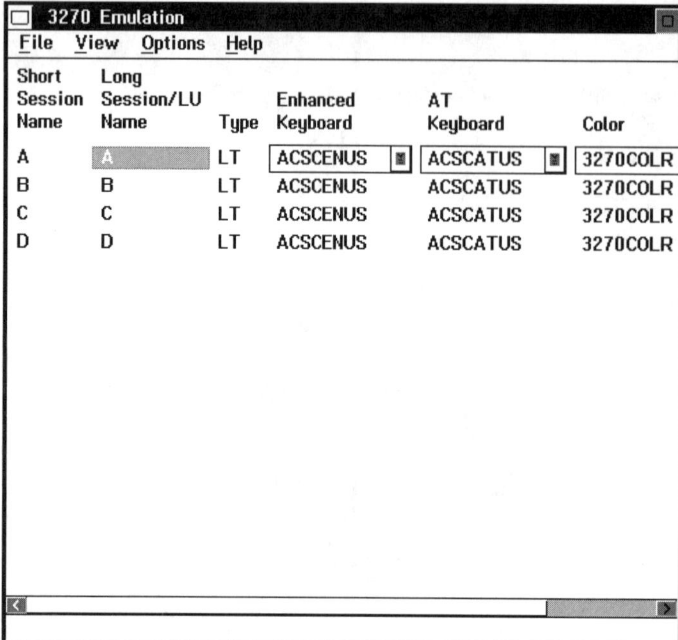

Figure 11.10 Viewing the 3270 sessions defined. [*Reprinted by permission from IBM's OS/2 2.0, Copyright (1988, 1992) International Business Machines Corporation.*]

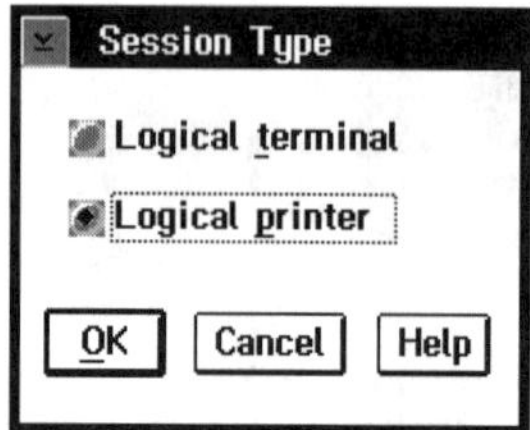

Figure 11.11 Adding a 3270 printer. [*Reprinted by permission from IBM's OS/2 2.0, Copyright (1988, 1992) International Business Machines Corporation.*]

Step 11 The 3270 Emulation screen will be redisplayed. Close this by double-clicking on the upper left-hand corner.

Step 12 The Communications Manager Profile List Sheet screen will be redisplayed. Click on Close to close this window.

Step 13 The Communications Manager Configuration Definition screen will be redisplayed. Click on Close. At this time the configuration will be verified by the setup program.

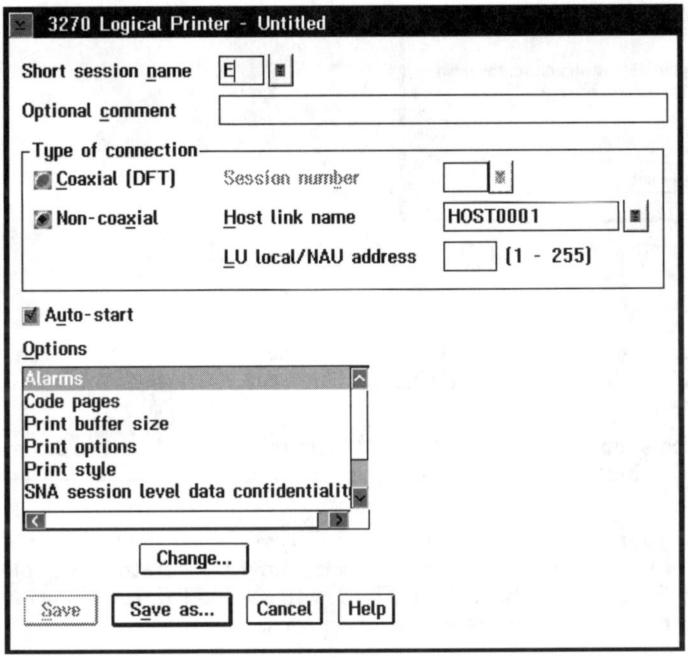

Figure 11.12 Assigning the printer LU address. [*Reprinted by permission from IBM's OS/2 2.0, Copyright (1988, 1992) International Business Machines Corporation.*]

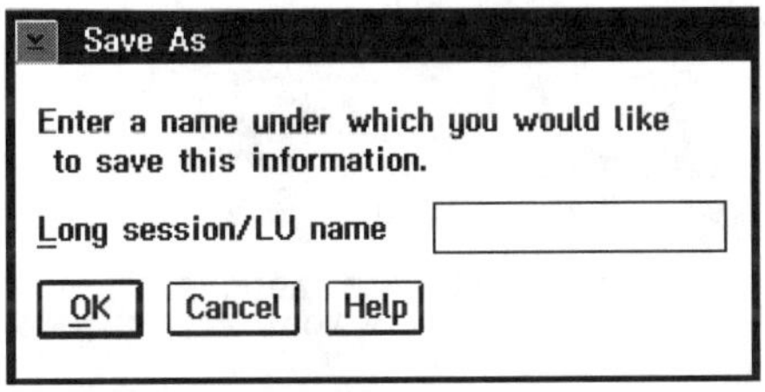

Figure 11.13 Naming the printer session. [*Reprinted by permission from IBM's OS/2 2.0, Copyright (1988, 1992) International Business Machines Corporation.*]

Step 14 Next you will be asked if you would like to either update the system files or dynamically update your SNA resources, as illustrated in Fig. 11.14. In either case click on Yes.

Step 15 Close the Communications Manager setup.

Step 16 Now it is time to modify your host VTAM definition for your new printer. Figure 11.15 is a VTAM definition that was used for this example.

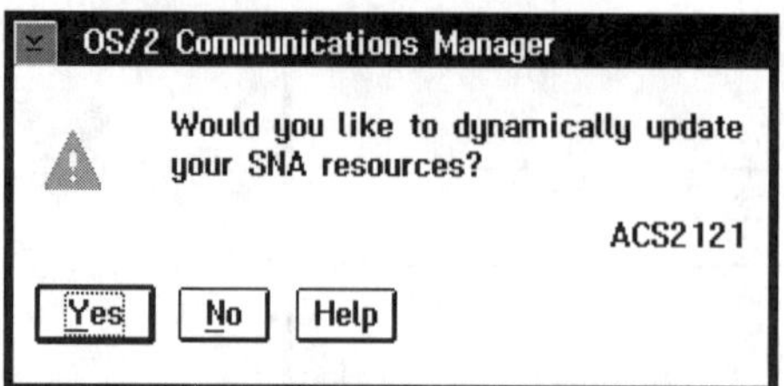

Figure 11.14 Dynamically updating the CM/2 SNA resources.

We chose LU address 11 for our printer. Look at Fig. 11.15 and find the line with LOCADDR=11. This is the line that defines our printer.

Each shop defines terminals and printers to VTAM a little differently. Make sure you follow the guidelines established at your shop.

Step 17 For your VTAM changes to take effect, you must deactivate and then reactivate the PU that controls your LU(s). In this example the PU is named LSNA1A61. To deactivate the PU, the following command is issued through the host console:

```
V NET,INACT,ID=LSNA1A61,F
```

To reactivate the PU, the following command is issued:

```
V NET,ACT,ID=LSNA1A61,SCOPE=ALL
```

```
LSNA1A61 VBUILD TYPE=LOCAL
A01CA61  PU     CUADDR=A61,         ** PHYSICAL UNIT ADDRESS
                DLOGMOD=M2SDLCQ,   ** DEFAULT LOGON MODE ENTRY NAME
                MAXBFRU=4,          **
                PACING=1,           ** FOR SNA GATEWAY
                USSTAB=USSSNA,      ** USE SNA USS TABLE
                MODETAB=AMODETAB    ** LOGON MODE TABLE NAME
*               STATOPT='OS2    GATEWAY'
A010A502 LU     LOCADDR=2
A010A503 LU     LOCADDR=3
A010A504 LU     LOCADDR=4
A010A505 LU     LOCADDR=5
A010A506 LU     LOCADDR=6
A010A507 LU     LOCADDR=7
A010A508 LU     LOCADDR=8
A010A509 LU     LOCADDR=9
A010A50A LU     LOCADDR=10
A010A50B LU     LOCADDR=11,DLOGMOD=S3270,SSCPFM=USSSCS
A010A50C LU     LOCADDR=12
A010A50D LU     LOCADDR=13
A010A50E LU     LOCADDR=14
```

Figure 11.15 The host VTAM definitions.

Be careful. If you are accessing the host via a gateway, all users who access the host via the gateway will be interrupted when you recycle the PU. If you are using the host PU emulation option of CM/2 for each user on your network, this deactivation and reactivation of the PU will affect only that user.

Step 18 Shut down and reboot your workstation. After your PC reboots, go into the Communications Manager/2 icon and double-click on the Start communications icon. If everything was configured correctly, your printer session will be active.

Step 19 It is time to test your 3270 print support. Each shop is configured a little differently and runs different applications. You should access one of the applications on your mainframe that utilizes VTAM 3270 printers and direct the print to your newly defined CM/2 3270 printer emulator.

Customizing 3270 Print Output

You can easily customize the way your 3270 print looks by using the Communications Manager/2 emulator print control function. To access the emulator print control function, do the following:

- From the OS/2 desktop, press both mouse buttons simultaneously to bring up your active window list. A sample of this list is shown in Fig. 11.16.
- Double-click on Emulator print control, and the panel illustrated in Fig. 11.17 will be displayed.

Some of these customization options available under the emulator print control are not available for certain printers. Check the capabilities of your printer to determine which options are valid for your environment. We will look at two of the most commonly changed customization options: modifying the lines per inch and modifying the characters per inch.

If you bring up the emulator print control function, you will notice that all your terminal and printer sessions are displayed. If you look further, you will notice that you can modify the print characteristics of both terminal and printer sessions. At first thought, this does not seem to make much sense; how could I (or why would I want to) change the print characteristics of a terminal session? The answer is simple. If you are in a host session and hit the Print Screen key, you will get a graphical picture of your screen sent to your printer. In most cases this graphical image looks like a big mess. If you press Shift+Print Screen, you will get a character-based picture of your screen. Changing the print characteristics of your terminal session will modify how this character-based print screen image is printed.

Figure 11.16 Viewing the OS/2 active window list. [*Reprinted by permission from IBM's OS/2 2.0, Copyright (1988, 1992) International Business Machines Corporation.*]

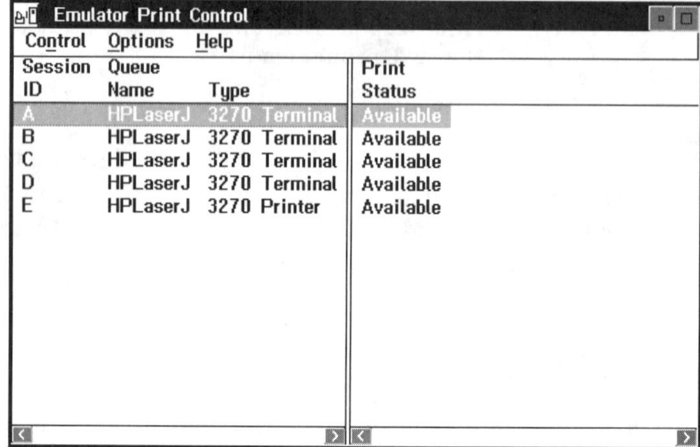

Figure 11.17 The CM/2 emulator print control function. [*Reprinted by permission from IBM's OS/2 2.0, Copyright (1988, 1992) International Business Machines Corporation.*]

Modifying your printer session print characteristics will change the print output of VTAM-based application print output. CICS and JES328X are two VTAM-based applications whose print can be tailored by modifying your printer session print options.

Changing the lines printed per inch

Most mainframe applications are designed to print either 6 or 8 lines per inch. CM/2 supports from 1 to 255 lines per page. To modify this setting for your terminal or printer session, do this:

Step 1 Bring up the emulator print control function as described earlier.

Step 2 Click on the session you wish to modify to highlight it, then click on Options. The panel shown in Fig. 11.18 will be displayed.

Step 3 Click on Print style to bring up Fig. 11.19.

Step 4 Enter the number of lines per inch you wish to use in the Lines per inch box; then click on OK.

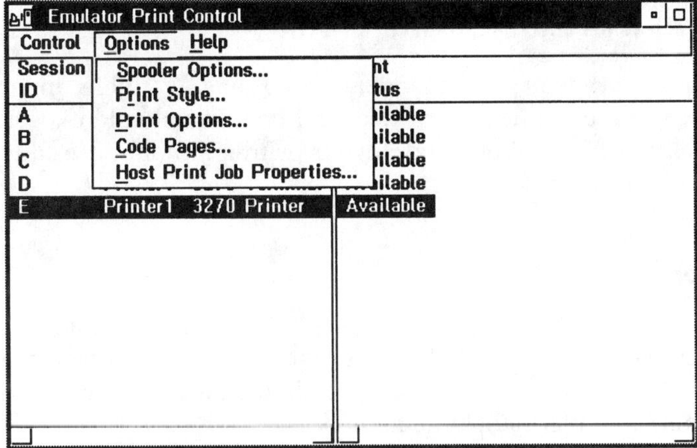

Figure 11.18 Changing the 3270 print options. [*Reprinted by permission from IBM's OS/2 2.0, Copyright (1988, 1992) International Business Machines Corporation.*]

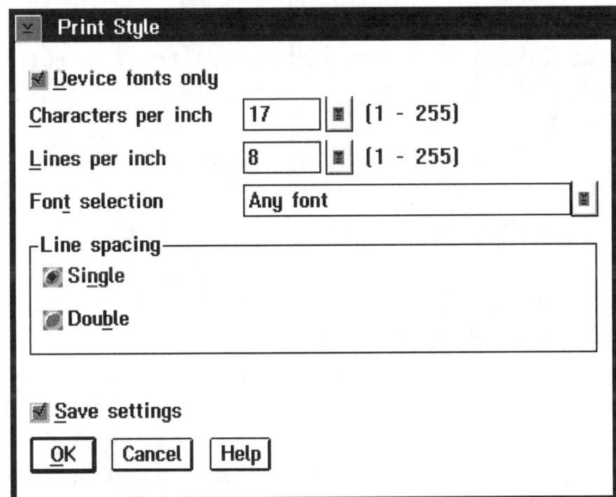

Figure 11.19 Modifying the 3270 print style. [*Reprinted by permission from IBM's OS/2 2.0, Copyright (1988, 1992) International Business Machines Corporation.*]

Changing the characters per inch

To modify the number of characters that the emulator prints per inch, use the following procedure:

Step 1 Bring up the emulator print control function as described earlier.

Step 2 Click on the session you wish to modify to highlight it, then click on Options. The panel shown in Fig. 11.18 will be displayed.

Step 3 Click on Print style to bring up Fig. 11.19.

Step 4 Enter the number of characters per inch you wish to use in the Characters per inch box; then click on OK.

There are many other print customization options available under the Options bar in the emulator print control box. You should experiment to determine which options match your printer's capabilities and your host print characteristics.

Troubleshooting the 3270 Printer

As you have seen, there are many components involved in providing 3270 printer support on an OS/2-CM/2 workstation. If you experience problems with the printing of host data, you should perform your troubleshooting effort in a methodical fashion.

The first area you should check is the native OS/2 printing setup. Send some printed output to the printer, using native DOS or OS/2 applications and/or commands. If these methods do not print, there are two areas that you should investigate next. Look into the OS/2 spool to see if the print made it that far. To check the spool, you simply double-click on the printer icon that you created when defining the printer to OS/2. A presentation manager box will open. If there are any jobs waiting to be printed, they will be shown in this box. If jobs are waiting in the spool, you most likely have a hardware-related problem with either your printer or the cable connections between the printer and the PC.

After you are sure that your OS/2 printer setup is operating correctly, begin looking at the mainframe connectivity. Each LU defined in CM/2 has a corresponding mainframe VTAM address. Display this VTAM address, using the following VTAM command:

```
D NET,ID=address,E
```

The LU associated with your CM/2 printer emulator should show a status of ACT or ACT/S. A status of INACT or NEVACT indicates a problem with your CM/2 configuration or your VTAM definition of the LU. Before you make any changes in your CM/2 configuration, enter the following VTAM in an attempt to activate the LU:

```
V NET,ACT,ID=address
```

After you issue the command, reissue the display command shown above. If the status changed to ACT or ACT/S, try resending the print from the host application. If the LU remained in the INACT or NEVACT state, we must look deeper into the problem.

The NEVACT status tells us that VTAM never tried to activate the LU. This is most likely a CM/2 configuration error. A good place to start looking for the error is in the LU address within the CM/2 configuration. If you placed an invalid address in this field, the NEVACT status could result.

The INACT status could be a mismatch between the LU definition on the mainframe and the printer definition within CM/2. Perhaps the CM/2 configuration specifies a printer LU type 1 while the VTAM definition reflects an LU type 3. To troubleshoot the INACT status, you should use the VTAM VARY command to activate the LU and then watch the mainframe console closely for errors. These errors will provide a sense code that will help you find the source of the problem.

Netports, NetWare, and Mainframe Print

Many networks use devices such as Netport to drive the printers on their local-area networks. Netport is a device, manufactured by Intel, that acts as a small NetWare print server. Netport can drive one or two network printers. If you are planning to utilize these types of devices for your host print, you may be facing a problem. Host print is always directed to LUs or LU emulators such as CM/2. In order to allow a Netport on a Novell LAN to print mainframe print, we must find a way to move the host print into a NetWare print queue. Two methods can be used to accomplish this goal.

There are two products from Levi, Ray and Shoup, Inc., named VPS and VPS/PC. These two software packages work hand in hand to perform the task of moving host print into NetWare print queues.

The second method is much cheaper, but less reliable. Configure the mainframe printer emulator in a CM/2 workstation as defined earlier in this chapter. Next issue a Novell CAPTURE command to capture the output of the LPT1: port and direct it to a NetWare print queue. Now when mainframe print is generated, first it goes to the CM/2 printer emulator. Then when it is shipped to the LPT1 port by the OS/2 printer driver, it is rerouted into a NetWare print queue. The obvious flaw with this method is that all the output from the workstation's LPT1 port would be directed to the NetWare print queue. While this method works, it can be slower than the VPS method.

Conclusion

There is a substantial computer downsizing trend sweeping corporate America. Even with this trend, many corporations still have their mission critical application running on mainframes. The last thing a network administrator needs is problems with the printing of these important data. The multitasking capabilities of OS/2 and its superb print spooling system make the OS/2-CM/2 workstation a fine vehicle for providing mainframe printed output. We also saw in this chapter that printer component manufacturers are beginning to see the light. Hardware and software components are being developed that will help us route mainframe print throughout a local-area network.

Part

3

NetWare Connectivity

Now we are ready to enter the realm of coexistence. We have established our host connectivity, and now we need to provide access to a Novell network. This is easier said than done. There are several methods available for providing coexistence. You will learn the concepts behind each of these coexistence methods.

Once we know the concepts behind coexistence, we can use this information in practice. We will go through several step-by-step procedures to implement each of the coexistence methods. After completing this part of the book, you will have a clear understanding of the intricacies involved in providing coexistence, and you will be able to make an informed decision on which option best suits your particular needs.

We will also explore the functions provided by the OS/2 NetWare Requester product. There are several utilities included with this product that can make your job much easier.

We will finish this part of the book with a chapter dedicated to network print routing methods (Chap. 15). We will look at all the NetWare printing components and will learn how OS/2 and CM/2 can mesh with NetWare. We will also look at ways to automate the routing of print through your network.

Chapter

12

Communications Manager/2 and NetWare Coexistence

What Is Coexistence?

Multiprotocol networks present some special problems for the network designer. It is very common today for a user to require access to many disparate systems concurrently. These systems include mainframes, minicomputers, and networked file servers, each of which speaks a different language (protocol). One solution to this problem is to place multiple terminals on the user's desk, one for each system. The user (and your boss) will probably not like that solution. Another solution is to define a separate CONFIG.SYS and AUTOEXEC.BAT for each system which load the particular drivers for that system and have the user reboot the workstation when switching between systems. This solution is not much better than the first.

Another solution is to use drivers that can share the NIC adapter in the PC in a manner where each application can *coexist* with the others. Using the coexistence solution allows the user to access multiple systems concurrently. To provide this coexistence, a networking system must be implemented that can transport the various protocols used by these various systems. Once we have a network cabling system in place that can handle these multiple protocols, we still have a major hurdle to tackle. Software must be implemented that can time-slice the use of the network interface card. This software must be able to send and receive the different protocol packets and direct them to the appropriate application. As you can surmise, this is not a simple task. This is the heart of what makes coexistence such a difficult goal to achieve.

The two most commonly used methods to allow multiple protocols to share a common NIC adapter concurrently are

- The Open Data-Link Interface (ODI)
- Demand Protocol Architecture (DPA) in combination with the Network Driver Interface Standard (NDIS)

If you are in the process of designing a multiprotocol network, you will probably be required to choose between ODI and the DPA/NDIS coexistence methods. Each of these two coexistence methods has its advantages and drawbacks. Depending upon your particular network configuration, one will be a better fit in your organization than the other. It is very important that you understand all the theories and techniques used by these two coexistence methods in order to make an informed decision. The remainder of this chapter will show you how each of these systems operates and will explain the benefits of each.

Let's take a look at the ODI coexistence methodology first.

Open Data-Link Interface

Older versions of NetWare bound the LAN NIC adapter to the IPX protocol (IPX.COM). This binding process prevented the NIC from being shared by other protocols. This worked fine as long as every application that was run on the workstation used the IPX/SPX protocol. If a TCP/IP system was on the network, the user could not access it without reconfiguring his or her workstation to remove the IPX driver and load a TCP/IP network interface driver.

Novell and Apple Computer developed the Open Data-Link Interface (ODI) to get around this problem. ODI decouples the LAN hardware from the protocol(s). This decoupling allows multiple protocols to share a common NIC adapter. The method used by ODI to perform this decoupling is rather impressive. Let's take a closer look at the individual components that allow the sharing of the NIC adapter between protocols.

ODI Components

The ODI architecture consists of three major components:

- Multilink interface driver (MLID)
- Link support layer (LSL)
- Protocol stacks

Multilink interface driver

The multilink interface driver is the closest software component to the hardware (NIC adapter). The MLID takes packets from the NIC adapter, removes the media access (MAC) headers, and passes the data to the link support layer.

Every packet retrieved by the NIC adapter is touched by the MLID. This function decouples the protocols from the hardware. The layers above the MLID know nothing about the MAC details. The beauty of this is that the protocol drivers (or interpreters) that run on the workstation no longer have to concern themselves with the lower-level hardware access. The MLID takes care of all the accesses to and from the NIC adapter for the protocol drivers.

Novell provides many ODI MLIDs. Since the MLID talks directly to the NIC adapter, each different NIC must have a specialized MLID. The naming convention used most often for these drivers is the name of the network interface adapter followed by ".COM," such as

NE1000.COM

NE2.COM

TOKEN.COM

Link support layer

The link support layer is the heart of ODI. The LSL can be viewed as a switchboard operator, as illustrated in Fig. 12.1. LSL receives packets from the MLID. LSL then looks into each individual packet and deter-

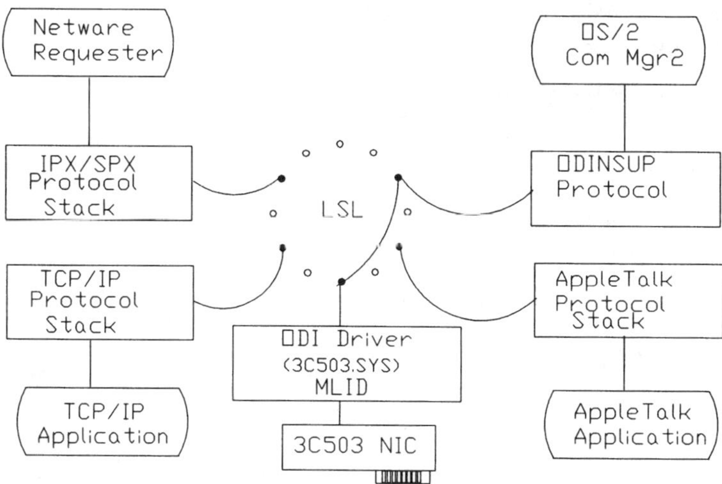

Figure 12.1 The Open Data-Link Interface (ODI).

mines which protocol the packet is using. LSL then routes the packet to the appropriate protocol stack.

So, let's see what we have so far. A packet is sent to our workstation. The NIC adapter, in conjunction with the MLID, receives the packet from the network wire. The MLID strips the hardware information (the MAC headers) from the packet and passes the packet to the link support layer. The LSL then looks to determine the protocol type of the packet and passes the packet to the appropriate protocol stack.

Protocol stacks

The protocol stacks take the packets from the LSL layer, remove the protocol header information, and pass the data on to the application. Some of the more common protocol stacks are TCP/IP, IPX/SPX, and APPLETALK.

Step back and think about the ODI theory and how its components bring this theory to life. ODI's goal is to allow one NIC adapter to be used by multiple applications using different protocols. There are two factors that must be addressed to attain this goal.

First, the tie between the NIC and the protocol must be severed. Breaking this tie allows the NIC to be used by other protocols. The MLID component performs this function.

Second, multiple protocols will use the same MLID to access the hardware. The LSL performs this sharing function by switching the connection between the MLID and the various protocol stacks.

Demand Protocol Architecture

The Demand Protocol Architecture (DPA) is designed to allow multiple protocols to share a common NIC adapter, just as ODI was designed to do. The method used by DPA is much different from ODI.

The DPA consists of the following components:

- Primary protocol
- Secondary protocol(s)
- Protocol manager
- Media access network driver interface standard NIC driver

Refer to Fig. 12.2 for a conceptual diagram of the DPA.

Primary protocol

The primary protocol is a memory resident portion of DPA. The primary protocol is used to communicate between the servers and the

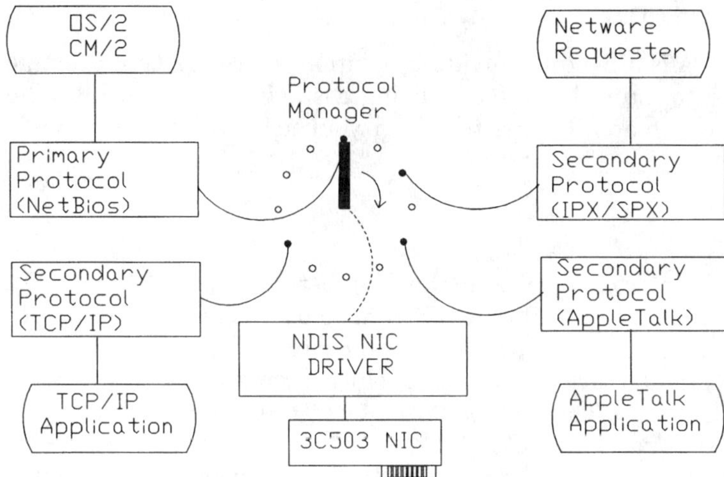

Figure 12.2 The Demand Protocol Architecture and NDIS.

workstations. The primary protocol is usually NETBIOS, but TCP and XNS are also available as primary protocols.

Secondary protocols

The secondary protocols are used to support multiple protocols. These drivers can be loaded and unloaded as required by the applications. Secondary protocols include TCP, IPX, and OSI.

Protocol manager

The protocol manager provides two functions: it loads and unloads the secondary protocol drivers and interrogates and directs the packets to the appropriate secondary (or primary) protocol drivers. These two functions, performed by the protocol manager, allow the NIC adapter to be shared by multiple applications using different protocols. The protocol manager is a memory resident component of DPA.

Media access network driver interface standard NIC drivers

The media access (MAC) network driver interface standard NIC drivers talk directly to the NIC adapter hardware. These drivers pass packets from the NIC to the protocol manager for incoming packets and from the protocol manager to the NIC for outgoing packets. The drivers are written to specifications developed by Microsoft and 3Com which outline a standard interface between the NIC adapters and the protocols. This standard is known as the Network Driver Interface Standard (NDIS).

A Comparison Between ODI and NDIS

ODI and DPA/NDIS both provide a solution for connecting a single workstation to multiple protocols using a single network cable. The decision of which architecture to use for your network should be made carefully.

Performance

One of the primary concerns in choosing between the DPA and ODI methods is performance. Both options have overhead associated with them. The majority of the overhead is incurred by the components of both these architectures that decide which protocol stack the packet should be routed to. The methods used by ODI and DPA differ widely in the way they route the packets.

Using the ODI method, the LSL acts as a switchboard operator, as illustrated in Fig. 12.1. The LSL looks at each frame and then sends it to the appropriate protocol stack. If the frame type is not recognized, the packet is sent to the ODINSUP driver. We will discuss ODINSUP in detail later in this chapter.

Using the DPA/NDIS method, the protocol manager acts as a distributor rotor on a car, as illustrated in Fig. 12.2. The rotor always starts at the primary protocol and sends the packet there. If the primary protocol rejects the packet, the rotor tries the secondary protocol that was loaded first. If this secondary protocol rejects the packet, the protocol manager tries the next secondary protocol. This process continues until one of the protocols accepts the packet.

The order in which the secondary protocols are loaded in the DPA/NDIS method can alter the performance of your system. If most of your traffic is going to the last loaded secondary protocol, the protocol manager will be creating a substantial amount of overhead in finding the right protocol. You can load the secondary protocols in any order you wish, but you must be aware of the type of traffic on your network in order to optimize the DPA/NDIS method. If most of your traffic is accepted by the primary protocol, the DPA method could outperform the ODI method.

Future compatibility

Compatibility with current and future hardware and software is of even greater concern than the performance issue in choosing between ODI and DPA. There is nothing as devastating to a network designer as finding out that an application cannot be implemented because of incompatibilities with the network software.

It appears that the NDIS method is being embraced by more vendors than the ODI method. This is probably occurring because Microsoft codeveloped the standard and is such a strong vendor of PC software.

Coexistence of NetWare and CM/2

OS/2 and Communications Manager/2 were designed to use NDIS NIC drivers. The Novell Requester was designed to use the ODI specifications. Already, you can see that we have a problem. We talked before about the two methods that can be used to allow a single NIC adapter to be shared by multiple protocols and applications. Now we see that this is not enough. What can we do when the applications that we must make coexist in the same workstation and each use a different coexistence method? This is the dilemma we face in trying to make CM/2 and the Novell Requester coexist on the same PC.

So, to complicate our lives a little more (and to keep those of us who understand this stuff employed), two methods were developed to allow DPA/NDIS applications and ODI applications to coexist. In other words, two solutions were developed to allow the two coexistence methods to coexist. Nothing is simple in the world of multiprotocol networking.

IBM developed a method to allow DPA/NDIS applications to coexist with ODI applications. The IBM product Network Transport Services/2 (NTS/2) provides a driver called ODI2NDI which, as its name implies, converts ODI packets to the NDIS format. NTS/2 must be installed on every CM/2 workstation that will be accessing a host via an Ethernet or Token Ring local-area network.

Novell is pushing ODI as the internetworking solution. Novell also developed a method to allow NDIS applications to coexist with ODI applications. The design of ODI allows it to support any protocol stack, including NDIS. This is done by using a shim to ODI called ODINSUP.

Let's take a closer look at how these two coexistence drivers operate. This is important, because we must make a decision between the two to solve our networking coexistence problems.

ODINSUP

Novell recommends using ODI drivers and the ODINSUP shim on all OS/2-CM/2 systems to allow the Novell OS/2 Requester and the OS/2 Communications Manager to coexist. Let's take a look at the theory behind ODINSUP.

Figure 12.3 shows the LAN adapter and protocol support for OS/2 and Communications Manager/2. ODINSUP translates the NDIS packets generated by Communications Manager/2 into the ODI speci-

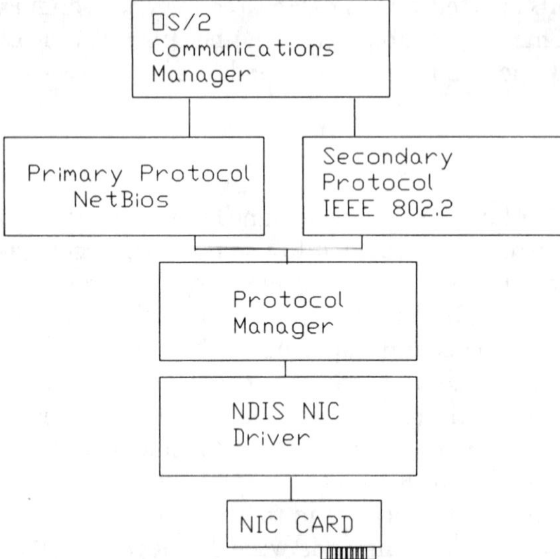

Figure 12.3 CM/2 protocol support.

fication. Packets destined for Communications Manager/2 from the network are converted by ODINSUP back to the NDIS format.

Figure 12.4 illustrates how ODINSUP is "shimmed" into the system to intercept the NDIS traffic. As you can see, using ODINSUP forces CM/2 traffic to go through more layers of drivers to get to the NIC while IPX/SPX traffic goes directly to the LSL.

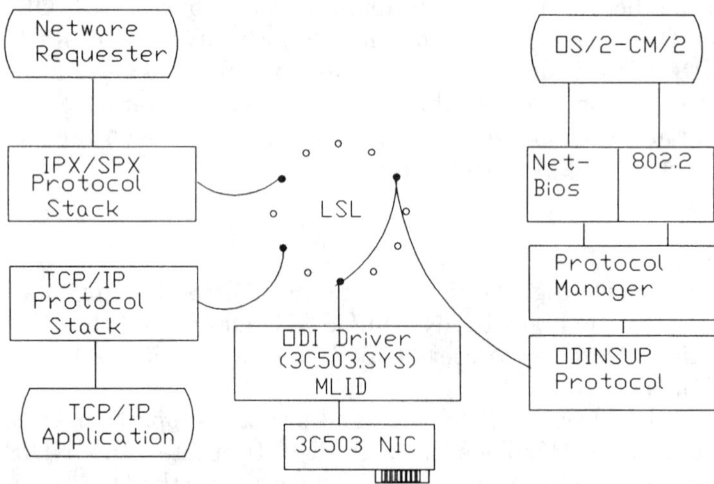

Figure 12.4 CM/2 ODINSUP intercept.

ODI2NDI

IBM, not to be outdone by Microsoft, developed the ODI2NDI driver to convert applications using the ODI specification to the use of the NDIS. Figure 12.5 shows how using ODI2NDI places a substantial amount of overhead on IPX/SPX packets while CM/2 traffic flows unimpeded.

Figure 12.5 illustrates how the ODI2NDI driver intercepts ODI packets and converts them to the NDIS protocol.

Conclusion

There is no clear right or wrong answer in the choice between DPA/NDIS and ODI to support a multiprotocol LAN. Here are a few additional points to keep in mind:

- Novell is pushing ODI. If you plan to use only Novell file servers, ODI is a fairly safe option.
- ODI has a method to support NDIS-only applications by using the ODINSUP driver.
- NDIS has a method to support ODI-only applications by using the ODI2NDI driver.
- To support ODI, you *must* have an ODI driver for the NIC adapter. You cannot use the NDIS driver, even with ODINSUP! Sometimes these drivers are difficult to locate.
- Many vendors currently support NDIS.

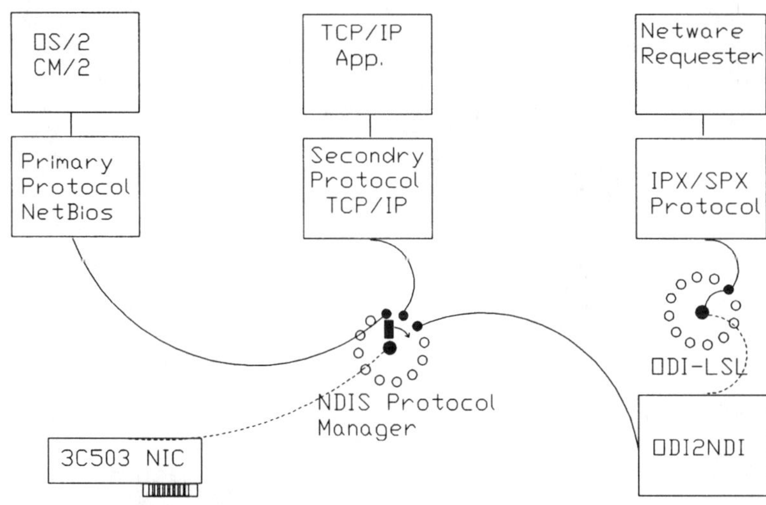

Figure 12.5 NDIS protocol with ODI support.

One final and very important factor to consider when you are choosing between the ODINSUP and the ODI2NDI coexistence methods is that ODI2NDI is much, much simpler to implement. To implement the ODI2NDI driver, you simply select the ODI2NDI driver from a panel in the NTS/2 configuration program. That is all there is to it.

To implement the ODINSUP coexistence method, you must manually change the OS/2 CONFIG.SYS file and the NET.CFG file. Some drivers must be removed from these files while others are added. The sequence of the loading of several drivers must also be modified. This cumbersome implementation is very prone to errors. To make things worse, sometimes when the CM/2 configuration screens are invoked to change minor items, such as 3270 emulation model types, the sequence of the drivers is rearranged, forcing you to manually change them back. This has caused many problems for OS/2 network administrators.

With the current battle that is brewing between Novell and Microsoft, I suspect that the ODI versus NDIS decision will not get any easier in the foreseeable future.

The details of implementing OS/2 Communications Manager/2 and the Novell Requester by using both ODINSUP and ODI2NDI are discussed in the next chapter.

Chapter

13

Implementing CM/2, NTS/2, and NetWare Coexistence

In this chapter we will explore two methods for implementing NetWare and CM/2 coexistence. Coexistence between these products allows the user at the OS/2 workstation to log in to NetWare file servers and host sessions concurrently, using the same NIC adapter.

There are three methods available to provide NetWare and CM/2 coexistence: ODI, NDIS, and LANSUP. The choice of which coexistence method to implement is very important in your network design. Each coexistence method has advantages and drawbacks. Some network configurations will benefit more from using the ODI method while other setups will benefit more from using the NDIS methodology. You should have a thorough understanding of both before you implement either ODI or NDIS. For more detailed information on the theories behind these technologies, see Chap. 12, Communications Manager/2 and NetWare Coexistence.

The LANSUP coexistence method will not be discussed in this chapter. LANSUP is very similar to the NDIS method, but is much more complicated to implement and troubleshoot. The LANSUP method will probably be phased out as more users migrate to the ODI and NDIS methods. The LANSUP method can be used only in Token Ring environments while ODI and NDIS can be used in both Ethernet and Token Ring local-area networks.

Which Version of the OS/2 Requester to Use

If you are using OS/2 version 2.1, you should use the OS/2 Requester version 2.01. If you are using OS/2 version 2.0, you should use the OS/2 Requester version 2.0.

All the examples shown in this book use OS/2 version 2.1 and the OS/2 NetWare Requester version 2.01.

Establish the Communications Manager/2 Host Link

Implementing NetWare coexistence is much simpler, no matter which coexistence method you choose, if first you implement and test the CM/2 host connection. Both the ODI and NDIS coexistence methods will work with any type of CM/2 host connection that you choose. This includes PU access via Token Ring or Ethernet topologies or gateway access via Token Ring or Ethernet.

The previous chapters describe each of these CM/2 host links. If you do not already have your host connection established, do so now, before you try to implement the OS/2 Requester or any of the coexistence methods.

Installing the OS/2 Requester

The OS/2 NetWare Requester can be obtained in a blue box from IBM or in a red box from Novell. The actual code for Requester was written by Novell and is identical whether the Requester is ordered from IBM or Novell. Novell also develops all the corrective service and future release upgrades for the product.

Support for the OS/2 Requester is provided by both IBM and Novell. If you purchase the product from IBM, you have access to the IBM support center for problem resolution. If you purchase Requester from Novell, you can obtain support via the NetWare CompuServe forum or by calling Novell technical support. Keep in mind that *each* time you call Novell technical support, you will be charged $125. For more information on IBM and Novell support, refer to Chap. 18.

The installation of OS/2 Requester version 2.01 software is fairly simple, so let's get started.

Step 1 Insert the WSOS2_1 diskette into your A: disk drive.

Step 2 Double-click on the Drive A icon. Figure 13.1 will be displayed.

Step 3 Double-click on Drive A to bring up Fig. 13.2.

Step 4 Double-click on Install EXE to bring up Fig. 13.3.

Step 5 Click on Installation, then click on Requester on workstation. You will be prompted for a target directory for the Requester software. Select the default of C:\NETWARE.

Step 6 Figure 13.4 should be displayed on your screen. Select Edit CONFIG.SYS and copy all files from this panel.

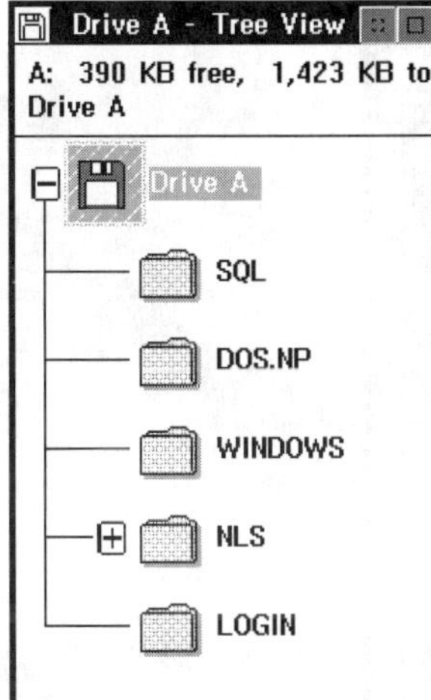

Figure 13.1 Opening the Drive A icon.

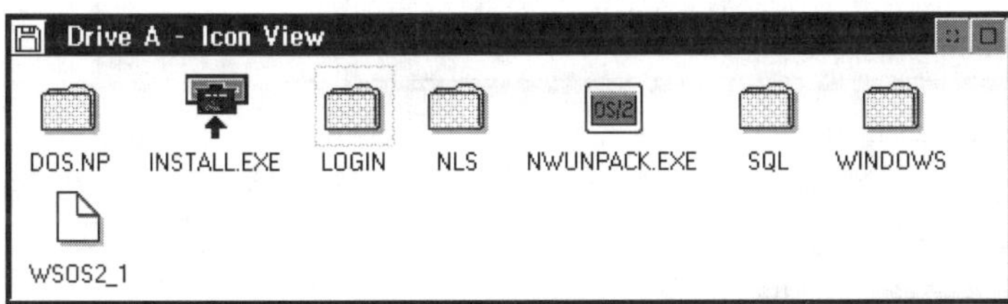

Figure 13.2 Viewing the contents of the Requester installation diskette.

Step 7 Figure 13.5 will be displayed, prompting you for an ODI LAN driver. You should choose the driver that corresponds to your NIC adapter. In this example, the 3C503.SYS driver was selected.

Step 8 You will be prompted for several diskettes, then Fig. 13.6 will be displayed. Choose IPX support for DOS and Windows and Private NetWare shell support for the default shell support.

Step 9 Figure 13.7 will be displayed. Choose SPX support for OS/2 sessions and NETBIOS emulation for OS/2 sessions, as shown in the figure.

Step 10 Figure 13.8 will be displayed, asking you if you wish to only copy the default driver or copy all the drivers on the diskette. Copy all the drivers. This will save time if you ever change your NIC adapter and need to reconfigure Requester.

Step 11 The installation program will copy the files from the diskette to your C: drive. When the installation program is completed, close the installation session.

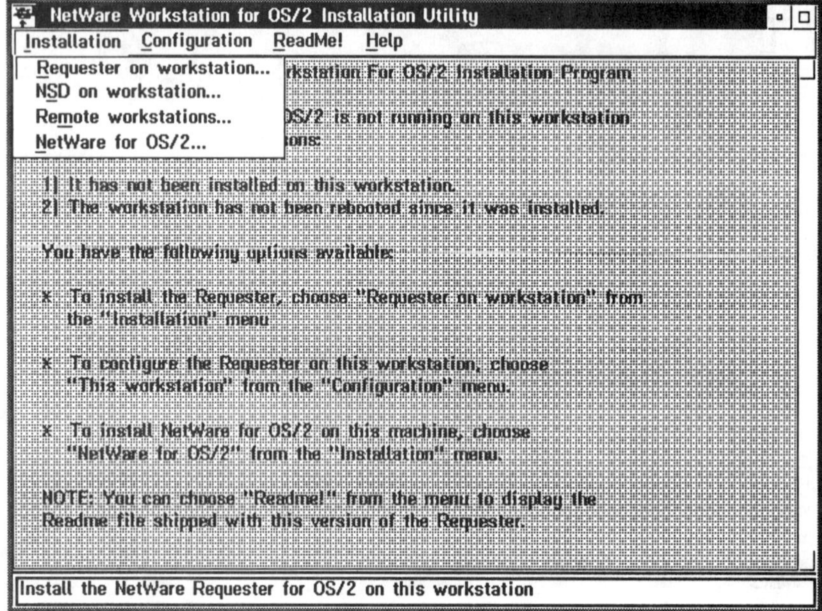

Figure 13.3 Initiating the NetWare Requester installation utility.

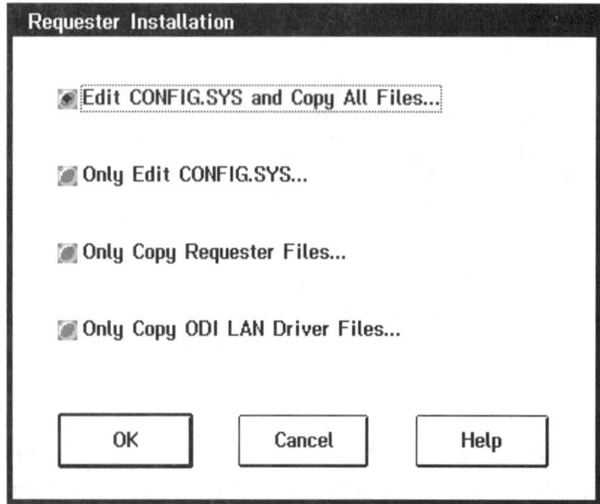

Figure 13.4 Selecting the type of installation.

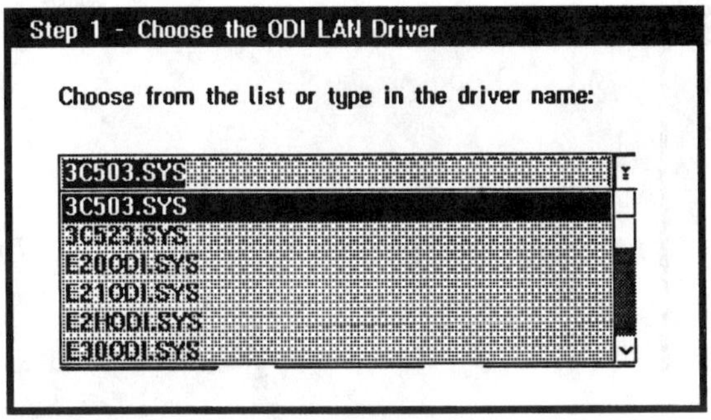

Step 1 - Choose the ODI LAN Driver

Choose from the list or type in the driver name:

3C503.SYS
3C503.SYS
3C523.SYS
E20ODI.SYS
E21ODI.SYS
E2HODI.SYS
E30ODI.SYS

Figure 13.5 Selecting the NIC driver.

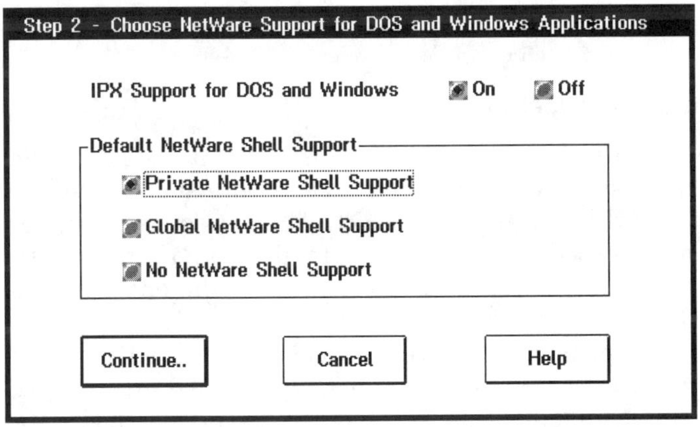

Step 2 - Choose NetWare Support for DOS and Windows Applications

IPX Support for DOS and Windows On Off

Default NetWare Shell Support
Private NetWare Shell Support
Global NetWare Shell Support
No NetWare Shell Support

Continue.. Cancel Help

Figure 13.6 Choosing the type of NetWare support.

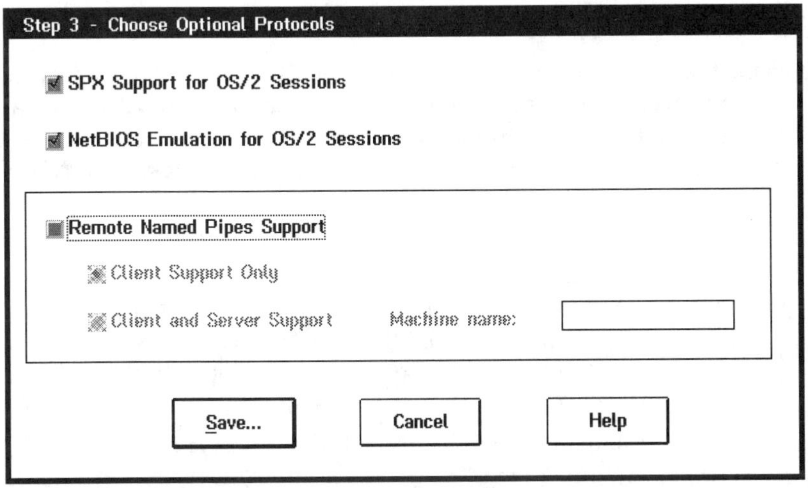

Step 3 - Choose Optional Protocols

SPX Support for OS/2 Sessions

NetBIOS Emulation for OS/2 Sessions

Remote Named Pipes Support
Client Support Only
Client and Server Support Machine name:

Save... Cancel Help

Figure 13.7 Selecting optional protocols.

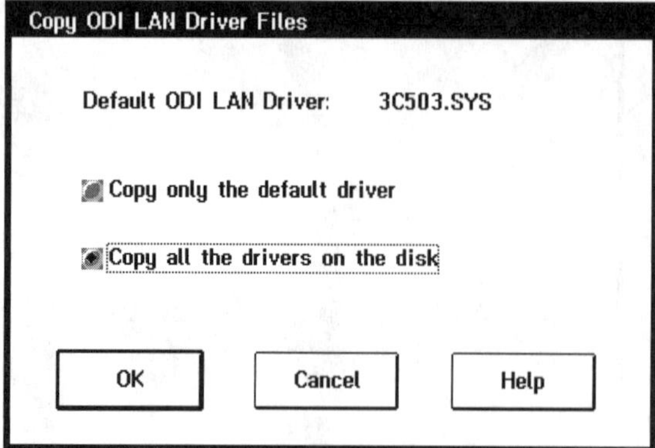

Figure 13.8 Copying the LAN drivers.

Choosing the CM/2-NetWare Coexistence Method

You are now at a critical point in the NetWare OS/2 Requester implementation. You must now decide which coexistence method to use. Chapter 12 outlined the pros and cons of each of the coexistence methods.

Do not be too concerned with choosing the right method. You can try both the ODI and NDIS methods and then choose the one that best suits your needs.

If you choose to implement the NDIS method, continue with the next section in this chapter. If you wish to implement the ODI method, proceed to the section "Implementing the ODI Coexistence Method" later in this chapter.

Implementing the NDIS Coexistence Method

The easiest way to obtain NetWare and CM/2 coexistence is to implement the NDIS coexistence method. As explained in Chap. 12, a special driver named ODI2NDI is provided with the NTS/2 product. This driver, as the name implies, converts the NetWare ODI packets to NDIS packets.

To implement the NDIS ODI2NDI driver, follow these steps:

Step 1 Open an OS/2 full-screen session.

Step 2 Change directories to C:\IBMCOM. If the IBMCOM directory does not exist, it means that the NTS/2 product is not installed on your workstation. If this is the case, stop now and install NTS/2.

Step 3 Enter LAPS at the C:\IBMCOM prompt.

Step 4 Select Configure when the initial LAPS screen is displayed.

Step 5 Figure 13.9 should be displayed on your screen. Select Configure LAN transports.

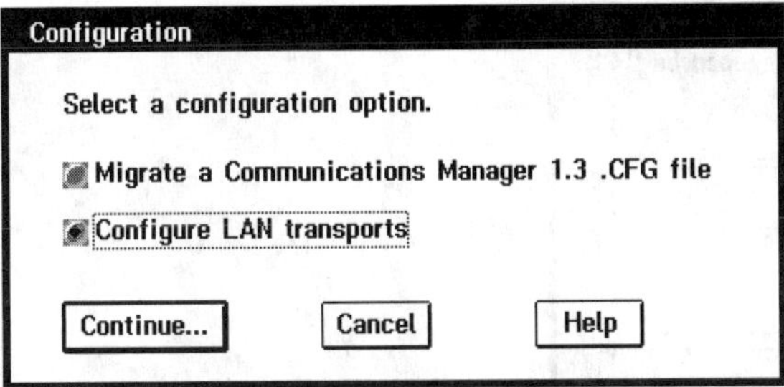

Figure 13.9 Entering the LAPS configuration utility. [*Reprinted by permission from IBM's OS/2 2.0, Copyright (1988, 1992) International Business Machines Corporation.*]

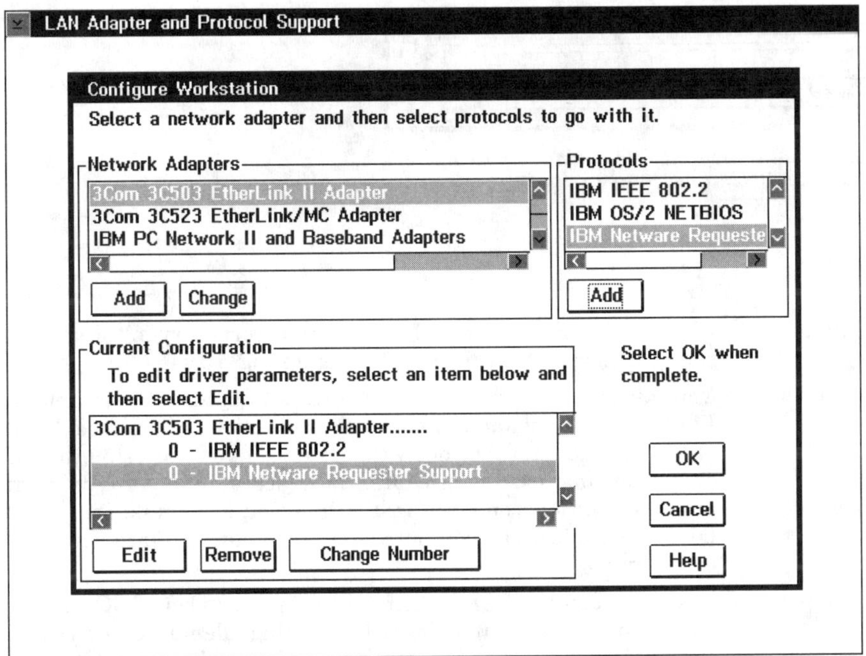

Figure 13.10 Adding NetWare Requester support to the NIC adapter. [*Reprinted by permission from IBM's OS/2 2.0, Copyright (1988, 1992) International Business Machines Corporation.*]

Step 6 Figure 13.10 will now be displayed on your screen. The current configuration area should already have a NIC adapter and the IBM 802.2 protocol selected. This was defined when you implemented your host connection. Click on the IBM NetWare Requester driver in the protocols section, then click on Add. This will move the driver to the current configuration section.

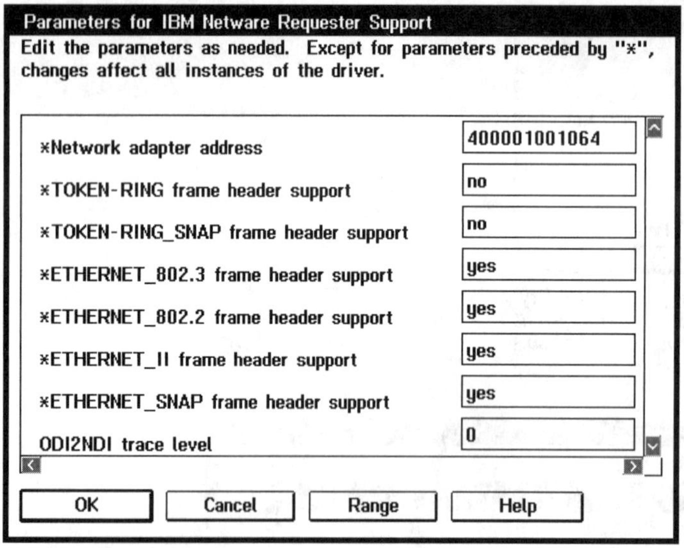

Parameters for IBM Netware Requester Support

Edit the parameters as needed. Except for parameters preceded by "*", changes affect all instances of the driver.

*Network adapter address	400001001064
*TOKEN-RING frame header support	no
*TOKEN-RING_SNAP frame header support	no
*ETHERNET_802.3 frame header support	yes
*ETHERNET_802.2 frame header support	yes
*ETHERNET_II frame header support	yes
*ETHERNET_SNAP frame header support	yes
ODI2NDI trace level	0

OK Cancel Range Help

Figure 13.11 Assigning the LAA. [*Reprinted by permission from IBM's OS/2 2.0, Copyright (1988, 1992) International Business Machines Corporation.*]

Step 7 Click on the IBM NetWare Requester support entry in the current configuration section. This will bring up Fig. 13.11.

Step 8 You must enter a value in the Network adapter address field in Fig. 13.11. This value is your locally administered address (LAA) of the NIC adapter for your workstation. If you are using the PU emulation method for providing host access, this LAA is what enables you to become the DSPU that you are emulating. CM/2 host communications will not work if this parameter is not coded correctly.

Step 9 Now you must tell LAPS which types of packets your NIC adapter will support. If you are using a Token Ring adapter, enter Yes for Token Ring frame header support and Token Ring–SNAP frame header support.

If you are using an Ethernet adapter, enter Yes for Ethernet–802.3, Ethernet–802.2, Ethernet–II, and Ethernet–SNAP frame header support.

Click on OK after you select the appropriate frame supports.

Step 10 Exit out of the LAPS configuration and reboot.

The LAPS configuration will update the C:\CONFIG.SYS file and the C:\IBMCOM\PROTOCOL.INI file. Figures 13.12 and 13.13 illustrate the CONFIG.SYS and PROTOCOL.INI files that will provide NetWare and CM/2 coexistence using the ODI2NDI/NDIS method.

```
IFS=C:\OS2\HPFS.IFS  /CACHE:64 /CRECL:4
DEVICE=C:\CMLIB\ROCSDD.SYS
DEVICE=C:\IBMCOM\LANMSGDD.OS2 /I:C:\IBMCOM
DEVICE=C:\IBMCOM\PROTMAN.OS2 /I:C:\IBMCOM
PROTSHELL=C:\OS2\PMSHELL.EXE
SET USER_INI=C:\OS2\OS2.INI
SET SYSTEM_INI=C:\OS2\OS2SYS.INI
SET OS2_SHELL=C:\OS2\CMD.EXE
SET AUTOSTART=PROGRAMS,TASKLIST,FOLDERS,CONNECTIONS
SET RUNWORKPLACE=C:\OS2\PMSHELL.EXE
SET COMSPEC=C:\OS2\CMD.EXE
LIBPATH=C:\IBMCOM\DLL;.;C:\OS2\DLL;C:\OS2\MDOS;C:\;C:\OS2\APPS\DLL;C:\MUGLIB\DLL;C:\CMLIB\DLL;C:\NETWARE;
SET PATH=C:\OS2;C:\OS2\SYSTEM;C:\OS2\MDOS\WINOS2;C:\OS2\INSTALL;C:\;C:\OS2\MDOS;C:\OS2\APPS;C:\MUGLIB;C:\CMLIB;C:\NETWARE;L:\OS2;P:\OS
SET DPATH=C:\IBMCOM;C:\OS2;C:\OS2\SYSTEM;C:\OS2\MDOS\WINOS2;C:\OS2\INSTALL;C:\;C:\OS2\BITMAP;C:\OS2\MDOS;C:\OS2\APPS;C:\MUGLIB\DLL;C:\
SET PROMPT=$i[$p]
SET HELP=C:\OS2\HELP;C:\OS2\HELP\TUTORIAL;C:\CMLIB;
SET GLOSSARY=C:\OS2\HELP\GLOSS;
SET IPF_KEYS=SBCS
PRIORITY_DISK_IO=YES
FILES=20
DEVICE=C:\OS2\TESTCFG.SYS
DEVICE=C:\OS2\DOS.SYS
DEVICE=C:\OS2\PMDD.SYS
BUFFERS=30
IOPL=YES
DISKCACHE=512,LW,AC:C
MAXWAIT=3
MEMMAN=SWAP,PROTECT
SWAPPATH=C:\OS2\SYSTEM 2048 2048
BREAK=OFF
THREADS=256
PRINTMONBUFSIZE=134,134,134
COUNTRY=001,C:\OS2\SYSTEM\COUNTRY.SYS
SET KEYS=ON
REM SET DELDIR=C:\DELETE,512;
BASEDEV=PRINT01.SYS
BASEDEV=IBM1FLPY.ADD
BASEDEV=IBM1S506.ADD
BASEDEV=OS2DASD.DMD
SET BOOKSHELF=C:\OS2\BOOK;C:\CMLIB\BOOK;
SET EPMPATH=C:\OS2\APPS
SET FAXPM=C:\OS2\APPS
REM DEVICE=C:\OS2\APPS\SASYNCDA.SYS
PROTECTONLY=NO
SHELL=C:\OS2\MDOS\COMMAND.COM C:\OS2\MDOS
FCBS=16,8
RMSIZE=640
DEVICE=C:\OS2\MDOS\VEMM.SYS
DOS=LOW,NOUMB
DEVICE=C:\OS2\MDOS\VDPX.SYS
DEVICE=C:\OS2\MDOS\VXMS.SYS /UMB
DEVICE=C:\OS2\MDOS\VDPMI.SYS
DEVICE=C:\OS2\MDOS\VWIN.SYS
DEVICE=C:\OS2\MDOS\VCDROM.SYS
REM DEVICE=C:\OS2\PCMCIA.SYS
REM DEVICE=C:\OS2\MDOS\VPCMCIA.SYS
DEVICE=C:\OS2\MDOS\VMOUSE.SYS
DEVICE=C:\OS2\POINTDD.SYS
DEVICE=C:\OS2\MOUSE.SYS
DEVICE=C:\OS2\COM.SYS
DEVICE=C:\OS2\MDOS\VCOM.SYS
CODEPAGE=437,850
DEVINFO=KBD,US,C:\OS2\KEYBOARD.DCP
DEVINFO=SCR,VGA,C:\OS2\VIOTBL.DCP
SET VIDEO_DEVICES=VIO_SVGA
SET VIO_SVGA=DEVICE(BVHVGA,BVHSVGA)
```

Figure 13.12 Sample CONFIG.SYS file.

Testing the NDIS coexistence method

Now we are ready to reboot the workstation and test the CM/2-NetWare coexistence. Shut down your PC and reboot. Watch carefully for errors as your PC reboots.

If you do not start CM/2 automatically, start it manually after your PC is rebooted. If your host sessions do not come up, review the C:\IBMCOM\LANTRAN.LOG file for errors. Figure 13.14 is a sample LANTRAN.LOG file that contains errors caused by enabling Token Ring frame support for an Ethernet adapter.

```
DEVICE=C:\OS2\MDOS\VSVGA.SYS

DEVICE=C:\OS2\LOG.SYS
RUN=C:\OS2\SYSTEM\LOGDAEM.EXE
RUN=C:\OS2\EPWROUT.EXE 1
RUN=C:\OS2\EPW.EXE

DEVICE=C:\OS2\MDOS\LPTDD.SYS

DEVICE=C:\CMLIB\ACSLANDD.SYS
DEVICE=C:\CMLIB\CMKFMDE.SYS
RUN=C:\IBMCOM\PROTOCOL\NETBIND.EXE
RUN=C:\IBMCOM\LANMSGEX.EXE
DEVICE=C:\IBMCOM\MACS\ELNKII.OS2
DEVICE=C:\IBMCOM\PROTOCOL\LANDD.OS2
DEVICE=C:\IBMCOM\PROTOCOL\LANDLLDD.OS2
RUN=C:\IBMCOM\PROTOCOL\LANDLL.EXE

REM --- NetWare Requester statements BEGIN ---
SET NWLANGUAGE=ENGLISH
DEVICE=C:\NETWARE\LSL.SYS
RUN=C:\NETWARE\DDAEMON.EXE
device = C:\ibmcom\protocol\odi2ndi.os2
REM DEVICE=C:\NETWARE\3C503.SYS
DEVICE=C:\NETWARE\IPX.SYS
DEVICE=C:\NETWARE\SPX.SYS
RUN=C:\NETWARE\SPDAEMON.EXE
rem DEVICE=C:\NETWARE\NMPIPE.SYS
rem DEVICE=C:\NETWARE\NPSERVER.SYS
rem RUN=C:\NETWARE\NPDAEMON.EXE
DEVICE=C:\NETWARE\NWREQ.SYS
IFS=C:\NETWARE\NWIFS.IFS
RUN=C:\NETWARE\NWDAEMON.EXE
DEVICE=C:\NETWARE\NETBIOS.SYS
RUN=C:\NETWARE\NBDAEMON.EXE
DEVICE=C:\NETWARE\VIPX.SYS
DEVICE=C:\NETWARE\VSHELL.SYS PRIVATE
REM --- NetWare Requester statements END ---
```

Figure 13.12 Sample CONFIG.SYS file (*Continued*).

After you successfully obtain access to the host via the CM/2 software, you are ready to test the connectivity to your NetWare LAN. Before you can log in the NetWare server from a DOS session, you must make a couple of modifications to your DOS session.

Step 1 Open the setting on your DOS session by moving your cursor to the DOS icon and pressing the right mouse button. Click on the arrow by the word Open, then select the Settings option.

Step 2 Figure 13.15 will be displayed. Click on the Session tab.

Step 3 Figure 13.16 will be displayed. Click on DOS settings.

Step 4 Figure 13.17 will be displayed. Click on DOS_LASTDRIVE, then enter E in the Value field.

Step 5 Scroll down the list of settings by clicking on the bottom arrow until you see the NETWARE_RESOURCES entry. Click on this entry.

Step 6 Figure 13.18 will be displayed. Enter PRIVATE in the Value field. More information on private and global NetWare sessions is included in the next chapter.

Step 7 Scroll through the list until you see DOS_VERSION. Click on DOS_VERSION, and a list of values will be displayed, as shown in Fig. 13.19. Scroll through the list of values until you see NETX.EXE. Modify the NETX.EXE value, by overtyping the current values, to

```
NETX.EXE,5,00,214
```

```
[PROT_MAN]

  DRIVERNAME = PROTMAN$

[IBMLXCFG]

  ELNKII_nif = ELNKII.nif
  LANDD_nif = LANDD.NIF
  ODI2NDI_nif = ODI2NDI.NIF

[LANDD_nif]

  DriverName = LANDD$
  Bindings = ELNKII_nif
  NETADDRESS = "400001001064"
  ETHERAND_TYPE = "I"
  SYSTEM_KEY = 0x0
  OPEN_OPTIONS = 0x2000
  TRACE = 0x0
  LINKS = 8
  MAX_SAPS = 3
  MAX_G_SAPS = 0
  USERS = 3
  TI_TICK_G1 = 255
  T1_TICK_G1 = 15
  T2_TICK_G1 = 3
  TI_TICK_G2 = 255
  T1_TICK_G2 = 25
  T2_TICK_G2 = 10
  IPACKETS = 250
  UIPACKETS = 100
  MAXTRANSMITS = 6
  MINTRANSMITS = 2
  TCBS = 64
  GDTS = 30
  ELEMENTS = 800

[ODI2NDI_nif]

  DriverName = odi2ndi$
  Bindings = ELNKII_nif
  NETADDRESS = "400001001064"
  TOKEN-RING = "no"
  TOKEN-RING_SNAP = "no"
  ETHERNET_802.3 = "yes"
  ETHERNET_802.2 = "yes"
  ETHERNET_II = "yes"
  ETHERNET_SNAP = "yes"
  TRACE = 0x0

[ELNKII_nif]

  DriverName = ELNKII$
  netaddress = "400001001064"
  interrupt = 3
  ioaddress = 0x300
  transceiver = "ONBOARD"
  maxtransmits = 8
  xmitbufs = 2
```

Figure 13.13 Sample PROTOCOL.INI file.

```
IBM OS/2 LANMSGDD [09/01/92] 2.01 is loaded and operational.
IBM OS/2 LAN Protocol Manager
IBM OS/2 LANDD [09/01/92] 2.01.2
IBM OS/2 LANDLLDD 2.01
IBM OS/2 LANDLLDD is loaded and operational.
IBM OS/2 ODI2NDI v1.0 [09/01/92]
IBM OS/2 LAN Netbind
IBM LANDD is accessing IBM 802.3 LAN Interface.
Adapter 0 was initialized and opened successfully.
Adapter 0 is using node address 400001001064.  The Token-Ring format is 020080000826.
IBM LANDD was successfully bound to MAC: ELNKII_nif->VECTOR.
LT80225: The frame types configured for ODI2NDI.OS2 are not supported by adapter 0.  Adapter 0 cannot be used by ODI2NDI.OS2.
LT80213: ODI2NDI.OS2 was unable to bind to MAC VECTOR.  Adapter 0 cannot be used by ODI2NDI.OS2.
PRO0029: A configuration parameter failure occurred when the program tried to bind ODI2NDI$ to VECTOR.
```

Figure 13.14 Looking for errors in LANTRAN.LOG file.

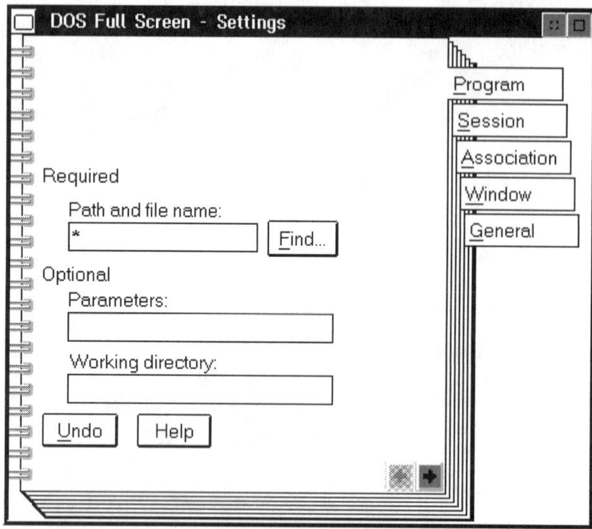

Figure 13.15 Entering the settings for a DOS full-screen. [*Reprinted by permission from IBM's OS/2 2.0, Copyright (1988, 1992) International Business Machines Corporation.*]

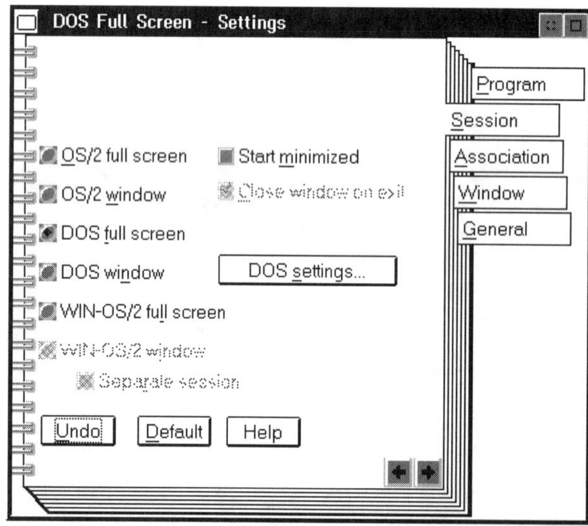

Figure 13.16 Choosing the DOS setting parameter. [*Reprinted by permission from IBM's OS/2 2.0, Copyright (1988, 1992) International Business Machines Corporation.*]

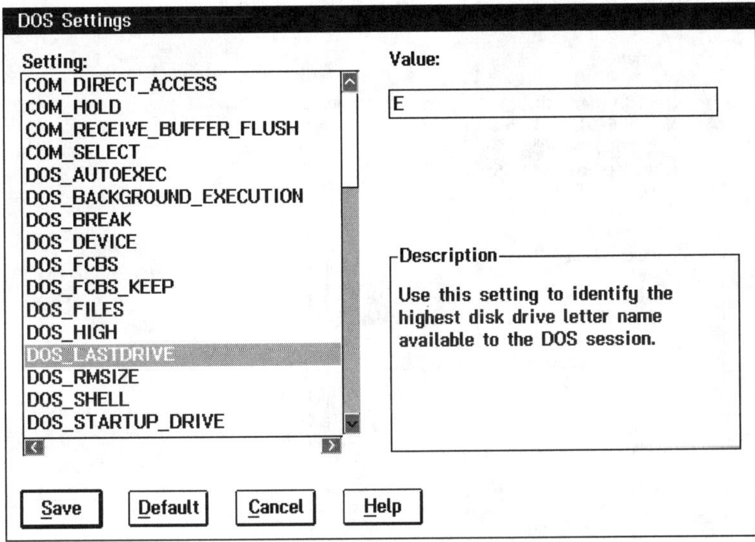

Figure 13.17 Modifying the DOS_LASTDRIVE parameter for private NetWare sessions. [*Reprinted by permission from IBM's OS/2 2.0, Copyright (1988, 1992) International Business Machines Corporation.*]

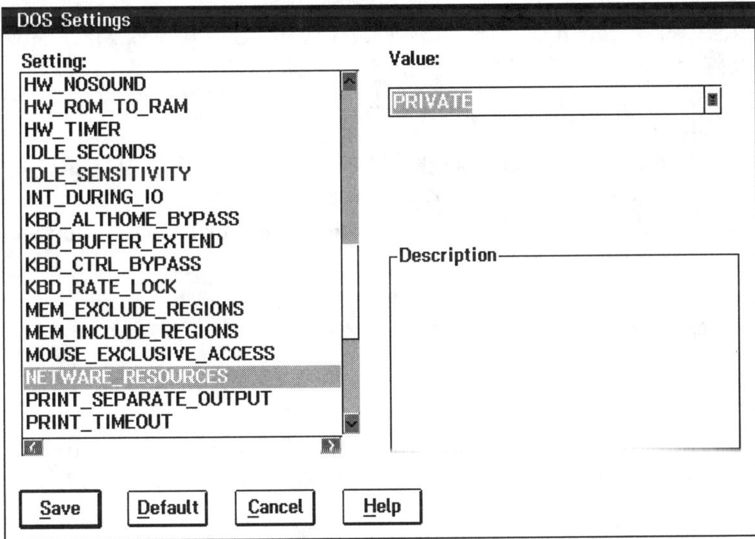

Figure 13.18 Modifying the NETWARE_RESOURCES parameter for private NetWare access. [*Reprinted by permission from IBM's OS/2 2.0, Copyright (1988, 1992) International Business Machines Corporation.*]

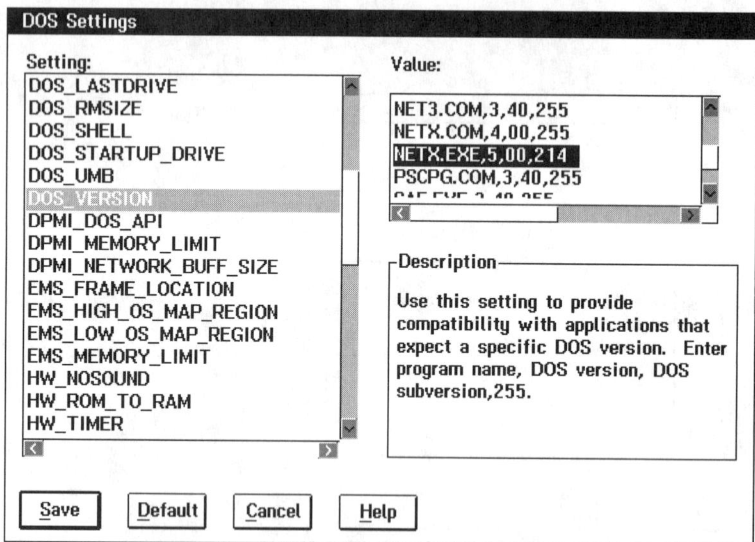

Figure 13.19 Modifying the DOS_VERSION parameters. [*Reprinted by permission from IBM's OS/2 2.0, Copyright (1988, 1992) International Business Machines Corporation.*]

Step 8 Scroll through the list and click on VIPX_ENABLED. Make sure the value is set to On.

Step 9 Scroll through the list, and click on IDLE_SENSITIVITY. Change the value to 100.

Step 10 Click on Save, then close the DOS Settings box by double-clicking on the upper left-hand corner of the box.

Step 11 Open the DOS session by double-clicking on the DOS icon that you just modified.

Step 12 Enter NETX at the C:\ prompt.

Step 13 Enter F: to get to the F:\LOGIN directory.

Step 14 Log in to the NetWare server just as you would from a DOS workstation.

Congratulations! If all went well, you should now have concurrent access to your CM/2 host sessions and your NetWare file server(s).

Implementing the ODI Coexistence Method

Obtaining coexistence between CM/2 host communications and NetWare resources can also be accomplished by using the ODI method. The ODINSUP driver, provided with the Requester product, is used to convert the CM/2 NDIS packets to the ODI format.

Three steps are required to implement the ODINSUP driver:

- Modify CONFIG.SYS.
- Modify NET.CFG.
- Modify PROTOCOL.INI.

Modifying CONFIG.SYS for ODINSUP

We must make several changes to the OS/2 CONFIG.SYS file in order to implement the ODINSUP driver. To perform these modifications, use any DOS editor through a DOS window, or use the OS/2 System Editor provided by OS/2.

To access the OS/2 System Editor, open the OS/2 system icon. You will see a Productivity icon inside the system folder. Double-click on the Productivity icon. Inside this folder you will see the OS/2 System Editor icon. Double-click on this icon to access the editor.

The OS/2 System Editor is fairly simple to use. To open a file, click on the File pull-down menu. You will see a list of drives, directories, and files. To navigate through these items, simply point to the directory, drive, or file that you wish to update and double-click.

The following steps will guide you through the changes needed on the CONFIG.SYS file to implement the ODINSUP driver.

Step 1 Change the statements in CONFIG.SYS that load the MAC level drivers into comment statements by placing the characters "REM" in the first position of the statement. These can be identified by looking for the drivers that are loaded from C:\IBMCOM\MACS\xxxxx.xxx. These statements should be near the end of the CONFIG.SYS file.

Step 2 Next you must add a line in the CONFIG.SYS file to load the ODINSUP driver. The line should look like this:

```
DEVICE=C:\NETWARE\ODINSUP.SYS
```

You must load the ODINSUP driver not only after PROTMAN.OS2 and LSL.SYS, but also after the NDIS NIC driver. The line in CONFIG.SYS that loads the NDIS NIC driver can be located by looking for a line that looks like

```
DEVICE=C:\NETWARE\xxxxx.SYS
```

where xxxxx.SYS is replaced with the driver you selected in step 7 of the Requester software installation.

Figure 13.20 is a sample CONFIG.SYS file with the modifications required to load the ODINSUP driver.

Step 3 Save the CONFIG.SYS file.

```
IFS=C:\OS2\HPFS.IFS  /CACHE:64 /CRECL:4
DEVICE=C:\CMLIB\ROCSDD.SYS
DEVICE=C:\IBMCOM\LANMSGDD.OS2 /I:C:\IBMCOM
DEVICE=C:\IBMCOM\PROTMAN.OS2 /I:C:\IBMCOM
PROTSHELL=C:\OS2\PMSHELL.EXE
SET USER_INI=C:\OS2\OS2.INI
SET SYSTEM_INI=C:\OS2\OS2SYS.INI
SET OS2_SHELL=C:\OS2\CMD.EXE
SET AUTOSTART=PROGRAMS,TASKLIST,FOLDERS,CONNECTIONS
SET RUNWORKPLACE=C:\OS2\PMSHELL.EXE
SET COMSPEC=C:\OS2\CMD.EXE
LIBPATH=C:\IBMCOM\DLL;.;C:\OS2\DLL;C:\OS2\MDOS;C:\;C:\OS2\APPS\DLL;C:\MUGLIB\DLL;C:\CMLIB\DLL;C:\NETWARE;
SET PATH=C:\OS2;C:\OS2\SYSTEM;C:\OS2\MDOS\WINOS2;C:\OS2\INSTALL;C:\;C:\OS2\MDOS;C:\OS2\APPS;C:\MUGLIB;C:\CMLIB;C:\NETWARE;L:\OS2;P:\OS
SET DPATH=C:\IBMCOM;C:\OS2;C:\OS2\SYSTEM;C:\OS2\MDOS\WINOS2;C:\OS2\INSTALL;C:\;C:\OS2\BITMAP;C:\OS2\MDOS;C:\OS2\APPS;C:\MUGLIB\DLL;C:\
SET PROMPT=$i[$p]
SET HELP=C:\OS2\HELP;C:\OS2\HELP\TUTORIAL;C:\CMLIB;
SET GLOSSARY=C:\OS2\HELP\GLOSS;
SET IPF_KEYS=SBCS
PRIORITY_DISK_IO=YES
FILES=20
DEVICE=C:\OS2\TESTCFG.SYS
DEVICE=C:\OS2\DOS.SYS
DEVICE=C:\OS2\PMDD.SYS
BUFFERS=30
IOPL=YES
DISKCACHE=512,LW,AC:C
MAXWAIT=3
MEMMAN=SWAP,PROTECT
SWAPPATH=C:\OS2\SYSTEM 2048 2048
BREAK=OFF
THREADS=256
PRINTMONBUFSIZE=134,134,134
COUNTRY=001,C:\OS2\SYSTEM\COUNTRY.SYS
SET KEYS=ON
REM SET DELDIR=C:\DELETE,512;
BASEDEV=PRINT01.SYS
BASEDEV=IBM1FLPY.ADD
BASEDEV=IBM1S506.ADD
BASEDEV=OS2DASD.DMD
SET BOOKSHELF=C:\OS2\BOOK;C:\CMLIB\BOOK;
SET EPMPATH=C:\OS2\APPS
SET FAXPM=C:\OS2\APPS
REM DEVICE=C:\OS2\APPS\SASYNCDA.SYS
PROTECTONLY=NO
SHELL=C:\OS2\MDOS\COMMAND.COM C:\OS2\MDOS
FCBS=16,8
RMSIZE=640
DEVICE=C:\OS2\MDOS\VEMM.SYS
DOS=LOW,NOUMB
DEVICE=C:\OS2\MDOS\VDPX.SYS
DEVICE=C:\OS2\MDOS\VXMS.SYS /UMB
DEVICE=C:\OS2\MDOS\VDPMI.SYS
DEVICE=C:\OS2\MDOS\VWIN.SYS
DEVICE=C:\OS2\MDOS\VCDROM.SYS
REM DEVICE=C:\OS2\PCMCIA.SYS
REM DEVICE=C:\OS2\MDOS\VPCMCIA.SYS
DEVICE=C:\OS2\MDOS\VMOUSE.SYS
DEVICE=C:\OS2\POINTDD.SYS
DEVICE=C:\OS2\MOUSE.SYS
DEVICE=C:\OS2\COM.SYS
DEVICE=C:\OS2\MDOS\VCOM.SYS
CODEPAGE=437,850
DEVINFO=KBD,US,C:\OS2\KEYBOARD.DCP
DEVINFO=SCR,VGA,C:\OS2\VIOTBL.DCP
SET VIDEO_DEVICES=VIO_SVGA
SET VIO_SVGA=DEVICE(BVHVGA,BVHSVGA)
```

Figure 13.20 Sample CONFIG.SYS file.

Suggestion Whenever you modify your Communications Manager configuration, always check the CONFIG.SYS file for the MAC drivers. Even minor changes to your configuration will cause the MAC driver statements to be reinserted into CONFIG.SYS.

Modify (or create) the NET.CFG file

You must create or modify C:\NET.CFG for Requester to operate properly. The lines you type into NET.CFG will vary depending upon

```
DEVICE=C:\OS2\MDOS\VSVGA.SYS

DEVICE=C:\OS2\LOG.SYS
RUN=C:\OS2\SYSTEM\LOGDAEM.EXE
RUN=C:\OS2\EPWROUT.EXE 1
RUN=C:\OS2\EPW.EXE

DEVICE=C:\OS2\MDOS\LPTDD.SYS

DEVICE=C:\CMLIB\ACSLANDD.SYS
DEVICE=C:\CMLIB\CMKFMDE.SYS
RUN=C:\IBMCOM\PROTOCOL\NETBIND.EXE
RUN=C:\IBMCOM\LANMSGEX.EXE
rem DEVICE=C:\IBMCOM\MACS\ELNKII.OS2
REM --- NetWare Requester statements BEGIN ---
SET NWLANGUAGE=ENGLISH
DEVICE=C:\NETWARE\LSL.SYS
RUN=C:\NETWARE\DDAEMON.EXE
DEVICE=C:\NETWARE\3C503.SYS
DEVICE=C:\NETWARE\ODINSUP.SYS
DEVICE=C:\NETWARE\IPX.SYS
DEVICE=C:\NETWARE\SPX.SYS
RUN=C:\NETWARE\SPDAEMON.EXE
rem DEVICE=C:\NETWARE\NMPIPE.SYS
rem DEVICE=C:\NETWARE\NPSERVER.SYS
rem RUN=C:\NETWARE\NPDAEMON.EXE
DEVICE=C:\NETWARE\NWREQ.SYS
IFS=C:\NETWARE\NWIFS.IFS
RUN=C:\NETWARE\NWDAEMON.EXE
DEVICE=C:\NETWARE\NETBIOS.SYS
RUN=C:\NETWARE\NBDAEMON.EXE
DEVICE=C:\NETWARE\VIPX.SYS
DEVICE=C:\NETWARE\VSHELL.SYS PRIVATE
REM --- NetWare Requester statements END ---
DEVICE=C:\IBMCOM\PROTOCOL\LANDD.OS2
DEVICE=C:\IBMCOM\PROTOCOL\LANDLLDD.OS2
RUN=C:\IBMCOM\PROTOCOL\LANDLL.EXE
```

Figure 13.20 Sample CONFIG.SYS file *(Continued)*.

whether you are using a Token Ring NIC or an Ethernet NIC adapter. The NET.CFG is divided into three main sections: the link driver, link support, and protocol option.

Link driver section

The link driver section is used to specify the various frame types used by your NIC adapter. If you are using an Ethernet NIC adapter, specify all the frame types shown in Fig. 13.21.

If you are using a Token Ring adapter, the following statements should be coded behind the link driver statement:

```
frame token-ring
frame token-ring_snap
```

The driver name on the first statement of the NET.CFG file must match the name of the NDIS NIC driver that you are using.

If you are using locally administered addressing, you must add the node address statement in the link driver section of your NET.CFG file. To obtain this address, you should look in your current C:\IBMCOM\PROTOCOL.INI file. You will see a statement resembling

```
NetAddress = "T400001001064"
```

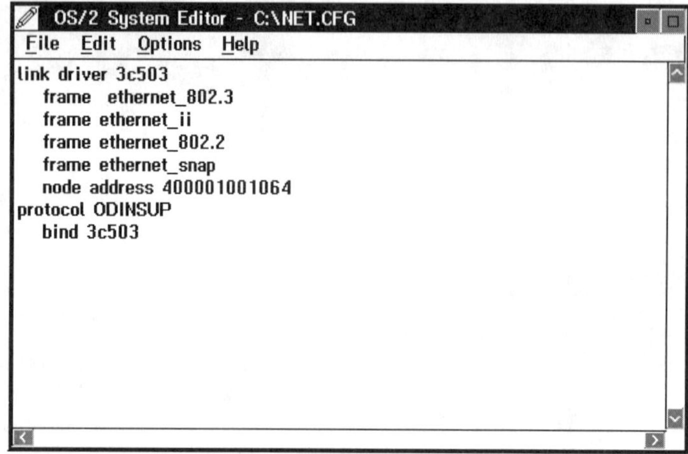
OS/2 System Editor - C:\NET.CFG
File Edit Options Help

```
link driver 3c503
   frame  ethernet_802.3
   frame ethernet_ii
   frame ethernet_802.2
   frame ethernet_snap
   node address 400001001064
protocol ODINSUP
   bind 3c503
```

Figure 13.21 Modifying the NET.CFG file.

Remove the T and include the remaining characters in the node address statement as follows:

```
node address 400001001064
```

See Fig. 13.21 for a sample NET.CFG file with the node address parameter.

Link support section

The link support section of NET.CFG is used to specify the number and size of the link support buffers. The default is buffers 20 1514.

In our example we chose the default by not coding the link support section.

Protocol option

This section is used to bind ODINSUP to the Ethernet or Token Ring driver. To do this, simply code a *bind* statement after the protocol ODINSUP statement. The name following the word "bind" must match the name specified on the link driver statement at the beginning of the NET.CFG file.

Figure 13.21 shows a sample NET.CFG file with all the changes required for the ODI coexistence method.

Modify PROTOCOL.INI

The PROTOCOL.INI file must be modified to use the ODI driver defined in the NET.CFG file. This change will direct Communications Manager to use the ODINSUP driver.

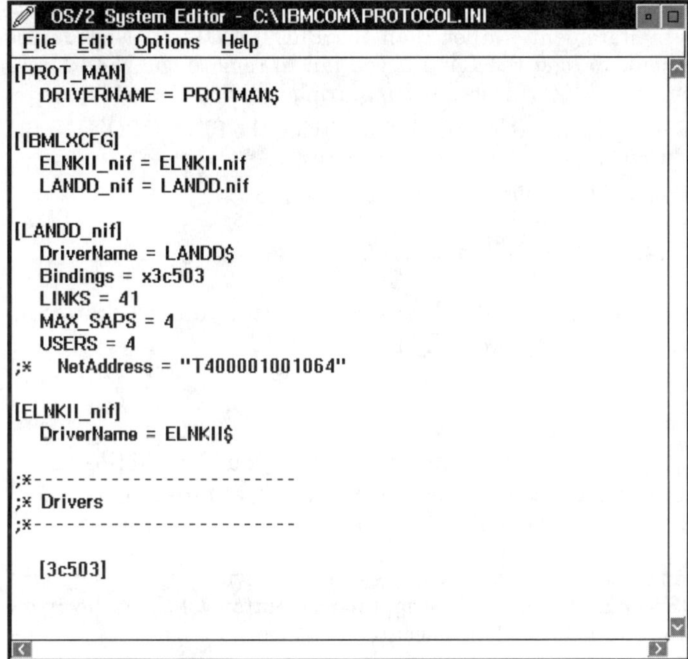

Figure 13.22 Modifying the PROTOCOL.INI file.

The PROTOCOL.INI file resides in the C:\IBMCOM directory. Two changes must be made to PROTOCOL.INI.

Step 1 Modify the BINDINGS= line by replacing the NDIS MAC driver name with the ODI driver name. See Fig. 13.22. The BINDINGS= parameter was changed from BINDINGS=ELNKII_nif to BINDINGS=X3C503. Place the name of the driver you selected during the installation into the BINDINGS statement.

Driver names in PROTOCOL.INI cannot begin with a number, so the 3C503 name was preceded by an X.

Step 2 You must now add a driver section at the end of the PROTOCOL.INI file. To do this, you simply place the following line at the end of the file:

```
[xxxxxxx]
```

where xxxxxx is replaced with the name of the driver you placed in the BINDINGS statement.

You must insert a blank line after the statement above.

Driver names that start with a number do not need to be prefaced by an X.

Step 3 You must remove the NetAddress statement in the PROTOCOL.INI file. The NetAddress statement is used to set the LAA of the adapter. The ODI coexistence method uses the NET.CFG node address statement, rather than the PROTOCOL.INI NetAddress statement, to load the LAA. If you fail to remove the NetAddress statement, CM/2 will get an error during initialization.

See Fig. 13.22 for an example of modifying the PROTOCOL.INI file for a 3C503 driver.

Step 4 Save the C:\IBMCOM\PROTOCOL.INI file.

Test the ODINSUP driver

Now comes the moment of truth. It's time to reboot your workstation. When you boot, watch very carefully for errors.

Modify the DOS settings

To test the Requester, we will attempt to log in to your Novell file server from a DOS full-screen session. Before we do this, we must make a couple of changes to the DOS settings for the session.

Step 1 Open the setting on your DOS session by moving your cursor to the DOS icon and pressing the right mouse button. Click on the arrow by the word Open, then select the Settings option.

Step 2 Figure 13.15 will be displayed. Click on the Session tab.

Step 3 Figure 13.16 will be displayed. Click on DOS Settings.

Step 4 Figure 13.17 will be displayed. Click on DOS_LASTDRIVE, then enter E in the Value field.

Step 5 Scroll down the list of settings by clicking on the bottom arrow until you see the NETWARE_RESOURCES entry. Click on this entry.

Step 6 Figure 13.18 will be displayed. Enter PRIVATE in the Value field. More information on private and global NetWare sessions is included in the next chapter.

Step 7 Scroll through the list until you see DOS_VERSION. Click on DOS_VERSION, and a list of values will be displayed, as shown in Fig. 13.19. Scroll through the list of values until you see NETX.EXE. Modify the NETX.EXE value, by overtyping the current values, to

```
NETX.EXE,5,00,214
```

Step 8 Scroll through the list, and click on VIPX_ENABLED. Make sure the value is set to On.

Step 9 Scroll through the list, and click on IDLE_SENSITIVITY. Change the value to 100.

Step 10 Click on Save, then close the DOS Settings box by double-clicking on the upper left-hand corner of the box.

Step 11 Open the DOS session by double-clicking on the DOS icon that you just modified.

Step 12 Enter NETX at the C:\ prompt.

Step 13 Enter F: to get to the F:\LOGIN directory.

Step 14 Log in to the NetWare server just as you would from a DOS workstation.

You should be able to log in to your NetWare file server. If you cannot log in to the server, stop now and correct the problem.

Accessing the host

If you do not start CM/2 automatically, start it manually after your PC is rebooted. If your host sessions do not come up, review the C:\IBMCOM\LANTRAN.LOG file for errors.

Congratulations! If all went well, you should now have concurrent access to your CM/2 host sessions and your NetWare file server(s).

Conclusion

Now we are delving into the nitty-gritty of interoperability. We have learned that there are many components involved in providing coexistence between two dissimilar systems. We are also beginning to see just how valuable a true multitasking operating system is. Our goal of providing a universal workstation and printer could not be achieved without it.

Chapter

14

Using the NetWare OS/2 Requester

NetWare OS/2 Requester is a set of programs that allow an OS/2 workstation to utilize the services of Novell file servers. Native OS/2 sessions, OS/2 DOS sessions, and OS/2 Windows sessions can log in to Novell file servers by using the services of the NetWare OS/2 Requester.

This chapter will explain how to set up and use the NetWare Requester. We will examine global and private NetWare support and the pros and cons of each of these log-in methods. We will also explore the NetWare services, provided by Requester, under native OS/2 sessions, OS/2 DOS, and OS/2 Windows sessions. We will discuss global and private network print-routing methods.

All the examples in this chapter assume that you already have OS/2 Requester installed on the workstation. The examples were implemented by using NetWare Requester version 2.01. Most of the material will work for earlier versions of Requester as well.

Virtual DOS Machines

OS/2 uses its multitasking capabilities and the memory protection and multitasking capabilities of the Intel 80386 and 80486 chips to implement a feature known as *virtual DOS machines,* or VDMs. A VDM is a DOS session that runs under the OS/2 operating system. The memory that is provided for each VDM is protected from other VDMs and other OS/2 programs and components. This protection mechanism allows OS/2 to stay active even though a DOS program running in a VDM goes haywire. The DOS program will not be allowed to corrupt the memory outside its given allotment.

NetWare Requester provides support for both VDMs and native OS/2 sessions. Two types of support are provided by Requester for VDMs: global NetWare access and private NetWare access. You may choose either method for your application, or you can use a combination of private and global NetWare access. Let's take a look at each of these NetWare VDM connectivity options in detail.

Global NetWare Access

OS/2 is a true multitasking operating system. You may have several DOS sessions, Windows sessions, and native OS/2 sessions running concurrently under the operating system. A global NetWare session allows you to log in to a NetWare file server one time and map all the drives you need access to. Once these mappings have been established, all other DOS, OS/2, and Windows sessions can access these drives. These sessions will also have access to all the other NetWare resources, such as the NetWare printing services. We will talk more about the global printing support a little later in this section.

Before you can implement global NetWare access, you must install the NetWare Requester utilities onto a file server on your local-area network. The installation adds a directory named OS2 to the NetWare LOGIN, PUBLIC, and SYSTEM directories on your file server. Next the installation places the OS/2 versions of certain NetWare programs into these OS2 directories. For example, the LOGIN.EXE and SLIST.EXE programs are placed into the LOGIN\OS2 directory. FILER.EXE and SYSCON.EXE are installed into the PUBLIC\OS2 directory. Global NetWare access requires that you log in to a NetWare file server from a native OS/2 session. That is why these OS2 versions of the NetWare utilities are placed in the various NetWare directories.

At the time of this writing, the latest version of OS/2 Requester does not contain the utilities that are supposed to be installed on the file server. If this is the case with the version of Requester that you have, you can obtain the utilities from the NetWare CompuServe forums. Chapter 18 explains how you can access and utilize the NetWare forums.

How to perform a global NetWare log-in

The following steps can be used to establish a global NetWare log-in:

Step 1 Open an OS/2 full-screen session.

Step 2 Change to the L: drive. If the L: drive does not exist, it means that Requester utilities are not installed on the file server that you are attached to. If you have multiple file servers on your network and only one has the NetWare Requester utilities installed on it, you can modify the NET.CFG file to specify a "preferred server." This will direct OS/2 to connect to the file server that contains NetWare Requester utilities at OS/2 boot time.

Step 3 Change directories to the L:\OS2 directory by entering CD OS2.

The L: drive is established after NetWare Requester is installed. The L: drive is actually pointing to the LOGIN directory of your file server. Within the LOGIN directory is an OS2 directory. This directory contains the OS/2 versions of the LOGIN.EXE, ATTACH, SLIST, and MAP NetWare utilities.

Step 4 Enter LOGIN user name.

OS/2 log-in scripts

When you log in to a NetWare file server from an OS/2 session, two log-in scripts are executed, a system log-in script and a user log-in script. These log-in scripts are completely separate log-in scripts from the DOS user and system log-in scripts.

To modify the OS/2 system and user log-in scripts, you must first log in to NetWare from an OS/2 session. Next you must switch to the PUBLIC\OS2 directory and execute the SYSCON utility. The facilities, use, and look of the OS/2 version of SYSCON are almost identical to those of the DOS version of the utility.

When you change the system log-in script by using the OS/2 version of SYSCON, you are modifying (or creating) a log-in script that will be executed by all OS/2 sessions that log in to that server. A DOS session will not execute this log-in script. In other words, there are two completely separate system log-in scripts, one for DOS users and one for OS/2 users.

Just as there are two completely separate system log-in scripts, each NetWare user can have two separate user log-in scripts. When the user logs in from a DOS workstation, the DOS log-in script is executed. When that same user logs in from an OS/2 workstation, the OS/2 user log-in script is executed. When you modify the user log-in script from the OS/2 version of SYSCON, you are modifying the OS/2 user log-in script. Conversely, when you execute the DOS version of SYSCON, you are modifying the DOS user log-in script.

Finding the OS/2 SYSCON utility can be a little difficult because of the way in which OS/2 search drive mappings are performed. After you log in to a NetWare server from an OS/2 session, enter MAP. A drive mapping for the PUBLIC\OS2 directory should exist. To execute SYSCON, you must change drives to the drive that is mapped to PUBLIC\OS2, then enter SYSCON.

OS/2 search drives

There are two types of mappings under NetWare, search mappings and drive mappings. Search drive mappings are directory paths that are added to the DOS path list. When a DOS command is issued, the search drives are scanned to find the requested program. Under DOS you can issue a MAP command to add a search path as follows:

```
MAP INS S16:=TRSERVER\VOL1:\WP51
```

This command would add the WP51 directory to the DOS search path list.

Regular drive mappings are used to establish a drive letter with a particular directory path. The following MAP command established drive J: with the WP51 directory:

```
MAP J:=TRSERVER\VOL1:\WP51
```

The above mapping does not add the WP51 directory to the DOS path list. The mapping simply gives you an easy way to access the directory. To access the WP51 directory, enter J: to switch to that directory.

One of the major differences between DOS and OS/2 NetWare sessions is the use of search drives.

Under OS/2, the search drive mapping is not supported. There are two alternatives you can use. You could establish regular drive mappings to all the directories you needed access to, then enter the drive letter followed by the command you wish to execute. If you absolutely need certain directories in your OS/2 path list, you can establish the regular drive mappings, as illustrated above, then add these mappings to your OS/2 PATH and DPATH statements in the OS/2 CONFIG.SYS file.

DOS global NetWare access

Now that you have logged in to a NetWare file server globally from an OS/2 session, we are ready to utilize the functions of the global log-in. All the drive mappings that you established in the OS/2 global log-in can be accessed by each DOS session that you open. Before this can happen, we must make a few changes to our DOS sessions.

Step 1 Open the setting on your DOS session by moving your cursor to the DOS icon and pressing the right mouse button. Click on the arrow by the word Open, then select the Settings option.

Step 2 Figure 14.1 will be displayed. Click on the session tab.

Step 3 Figure 14.2 will be displayed. Click on DOS settings.

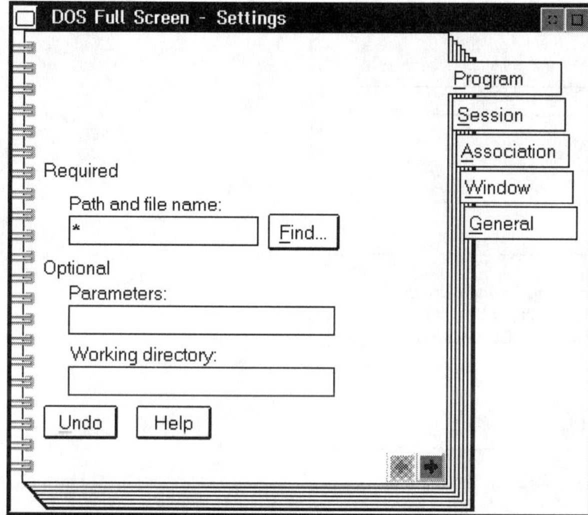

Figure 14.1 Opening the DOS full-screen settings. [*Reprinted by permission from IBM's OS/2 2.0, Copyright (1988, 1992) International Business Machines Corporation.*]

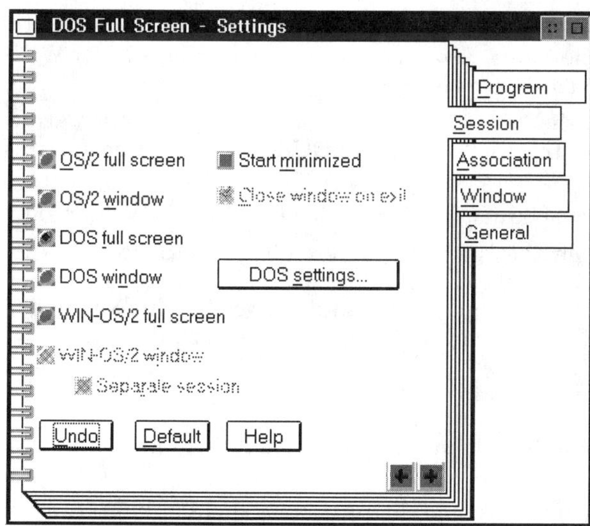

Figure 14.2 Accessing the DOS settings. [*Reprinted by permission from IBM's OS/2 2.0, Copyright (1988, 1992) International Business Machines Corporation.*]

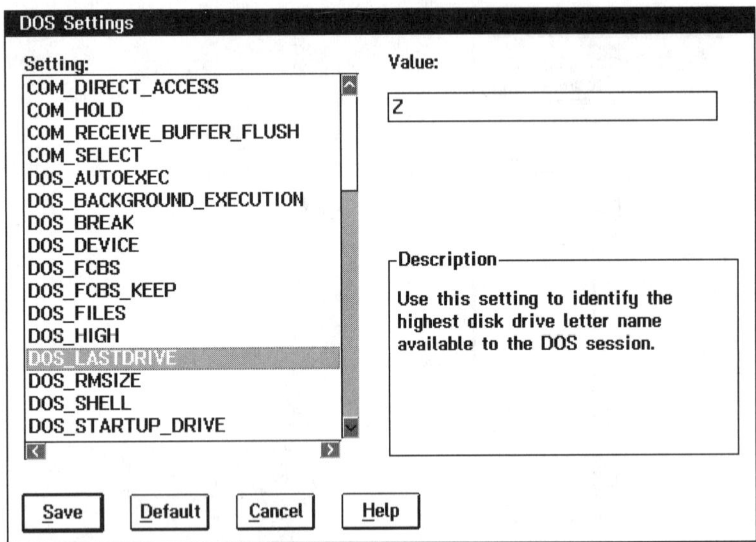

Figure 14.3 Modifying the DOS-LASTDRIVE for global NetWare access. [*Reprinted by permission from IBM's OS/2 2.0, Copyright (1988, 1992) International Business Machines Corporation.*]

Step 4 Figure 14.3 will be displayed. Click on DOS_LASTDRIVE, then enter Z in the Value field. This setting allows the DOS (or WIN-OS/2) session access to all the globally mapped drives.

Step 5 Scroll down the list of settings by clicking on the bottom arrow until you see the NETWARE_RESOURCES entry. Click on this entry.

Step 6 Figure 14.4 will be displayed. Enter GLOBAL in the Value field.

Step 7 Scroll through the list until you see DOS_VERSION. Click on DOS_VERSION, and a list of values will be displayed, as shown in Fig. 14.5. Scroll through the list until you see NETX.EXE. Modify the NETX.EXE value, by overtyping the current values, to

```
NETX.EXE,5,00,214
```

Step 8 Scroll through the list, and click on VIPX_ENABLED. Make sure the value is set to On.

Step 9 Scroll through the list, and click on IDLE_SENSITIVITY. Change the value to 100.

Step 10 Scroll through the list until you find DOS_FILES. Click on DOS_FILES, and change the value to 214, as illustrated in Fig. 14.6.

Step 11 Click on Save, then close the DOS Settings box by double-clicking on the upper left-hand corner of the box.

Step 12 Open the DOS session by double-clicking on the DOS icon that you just modified.

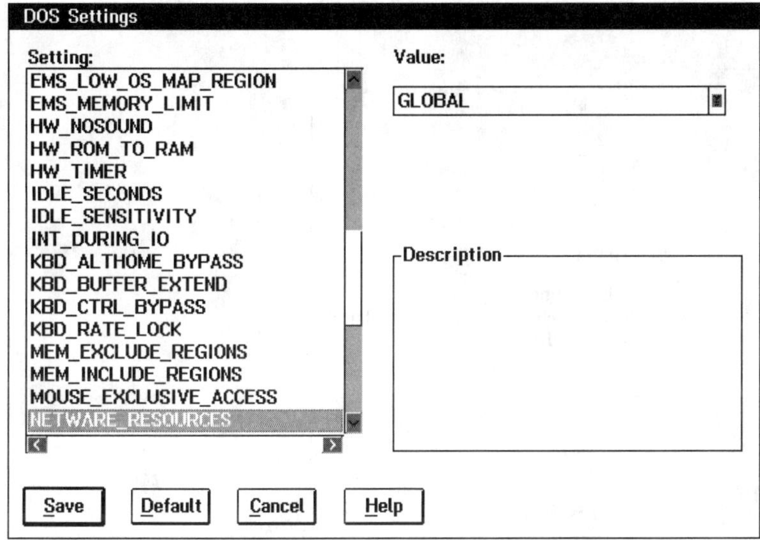

Figure 14.4 Enabling the global NetWare resources. [*Reprinted by permission from IBM's OS/2 2.0, Copyright (1988, 1992) International Business Machines Corporation.*]

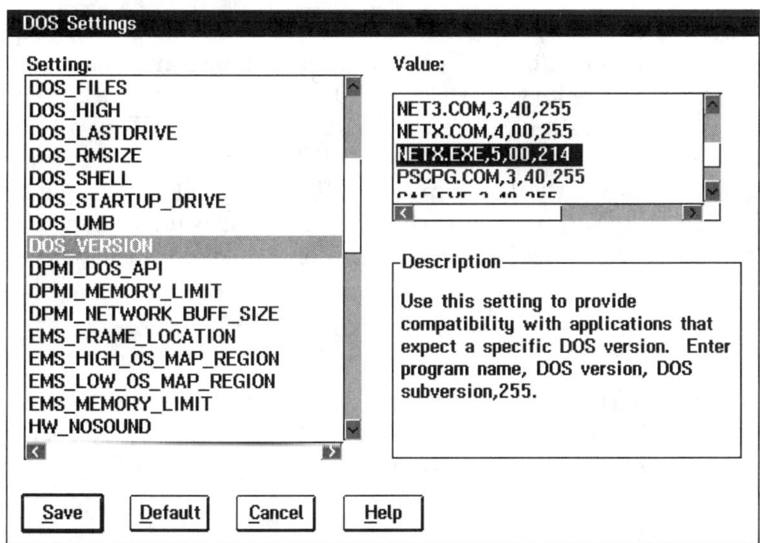

Figure 14.5 Modifying the DOS_VERSION settings. [*Reprinted by permission from IBM's OS/2 2.0, Copyright (1988, 1992) International Business Machines Corporation.*]

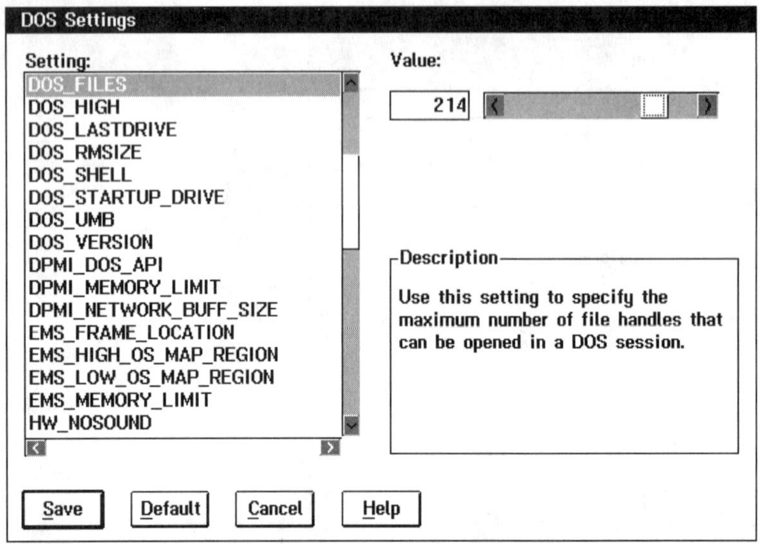

Figure 14.6 Modifying the DOS_FILES parameter for global access. [*Reprinted by permission from IBM's OS/2 2.0, Copyright (1988, 1992) International Business Machines Corporation.*]

Try switching drives to one of the drives that was mapped in your OS/2 session. You should be able to access them. There are a couple of tricks you can use to make your DOS global sessions easier to use. Once you are in the DOS session, you can once again use the NetWare search mapping to add directories to your DOS path. To do this, you must have access to the NetWare PUBLIC directory. The simplest way to get to the PUBLIC directory is to include the following map command in your OS/2 log-in script which will be executed when you log in through your global OS/2 session:

```
MAP F:=SYS:\
```

This will allow the DOS session access to the entire SYS: drive (assuming the user has NetWare rights to the volume). From the DOS session you can insert a search mapping by entering the following commands:

```
F:
CD\PUBLIC
MAP INS S16:=VOL1:\WP51
```

These commands can be placed in the AUTOEXEC.BAT file for the DOS session so that they are automatically executed when the DOS session is opened. Keep in mind, each DOS session can have its own AUTOEXEC.BAT file. This is accomplished by modifying the

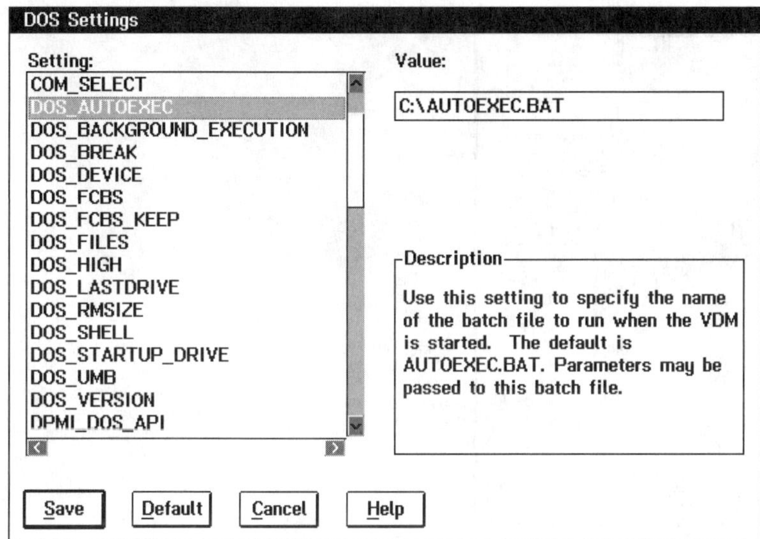

Figure 14.7 Selecting the AUTOEXEC.BAT file. [*Reprinted by permission from IBM's OS/2 2.0, Copyright (1988, 1992) International Business Machines Corporation.*]

DOS_AUTOEXEC value in the DOS Settings box, as illustrated in Fig. 14.7.

Windows global NetWare access

WIN-OS2 sessions can also utilize the global NetWare log-in facility. The process works in much the same way as the DOS sessions. The drive mappings are established by a global OS/2 log-in, and these mappings are available to the WIN-OS2 sessions.

You must make the following changes in your WIN-OS2 session to utilize the global log-in facility:

Step 1 Open the setting on your WIN-OS/2 session by moving your cursor to the WIN-OS/2 icon and pressing the right mouse button. Click on the arrow by the word Open, then select the Settings option.

Step 2 Figure 14.8 will be displayed. Click on the Session tab.

Step 3 Figure 14.9 will be displayed. Click on WIN-OS/2 settings.

Step 4 Follow steps 4 through 11 of the DOS global NetWare access setup example above to modify the DOS_LASTDRIVE, NETWARE_RESOURCES, DOS_VERSION, DOS_FILES, VIPX_ENABLED, and IDLE_SENSITIVITY parameters.

After you have made these changes, your WIN-OS/2 session will have access to all the drives mapped by the OS/2 global NetWare log-in.

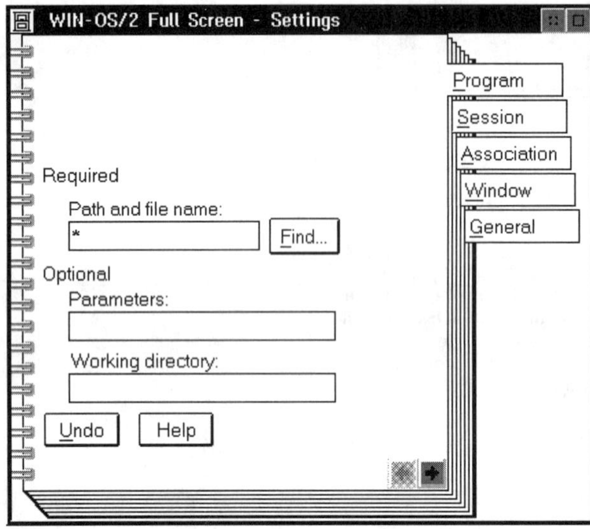

Figure 14.8 Opening the WIN-OS2 full-screen settings. [*Reprinted by permission from IBM's OS/2 2.0, Copyright (1988, 1992) International Business Machines Corporation.*]

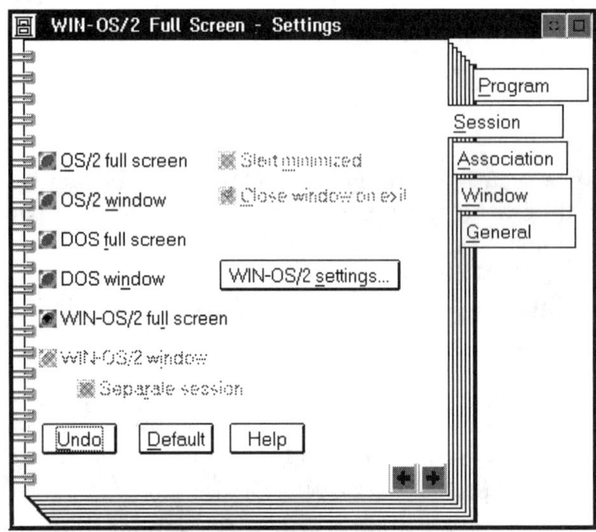

Figure 14.9 Entering the WIN-OS/2 settings. [*Reprinted by permission from IBM's OS/2 2.0, Copyright (1988, 1992) International Business Machines Corporation.*]

Global print capture

One of the nicest features of the global log-in facility is the ability to execute the global CAPTURE command. Capture is a NetWare utility that allows you to redirect the output from the LPTx: port directly into a NetWare print queue. Capture allows users who do not have a printer connected to their workstations to route print to network printers. A global CAPTURE will direct the print for all DOS and OS/2 sessions to the same NetWare print queue.

Some sites use the global log-in facility just to implement the global CAPTURE command. Workstations that do not have a printer attached have their STARTUP.CMD file modified to log in to a file server and invoke the Capture utility to route their print to their neighbor's workstation. (STARTUP.CMD is a command file that is executed each time an OS/2 workstation is rebooted.)

Implementing the global print Capture utility

The global Capture utility is implemented by following these steps:

Step 1 Globally log in to a NetWare server from an OS/2 session, as explained above.

Step 2 Enter the CAPTURE command. The format and use of the NetWare CAPTURE command are explained in detail in Chap. 15, Printing through a Novell Network.

This process can be automated by placing the CAPTURE command into the OS/2 system or user log-in script.

Pros and cons of global NetWare access

There are several pros and cons to using global NetWare access to link to your NetWare servers.
Pros:

- The user needs to log in to NetWare only once for all sessions.
- Fewer log-in connections are required for the network. This can be a primary concern if you are trying to support 100 users with a 50-user NetWare license.
- The global Capture utility can be utilized.

Con:

- Some programs cannot run in global sessions.

Performing a global log-in automatically at boot time

You may need to automatically perform a global log-in each time the user reboots her or his workstation. This can be accomplished by adding the following line to the CONFIG.SYS file:

```
CALL=C:\NETWARE\LOGIN.EXE SERVER\USER
```

You must substitute a valid user and server name in the statement. If the user has a password, the password prompt will be displayed. After the password is entered, the OS/2 log-in scripts will be executed. You can place drive mappings in these log-in scripts. These mappings will be accessible by other global DOS and OS/2 sessions.

Private NetWare Access

Private NetWare access establishes a separate log-in connection for each DOS, OS/2, and WIN-OS2 session that is opened by the user. Private NetWare access "feels" like the standard DOS-to-NetWare log-in mechanism. The DOS session is opened; the user enters NETX to load the NetWare shell and then logs in to a NetWare file server.

DOS private NetWare access

Again, we must make changes to the DOS session in order to utilize the private NetWare access utility.

Step 1 Open the setting on your DOS session by moving your cursor to the DOS icon and pressing the right mouse button. Click on the arrow by the word Open, then select the Settings option.

Step 2 Figure 14.1 will be displayed. Click on the Session tab.

Step 3 Figure 14.2 will be displayed. Click on DOS settings.

Step 4 Figure 14.3 will be displayed. Click on DOS_LASTDRIVE, then enter E in the Value field.

Step 5 Scroll down the list of settings by clicking on the bottom arrow until you see the NETWARE_RESOURCES entry. Click on this entry.

Step 6 Figure 14.4 will be displayed. Enter PRIVATE in the Value field.

Step 7 Scroll through the list until you see DOS_VERSION. Click on DOS_VERSION, and a list of values will be displayed, as shown in Fig. 14.5. Scroll through the list of values until you see NETX.EXE. Modify the NETX.EXE value, by overtyping the current value, to

```
NETX.EXE,5,00,214
```

Step 8 Scroll through the list until you find DOS_FILES. Click on DOS_FILES, and change the value to 214, as illustrated in Fig. 14.6.

Step 9 Scroll through the list, and click on VIPX_ENABLED. Make sure the value is set to On.

Step 10 Scroll through the list, and click on IDLE_SENSITIVITY. Change the value to 100.

Step 11 Click on Save, then close the DOS Settings box by double-clicking on the upper left-hand corner of the box.

Step 12 Open the DOS session by double-clicking on the DOS icon that you just modified.

When you open the DOS session, you will notice that an IPX/SPX driver is automatically loaded, as illustrated in Fig. 14.10.

Next enter the following command from the C:\ prompt to load the DOS NetWare shell:

```
NETX
```

Now switch to the LOGIN directory by changing to the F: drive. You should now be able to log in to your Novell file server.

> **Note** If you placed a value other than E in the DOS_LASTDRIVE, you will not have an F: drive. To log in to the network, you must switch to the drive which is one letter higher than the DOS_LASTDRIVE setting. For example, if you placed an L in the DOS_LASTDRIVE parameter, enter M: to get to the LOGIN directory.

After you log in by using a DOS private session, the session should look and feel just like any other DOS workstation on your network. The DOS system and user log-in scripts are executed, and all the search and drive mappings will be established just as with a DOS workstation.

You may use the NetWare CAPTURE command to route the print for the DOS session to a NetWare print queue. Keep in mind that the CAPTURE command will affect only this DOS session, since this is a private log-in. The CAPTURE command will not route the print from other DOS or WIN-OS/2 sessions.

```
Netware for OS/2 v2.0 (930204)
Virtual IPX/SPX Driver for MVDM Support
(c) Copyright 1992, 1993 Novell, Inc.  All Rights Reserved
```

Figure 14.10 The VIPX driver message.

Windows private NetWare access

WIN-OS2 sessions can also utilize the private NetWare log-in facility. The process works in much the same way as the DOS sessions. When using the private NetWare log-in for WIN-OS/2 sessions, you must log in to the NetWare server(s) before you enter into Windows. Standard Windows works in this same manner. The following steps must be taken to log in to the server before entering into Windows:

Step 1 Create a BAT file that issues the NETX command and logs in to a NetWare server. Figure 14.11 illustrates a modified version of the BAT file that came with OS/2 2.1 that launches the WIN-OS/2 session. Notice the last three lines of the BAT file. These lines perform the log-in into a NetWare file server.

Step 2 Save the BAT file with a unique name.

Step 3 Now we must tell the WIN-OS/2 session to use our newly created BAT file as its AUTOEXEC.BAT file. Open the setting on your WIN-OS/2 session by moving the cursor to the WIN-OS/2 icon and pressing the right mouse button. Click on the arrow by the word Open, then select the Settings option.

Step 4 Figure 14.8 will be displayed. Click on the Session tab.

Step 5 Figure 14.9 will be displayed. Click on WIN-OS/2 settings.

Step 6 Click on the DOS_AUTOEXEC parameter, and change the value to the name of the BAT file you just created. See Fig. 14.12.

Step 7 Click on Save, then exit the settings box.

Step 8 Follow steps 4 through 11 of the DOS private NetWare access setup example above to set the DOS_LASTDRIVE to E, the NETWARE_RESOURCES to PRIVATE, the DOS_FILES to 214, the DOS_VERSION to NETX.EXE,5,00,214, VIPX_ENABLED to ON, and IDLE_SENSITIVITY to 100.

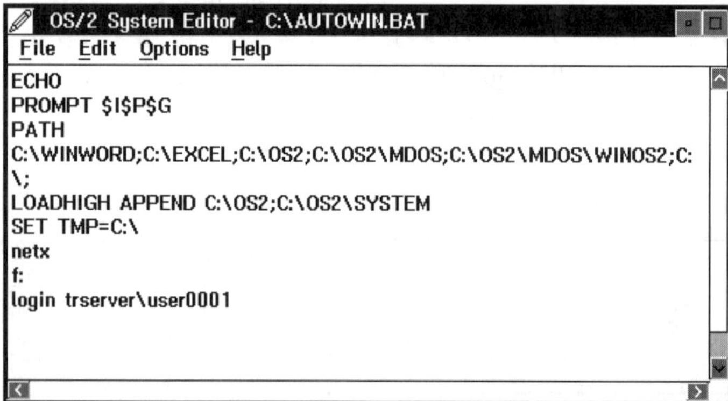

Figure 14.11 Modifying the AUTOEXEC.BAT file for Windows.

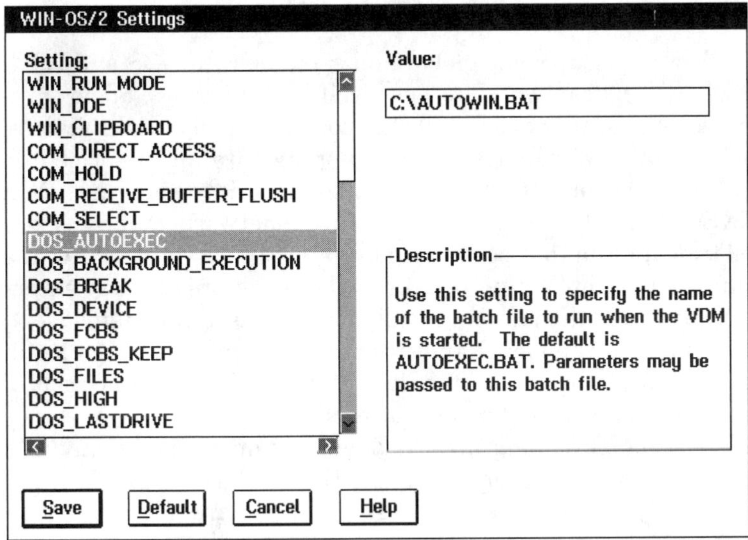

Figure 14.12 Specifying the name of the WIN-OS/2 AUTOEXEC.BAT file.

When you open the WIN-OS/2 session, you should have access to all the NetWare resources, including NetWare print services. The WIN-OS/2 session should look and feel just like a native Windows workstation on a Novell network.

Pros and cons of private NetWare access

There are pros and cons to using private NetWare access to link to your NetWare servers.

Pros:

- The sessions “look and feel” like standard DOS and Windows networked sessions to the user.
- Almost every program will work in a private session.
- You can use the NetWare CAPTURE command to route the print, by session, to a network printer.
- The private log-in facility is less complex and easier to set up and maintain than the global log-in facility.

Con:

- The user must log in to NetWare each time a new session is established. This could cause problems if you are currently pushing the number of concurrent NetWare users set by your NetWare license.

Combining Private and Global Log-ins

You may elect to set up some global and some private DOS and WIN-OS/2 sessions. This can work out very well in some cases. Some organizations use global sessions for all the most commonly used software, such as Lotus and WordPerfect. The mappings are all performed by using a combination of the OS/2 log-in script and the DOS AUTOEXEC.BAT file. Less frequently used network programs are launched from an icon that performs a private DOS log-in. The BAT file that launches the application logs in to the Novell file server, enters into the application, then automatically logs the user out again.

Experiment with the global and private DOS and WIN-OS/2 log-in utilities. As you become more familiar with the functions of each of these methods, you will find niches for each type of log-in.

There are some DOS programs that will not operate correctly in a global DOS session, and there are some DOS programs that will not operate correctly in a private DOS session. If you are having difficulties making a DOS program run under an OS/2 VDM, experiment with the NetWare Requester global and private settings.

Novell Folder

After you install the OS/2 Requester, you will notice that the Novell icon was added to your OS/2 desktop. If you open this folder, you will find that three utilities are provided with Requester: the Network Printer, the NetWare Target Service Agent, and the NetWare Tools. Let's take a look at each of these utilities.

Network Printer utility

The Novell Network Printer utility is a program that runs on an OS/2 workstation that allows you to use the printer attached to the OS/2 workstation as a network printer. This utility is known as the Network Printer or NPRINTER. Older releases of the OS/2 NetWare Requester provided this same function under the name of Remote Printer, or RPRINTER.

When an OS/2 workstation activates the Network Printer utility, other network users can direct their print to Network Printer, just as they would to a printer that is connected directly to a print server. This function gives the network administrator a lot of flexibility in designing the network. The administrator no longer needs to be concerned with placing print servers in strategic locations throughout the organization.

More information on setting up and using the Network Printer utility is provided in Chap. 15, Printing through a Novell Network.

Before you decide to implement the Network Printer solution throughout your local-area network, test all the types of print that your LAN must support. OS/2 in conjunction with the NPRINTER utility has problems with some types of printed output. Graphical print can cause problems as well as print output that contains special printer control commands. An example of a print job that has problems with OS/2 and NPRINTER is an application that loads a form design into the memory of an HP LaserJet printer and then sends multiple print data streams to the printer with special printer codes telling it to utilize the form design loaded into the printer's memory.

NetWare Target Service Agent

Networks seem to expand at a tremendous pace, and keeping up with this expansion can be overwhelming to network administrators. One of the areas that is commonly overlooked in designing networks is the backup of critical data. Many shops tell their users that the data on the file server will be backed up by the data processing department, but all local data are the responsibility of the user. The NetWare Target Service Agent (TSA) is a utility that can change the way we back up the user's data.

The NetWare TSA is a utility that runs in an OS/2 session that allows your workstation's local drive to be backed up, automatically, on the network.

The TSA utility works hand in hand with the Novell SBACKUP utility. When you load TSA on your workstation, you tell TSA (1) which users are allowed to access your local drive, (2) a password that those users must enter to access your drive, and (3) which drives users are allowed to back up. The SBACKUP utility can then perform a backup of your workstation's local data.

If you do not wish to implement the TSA backup utility, there are other ways to back up your user's hard drives onto the network. One method that can be used is to place a "daily backup" icon on each user's system. Clicking on this daily backup icon will invoke a BAT file within a private or global VDM. The BAT file could copy certain directories or the entire hard drive to a directory on the file server. This type of backup system is still at the mercy of the end-user, as he or she must initiate the backup. By making the backup as simple as clicking on an icon, the chances of users actually performing the backup are greatly enhanced. This backup method has one glaring requirement: lots of file server disk space. Clearly, if you are backing up hundreds or thousands of PCs to a file server disk drive, this will consume a considerable amount of space. A product such as IBM's LANRES is perfect for this type of application. LANRES allows mainframe direct access storage device (DASD) to be utilized as native NetWare file server drives.

NetWare Tools utility

The NetWare Tools utility is a *graphical user interface* (GUI) that allows the user to access the network resources. The user can log in to servers and map drives and can look at print queues and see which users are currently logged in to the network. All these functions can be performed without the GUI, but some users prefer the graphical interaction to native DOS or OS/2 commands. Let's take a look at some of the functions available through the NetWare Tools utility.

The GUI log-in

To log in to a file server by using the NetWare Tools GUI, do the following:

Step 1 Open the Novell folder by double-clicking on the Novell folder icon.

Step 2 Open the NetWare Tools utility by double-clicking on the NetWare tools icon.

Step 3 The Disk Drives utility should be displayed on your screen, as illustrated in Fig. 14.13.

Step 4 Double-click on the L:SERVERCC\SYS:\LOGIN drive, and Fig. 14.14 will be displayed.

Step 5 Click on Attach, and Fig. 14.15 will be displayed. Enter a user name and password to log in to the network.

This procedure performs a global network log-in. See the previous sections in this chapter for more information on global and private network log-ins.

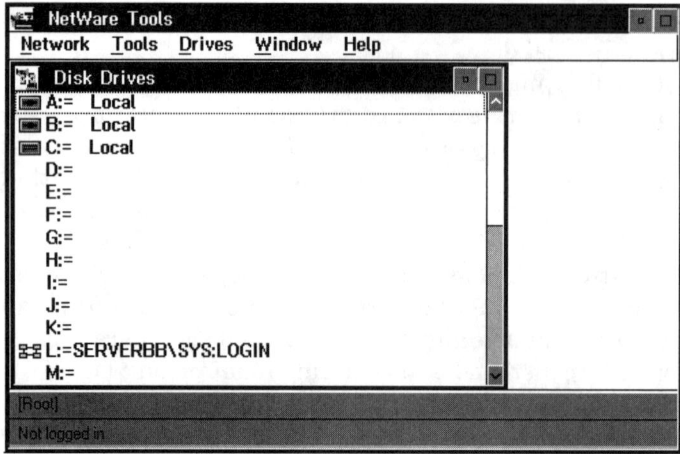

Figure 14.13 NetWare Tools disk utility.

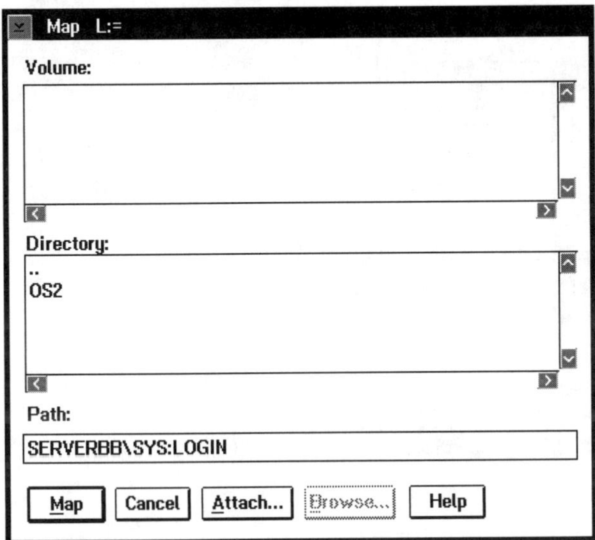

Figure 14.14 Attaching to a file server.

Figure 14.15 Entering the user name and password.

The GUI map utility

To map a drive using the NetWare Tools interface, do the following:

Step 1 Go to the Disk Drive utility, as shown in Fig. 14.16.

Step 2 Double-click on an available drive letter. Figure 14.17 will be displayed.

Step 3 Click on a volume entry from the top section of Fig. 14.17, then click on a directory entry from the bottom section. Click on Map, and the selected drive will be mapped to the directory. This drive can then be accessed by other global DOS and OS/2 sessions.

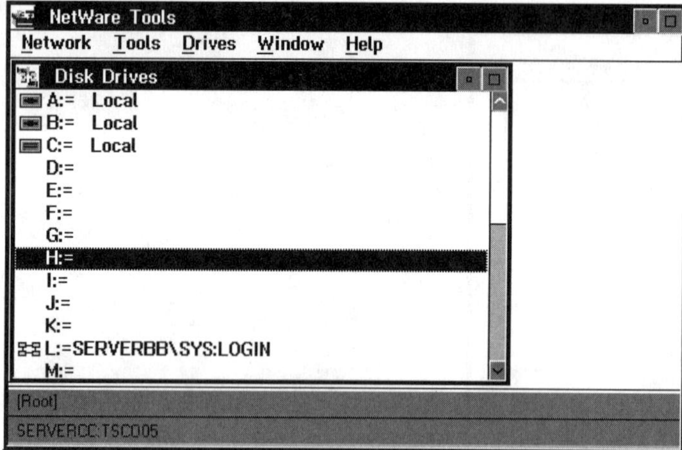

Figure 14.16 Preparing to map a network drive.

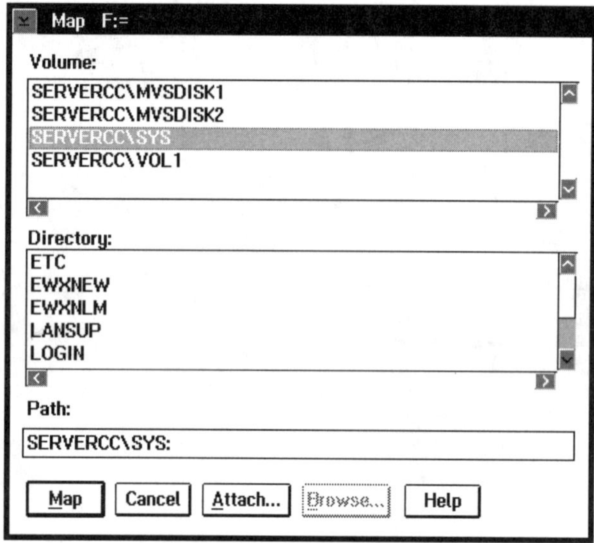

Figure 14.17 Mapping F: to a network volume.

The GUI user list

You can also use the NetWare Tools utility to view which users are currently logged in to a file server. To perform this function:

Step 1 Use the NetWare Tools utility to log in to a file server, as explained earlier.

Step 2 Click on the Tools menu bar to access the pop-up menu shown in Fig. 14.18.

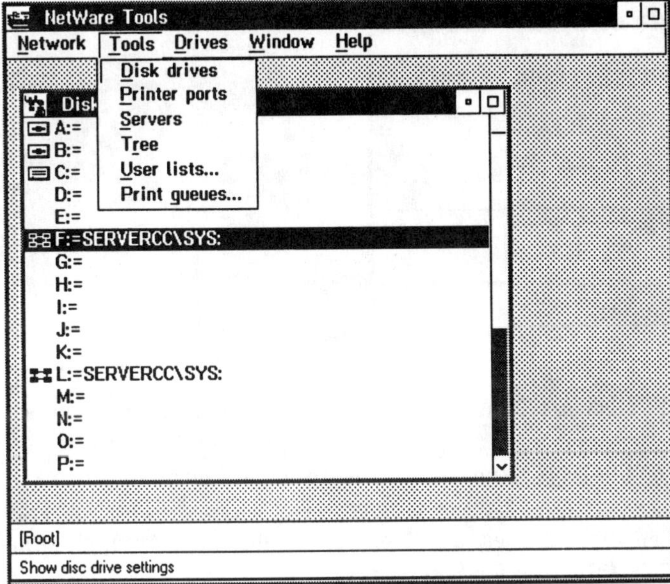

Figure 14.18 Accessing the NetWare Tools menu.

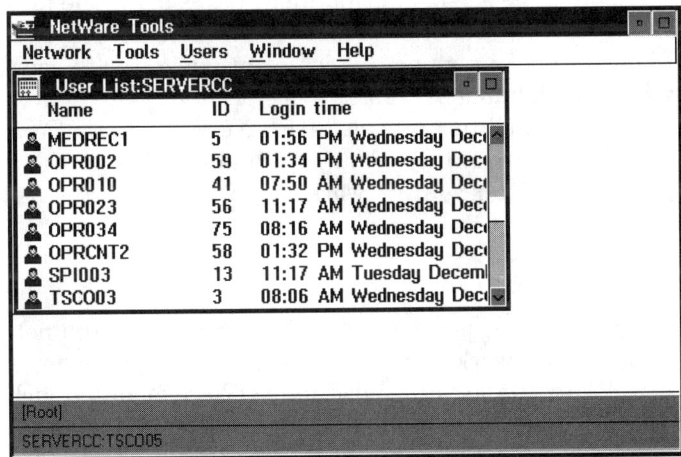

Figure 14.19 Viewing the user list tool.

Step 3 Click on User lists, and Fig. 14.19 will be displayed, showing you the users who are currently logged in to your file server.

The GUI print queue list

The NetWare Tools utility also provides a utility to graphically view your NetWare print queues. To do this:

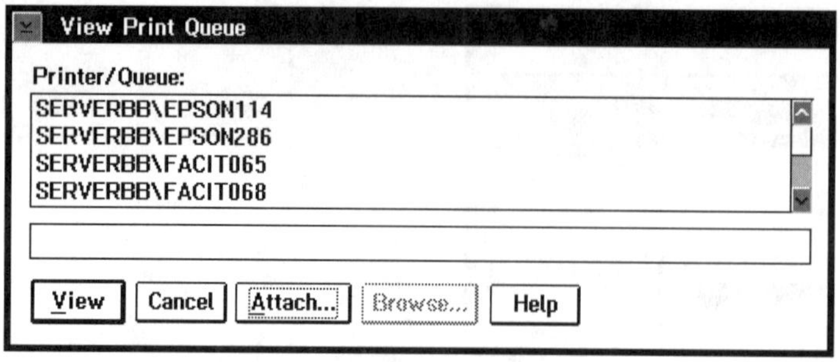

Figure 14.20 Viewing the NetWare print queues.

Step 1 Use the NetWare Tools utility to log in to a file server, as explained earlier.

Step 2 Click on the Tools menu bar to access the pop-up menu shown in Fig. 14.18.

Step 3 Click on Print queues, and Fig. 14.20 will be displayed, showing your NetWare print queues.

You can also use the NetWare Tools print queues utility to determine if a print queue is backed up, indicating a problem in the network printing system. You can arrange a grid of print queue boxes using the utilities of NetWare Tools and the OS/2 presentation manager services. This grid would show you, at a glance, which print queues were operating normally and which had jobs waiting to be printed.

There are many other facilities provided with NetWare Tools. Take your time and explore these utilities. You may find a utility in there that could help you administer your network.

Conclusion

The OS/2 NetWare Requester is an extremely robust tool for the network designer and the network administrator. Requester provides a means to access NetWare file servers and other NetWare facilities such as print services. OS/2 and NetWare Requester are still evolving. Some DOS applications do not work correctly in private VDMs while other DOS applications do not work correctly in global VDMs. As OS/2 and NetWare Requester mature, hopefully these types of problems will become a thing of the past. The NetWare Tools utility functions provide several utilities that can be used to monitor the status of your network, including the status of your network printing system.

Chapter

15

Printing Through a Novell Network

The routing of network print is one area of network design and administration that causes the most problems. Network printing is also one of the most visible aspects of network administration. When the network print stops, users get upset and can make your life difficult.

The real challenge is not simply designing a system to route network print around the corporation. The printing system must also be able to support print jobs from all the hardware and software platforms on your LAN. A typical network could require print support for a mainframe, a minicomputer, DOS, Windows, OS/2, and Novell applications.

Printing Basics

To see why this is such a challenge, we must first have a clear understanding of the components available to design a network printing subsystem. Figure 15.1 illustrates the major printing components provided by NetWare and OS/2.

Let's look at how a simple print job is routed through the network by using NetWare and OS/2. The user workstation, in the upper left-hand corner of Fig. 15.1, does not have a local printer attached to its PC. This user wishes to route print to the printer attached to a coworker's OS/2 workstation, which is shown on the right half of Fig. 15.1.

The print from the user's workstation is first redirected to a Novell print queue by using the NetWare CAPTURE command. The CAPTURE command will be discussed, in detail, later in this chapter.

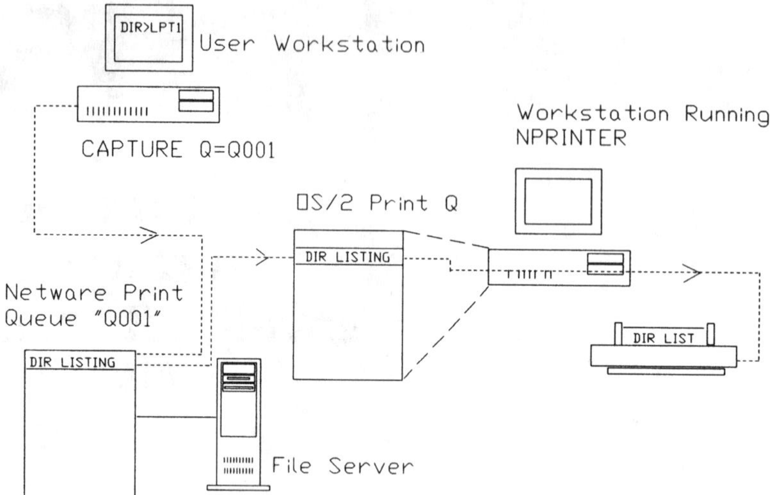

Figure 15.1 Routing print by using Nprinter.

Once the print is in the Novell print queue, a print server will process the print job. A Novell print server is a program that can run either on a file server as a NetWare loadable module (NLM) or on a dedicated PC. The print server will do one of two things with the print job. The print server could, depending upon how it is configured, print the job on a printer connected to the print server's LPTx: or COMx: ports. The print server could also send the print job to an OS/2 Network Printer (NPRINTER) or a DOS Remote Printer (RPRINTER) for processing.

The OS/2 Network Printer (NPRINTER) is a program that comes with the Novell OS/2 Requester product. NPRINTER runs on OS/2-based machines. NPRINTER receives print output from a print server and directs the print to the workstation's printer port. The NPRINTER for OS/2 does not direct the print directly to the printer port. OS/2 uses a special printing subsystem of its own. The OS/2 NPRINTER program directs the network print job to the OS/2 print subsystem. The OS/2 print subsystem queues the jobs in a spool file. The print driver then selects these jobs, one at a time, and directs them to the local printer.

The Remote Printer (RPRINTER) provides the same function as NPRINTER, but it runs on DOS-based machines. RPRINTER is a *terminate and stay resident* (TSR) program that is provided with NetWare. The DOS RPRINTER has been plagued with problems since its inception. One of RPRINTER's most annoying problems is that when a user running RPRINTER reboots his or her workstation and

RPRINTER tries to restart, it fails to initialize. This failure occurs because the print server takes several minutes to time out the device. When RPRINTER tries to restart, it fails because the print server tells it that the printer is currently active. The user must wait for a couple of minutes, then try to reestablish the RPRINTER connection.

Note The OS/2 Network Printer was called RPRINTER in earlier releases of OS/2 Requester. The name was changed to Network Printer with version 2.01 of the Requester product.

The OS/2 print subsystem is one of the strong points of the OS/2 operating system. OS/2 is a true multitasking operating system in which multiple DOS and OS/2 programs can be running concurrently. Without some type of store-and-forward print mechanism, print jobs would be interlaced if these concurrently running programs all tried to print at the same time.

OS/2 uses a spooling mechanism to store and then print the output from the various tasks. Print jobs are stored in a special directory on the local C: drive; then the print driver takes these jobs, one at a time, and ships them to the printer.

This OS/2 print spooling feature is especially nice for mainframe print. In the DOS world, mainframe print LU emulators receive print from the host and then direct the print to the LPTx: port on the PC. Many host applications print at random intervals, not under the control of the user. If the poor DOS user is in the middle of printing a large word processing document, the host print jumps right in there, interleaving the host print with the word processing print. CM/2 host print LU emulators direct their print to the OS/2 print spooler, eliminating this problem.

Now that we have a general understanding of how host and network print is routed through the network, let's take a closer look at each of the components of the network and OS/2 printing subsystems.

NetWare Capture Utility

NetWare provides a utility known as Capture. Capture allows you to take the print that would normally go to a workstation's LPTx: port and place it directly into a NetWare print queue. The Capture utility is provided with NetWare.

There are two types of CAPTURE commands available with OS/2 workstations: global and local captures. Global captures, as the name implies, affects the entire workstation and all its OS/2 and DOS sessions. Local captures intercept and route the print for a particular OS/2 or DOS session to a Novell print queue.

Global NetWare CAPTURE command

To implement a global CAPTURE command, the following steps must be performed. You must have NetWare Requester installed on the workstation in order to perform this procedure.

- Open an OS/2 session.
- Log in to a NetWare server from the OS/2 session.
- Switch drives to the F:\PUBLIC\OS2 directory.
- Enter the CAPTURE command.

The global CAPTURE command has the following format:

```
CAPTURE S=fileserver Q=qname L=x NFF NB TI=nn
```

where S = name of file server to where print should be routed
qname = name of NetWare print queue where print is to be routed
L = LPTx: port number that is to be captured. A 1 specifies LPT1:; a 2 specifies LPT2:; and so on.
NFF = no form feed. If you do not code this parameter, a blank page will be inserted after each print job.
NB = no banner page. If you do not code this parameter, each job will be preceded by a banner page containing the NetWare user ID of the user who printed the job.
TI = number of seconds to wait after application last writes to print file

There are many other options available with the Capture utility. The Novell print server manual explains these options in detail.

Once you have issued the global CAPTURE command, all the output that was destined for the printer port, from all OS/2 and DOS sessions, will be redirected to the NetWare print queue specified in the CAPTURE command.

You can automatically issue the global CAPTURE command by placing the NetWare log-in and CAPTURE commands in the C:\STARTUP.CMD file. The STARTUP.CMD file is an OS/2 command file that is run each time OS/2 is booted. The STARTUP.CMD file is equivalent in function to the DOS AUTOEXEC.BAT file. Placing the log-in and CAPTURE commands in this file ensures that they will be issued for the end-user each time she or he reboots the workstation.

Figure 15.2 illustrates a sample STARTUP.CMD file to automatically log the user into a NetWare server and globally capture the LPT1: port and direct it to NetWare queue HPLAS003.

```
REM - Sample C:\STARTUP.CMD to
REM - automatically login to a
REM - Novell File server and
REM - issue a Global Capture
REM - command

L:
cd os2
login TRSERVER\USER001
E:
capture q=hplas003 nff nb l=1
```

Figure 15.2 STARTUP.CMD to issue global Capture.

Local NetWare CAPTURE command

A local NetWare CAPTURE command reroutes the print from a single OS/2 DOS session to a NetWare queue. You must have NetWare Requester installed on the workstation to perform the local capture. To use the local CAPTURE command, do as follows:

- Log in to a NetWare server from an OS/2 DOS session.
- Enter the CAPTURE command, using the same format as described in the "Global NetWare CAPTURE Command" section above.

The NetWare Print Subsystem

The NetWare printing system consists of three major components: print queues, print servers, and the Network Printer facility. These components work together to route network print throughout the network.

NetWare print queues

NetWare print queues are holding areas for print. Multiple users can route print to these queues, and the data will be stored there until a print server processes the print. NetWare print queues are created by using the NetWare PCONSOLE utility. The actual print jobs are held in a subdirectory in the SYS:SYSTEM directory of the file server.

NetWare print server

The NetWare print server is a program that takes the print job from the NetWare print queues and routes the print to a printer. The print server program can run as an NLM on the NetWare file server, or it can be run on a dedicated PC. Each print server can control up to 16 printers. These printers can be connected to the print server's parallel ports or serial ports, or the NPRINTER utility can be used.

The NetWare PCONSOLE utility is used to define print servers. Up to five local printers can be defined for each print server, which should be connected to the LPT1:, LPT2:, LPT3:, COM1:, and COM2: ports. The print server can also process print queues defined in other NetWare print servers.

OS/2 Print Subsystem

The OS/2 print subsystem works according to the print queuing theory, much like the NetWare print system. Print output from the various tasks running under OS/2 is placed in a queue. The print driver selects the print jobs, one at a time, and routes them to the printer.

> **Suggestion** Before you attempt to implement the NetWare NPRINTER utility on an OS/2 workstation, first make sure that the OS/2 print system is working properly. Failure to do so will impede troubleshooting efforts.

For information on setting up the OS/2 print subsystem, refer to Chap. 11.

NetWare Network Printer

The NetWare Network Printer (NPRINTER) is a program that runs on a user's OS/2 workstation, receives print jobs from a print server, and prints that job on the workstation's local printer.

Setting up the OS/2 Network Printer utility

Before you can implement the OS/2 Network Printer, you must configure the NPRINTER program. During the configuration process we must tell the Novell print server which printer we will be using as a Network Printer. We must also tell the NPRINTER program which Novell printer we will be utilizing.

OS/2 Network Printers are defined to Novell in the same manner as any other printer. The print server must first be created by using the PCONSOLE utility. Next we use PCONSOLE to define the print queue(s) that Network Printer will be using. The creation of the print queues is performed in the same manner as any other print queue. When we use PCONSOLE to define the printer to the print server, we must make sure we choose the correct printer type. The Network Printer uses one of the following printer types:

Remote parallel, LPT1

Remote parallel, LPT2

Remote parallel, LPT3

Remote serial, COM1

Remote serial, COM2

Remote serial, COM3

Remote serial, COM4

If your Network Printer is attached to the workstation's LPT1: port, choose the remote parallel LPT1 setting. If the printer is connected to the COM2 port of the workstation, choose remote serial COM2, and so on.

After choosing the printer type, you must tell the print server which print queue(s) will be serviced by Network Printer. This is accomplished with the PCONSOLE utility just like any other printer in a Novell network.

Now we are ready to configure the NPRINTER program.

Step 1 Open the Novell folder by double-clicking on the Novell icon.

Step 2 Double-click on the Network Printer icon.

Step 3 Click on Printers to access the pull-down menu shown in Fig. 15.3.

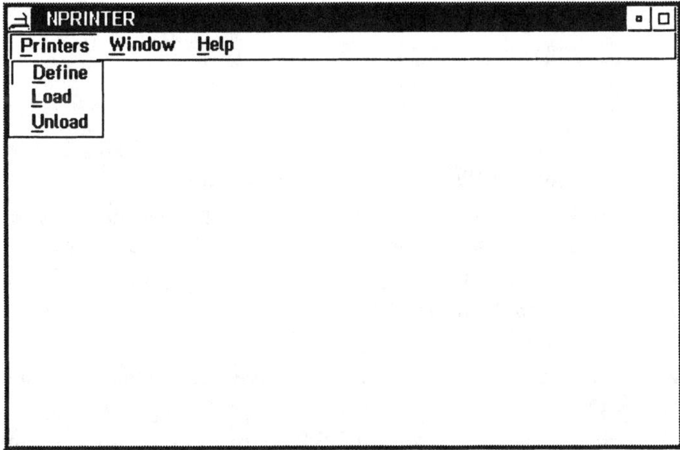

Figure 15.3 Invoking the Nprinter define utility.

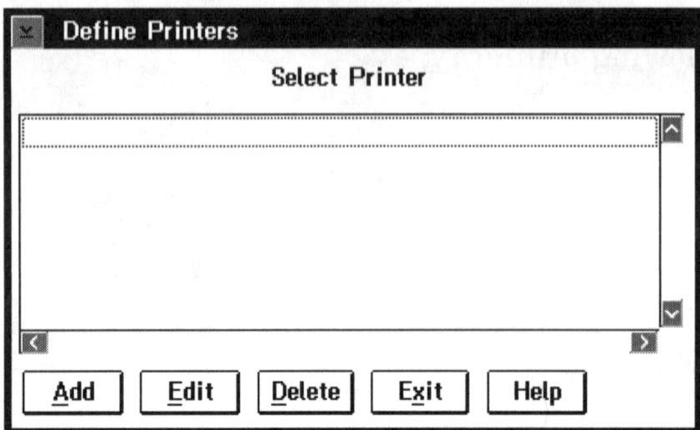

Figure 15.4 Adding a network printer to the desktop.

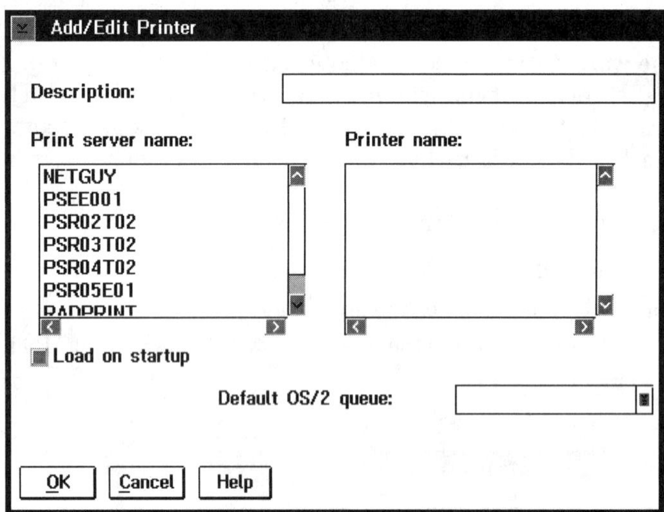

Figure 15.5 Selecting a print server.

Step 4 Click on Define, and Fig. 15.4 will be displayed.

Step 5 Click on Add, and Fig. 15.5 will be displayed. Notice that all your NetWare print servers will be listed in the left-hand column.

Step 6 Double-click on the print server where you defined your Network Printer. Figure 15.6 will be displayed, showing you all the printer names available.

Step 7 Click on the printer name that you specified when defining Network Printer to the file server.

Step 8 Click on the arrow by the Default OS/2 queue field. A panel resembling Fig. 15.7 will be displayed. Select the OS/2 print queue name of where you wish the network print to be routed.

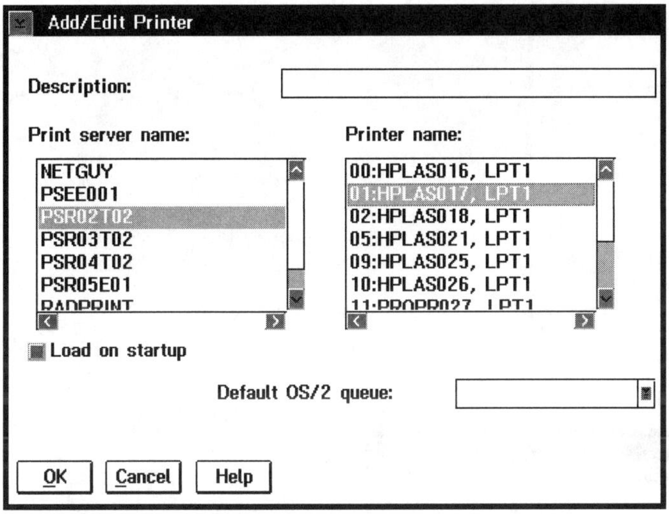

Figure 15.6 Selecting a NetWare printer.

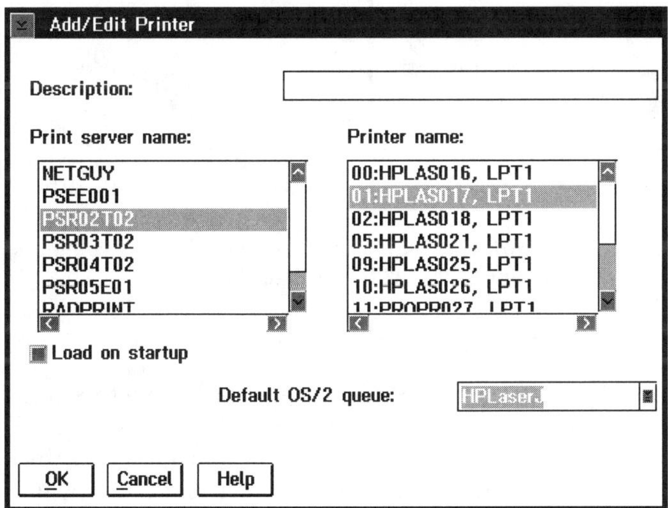

Figure 15.7 Selecting the OS/2 print queue.

Step 9 Enter a description in the Description field, then click on OK. Figure 15.8 will now be displayed. Click on Exit.

Step 10 Click on Printers to access the pull-down menu shown in Fig. 15.3.

Step 11 Click on Load. Figure 15.9 will be displayed. Click on the printer you just defined (Network Printer in this example) to highlight it, then click on Load.

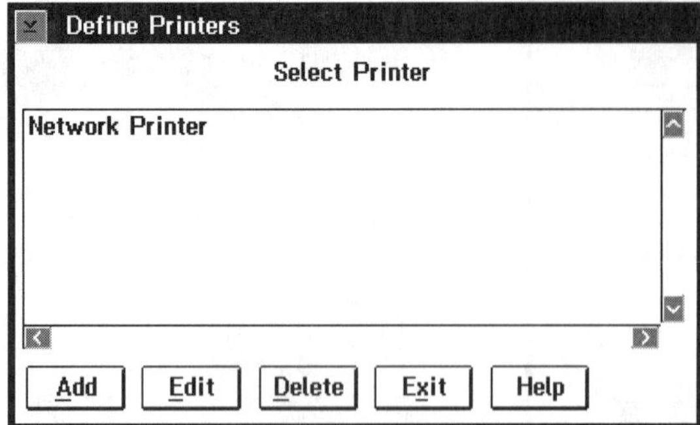

Figure 15.8 Naming the Nprinter.

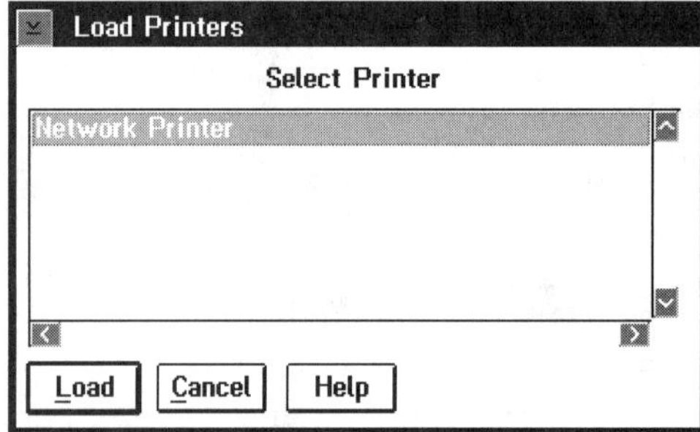

Figure 15.9 Loading the Nprinter.

Step 12 To test your Network Printer, you can use the following command to ship a copy of your CONFIG.SYS file to the printer:

```
NPRINT C:\CONFIG.SYS q=queuename
```

You can load the Network Printer automatically each time the workstation is rebooted by making these changes:

On Fig. 15.5 click on the Load on startup option. Move the Network Printer icon to the startup folder. The startup folder is a folder whose members are activated at boot time. The startup folder is located in the OS/2 system folder.

LANRES Print Facility

LANRES is a relatively new product from IBM providing several functions which allow mainframe and NetWare LANs to share devices. The heart of LANRES is its ability to store NetWare files on mainframe DASD. The mainframe DASD looks just like a native NetWare drive to both NetWare and the end-users. In a properly configured LANRES environment, the mainframe volumes can actually outperform the native file server volumes.

LANRES also provides host-to-LAN and LAN-to-host print facilities. Host output can be sent directly to NetWare print queues. Conversely, Network print can be sent directly to host printers.

The facilities of LANRES, both the print- and file-sharing options, greatly expand the horizons of integrating mainframes and networks.

VPS and VPS/PC

Levi Ray and Shoup provide two software products that work hand in hand to route mainframe print through a Novell network: VPS and VPS/PC. These products take all types of mainframe print and place the print into Novell print queues. This a very good solution for mainframe sites that require this functionality.

The Cheaper Way to Route Mainframe Print Through Novell

All the methods of placing mainframe print into NetWare print queues are rather expensive. There is an alternative for those sites on a limited hardware and software budget. The method we are about to explore is slower and can be less reliable than the other methods, but it is almost cost-free. Using either an OS/2 or DOS PC, configure the terminal emulator (CM/2 in the case of an OS/2 workstation) so that it has three mainframe printers defined. These mainframe print emulator sessions should be directed to ports LPT1, LPT2, and LPT3. Before starting the emulator, issue the following CAPTURE commands:

```
Capture Q=NETPRT01 L=1 NFF NB
Capture Q=NETPRT02 L=2 NFF NB
Capture Q=NETPRT03 L=3 NFF NB
```

The above CAPTURE commands will direct the print from the three LPT ports into NetWare queues NETPRT01, NETPRT02, and NETPRT03. When mainframe print is sent to the emulators, the print will be redirected for you.

Netport

Netport is a small hardware device developed by Intel which acts as a small Novell print server. Netport can drive up to two printers. Netport has two parallel ports and one serial port, but can drive only two printers. You can connect two parallel printers or one parallel printer and one serial printer. One of Netport's primary advantages is that it can be used in place of a standard Novell print server in areas where a dedicated print server is overkill. Netport is extremely reliable. Once you have it installed and configured, it rarely has problems. One of Netport's disadvantages is that it cannot be used to route host print unless a third-party product, such as LANRES, is used to direct the host print into NetWare print queues.

NetWare-Ready Printers

Many of the major printer manufacturers, including Hewlett-Packard, have developed or are in the process of developing NetWare-ready print devices. A NetWare-ready printer is directly attached to the network and can then accept print jobs from the network. These NetWare-ready printers perform both the print server function and the printer function. This type of configuration can be cost-effective in sites where a full-blown print server would be overkill.

Multiprotocol Print Servers

Many companies are making new strides in the network printing arena. Several of these companies, including Axis Communications (Danvers, Massachusetts), has developed a multiprotocol Token Ring print server that supports TCP/IP, NetWare, LAN Manager, and LAN Server and that has built-in SNA/SDLC support. This is a great improvement in LAN printing, and other vendors are sure to follow suit.

Common Printer Problems

The Capture utility has several problems. The most aggravating problem is the use of the time-out (TI) parameter. You will know if you are experiencing time-out-related problems when print jobs do not get sent to the printer until the user exits the application. If this happens, you must begin tinkering with Capture's time-out parameter. Keep in mind that the time-out parameter specifies the number of seconds that must pass after the application last writes to the print file. There are some applications that write column headers to the print file, then process the data before once again writing to the print file. If the number you specify in the TI parameter is too low, you will get a single page with the column headings, then other pages with the actual data. Graphical print can also have a problem with a time-out value that is set too low. A good starting value is TI=10. To the end-user, the specification of a 10-second time-out will appear as if the print is slow to start.

Under OS/2 there is also a time-out parameter for the LPTx port. The OS/2 time-out parameter performs a totally different type of function than the Capture time-out parameter. The OS/2 time-out is the number of seconds that the PC retries a print job before changing the print job to an error status.

Many sites configure their NetWare servers with a relatively small SYS: volume and a large VOL1: volume. By default, all NetWare print queues are placed on the SYS: volume. Large volumes of print can cause the SYS: volume to fill up. Infinite Technologies developed a program called CREATEQ which allows the user to create Novell print queues on volumes other than SYS:. The software can be downloaded and used free of charge from the NOVVEN CompuServe forum.

DOS applications running in OS/2 DOS sessions, such as WordPerfect and some Clipper applications, require the loading of a special driver in order to use the CAPTURE command. The symptoms of this missing driver are print screens that are successfully captured and routed while DOS application print seems to disappear. To correct this problem, enter the following statement in your OS/2 CONFIG.SYS file:

```
DEVICE=C:\OS2\MDOS\LPTDD.SYS
```

Some DOS applications running under OS/2 require access to the LPTx port during their initialization process. These programs will not function if the share-access option is not set in the printer object. To set the share-access option, do as follows:

- Open the setting on the printer object by moving the cursor to the Printer icon and clicking the right mouse button once.
- Click on the arrow by the Open entry, then click on Settings.
- Go to the Output page in the settings.
- Double-click on the LPTx port that is active (the one with the hash marks).
- Click on the Share-Access box.
- Close the printer settings window.

Some applications write a form template to the memory of a laser printer. Using printer commands, the application then sends data to the printer, using the form stored in memory. These types of applications do not lend themselves to printing through a network.

A user on a network may have access to many different types of printers which are network-attached. Using products such as WordPerfect requires that the user select the print driver to match the printer being used. Many times the user will select the wrong print driver for the printer receiving the print. The selection of the wrong print driver can cause very strange results to be printed at the printer.

When RPRINTER is restarted immediately after a system crash or system reboot, it does not always reconnect. The problem is caused because the print server has not realized that the previously running RPRINTER terminated. The print server will time the old RPRINTER session out after a couple of minutes. The new RPRINTER session cannot be established until the time-out occurs.

The printer's printing an extra sheet of paper is a problem that nags at many network administrators. Many factors can cause this. First, if you are using the CAPTURE command, make sure that NFF (no form feed) is specified on the command that invokes the Capture utility. Next the software generating the print should be checked.

When the Print Screen key is pressed from a CM/2 3270 screen, a graphical image is sent to the printer. This graphical image looks terrible. The character print screen is invoked by pressing ALT-Print Screen. The image from this key combination will look like a standard 3270 print screen. The CM/2 keyboard configuration utility can be used to remap the Print Screen key to invoke the character print screen function, reducing the complexity of the system to the end-users.

Conclusion

Using the services of the NetWare operating system to route print throughout a multiprotocol network can be a great benefit to a network administrator. We can capture data from any system on the network and route them anywhere within the local- or wide-area network by using the services of NetWare. Better yet, we do not have to worry about the mechanics of making a PC printer print mainframe-printed output. We let NetWare handle that for us. We also saw that printer vendors are beginning to see the light. These vendors are developing printers that will support multiple print data streams from a multiprotocol network. This type of printer promises to further simplify the job of the network administrator.

Part

4

DEC Connectivity

Showing you how to access the DEC/VAX machine from an OS/2 workstation is the goal of this part of the book. We will take a look at providing VT220 terminal emulation, using the IPX protocol as our transport mechanism.

We will then look at how DEC print can be routed throughout the network by using the NetWare printing components.

We will close with a look at the support options available for OS/2, CM/2, and NetWare. Some of these options can be very expensive, while others are relatively cost-effective.

Chapter

16

DEC VT220 Emulation

In the past, organizations that utilized both a DEC/VAX and an IBM mainframe would keep these two systems completely separate. Each system would use its own network to drive its own terminals and printers. An end-user who needed access to both systems would have both a mainframe terminal and a DEC terminal placed on the desk. Even when local-area networks began infiltrating corporate America, the DEC was often still left completely isolated on its own separate network. The goal of this book is to show you how to incorporate different systems, such as the DEC and the mainframe, so that a single workstation and printer can be used to access each of them. This universal workstation and printer can stop the implementation of multiple terminals at the end-user's desk and can also allow you to consolidate all your network traffic on one cabling system.

OS/2 DEC Connectivity Services

Providing connectivity to a DEC/VAX machine by using the services of OS/2 and CM/2 requires the use of the CM/2 Asynchronous Communication Device Interface (ACDI). The ACDI uses the asynchronous ports on the PC to provide communications. The ACDI can be redirected to an IBM Local-Area Network Asynchronous Communications Server (LANACS). LANACS allows you to share asynchronous resources between the workstations on your LAN.

There are alternatives to using ACDI or LANACS for DEC connectivity. One of the best options is the Terminal Emulation Services (TES) product from InterConnections.

Terminal Emulation Services

TES provides asynchronous DEC connections to workstations on Novell LANs. TES uses the services of IPX to route DEC traffic throughout the network. Using TES along with terminal emulation software allows the users on a Novell LAN (DOS, OS/2, or Windows workstations) to log in to DEC/VAX systems. The TES system is composed of two software components, the server software and the client software.

The TES server software runs on the VAX and coordinates the communications between the clients and VMS. The server software converts the DEC on-line screens to IPX packets. These packets are then directed to the LAN and are received by the client software. The TES server software requires that VMS version 5.0 or above be installed on the VAX. A DEC Ethernet controller must also be installed on the VAX.

The client software is a terminate-and-stay-resident (TSR) program that intercepts the serial port services of the client workstation and redirects them over the LAN. The client TSR program can be run from an OS/2 DOS full-screen session or a DOS window session.

TES Software

The TES workstation must also run a terminal emulation software package to emulate the VTxx DEC terminal. InterConnections packages Kermit with the TES product for terminal emulation.

TES Network Configuration Requirements

TES uses the Ethernet protocol and supports both the NetWare 802.3 and Ethernet type II protocols. InterConnections recommends that the network be configured for the 802.3 protocol rather than Ethernet type II. Future enhancements are expected to be made only to the 802.3 protocol.

DEC to LAN: The Physical Connection

Before you can use TES to connect to your DEC/VAX system, a physical connection between the DEC and your Novell network must be established. The manner in which this connection is made depends upon the type of topology you are using.

DEC/VAX systems use Ethernet to communicate between the DEC machine and its terminals. If your Novell network uses the same Ethernet network as your DEC, you are already home free. The physical connection is already there.

If your Novell network is running on a separate Ethernet network from your DEC, you can bridge these two networks together.

If you are using Ethernet wiring concentrators, you can simply connect your DEC up to the concentrator. This type of connection simply adds the DEC segment to your existing Novell Ethernet segment.

You can use the TES product on a Token Ring network if you implement a bridge or router, which supports IPX, between the Ethernet and Token Ring networks, as illustrated in Fig. 16.1. The Novell internal bridge program (which is actually a router) can be used to pass TES data between Ethernet and Token Ring.

Installing the TES Server Software

The TES server software is installed on the DEC by using the VMSINSTAL utility. You will be prompted for such items as the TES directory name, Ethernet controller type, Ethernet device type, and protocol to be used (either 802.3 or Ethernet type II). For most installations, the default values may be selected during the installation. There are two options that require special attention, the Ethernet protocol and the network address.

Ethernet protocol

The standard protocol used by NetWare is 802.3. If you do not have any earlier version of InterConnections VMS/NetWare products, you should choose 802.3 for the protocol. Earlier versions of InterConnections software require the use of the Ethernet type II protocol.

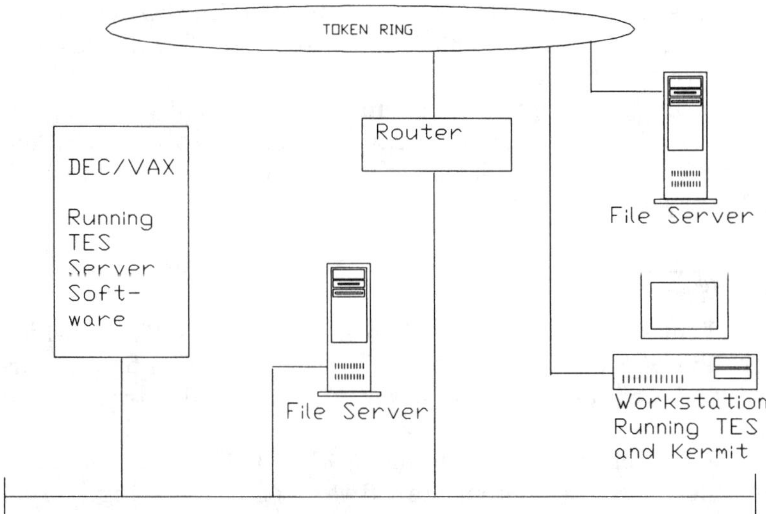

Figure 16.1 TES sample network configuration.

```
System AUTOEXEC File

file server name ETSERVER
ipx internal net 10001990
load NE2 slot=5 frame=ETHERNET_802.3
bind ipx to NE2 net=10000001
load monitor
```

Figure 16.2 Finding the physical network address.

You must also check your NetWare server(s) to make sure they support the protocol you select. To check the protocols in use on your NetWare server, use the SYSCON utility to edit the AUTOEXEC.NCF file. You should see a screen that resembles Fig. 16.2. Notice the load of the NE2 Ethernet adapter in Fig. 16.2. The frame type supported in this example is 802.3.

Network address

The network address you specify during the TES server software installation must match the IPX physical network address specified in the Novell file server's AUTOEXEC.NCF file. Notice the bind statement in Fig. 16.2. The net=10000001 parameter specifies the physical network address of the Ethernet segment.

TES will operate even if you have a router installed at your site and you use the router to tie multiple Ethernet networks together. You should specify the network address of the Ethernet network to which the DEC is physically connected.

Using the TES Client Software

The TES client software consists of several layers of software which run under the DOS operating system. This software, if configured correctly, will work under OS/2 DOS boxes. Figure 16.3 illustrates these layers of software.

To use the TES client software from an OS/2 DOS box, you must create a BAT file to load the appropriate software components. Figure 16.4 illustrates a sample BAT file to load the TES client software. To execute the BAT file, the user simply opens an OS/2 DOS session and then

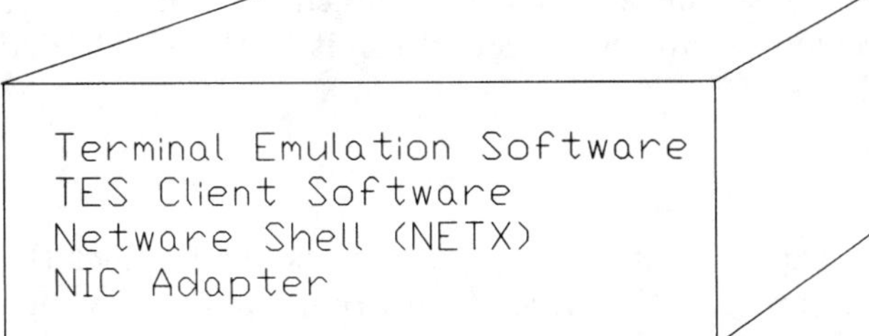

Figure 16.3 TES client software components.

```
@ECHO OFF
PATH
C:\OS2;C:\OS2\MDOS;C:\OS2\MDOS\WINOS2;C:\;C:\NETWARE;
LOADHIGH APPEND C:\OS2;C:\OS2\SYSTEM;C:\NETWARE;
C:
NETX
CD\TESKERMT
TES PORT LABA
KERMIT SETUP
TES U
EXIT
```

Figure 16.4 BAT file to load the TES software on the client node.

enters the name of the BAT file. You can set up a special icon for your users which issues the BAT file when the user double-clicks on the icon. The BAT file performs the following functions:

- Sets the DOS path
- Loads NetWare shell (NETX)
- Changes to the directory where TES and Kermit reside
- Loads TES
- Loads Kermit

After TES and Kermit are loaded, you should see your DEC/VAX sign-on screen. When the user signs off the DEC, the ALT-X key combination is pressed to exit Kermit and return control to the BAT file. The TES U line in the BAT file unloads Kermit, and the exit statement closes the DOS session.

InterConnections does not officially support the use of OS/2 DOS boxes for the TES product. They will provide support if a problem arises that can be recreated on a native DOS machine. I have never experienced any problems running TES or Kermit in the OS/2 DOS compatibility boxes.

Kermit keyboard remapping

Kermit provides the capability to remap your keyboard to meet the needs of your particular application. A keyboard-remapping file, which is included with the Kermit product, sets the keyboard up to look like a VT200 or VT300 LK201 keyboard. A partial listing of the VT300.INI keyboard-remapping file is shown in Fig. 16.5. Notice the second "set

```
; Automatic keyboard test
;
:kbtest
if equal "\v(keyboard)" "88" goto kb88
if equal "\v(keyboard)" "101" goto kb101
echo Keyboard type "\v(keyboard)" not supported by
VT300.INI.
pop

:kb101
echo VT300.INI: IBM-101 Extended Keyboard Setup...
;
; *********** IBM-101 Extended Keyboard Definitions
;                       IBM KEY          DEC KEY
set key \319 \kbreak            ; F5        Break
set key \320 \Kdecf6            ; F6        DEC F6
set key \321 \Kdecf7            ; F7        DEC F7
set key \322 \KdecF8            ; F8        DEC F8
set key \323 \KdecF9            ; F9        DEC F9
set key \324 \KdecF10           ; F10       DEC F10
set key \389 \kdecF11           ; F11       DEC F11
set key \390 \kdecdo            ; F12       DEC Do
set key \2408 \kdecF11          ; Alt-F1    F11
set key \2409 \kdecF12          ; Alt-F2    F12
set key \2410 \kdecF13          ; Alt-F3    F13
set key \2411 \kdecF14          ; Alt-F4    F14
set key \2412 \kdechelp         ; Alt-F5    Help (F15)
set key \2413 \kdecdo           ; Alt-F6    Do (F16)
set key \2414 \kdecF17          ; Alt-F7    F17
set key \2415 \kdecF18          ; Alt-F8    F18
set key \2416 \kdecF19          ; Alt-F9    F19
set key \2417 \kdecF20          ; Alt-F10   F20
```

Figure 16.5 TES keyboard definition file.

key" statement. The scan code for the F6 key is 320. The set key command remaps the F6 key to the DEC F6 function.

Conclusion

Most local-area networks are not composed of only OS/2 workstations. Most network designers and administrators are required to support OS/2, DOS, and Windows clients. The information we presented in this chapter allows you to implement one solution for DEC/VAX connectivity for all these PC operating system platforms. The Terminal Emulation Services product is very reliable and robust. It uses the services of Novell's IPX protocol to route DEC traffic through the local-area network. Since the IPX protocol is routable, you are given a great deal of flexibility in designing both local- and wide-area networks.

Chapter

17

DEC Print Support

We have discussed implementing the global workstation, where one workstation can be used to access multiple systems regardless of their hardware or software platform. To establish the universal workstation, we used the facilities of OS/2, CM/2, NTS/2, and TES. Your users need not only a universal workstation but also a universal printer. This universal printer should be able to print data from all the different platforms on your network.

Providing printer support is always more difficult than providing terminal emulation. Typically there are more hardware and software components involved in the printing systems, and there are so many PC printer models on the market that it is mind-boggling. Providing printer support from multiple disparate systems to the wide range of PC printer types can be rather difficult.

Routing print from multiple platforms throughout a network is a formidable goal. Each hardware and software platform handles print a little differently. So we need to find a common denominator, between these disparate systems, to perform the print routing for us. This common denominator is NetWare.

The NetWare print system is well suited for routing print from various platforms. The NetWare print system also supports myriad common PC printers. Once we get the print data into NetWare, we can route them anywhere we want through the entire network and print them on just about any type of printer. As new PC printer models are developed, we can use the NetWare print system to provide support for us. This alone can help reduce the number and force of the network administrator's headaches.

The trick to implementing the universal printer lies in getting the print from these platforms into NetWare. Once we have the data from the print-creating system in a NetWare print queue, we can simply let the NetWare printing system take over. In this chapter, we will concentrate on a method to route DEC print from the DEC system into a NetWare print queue.

Network Print Services

Network Print Services (NPS) is a product from InterConnections, Inc. The DEC/VAX machines utilize the VMS operating system. See Fig. 17.1. VMS provides a printing subsystem which is very similar to the NetWare printing subsystem. Under VMS, print queues are built and print data streams are directed into these print queues. NPS runs on the DEC/VAX and intercepts the print jobs that are destined to specific VMS print queues. NPS then reroutes these print jobs directly into NetWare print queues. To VMS, NPS looks like a print driver and is completely transparent.

NPS uses the IPX protocol to send the print jobs to Novell. IPX is Novell's primary protocol. Since NPS uses IPX, the complexity of the print routing is greatly reduced. The use of IPX also reduces the complexity of your entire network design. The fewer protocols you have to support on your network, the fewer occasions there are for things to get fouled up. Simplicity breeds success.

DEC to LAN: The Physical Connection

Before you can use NPS to route your VMS print into NetWare print queues, a physical connection between the DEC and your Novell net-

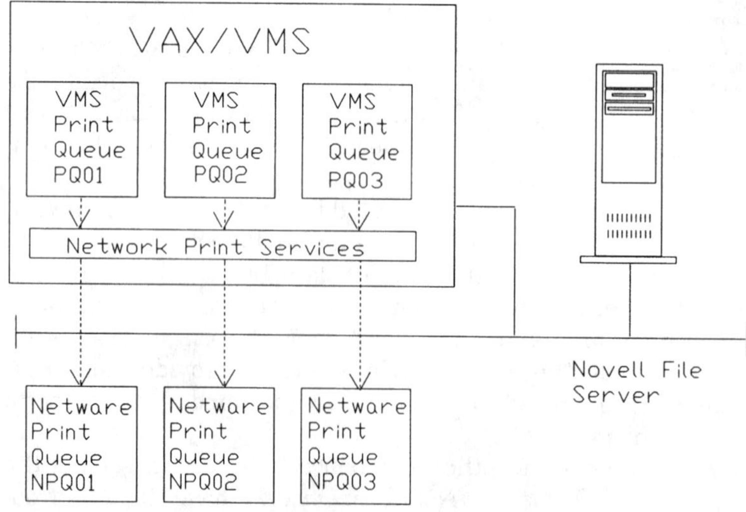

Figure 17.1 DEC network print service.

work must be established. The manner in which this connection is made depends upon the type of topology you are using.

DEC/VAX systems use Ethernet to communicate between the DEC and its terminals. If your Novell network uses the same Ethernet network as your DEC, you are home free. The physical connection is already there.

If your Novell network is running on a separate Ethernet network from your DEC, you can bridge these two networks together.

If you are using Ethernet wiring concentrators, you can simply connect your DEC up to the concentrator. This type of connection simply adds the DEC segment to your existing Novell Ethernet segment.

If your Novell system is running on a Token Ring, you must implement a router to connect the Token Ring to the DEC Ethernet segment in order to make the physical connection between the DEC and your Novell network. Refer to Fig. 17.2 for a sample Token Ring configuration.

Installing NPS

Installing NPS on the DEC/VAX is a simple process. The product is installed by using the standard DEC VMSINSTALL process. During the installation process you will be prompted for several pieces of information, including:

- The name of the directory to hold the NPS programs and configuration files. You can choose the default, and a new directory will be created for you.

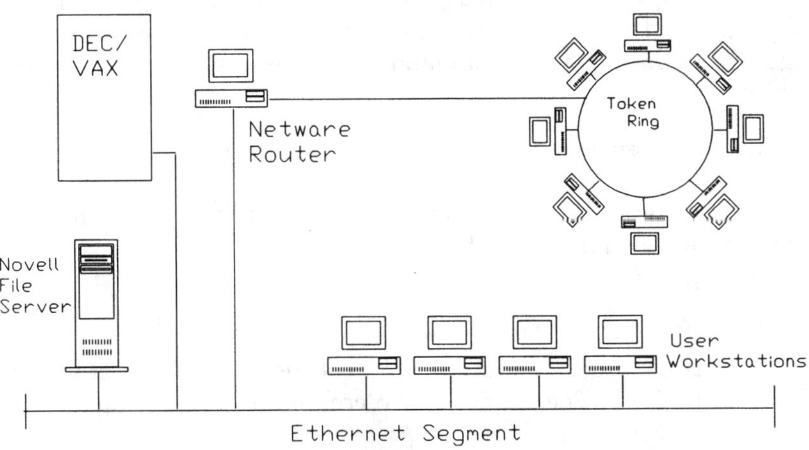

Figure 17.2 Using NPS to route print from Ethernet to Token Ring.

- The network number of your Novell Ethernet segment. This number is defined in the NetWare AUTOEXEC.NCF file on the Novell file server.
- The Ethernet protocol that you wish to use. The choices are 802.3 and Ethernet II.

Configuring NPS

Once you have NPS installed, it is time to customize the product. During the customization process, you tell NPS which VMS queues it is to control. Next you tell NPS the name of the NetWare print queues to which the VMS print is to be routed. Each VMS print queue can be routed to a corresponding NetWare queue, or multiple VMS queues can be routed to a single NetWare print queue.

Once you have NPS installed, place the NPS start-up command into the VMS system start-up file. This will cause NPS to be automatically started each time the DEC is rebooted. The instructions for this modification are detailed in the NPS manual.

NetWare modifications for NPS

A special user ID must be created on the NetWare file server for NPS's use. By default the name of the user ID is VMSPRINT. The only authority required for the VMSPRINT user ID is that it have access to the required Novell print queues.

Setting up VMS print queues

Initializing the VMS print queues, which are to be under the control of NPS, is performed in the same manner as for any other VMS print queue. The following VMS command can be used to initialize a VMS print queue:

```
$ INITIALIZE/QUEUE name DEFAULT=(NOBURST,NOFLAG,NOTRAIL,NOFEED)
```

Do not start the queue after you create it. NPS will start the VMS queue for you when it first comes up.

Setting up NetWare print queues

There is nothing special about the setup of the NetWare print queues to be used by NPS. These queues are created by using the NetWare PCONSOLE utility.

NetWare Print Routing

Once NPS places the DEC print into the specified NetWare print queues, you can use the facilities of NetWare to route the print anywhere you wish throughout the network. The print can be routed to any Novell print server you wish, including print servers attached to other file servers.

You can also use the NetWare Remote Printer (RPRINTER) or the new NetWare Network Printer (NPRINTER) to route the VMS print to printers attached directly to a user's workstation.

Refer to Chap. 15 for more information on setting up NetWare print services and the use of RPRINTER and NPRINTER.

Troubleshooting NPS

NPS provides several utility commands to help troubleshoot printing problems. Once you have NPS properly configured, you will rarely need these commands. NPS is a very stable printing system. The following NPS commands are available for troubleshooting:

SHOW STATUS	This command shows you whether NPS is running on the DEC/VAX.
SHOW CONNECTIONS	This command shows you the status of your connection to Novell.
SHOW SERVER	This command allows you to determine if the NetWare server exists.

As with any other system, you should approach troubleshooting in a methodical manner. Start at the top and work your way down. First you must determine whether NPS is active or not. You can use the SHOW STATUS command for this.

Next you must determine where the print is stopping. Remember that NPS takes the print from the VMS print queue and reroutes it to the appropriate Novell queue. You must look at the VMS print queue to determine whether the print gets that far. If the print is not in the VMS print queue, then either the job creating the print malfunctioned or the print was successfully rerouted to the Novell queue.

If there is print in the VMS print queue but it never makes it out of there, you should check the following items:

- Is the network number you specified in the NPS installation correct? This number must match the network number specified in the AUTOEXEC.NCF file on your Novell file server.
- Is the protocol you specified in the NPS installation correct?

- Was the NetWare VMSPRINT user ID properly configured?
- Was the Novell print queue created properly? To test this, route some print to the Novell print queue from a networked PC, using the Novell NPRINT command. A sample NPRINT command follows:

```
NPRINT C:\NET.CFG S=SERVER1 Q=NWQUEUE1
```

If all else fails, you can always read the manual or call the InterConnections technical support staff.

Conclusion

NPS is a strong player in the universal printer market. The product uses the native Novell IPX protocol which greatly simplifies the entire network printing mechanism. NPS requires very little overhead on both the DEC and Novell machines. The product is also extremely reliable. The concept of using NetWare as the print routing engine also reduces the complexity of the entire network. You can rely on the facilities of NetWare for all of your local and remote print routing.

Chapter

18

OS/2, CM/2, and Novell Support Avenues

There are several support channels available to you when you need technical assistance with the OS/2, CM/2, or Novell products. Some of these support options are free of charge, while others can be very expensive. It is important to explore each of these options to learn where you can find the best support for your situation. There is nothing more aggravating than having a major problem with your network and having your support avenues pass the buck to other vendors. Some of the support options listed in this chapter have expertise in a wide range of hardware and software issues.

OS/2 and CM/2 Support

Let's start with OS/2 and CM/2 support. There are three support channels supplied by IBM for OS/2 and CM/2 support: the IBM support center, the IBMLink online database, and the CompuServe OS/2 support forums. The type of support you can receive differs widely between the three support center options.

The IBM support center

The IBM support center provides voice support and can be reached by calling (800) 237–5511. If your site has purchased mainframe software, this support is free of charge for OS/2 and CM/2 products. If you purchased NetWare from IBM (in the blue box), you can also use the IBM support center for NetWare-related problems and issues. The support center also supports all the software sold by IBM. This includes mainframe operating systems and products, minicomputer operating system software such OS/400 and AIX, and their PC line of software.

When you call the toll-free number, the person who answers the telephone will ask you for your customer number and the component and operating system for which you are asking support. If you do not have an IBM customer number, tell the person who answers the telephone that you need OS/2 support. Officially, you only have 60 days of free support from the IBM support center when you purchase OS/2. However, I have never had them turn me down when I requested support for OS/2.

The IBM support center can help you with product defects. If you suspect a bug in the OS/2 operating system or CM/2 code, the support center will help you isolate the problem and will send you the corrective fixes.

You should be prepared, before you place the call to IBM. Be ready to provide the complete message number and text associated with the problem you are having. For CM/2-related problems, you should be prepared to provide the symptom codes provided by the FFST/2 utilities.

The first person you talk to at the IBM support center will gather the information you specify and will pass it on to the level 1 support personnel. Sometimes you will be transferred to level 1 support immediately, but most of the time they are busy and will call you back.

When you talk with level 1 support personnel, they will use the messages and symptoms you provide and will search their database of problems. Almost all problems are solved by level 1 support personnel. If level 1 support personnel cannot find the solution to your problem, the problem will be directed to level 2 support.

Level 2 support personnel are usually the developers of the product that you are having problems with. When level 2 support personnel call you, they will probably ask you to provide more information and to run a trace using the FFST/2 utilities.

The IBM support center assigns a priority to the problem calls that are received. Each call is given one of three severity levels. You, the customer, can tell the support center which severity level your problem should be placed in. If you do not specify the severity level of your problem, IBM will do it for you. If you let IBM personnel assign your priority level, they will most likely assign the lowest priority.

Severity level 3 calls are the lowest-priority calls. When your problem is assigned to severity 3 priority, you may be required to wait a couple of days for the level 1 support person to call you back. Severity level 3 is comprised of problems that do not affect the operation of your company's function. Severity 3 calls are generally minor problems.

Severity level 2 priority calls are for problems of a more critical nature to your business. When your problem is assigned to severity level 2 priority, you can expect a call back from the level 1 support person within a few hours.

Severity level 1 is the highest priority level within the IBM support center. You should use discretion when you escalate a problem to severity level 1 priority. Severity level 1 was designed to help customers with problems that are directly impacting their businesses. When you promote a problem to severity level 1, you should (and will) receive very good call-back response times from both support level 1 and support level 2. Be aware, however, that you must do your part to help the IBM support center solve your problem. When the support person asks you for more information, you must be able to provide the information in a timely manner. The IBM support center is a 24-hour operation. If you call in a problem at 5:00 p.m. and assign it to severity level 1, you are expected to have someone available to work with the IBM support person from the time you place the call until the problem is solved. If you do not live up to your end of the bargain by providing the information requested by the support personnel, then IBM will drop the severity of your problem from severity level 1 to a lower level.

Overall, the IBM support center is an outstanding support organization. The experience level of the IBM support personnel varies from person to person, as with any other support organization. Do not worry if you are connected with someone who seems to be a rookie. You are in control with the IBM support center. If you are not satisfied with the solution you are given, you can always escalate the problem. IBM support for OS/2 and CM/2 has improved dramatically since the products were first announced. The IBM support center also has some very strong network technicians on the support center staff. These technicians are knowledgeable in OS/2, CM/2, NetWare, LAN Server, and bridges and routers. If you experience a network-related problem with CM/2 or OS/2, give these folks a call.

IBMLink

When you call the IBM support center, the level 1 support person will scan a database to see if the problem that you are experiencing was reported previously by another customer. If the problem was reported previously and was corrected by the support department, the corrective action is also stored in the database.

IBMLink is an online system that allows you to scan the IBM problem database yourself, without calling the support center. If you are working in a shop that has IBM mainframe hardware or software, an IBMLink account has probably already been established for your site.

The use of IBMLink is a little complicated for the first-time user. You must know which problem libraries to search, and you must know the proper way to enter your search keywords. After signing on to IBMLink, enter SIS to get to the problem search database. Next you must select the OS/2 database by following the on-line menu selections.

Entering the search keywords correctly is the secret to finding the answers to your problem by using IBMLink. If you have a message associated with your problem, enter the characters MSG before the actual message number. For example, if you received message ACS3203, enter MSGACS3203 for your search criteria. You can also enter the symptom data provided in the FFST/2 utilities. These symptom codes should be entered exactly as they are displayed in the utility.

The IBMLink database is used primarily to help resolve defects in the product code. There is some information in IBMLink that can help you find ways to configure the products to meet your specific needs.

There is a wealth of information in the IBMLink database. You can find solutions to OS/2, CM/2, and Novell problems in this database. Connectivity solutions between CM/2 and other hardware and software platforms are also provided in the IBMLink database.

There are different levels of IBMLink access. The lowest level restricts your access to scanning the problem database. The highest level of IBMLink access allows you to also ask questions of the IBM software support personnel.

CompuServe Forums

CompuServe is a worldwide information network. To access the CompuServe system, you must first purchase a starter kit. These kits contain an initial user ID and password, a manual, and usually a $25 credit for CompuServe access. Included in the CompuServe manual is a list of telephone numbers that you can use to dial into the CompuServe network. Most large metropolitan areas have local telephone numbers that can be used without requiring you to pay long-distance tolls.

CompuServe charges you for the time that you are connected to the system. These charges are considerably lower during the weekends and late at night. If you do not live in or near a large metropolitan area, you may be required to call a long-distance number to access the CompuServe system. If this is the case, you will be billed for both the long-distance charges and the CompuServe connect-time charges. CompuServe bills you by charging your monthly connect-time charges to your credit card. You must have a credit card to open a CompuServe account. CompuServe does offer a corporate account. With this type of account, your corporation will be billed each month for the connect charges associated with your user ID.

One of the most widely used offerings of CompuServe is their forums. Forums can be viewed as individual bulletin board systems. Many software vendors maintain CompuServe forums to providc support for their products. The forums have areas where users can ask questions and read questions from other users. Most forums also have areas established for uploading and downloading files.

CompuServe Navigation Programs

If you plan to use CompuServe to access the various support forums, you will quickly see your connect-time charges build up. You cannot access the forums by using the basic flat monthly CompuServe charge option. You must use the hourly connect-time charge method. Investing in one of the CompuServe navigation programs could save you a substantial amount of connect-time charges.

There are several CompuServe navigation products. The two most popular are the CompuServe Information Manager, sold by CompuServe, and TAPCIS, which is sold by Support Group, Inc. The functionality of these two products varies greatly, and the connect-time savings vary as well.

The CompuServe Information Manager

The CompuServe Information Manager (CIM) provides a menu system to access the various CompuServe resources. Native CompuServe commands are cryptic, and a menu system such as CIM can save the novice user hours of connect-time charges. There are also certain CompuServe applications that take advantage of the graphical interface provided by CIM.

TAPCIS

TAPCIS is a CompuServe navigation program that was designed to minimize the amount of on-line connect time used. TAPCIS has the following advantages over CIM:

- Composing forum messages is performed off line and is then posted to the forum after the entire message has been written.
- New forum messages are retrieved from CompuServe and placed on your hard drive. You can then read through the messages off line without accruing connect charges.
- CompuServe E-Mail is retrieved and placed on your hard drive where it can be read off line.

TAPCIS can be obtained for a 21-day evaluation by calling 1-800-USA-GROUP. There is a $79 charge for TAPCIS if you decide to purchase the product.

OS/2 and CM/2 CompuServe Support

IBM provides several CompuServe forums for OS/2 and CM/2 support. There is no charge for the CompuServe forums other than the CompuServe connect charges. Using these forums, you can read other people's problems and questions and can ask your own questions. The questions asked in these forums are answered by both IBM personnel and other users of the OS/2 products. The IBM CompuServe forums are perhaps the best place to obtain OS/2- and CM/2-related support. There is almost always someone out there who can help you and who has faced the same problems that you are facing.

There are three major OS/2 and CM/2 CompuServe forums: OS2SUPPORT, OS2DF1, and OS2DF2.

OS2SUPPORT forum

The OS2SUPPORT forum is designed to provide support for the OS/2 operating system. Configuration questions and problem resolution for the base operating system are dealt with here. This forum covers a wide variety of OS/2 topics. Issues such as hardware compatibility and installation-type questions are covered. Most of the information in this forum is directed toward the first-time OS/2 user.

OS2DF1 forum

The OS2DF1 forum was designed for OS/2 developers. Questions about the internals of the operating system are discussed here. Do not worry if you are not a developer; go ahead and take a look at this forum. There is a wealth of information in here.

OS2DF2 forum

The OS2DF2 forum was designed for developers and advanced users of the OS/2 and CM/2. This forum focuses primarily on connectivity issues. This forum is where you should be if you have questions about configuring and using CM/2. The IBM staff who support this forum are some of the best technicians on staff. Some types of issues handled in this forum include

- Coexistence with CM/2 and Novell
- CM/2 and TCP/IP

- CM/2 and LAN Manager coexistence
- NIC driver availability
- WIN-OS2 connectivity problems
- EHLLAPI questions

Novell Support Avenues

Novell support was designed a little differently from IBM support. There are four avenues for Novell support:

- Novell CompuServe forums
- Novell direct support
- Software dealer support
- Third-party support lines

Novell CompuServe forums

Novell provides several CompuServe forums for you to obtain Novell-related support. There is no charge for this support other than the normal CompuServe connect charges. There are numerous Novell CompuServe forums, but only one deals with connectivity issues. This forum is NOVC.

The NOVC forum is just like any other CompuServe forum. Questions are answered by both Novell personnel and other users who have experienced similar problems. You have to be persistent in the Novell forums. Many times I have asked questions and received no response. As they say, the squeaky wheel gets greased. Just keep right on asking until you get an answer.

The NOVC forum is also a great place to get ideas on new ways to utilize your network. Many of the people who participate in the forum are on the leading edge of the networking industry. At times, you will gain insight on new ideas and new technologies that can be very beneficial to your organization.

Novell direct support

You can call Novell directly for support. You will be charged $150 per call for this support option. You must pay by credit card at the time of the call. I have only used this support avenue one time, and that was only because I was facing a major problem. Before I called, I wrote down every question I ever wanted to ask a Novell technician and fired them all off when I placed the call. If you're going to pay $150, you might as well try to get your money's worth. The Novell technicians on this support line are very professional and knowledgeable. You *will* get your problem solved when you call Novell directly.

Software dealer support

Most Novell resellers can call Novell directly for a reduced charge or no charge at all. It is a good idea to get to know your reseller and use this free support avenue before investing in the more expensive options.

Third-party support lines

Due to the exorbitant fees charged for Novell direct support, many third-party Novell support lines have been established. These organizations have Novell certified NetWare engineers (CNEs) on staff who will try to answer your questions. If they do not know the answer, they will contact Novell on your behalf. The charges for these third-party support lines vary, but all will be less than Novell direct support. The third-party organizations advertise in the PC and communications trade magazines.

Conclusion

You should get to know each of these support options. By learning what types of information can be found in each of the different support avenues, you will be able to solve your problems much more quickly. If you do not already have a CompuServe account, pick one up; or better yet, open a corporate account.

The information you receive from these avenues not only will help you solve your networking problems, but also will give you ideas of ways to better utilize your existing hardware and software resources.

Appendix

A

OS/2 and CM/2 Utility Programs

The OS/2 operating system and the Communications Manager/2 product provide some very useful utilities that can enhance the productivity of the network administrator and the network's end-users. In this chapter we will explore some of these utility programs and how they can be used to solve some of your day-to-day problems.

Keyboard Utilities

CM/2 provides several utility programs that allow you to view your keyboard layout and to remap the keys on your keyboard. To view your current keyboard mapping, do the following:

- Go into one of your 3270 terminal emulation sessions.
- Move the cursor to the upper left-hand corner of the emulator, and click the left button.
- Select Emulator operations.
- Select Display keyboard.

The panel illustrated in Fig. A.1 will be displayed on your screen. You can move the mouse cursor around and select the different keys that are displayed. In Fig. A.1 the ESC key was selected. The pop-up box shows you how the particular key is mapped and what functions are executed when the key is pressed with the ALT, ESC, and Shift keys.

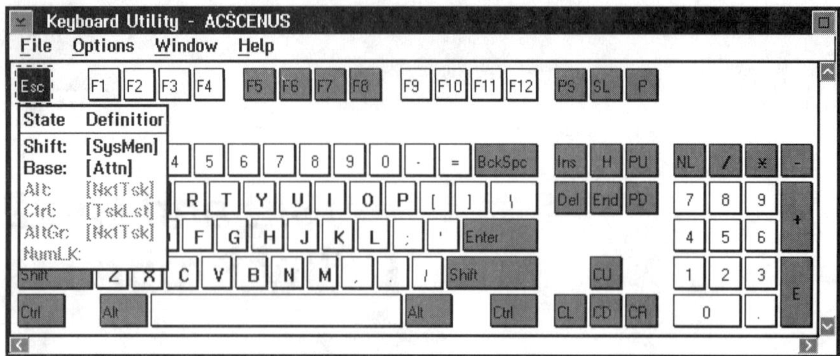

Figure A.1 CM/2 keyboard mapping utility. [*Reprinted by permission from IBM's OS/2 2.0, Copyright (1988, 1992) International Business Machines Corporation.*]

CM/2 also provides a utility that allows you to remap your keyboard. To perform the keyboard remapping, do the following:

- Go into one of your 3270 terminal emulation sessions.
- Move the cursor to the upper left-hand corner of the emulator, and click the left button.
- Select Emulator operations.
- Select Remap keyboard. A panel resembling Fig. A.1 will be displayed.
- Click on the key that you wish to remap. The key will be highlighted.
- Click on File, then click on Open key. The panel illustrated in Fig. A.2 will be displayed. Figure A.1 shows you that the F10 key issues the F22 function when pressed with the Shift key. When the F10 key is pressed by itself (BASE), the F10 function is invoked. When F10 is

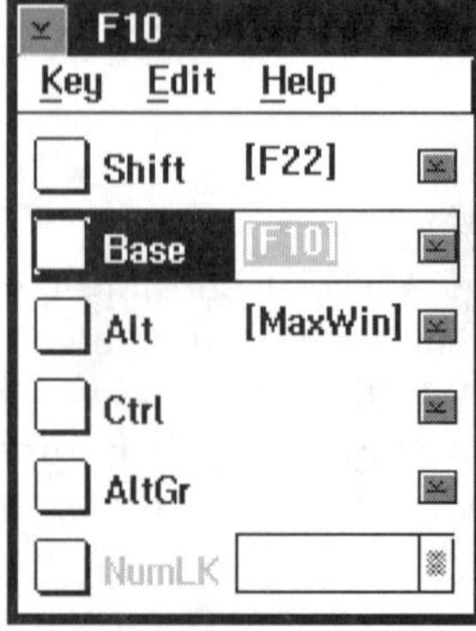

Figure A.2 Selecting a key to modify. [*Reprinted by permission from IBM's OS/2 2.0, Copyright (1988, 1992) International Business Machines Corporation.*]

pressed in conjunction with the ALT key, the MAXWIN function is invoked.

- You can key in the value that you wish the key to have in its various states by moving the cursor to the appropriate position and keying in the value.
- You can also use the pull-down selection beside each of the states to select a function from the available list.
- To save the key remapping, close the window that is illustrated in Fig. A.1. When you close the window, you will be prompted about whether you wish to save or cancel the changes.

The OS/2 Enhanced Editor

OS/2 provides two editors with the base operating system. One of these editors, Enhanced Editor, has special functions available for CM/2 users. Enhanced Editor allows a CM/2 user who has mainframe connectivity to a host with ISPF to edit mainframe datasets from within the editor. To accomplish this task, do the following:

- Log on to TSO from one of the 3270 emulators. Go to either ISPF option 6 or the TSO ready prompt. Make a mental note as to the 3270 session letter that you are using.
- Open the OS/2 system folder by double-clicking on the OS/2 system icon.
- Open the productivity folder by double-clicking on it.
- Double-click on the Enhanced Editor icon to start the utility.
- Click on File, then click on Open.
- Enter the following command in the Open Pop-up Dialog box, as illustrated in Fig. A.3:

  ```
  Hx:`data.set.name(member)'
  ```

  where x is the 3270 session letter that is waiting in ISPF option 6 or the TSO ready prompt.
- Click on OK.
- Behind the scenes, Enhanced Editor will perform a download from the TSO session to your editor session. Figure A.4 illustrates the results of a successful download.
- You can use all the features of Enhanced Editor to modify the host data set.

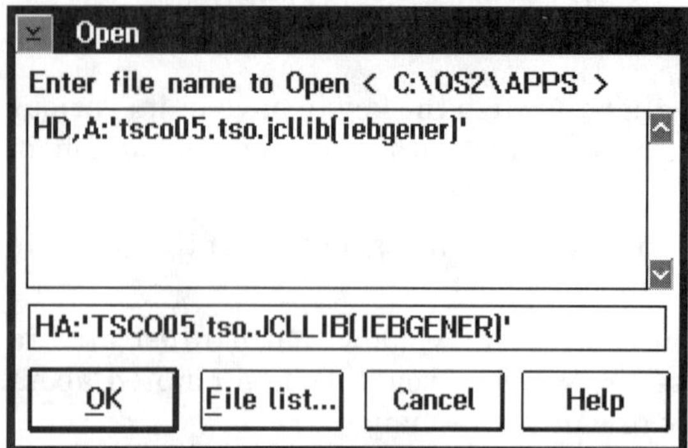

Figure A.3 Preparing to edit a host file by using the Enhanced Editor.

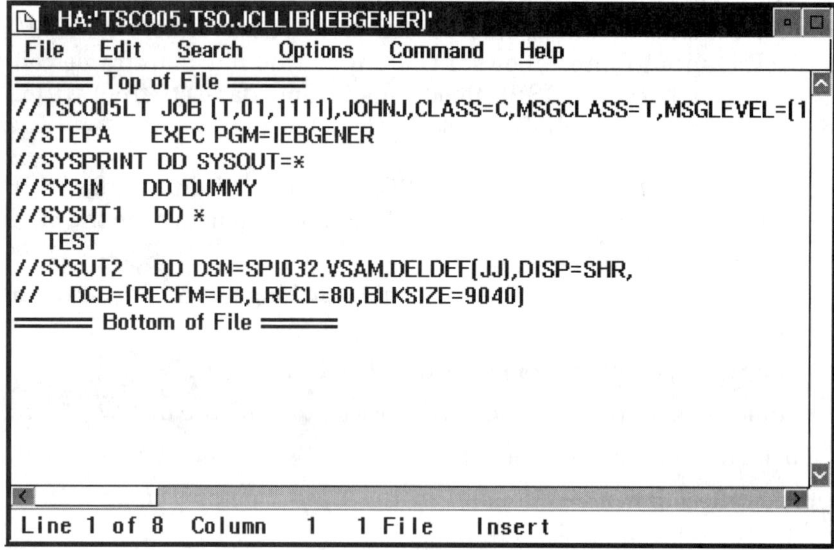

Figure A.4 Editing a host file via the Enhanced Editor.

- When you complete the editing process and wish to save the data set on the mainframe, click on File, then click on Save.
- Enhanced Editor will upload the modified file back to the mainframe. Notice also that Enhanced Editor performs all the ASCII-to-EBCDIC conversions for us.

Enhanced Editor has many more features available to you. Among other things, it can be used to modify files residing on a VM system.

Take your time and learn the functions of Enhanced Editor. The results are well worth the effort.

TSO File Transfer

You can use the services of CM/2 to transfer data from TSO to the local drive of the workstation. To receive a file from the host, perform the following steps:

Step 1 Open an OS/2 full-screen session.

Step 2 Enter TSO from one of the 3270 emulators.

Step 3 Go to either the TSO ready prompt or option 6 in ISPF.

Step 4 Enter the following command:

```
RECEIVE C:\dir\filen.ame a:dataset(member)
```

where dir = directory where you wish to place downloaded data
filen.ame = name of PC file that will contain downloaded data from TSO
a: = host session letter from which you are performing the download
dataset = data set name that is to be downloaded (quote marks not required)
member = member name if the data you are downloading reside in a partitioned data set (PDS) on the mainframe

You can also send data from your PC to the host, using the following procedure:

Step 1 Open an OS/2 full-screen session.

Step 2 Enter TSO from one of the 3270 emulators.

Step 3 Go to either the TSO ready prompt or option 6 in ISPF.

Step 4 Enter the following command:

```
SEND C:\dir\filen.ame a:dataset(member)
```

where dir = directory where data reside that is to be uploaded to mainframe
filen.ame = name of PC file that will be uploaded to mainframe
a: = host session letter from which you are performing the upload
dataset = data set name on the mainframe to where the data are to be uploaded
member = member name if you are uploading the data to a partitioned data set on mainframe

The send and receive commands can also be used to transfer data between an OS/2 workstation and a VM host or between an OS/2 workstation and a CICS mainframe session.

CM/2 Productivity Aids

When you purchase CM/2, you are given a diskette containing several productivity aids. These programs can help make your CM/2 workstation more robust and easier to use. Some of these productivity aids are actual working utility programs, while others are nonworking demonstration programs that give you a look at some of the third-party programs on the market today. We will focus primarily on the actual working utilities in this chapter.

CMMOUSE

CMMOUSE is a productivity aid included with CM/2. CMMOUSE allows you to custom-program the mouse buttons for mainframe use. CMMOUSE uses the EHLLAPI interface to communicate to the CM/2 3270 emulator sessions. All the mouse functions can be programmed to issue any command that you desire. The mouse functions that can be programmed are a single click on the left button, a single click on the right button, a double click on the left button, a double click on the right button, the left + right button click, and the right + left button click.

CMMOUSE uses a configuration file known as the button definition file (BDF). Figure A.5 illustrates a simple CMMOUSE BDF. Notice that the left mouse button is programmed to perform the SEEK function and then the CRSEL function. This is used to simulate the 3270 light-pen function. The SEEK command tells CMMOUSE to move the mainframe cursor to the position where the mouse cursor is found. The CRSEL function initiates the 3270 cursor select feature.

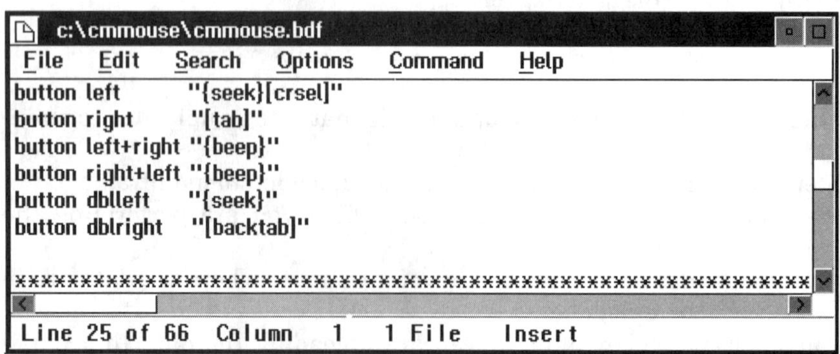

Figure A.5 Customizing the CMMOUSE buttons.

One of the added features of CMMOUSE is its ability to detect the type of host application that the user is in, and this can be programmed specifically for that application. CMMOUSE uses the EHLLAPI interface to look for certain character strings within the 3270 display area. If a match is found, the mouse buttons are reprogrammed accordingly. The character strings that are searched for are completely user-programmable. This allows you to use the CMMOUSE product for any custom applications. For example, a user could be using the mainframe ISPF utility. The mouse buttons can be programmed specifically for that application. For instance, the left button could be programmed to issue the ISPF END command while the right button could be programmed to issue the ISPF PAGE UP command. When the user switches to another application such as SDSF, a whole new set of mouse functions could be enabled, such as the left button issuing the SDSF DA command.

One common use for CMMOUSE is to emulate the light-pen function for CICS applications. This is accomplished by programming CMMOUSE to perform the cursor select function when either the left or right mouse button is pressed, as illustrated in Fig. A.5. CMMOUSE can be customized to meet any and all of your host or mouse requirements.

MOUSE3270

MOUSE3270 is another mouse utility that is provided with CM/2.

TOGGLE

TOGGLE is a productivity aid that allows you to quickly toggle between Communications Manager 3270 sessions. The user can use a single hot key to switch between the 3270 terminal emulation screens defined in his or her CM/2 host connectivity.

3270PDT—host print control via PDTS

This allows control over 3270 host printing to a PC printer.

CMWAIT

This is a utility that waits for Communications Manager/2 to complete its start-up processing.

NNLINK

This program keeps the APPN network node link active.

PD—Communications Manager/2 problem determination aids

This set of programs provides additional CM/2 problem determination. These utilities can be used in conjunction with the FFST/2 utilities.

SOFTTERM

This ASCII terminal emulation program can emulate a DEC VT320, VT220, VT100, VT52, IBM3101, and several other ASCII terminals. SOFTTERM can be used to dial into bulletin board services such as CompuServe.

Appendix

B

Networking Questions and Answers

When designing a network for the first time, you will find that as you begin the design, you will have many more questions than answers. This chapter is dedicated to help you find the answers to some of the most commonly asked networking questions. There are all types of questions about many different topics included in this section. Some of the major networking components discussed in this chapter include NetWare, CICS, OS/2, CM/2, Ethernet, Token Ring, and many others.

Some of these questions are intended for novice networking designers and administrators while other questions are for the advanced networking professional. There are many questions of concern to the individuals charged with developing a multiprotocol network that supports many dissimilar hardware and software platforms.

Take a look at these entries. There's something in this chapter for everyone.

How can I route CICS print into NetWare print queues?

First let's discuss the reasons why you would want to route CICS (or other mainframe print) into NetWare print queues. Mainframe printer emulators are usually provided with 3270 emulation packages. CM/2 also provides the 3270 printer emulation function. These 3270 printer emulators route the host print to the workstation's local printer. This causes two problems for the network administrator.

Problem 1 If you are using Netports, or other specialized print server mechanisms that do not connect to a workstation, you will not be able to use those devices for mainframe print.

Problem 2 If you are using DOS-based workstations with 3270 terminal and printer emulation, the host print could jump right in the middle of your local PC print output.

There are two ways to route CICS print to NetWare print queues.

Solution 1 Use combination of two products, from Levi, Ray and Shoup, Inc., called VPS and VPS/PC. These two products are rather expensive, but they will provide the functionality that you are looking for.

Solution 2 This solution is less expensive, but requires more effort on your part to set up. You can configure a DOS or OS/2 PC to have three host printer sessions. Printer session 1 should be directed to LPT1:, printer session 2 should be directed to LPT2:, and printer session 3 should be directed to LPT3:. Do not worry if your PC does not have an LPT2 and LPT3, because they will not actually be used. Before you start the 3270 emulator (which has these three host printers defined), enter CAPTURE commands for the three LPT ports. Each CAPTURE command can direct the output from the LPTx port to a different NetWare print queue. When host print (CICS or any other host application) is processed by the 3270 emulator, the print will be directed to NetWare for you. The only problem I have encountered with this approach is that it can be a little slow, and you may need to experiment with the print time-out parameters on the PC.

Should I purchase a router or a bridge?

Most corporations that purchase routers use them as bridges. This does not mean that you should not purchase a router. There are several things that you must consider before deciding on a direction to take.

If you purchase a bridge, the only thing that you will be able to use the device for is bridging. If you purchase a router, your options are open. You may still use the router as a bridge; but if the need arises, you can use its routing functions.

If you need to provide access to a wide-area network, a bridge will not help you. Most routers provide WAN support.

If you need to access Internet at some time in the future, you *must* have a router.

The whole issue of purchasing a bridge versus a router boils down to three issues: today's needs, tomorrow's needs, and cost. If you only need the functionality of a bridge today and money is scarce, perhaps a bridge is the best solution. If tomorrow you need the routing functionality, will management question your past decision on the bridge? Sometimes it is easier to go the safe route and purchase a router from the start.

I am setting up a new local area network. Should I use Ethernet or Token Ring?

This is an age-old question that is still being discussed. Let's look at the strengths and weaknesses of both topologies:

Token Ring strengths	There is simple, flexible IBM host access. Performance is consistent under high traffic loads.
Token Ring weaknesses	NIC adapters are considerably more expensive than Ethernet. Token Ring concentrator components (such as Synoptics concentrators) are considerably more expensive than Ethernet.
Ethernet strengths	NIC adapters are inexpensive. Ethernet concentrator components are inexpensive.
Ethernet weaknesses	Performance is erratic under high traffic loads.

In the past, network planners and managers chose Token Ring because of the easy IBM host connectivity. Ethernet has made tremendous strides in this area. The IBM 3172 and the Memorex 1174 provide host access to Ethernet LANs that are just as simple, reliable, and flexible as the standard Token Ring configurations.

To provide the best of both worlds, some shops set up a small Token Ring network to provide host access and then use a bridge or router to connect a large Ethernet network. The Ethernet network contains the bulk of the end-user workstations. This type of configuration works well, but you must invest in a good router that supports SNA in order to prevent headaches down the road.

I need to provide approximately 40 Gbytes of disk space on our LAN. Should I use the LANRES product to utilize the mainframe DASD or should I establish an SCSII farm?

The issue of using LANRES or SCSII drives depends upon your disaster recovery and backup needs. The current LAN backup systems claim up to a 10-Mbyte/min backup. In practice, the best you can do is about 7 Mbytes/min. So a 1-Gbyte SCSII drive would take about $2\frac{1}{2}$ hours to back up. Multiply that number by 40, and that is how much time it would take to back up your entire SCSII farm. Of course, multiple tape drives will speed this up, but we are still talking about a considerable amount of time. LAN backups are also operator-intensive tasks. The tapes must be manually located, mounted, and labeled.

A 1.5-Gbyte LANRES drive can be backed up in about 20 min, by using standard host backup procedures. These procedures are already in place at most mainframe sites. These procedures can also be automated to a large degree. Recovery of LANRES volumes is also simpler and faster than LAN-based backup and restore procedures. The only problem with LANRES is that it is still a new product, and not all the bugs have been worked out of it yet. As far as performance goes, the LANRES disks are just as fast as native SCSII drives.

To answer the question, LANRES should be used if you have the host resources to spare. But 40 Gbytes of SCSII drives is to hard to manage.

The security structure on my NetWare 3.11 file server is getting out of hand. Are there any techniques that I can use to keep the security structure manageable?

The best way to control security in a NetWare 3.11 system is by directories and groups. Try your absolute best not to assign trustee rights to individual files. You should assign the rights to directories only. Also beware not to assign trustee rights to entire volumes. It is very easy to forget that some users can read everything on a given NetWare volume. Security rights should be given to groups rather than to individual users. This can be harder to implement than it appears at first sight. Do not be afraid to create a lot of groups and make individual users members of multiple groups. For example, you could have a group named WPUSERS. You then assign read and file Scan rights to the WordPerfect directory to the WPUSERS group. To allow a user to access WordPerfect, you simply add the user to the WPUSERS group. To take this theory one step further, you can also assign search drives based on the group structure. You can add the following lines in your system log-in script to add the WordPerfect directory in the search path for the members of the WPUSERS group:

```
IF MEMBER OF "WPUSERS" THEN
  MAP INS S16:=SERVERA1:VOL1:\WP51
END
```

Keeping all the trustee rights assigned to groups rather than to individual users also makes the migration to new releases of NetWare much simpler, since you have fewer places to look for information.

One more word of advice about keeping your NetWare 3.11 system under control: Try not to use the user log-in scripts for anything. Try to use the system log-in script for everything. There are two reasons for this approach. First, by keeping all your drive mappings, etc., in the system log-in script, you can tell at a glance how the mappings will be set up for each individual user. If you use the user log-in scripts, you must scan the system log-in script and then look at the individual user log-in scripts to obtain the same information. Second, when you upgrade to a new release of NetWare, you must retrofit all the user log-in scripts into the new release. It is much simpler to upgrade if you have to worry about only the system log-in script.

I have the NetWare SNA gateway installed for our DOS users. I am about to implement several Windows workstations on our Novell network. Can I use the NetWare SNA gateway with the WSLAN DOS emulator for these Windows users?

Yes and no. You can start the WSLAN connection to the NetWare SNA gateway before you start Windows. This method does work, but the WSLAN program can consume a substantial amount of RAM below the 1-Mbyte line. Because of the RAM appetite of WSLAN, you may experience problems with other Windows applications, and you will most likely experience problems with DOS applications running under Windows. Another option is to run WSLAN under a DOS session under Windows. This option tends to hang up the entire Windows session. A more viable option is to purchase a true Windows 3270 emulation package. WallData has a product, RUMBA for NetWare, that will run as a native Windows application and can use both the NetWare SNA gateway and the NetWare systems applications architecture (SAA) gateway for its host connection.

How can I see what files a user has open on my NetWare file server?

For NetWare 3.1x systems, load the MONITOR NLM on your file server by typing

```
LOAD MONITOR
```

at the : prompt. Select the CONNECTIONS function within the monitor. Cursor down to the user in question, and hit Enter. You will be shown the list of files that the user has open.

I have a NetWare file server, and I forgot the password for Supervisor. What can I do?

Hopefully you have another Supervisor-level user ID that you can use to reset the password for Supervisor. If not, things get a little more complicated.

You must first boot the file server with DOS. Using a tool that can access the server's hard drive by sector, such as Norton Utilities 5.0, search the directory for the bindery files. These files are named NET$BIND.SYS and NET$BVAL.SYS. Change the extensions of these names to .OLD. Next reboot the server. When the server notices that the bindery files do not exist, a default bindery is created. This default bindery contains two users, Supervisor and Guest. Neither of these will have a password assigned. Once you log in as Supervisor, use BINDREST to restore the bindery. Now would be a good time to set up another Supervisor-level user.

The Novell service and support course provides a utility to provide this function.

I need to establish a wide area network. What are my options?

There are four basic types of WAN implementations:

LAN to LAN

Taking over a PC on a remote LAN

Becoming a node on a remote LAN

Internet

LAN to LAN communications are accomplished by connecting two routers together, using some type of telecommunications medium. The most common communications methods used are a leased synchronous line, a T1 line, or a dial-up synchronous line. Each of these communications links has different speed capabilities and costs.

Taking over a PC on a remote LAN is accomplished by using software such as the NetWare Access Server (NAS) or PCAywhere. These products run software on a node which is attached to a LAN. The node also contains a modem that a remote PC dials into. The software on the dialing node runs software that talks to the software on the LAN-attached node. The dialing node then takes over the operation of the LAN-attached node. This method is quite commonly used by software support personnel, but it can be impractical for large corporate uses. The drawbacks are that for each dialing node you must provide an unused LAN-attached node. In the case of the NAS, the software can support multiple dialing nodes on one 386 or 486 LAN-attached node.

Becoming a node on a remote LAN is becoming more popular. Several products provide this function including Shiva NetModem and Centrum. The dialing node dials up to a special hardware device. This device actually extends the LAN to the dialing node, making the dialing node another node on the LAN.

Internet was recently opened to commercial uses. If you have two LANs connected to Internet, these two LANs can communicate with each other over Internet. You must be very careful with security if you implement this type of WAN in your corporation.

What is Internet?

Internet is a worldwide network comprised of thousands of individual networks and workstations. Internet is used primarily for academic functions, but it has recently been opened up for commercial uses. To access Internet, you must obtain an Internet IP address. You must also utilize a router to connect to Internet. When you apply for an Internet address, you will be given more detailed instructions on how to perform the physical connection to the network. Be aware that performance on Internet can be erratic at times.

How can I obtain an Internet address?

Internet addresses are free and can be obtained from

InterNIC Registration Services
505 Hunter Park Drive
Herndon, VA 22070
(703) 742–4777
(800) 444–4345

Can I use the Internet for my WAN?

Yes. This can be a good idea, but you have to be careful. Internet has many thousands of users, with thousands of entry points. You must set up your router very carefully to keep any and all hackers out of your network. There are people out there on Internet just waiting for new, inexperienced users to connect to the network so that they can snoop around.

How can I implement remote IPL for my OS/2 NetWare clients?

Remote booting (RIPL) of OS/2 workstations under Novell is not currently supported, as of this writing. The NetWare Requester manual contains a chapter on the RIPL function, but if you read the README file that comes with Requester, you will find that the RIPL function is not currently supported.

I need to implement a gateway to the mainframe for the DOS users on my Novell network. Which product best serves this purpose?

NetWare SAA. This product is continually being upgraded and added to. For example, the LANRES product recently announced a method to use mainframe DASD on NetWare LANs by using a connection through NetWare SAA.

I need to implement a tape backup for our file server SCSII drives. Which tape backup software would be best?

Each tape backup system has its advantages and disadvantages, and you must weigh these very carefully. The single most important factor is the speed of the data transfer. What good is a tape backup system if it takes 10 hours to back up a 1-Gbyte drive?

We use the LIU/2 product from IBM to load our OS/2 version 2.0 workstations. We need to convert these workstations to OS/2 version 2.1. Can we use LIU/2 for this?

No. LIU/2 does not support version 2.1. The NTS/2 product does provide a similar function. This function is called CID and is explained in the NTS/2 manual.

What is the IDLE SENSITIVITY setting in the OS/2 DOS settings used for?

Many DOS programs enter a tight, endless loop, checking for keyboard input from the user. Why shouldn't they? They think they have the CPU all to themselves. OS/2 is a true multitasking operating system. If the user starts a DOS application which enters one of these keyboard loops and then switches to another application, the CPU could be consumed processing this loop. OS/2 provides the idle sensitivity parameter to prevent the CPU from being consumed by these loops. OS/2 looks for programs in these loops and reduces the amount of CPU allocated to them. The idle sensitivity parameter tells OS/2 when to lower the priority of these tasks.

The idle sensitivity can cause problems with communications programs. Communication programs must be able to process data received from the COM ports very quickly. If OS/2 reduces their CPU time slice, the program could lose data. Idle sensitivity should be disabled for communications programs.

Now that I have decided to implement a router, which router vendor should I purchase from?

There are several factors that you must consider when selecting a router vendor:

1. The vendor should have a reputation for keeping up with the changes in the industry. As new protocols such as FDDI and ATM arise, does the router vendor provide prompt support for these protocols?
2. Does the router support all the protocols that you wish to implement? For example, do you require source routing transparency to bridge Ethernet and Token Ring? Does the router support this?
3. Can you get replacement boards in a timely manner? Most shops rely heavily on their router(s). If a board failure occurs, can you get a replacement board in a time frame that is acceptable to you? If you purchase a router from local resellers, you may be able to

strike a deal with them so that they maintain a stock of extra boards for you.

4. How is the vendor's technical support? One of the major problems with multivendor, multiprotocol networks is that when things break, everyone points the finger at every one else. Will your router vendor stop the finger pointing and help you troubleshoot your problems, or will the vendor become part of the problem?

When selecting a router, you must also look at performance. Will the router be able to handle the traffic flow that you intend to manage?

I am setting up a network and am new in the field. Should I purchase a LAN analyzer in preparation for problems?

Yes, Yes, Yes.... You will encounter problems with your network at some time. If you purchase a LAN analyzer right from the start, you will have time to learn how to use the device before problems arise. The analyzer will also help those new to networking learn how the network operates and what "normal" operation looks like.

Should I implement OS/2 on the workstations or Windows?

This all depends upon the needs of your end-users. If they do not require the use of a multitasking operating system, Windows 3.1 should be sufficient. Windows NT does not appear to be a viable solution for the average corporate user. The hardware requirements require top-of-the-line personal computers to support the operating system. The memory and CPU resources for NT are considerably higher than those of OS/2. NT is still a new product, while OS/2 has become remarkably stable. As the critical mass for OS/2 continues, it is unlikely that IBM will drop OS/2. Food for thought: If IBM did drop OS/2, it would not just drop support; IBM would sell the product to another software vendor. OS/2 might even do better if another vendor took it over (i.e., of course, unless the MicroSoft folks got their hands on it).

Which trade shows are good for learning about multiprotocol networking issues and products?

InterOp is an excellent trade show. InterOp provides many two- and three-day tutorials on specific subjects. There are also hundreds of smaller (2-hour) miniclasses on specific applications and products. InterOp also has a showcase where a multitude of networking hardware and software vendors connect their products together on a large multiprotocol network. This allows you, the customer, to see how these products work in real life.

I have an OS/2 version 2.0 workstation with Extended Services set up as a mainframe gateway. The gateway seems to be allowing only eight concurrent users on. Is there a parameter that I have set wrong?

Yes. Check MAXIMUM NUMBER OF LINK STATIONS in your gateway's CM/2 configuration. This number limits the number of concurrent users that can access the gateway.

I have an OS/2 workstation on a Novell LAN. When the machine boots, a CAPTURE command is issued to capture the output of the LPT1 port and route it to a Novell print queue. When the user goes into a DOS session, the Print Screen function works fine, and the output is successfully routed to the proper print queue. When the user tries to print from one of the DOS applications, the print seems to disappear. Any ideas?

You must have the following statement in the workstation's CONFIG.SYS file in order for the DOS application's print to be routed successfully:

```
DEVICE=C:\OS2\MDOS\LPTDD.SYS
```

We have several OS/2 workstations on our network. Some of the DOS applications that run on the OS/2 machines require the ANSI.SYS driver. How can I implement this driver?

Insert the following statement in the OS/2 CONFIG.SYS file:

```
DEVICE=C:\OS2\MDOS\ANSI.SYS
```

My network consists of hundreds of OS/2 version 2.0 workstations. I have noticed that on the OS/2 workstations that run the Novell RPRINTER program, the screen saver does not work. How can I correct this?

This problem was corrected with OS/2 version 2.1 and the latest version of the OS/2 NetWare Requester.

I have three Novell 3.11 file servers at my site. Several users need to access all three of these servers. Is there any way I can attach these users to all these servers and have them enter their password only once, without compromising security or converting to NetWare 4.0?

Yes. You can place all the users that require access to all three servers into a group. For this example, let's call this group ATTACH3. In the system log-in script of server 1, enter the following lines:

```
IF MEMBER OF "ATTACH3" THEN
  ATTACH SERVER2\%LOGIN_NAME
  ATTACH SERVER3\%LOGIN_NAME
END
```

If the user's passwords are the same on all three file servers, the user will be attached to all three servers and will be prompted for the password for only the initial server.

I need to provide access to an IBM host from a small Ethernet LAN. I do not have a front-end processor or a Token Ring network to utilize our 3174 control units. What are my options?

There are several ways to accomplish this, each having its advantages and drawbacks:

1. Most gateway products allow you to physically attach to the host in several ways. One of these ways is to place a 3270 card in the gateway PC which is attached to a 3174 DFT port. This option is very inexpensive, but it can support only up to five concurrent users.
2. Some gateway products allow you to attach to the host on a Mux port on a 3174. This option is also very inexpensive, but it can support only up to 40 concurrent users.
3. You can purchase an IBM 3172 controller. This controller channel attaches to the host and also has an Ethernet port to connect to the LAN. This option, while more expensive than the others, supports many more concurrent users.

The thing I have the most trouble with on our NetWare network is problems keeping RPRINTER running on our OS/2 nodes. I need a way to monitor all the RPRINTERs to see when they are hung up. This should be a one-screen, self-updating monitor that our operators can view. Do you know of such a tool?

Yes, and you already have the tool. It is a component of NetWare Requester for OS/2. The NetWare Tools function within the OS/2 NetWare Requester provides a utility to graphically view your NetWare print queues. To do this:

Step 1 Use the NetWare Tools to log in to a file server.

Step 2 Click on the Tools menu bar to access the pop-up menu.

Step 3 Click on Print queues, and your print queues will be displayed.

You can arrange a grid of print queue boxes by using the facilities of the NetWare tools and the OS/2 presentation manager services. This grid would show you, at a glance, which print queues were operating normally and which had jobs waiting to be printed.

What is a translating bridge?

A translating bridge is a bridge that converts one topology to another, such as Ethernet to Token Ring.

What is a transparent bridge?

Transparent bridges are usually used on Ethernet networks. Transparent bridges examine the MAC addresses of the packets and forward packets based on their addresses. The transparent bridge keeps internal tables that correlate the MAC addresses to the ports where they are located. The bridge is continually learning about where the network nodes are located. Transparent bridges are protocol-independent, and their operation is transparent to the end-users.

What is a source routing bridge?

A source routing bridge is used on Token Ring networks to connect two token rings together.

What is a source routing transparent bridge?

A source routing transparent (SRT) bridge is a bridge that can act as a source routing bridge when talking to Token Ring networks and can act as a transparent bridge when talking to Ethernet LANs. Router vendors are just beginning to support SRT bridging. These types of bridges are useful when you need to bridge SNA from Token Ring to Ethernet. An example of when you would need to implement an SRT bridge is when you want OS/2 nodes on an Ethernet LAN to emulate the PU function (via CM/2) by using the downstream PU method to a 3174 or 3745 on a Token Ring network. See Chapters 9 and 10.

What is an encapsulating bridge?

An encapsulating bridge is a bridge that wraps a packet with another protocol (usually IP) and forwards the packet to another bridge. This other bridge must also be an encapsulating bridge. An example of where this is used very effectively occurs where you have an FDDI backbone to which numerous LANs are attached. Each LAN is connected to the FDDI backbone with an encapsulating bridge. When packets are routed from one LAN to another, the bridge wraps IP around the packet and sends it to the destination router. This router unwraps the packet and sends it to the destination LAN. For this configuration to work, the file servers cannot reside on the backbone FDDI LAN. The file servers must reside on the individual LANs that are connected to the backbone.

What is a root bridge?

When the spanning tree algorithm is implemented for either Token Ring or Ethernet LANs, the bridges talk to each other to determine which bridge will become the root bridge. This is determined by a combination of the priority setting in the bridge and the bridge's MAC address. The root bridge is used by the spanning tree to determine which bridge ports should be blocked (in the case of Ethernet/Transparent networks) or converted to all-routes bridges (in the case of Token Ring or source routing networks).

What is a universal address?

A universal address is a MAC address that is preset by the board manufacturer. Each board has a unique universal address. The first six digits (of the 12-digit universal address) are assigned to a manufacturer, and the last six digits are assigned by the manufacturer. For example, 0000A2 is assigned to WellFleet for its manufacturer code. The boards that WellFleet makes will all have these digits in the first six positions of their universal address. The remaining six digits are assigned by WellFleet. This address can be overridden with software. When the universal address is overridden, the address is called a locally administered address (LAA).

What causes beaconing?

One of the most common causes of beaconing on a Token Ring LAN is the introduction of an adapter to the ring with the wrong speed setting, e.g., inserting a NIC set to 4 Mbytes/s into a 16-Mbytes/s Token Ring LAN. Hardware errors can also cause beaconing.

I am setting up a new Ethernet network in a campus environment. This network will start with very light traffic, but will be expanded to handle very high traffic for an imaging project. I would like to keep all the file servers in a central location, but I am worried about the segmenting needs created by the high traffic. Should I decentralize the segments and keep the various file servers at the different buildings of the campus?

Since you are building a new network, all your options are open. There is a very successful network design that addresses your performance issues and centralized file server concerns. Each building in the campus contains a concentrator, such as the Synoptics concentrator. A fiber-optic cable is run from the remote concentrator back to a computer room. This fiber is plugged into a multiplane concentrator in the computer room. The multiplane concentrator is simply a concentrator that is broken down into multiple segments. This multiplane concentrator can be viewed as several individual concentrators, each supporting a separate network. The file servers connect to this multiport concentrator. The various network segments are connected by a router. Using this method, you are actually extending each separate LAN into a central computer room. This allows you to keep all the file servers in one room, while also keeping the traffic localized on each segment, as much as possible.

When should I implement the spanning tree bridging algorithm?

Let's review just what spanning tree does. If you have an internetwork that contains multiple paths to multiple networks which are connected via bridges, you must use spanning tree. Spanning tree will examine the various paths of the these multiple networks and will block (disable) certain paths to prevent network loops. Without this blocking you will encounter broadcast storms that could consume your entire network. Spanning tree can be used on Ethernet bridges (transparent bridges) and on Token Ring (source routing) bridges. The Token Ring spanning tree algorithm works a little differently from the Ethernet algorithm. On Token Ring, rather than blocking bridges, it converts some bridges to all-routes bridges and some to specific-route bridges. The end result of the Token Ring spanning tree and the Ethernet spanning tree is the same—broadcast storms are eliminated.

If you do not have any duplicate paths in your network that could cause loops, you do not need to implement spanning tree.

What is the difference between routing protocols and routable protocols?

A *routing protocol* is a protocol that is used by routers to communicate with each other. Routers talk to each other to pass information, such as which networks each other has access to. Routers use routing protocols to perform this router-to-router communication. Samples of routing protocols are Routing Information Protocol (RIP) and Open Shortest Path First (OSPF). These two particular protocols are used by the routers to share information about the IP networks. Again, a sample of what would be contained in the RIP or OSPF packets includes copies of the individual router's tables. These tables would contain the IP addresses of the networks to which the router has a path.

A *routable protocol* is a user protocol that can be routed. Two sample routable protocols are Internet Protocol (IP) and Novell's IPX. These protocols have information in the network layer of their packets that can be used by routers to forward the information through the network(s). There are also protocols that cannot be routed. These nonroutable (or bridgeable) protocols do not have information in the network portion of their packets. Samples of nonroutable protocols are NETBIOS and APPLETALK. These nonroutable protocols can be forwarded by bridges.

What is the difference between a router and a bridge?

A bridge looks at the MAC addresses in packets and uses this information to decide whether to forward or drop a packet. For instance, let's say we have a router with three Ethernet ports, each port attached to a LAN segment. A packet comes from port 1 (segment 1) into the bridge. The bridge looks at the MAC address field of the packet and gets the hardware address (universal or locally administered address) of the sender. Let's say the sender's address is 1. The bridge updates its internal table with an entry that says that address 1 can be accessed by port 1. The router then looks at the packet to get the address of the destination node. It searches its internal tables for ports 2 and 3 (notice it does not search the sending ports table; a router never forwards a packet to the port where it came from) for a match on the destination address. If it docs not find a match, it forwards the frame to both ports 2 and 3. When the destination node receives the packet and then sends a reply, the router performs the same function as above. Let's say that node 3 from port 3 (LAN 3) was the destination and it is now replying. The router then reads address 3 and updates its table for port 3 that node 3 can be reached from port 3. The bridges are constantly performing this learning process, discovering which nodes can be accessed by which ports.

A router looks deeper into the packets for network information. The data in the network portions of the packets cover such things as which IP network or IPX network the destination address resides on. The packet can also contain a trail of router addresses to where the destination address can be found. This information can be viewed as a road map to the destination address. Such things as "go to router 3 on ring 1 to router 5 on Ethernet network number 6 to router 10 to the node" are stored in the network layer of the packet. This information can help to reduce traffic on the network. A router can also be configured as a bridge. It can be configured as both a router and a bridge, on the same port. Using this configuration, the router would route the protocols it could, such as IP and IPX, and would bridge all the other protocols.

I am using IP and IPX on my Novell network. I have to assign an IP and an IPX address to each LAN segment. Is there an easy way to correlate these two addresses with each other?

Yes. First, I assume you are using class "C" IP addresses such as

```
192.2.3.0
```

The IPX address consists of 4 hexadecimal bytes. To keep the IP and IPX addresses in sync, simply convert each digit of the IP address to hexadecimal and use the result as your IPX LAN address. This makes sure that all your IPX addresses are unique and also provides a method to correlate the IPX address to the IP address. For example,

IP address 192 . 2 . 3 . 0

IPX address C0 . 02. 03 . 00

We are experiencing MACH690 errors on our Ethernet CM/2 connections to the mainframe. We are using the Ethernet PU emulation function of CM/2 to attach to a TIC that is installed in a 3174 control unit on a Token Ring LAN. A CISCO router is used to connect the Token Ring network to the Ethernet segments. What is causing the MACH690?

A MACH690 is an SNA timing error. The CM/2 workstation is not responding to the host quickly enough to keep SNA happy. There are several things that can cause this:

- An extremely busy Ethernet segment
- An extremely busy Token Ring network
- A bottleneck at the router
- Router software problem

MACH690s can also be caused by OS/2 problems. These errors have occurred when WordPerfect was started in a private DOS session before CM/2 was initialized.

Glossary

3172 A mainframe control unit that can be used to connect a mainframe to a Token Ring or Ethernet LAN. The 3172 can allow you to access mainframe systems from workstations on local-area networks.

3174 A mainframe control unit which controls terminals and printers. A TIC can be placed in a 3174 to connect the mainframe to a Token Ring LAN. It is also known as a control unit or cluster controller.

3274 A mainframe control unit which controls terminals and printers. Also known as a control unit or cluster controller.

3x74 A term meaning *either* the 3174 or 3274 terminal control unit.

3725 A mainframe communications controller. Also known as a front-end processor. The 3725 is used to control communications lines to remote sites (WAN). A TIC can be placed in the 3725 to connect the mainframe to a Token Ring LAN.

3270 The most common type of mainframe terminal or printer. These are known as 3270 devices.

3745 A mainframe communications controller. Also known as a front-end processor. The 3745 is used to control communications lines to remote sites (WAN). A TIC can be placed in the 3745 to connect the mainframe to a Token Ring LAN.

37x5 A shorthand term meaning *either* a 3725 or 3745.

8209 A bridge developed and sold by IBM. The bridge allows SNA to be passed between Token Ring and Ethernet LANs.

APPN Advanced Peer to Peer Networking. An IBM architecture.

AUTOEXEC.BAT A DOS file containing DOS commands that are executed when the DOS PC is booted.

Bandwidth The traffic capacity of a wire. The maximum number of bits that can be transmitted per second over the wire.

Bind The process of connecting a terminal, printer, or program to a host application through VTAM.

Bridge A communications device that can be used to extend a LAN. A bridge can also be used to isolate LAN traffic, thereby increasing overall network performance and capacity. A bridge examines the hardware or MAC addresses of the source and destination workstation within each packet. The bridge builds internal tables containing these MAC addresses and bases its packet-forwarding decisions on these tables.

Brouter A device that combines the functions of a bridge and a router in one box. The brouter will route all routable protocols, such as TCP/IP and IPX. The brouter will bridge all nonroutable protocols such as NETBIOS and SNA.

Capture A utility provided by NetWare that redirects print from the LPTx: port to a Novell print queue.

Channel In the mainframe world, a channel is a specialized hardware device that controls the data movement between a peripheral device, such as a disk drive, and the central processing unit.

Cluster controller A mainframe control unit which controls terminals and printers. See 3174 and 3274.

Coexistence Use of one NIC to access multiple systems concurrently.

Communications controller A front-end processor. See 3725 and 3745.

CUADDR Control unit address. The address, on the control unit, where a device is connected.

CUT Control unit terminal. A terminal (or a PC emulating a terminal) that has no brains. A dumb terminal.

DECLAT Digital Equipment Corporation's (DEC's) nonroutable protocol.

DECNET Digital Equipment Corporation's routable protocol.

DFT Distributed-function terminal. A terminal (or a PC emulating a terminal) that has brains. The terminal can perform some of the functions of the control unit. DFTs can perform advanced 3270 functions that cannot be performed by their CUT counterparts.

DPA Demand Protocol Architecture. An architecture that provides coexistence.

DSPU Downstream physical unit. An access address for a PU emulator to connect to a host via a TIC in a 3174 or 37x5. CM/2 workstations and gateways can use the DPSU as a means for accessing a mainframe.

Emulator A program that emulates a device or another program. For example, the software that runs on a PC to access a mainframe emulates the LU function and appears to be an LU to the mainframe.

End Node A specialized APPN node type. This node type requires the use of an APPN Network Node to gain access to an APPN or SNA network.

Etherand This is another word for Ethernet. IBM uses this word.

Ethernet A network technology that uses a collision detection method to control multiple concurrent network transmits. IEEE 802.3 defines the Ethernet architecture.

FEP Front-end processor. A 3725 or a 3745.

File server A specialized computer that stores files which can be accessed by multiple network users.

Front-end processor See FEP.

Gateway A networking device comprised of hardware and software that connects two dissimilar computer systems. An example of a gateway is the Novell SAA gateway that connects a mainframe to a local-area network. CM/2 can be configured as a gateway to a mainframe.

Global session All OS/2 and DOS sessions share a single NetWare log-in.

Hardware address An address that is burned into the network adapter by the hardware manufacturer. This address is also known as the universal address and the MAC address.

Host Host usually refers to a mainframe computer.

IEEE 802.3 The Institute of Electrical and Electronic Engineers (IEEE) developed this standard to define the rules for participating in an Ethernet local-area network.

ILAN A bridge manufactured by CrossComm that can be used to pass SNA traffic between a Token Ring and an Ethernet LAN. The ILAN performs the same function as the IBM 8209 bridge.

Internet A worldwide network comprised of thousands of interconnecting PCs and LANs. Internet is primarily used by universities, although commercial applications are expected to begin using the network soon.

Internetwork A network comprised of multiple LANs.

IOCP Input-Output Configuration Program. A mainframe utility that is used to tell the mainframe microcode what types of devices are connected to it.

IPX/SPX Internetwork Packet Exchange/Sequenced Packet Exchange. A protocol used by NetWare to transmit packets through a network.

LAA Locally administered address. The network administrator places an address in the NIC adapter rather than using the universal address provided by the NIC manufacturer. The LAA can be set by using a variety of methods, including the NET.CFG file and the PROTOCOL.INI file.

LAB Line attachment base. A 37x5 component which is used to connect communications lines and/or TICs to the 37x5.

LAN Local area network. A hardware and software setup that allows PCs to share resources and connect to different systems.

LANRES A product from IBM that provides a method to use mainframe DASD as native Novell file server drives. LANRES also provides utilities that allow you to route host print to NetWare printers and NetWare print to mainframe printers.

LANSUP A set of drivers from IBM that can be used to provide coexistence on Token Ring LANs.

LASTDRIVE A setting which tells DOS or OS/2 the last physical drive it has control over. The next higher drive letter will be the first network drive assigned by the network operating system. For example, if you set the LASTDRIVE parameter to E, the first network drive will be F.

Link support layer See LSL.

Logical unit See LU.

Log-in script A set of commands that are executed when a user logs in to a NetWare file server. There are a variety of log-in scripts. The DOS system log-in script is a single log-in script that is executed for every DOS user who logs in to a NetWare server. Each DOS user can optionally have a DOS log-in script that is executed after the DOS system log-in script. There are also OS/2 system and user log-in scripts that perform the same functions for OS/2 log-ins.

LSL Link support layer. A component of ODI that controls the multiple accesses to the NIC adapter.

LU Logical unit. An SNA program that controls devices such as printers and terminals. Many people refer to the actual devices as LUs.

MAP A NetWare utility that allows you to assign a drive letter to a particular directory path structure.

MAU Multistation access unit. A device used to connect Token Ring nodes to the network.

MLID Multilink interface driver. A component of ODI that controls the NIC adapter.

Modem Modulate/demodulate. A device that allows data to be passed over a telephone line. It converts digital data to analog signals. A modem is required on each end of the telephone line.

Multiprotocol router A router that can route packets from multiple protocols.

MVS Multiple virtual systems. A mainframe operating system.

MVSCP MVS Configuration Program. A mainframe program that is used to tell the operating system (MVS) what devices it has control over.

NCP Network Control Program. A program that is loaded in a 37x5 front-end processor to control mainframe communication lines and devices. There is also an NCP that runs on DEC/VMS systems and performs similar functions.

NDIS A NIC driver development standard that, when followed, allows the driver to coexist with other protocols.

Netport A device from Intel that acts as a small Print Server. Netport can connect two printers to a Novell network.

NetWare A network operating system developed by Novell.

NetWare Requester A product that runs on OS/2 workstations. Requester allows OS/2, DOS-OS/2, and WIN-OS/2 sessions to access Novell file servers and other Novell services.

Network address The address presented to the network by the NIC adapter. This can be an LAA or a universal address.

NETX.EXE A program interface with NOS to redirect DOS requests to NOS.

NIC Network interface card. A card that is placed into a personal computer to provide access to a local-area network.

Node A device that is attached to a local-area or wide-area network.

NOS Network operating system. NetWare is an example of a NOS.

NPRINTER A program provided with the OS/2 Requester that lets a printer attached to a PC become a network printer.

NPS Network Print Services. A product from InterConnections, Inc., that redirects print from DEC/VAX systems to Novell print queues.

NTS/2 Network Transport Services/2. An OS/2 package that is used to provide LAN communications.

ODI Open Data-Link Interface. An architecture developed by Novell and Apple to provide coexistence.

ODINSUP A driver that translates NDIS packets into ODI packets.

ODI2NDI A driver that translates ODI packets into NDIS packets.

Packet A group of information that is passed through a network. The packet contains control information, such as destination addresses and data.

PCONSOLE A NetWare utility that is used to define print servers and print queues.

Physical unit See PU.

Print queue An area on a file server that holds print jobs. The print server takes these jobs and routes them to the appropriate network printer.

Print server A program that controls network printers.

Private session Each DOS session under OS/2 has its own NetWare session.

Protocol An architecture that, when followed, allows two programs to communicate with each other.

PROTOCOL.INI A file used to configure NTS/2.

Protocol manager A component of DPA that interrogates the packets sent to the NIC and determines which protocol stack they belong to.

PU Physical unit. An SNA device that controls other devices. A 3174 cluster controller is an example of a PU.

Router A communication device that connects two or more LANs or WANs together. The router can be viewed as bridge with brains. It can perform all the functions of a bridge, plus it can delve into each packet and make forwarding decisions based on user-defined criteria. A router uses the network address field in the network packets to make its forwarding decisions.

RPRINTER A program provided with OS/2 Requester that lets a printer attached to a PC become a network printer.

SNA Systems Network Architecture. A set of rules that mainframe communications programs and devices follow in order to communicate with each other.

Source routing A routing methodology used in Token Ring networks.

Source routing transparency See SRT.

Spanning tree An algorithm used in transparent bridging that prevents redundant paths between the segments of the network. Spanning tree is implemented under transparent bridging. Transparent bridging cannot tolerate redundant network paths. Spanning tree prevents this by blocking certain bridges from participating in the network.

SPOOL A holding area for print jobs.

SRT Source routing transparency. A routing method that can be used to route SNA traffic between Token Ring and Ethernet LANs.

STARTUP.CMD A file containing OS/2 commands which are executed each time the OS/2 PC is booted. Comparable to the DOS AUTOEXEC.BAT file.

SYSCON A NetWare utility that provides many functions, such as adding users and groups and providing security access to files and directories.

SYS1.VTAMLST The file on a mainframe where the VTAM configurations are held.

TCP/IP Transmission control protocol/Internet protocol. These protocols were initially developed for Unix systems. TCP/IP has since been embraced by many other networking systems as the protocol of choice for interoperability.

TES Terminal Emulation Services. A product from InterConnections, Inc., that allows a workstation to access a DEC/VAX in terminal emulation mode.

TIC Token Ring interface coupler. A card that is placed in a 3174 or 37x5 controller that connects Token Ring networks to mainframes.

Token Ring A local-area network topology, created by IBM, that uses the concept of passing a token throughout the network. The node must wait for the token before the node can transmit.

Token Ring interface coupler See TIC.

Topology An arrangement of nodes on a local-area network. Ring, bus, and star are types of topologies.

TRA Token Ring adapter. A 37x5 component which is comprised of two TICs.

Transparent bridging A bridging method primarily used on Ethernet LANs.

TRSS Token Ring network attachment subsystem. A 37x5 component comprised of one to four Token Ring adapters.

Universal address A network address preset by the NIC manufacturer. This address can be overridden with an LAA.

UTP Unshielded twisted pair. A type of cabling that is quickly becoming the most common type used in new networks. Token Ring and Ethernet local-area networks can utilize UTP cables if the correct type of wiring concentrator is implemented.

VIPX Virtual/IPX. A driver used by OS/2 workstations to communicate with NetWare LANs. VIPX is provided with the NetWare Requester product.

VMS The operating system which is run on DEC/VAX machines.

VTAM Virtual Telecommunication Access Method. This software product controls terminals, printers, and other mainframe communications.

WAN Wide area network. A network that extends to remote sites and uses telephone lines, microwave, satellite, or other technology.

Index

ABOUT THE AUTHOR

John E. Johnston has more than 14 years of data processing experience encompassing mainframe systems and applications programming, LAN administration, PC programming, multiplatform connectivity, and technical management. Currently, he is the technical support manager for the Reading Hospital and Medical Center. In this capacity, he has designed and implemented numerous systems that connect a wide variety of hardware and software, including a campus wide LAN that can access an IBM 3090 mainframe, a DEC VAX, and multiple Novell LANs concurrently. He writes for *Enterprise Systems Journal* and is a part-time editor for *Technical Support* magazine. John can be reached for questions or comment: via CompuServe: 73473, 2146.

ABOUT THE SERIES

The J. Ranade Workstation Series is McGraw-Hill's primary vehicle for providing workstation professionals with timely concepts, solutions, and applications. Jay Ranade is also series editor in chief of more than 125 books in the J. Ranade IBM and DEC Series and series advisor to the McGraw-Hill Series on Computer Communications.
Jay Ranade, Series Editor in Chief and best-selling author, is a senior systems architect and assistant vice president at Merrill Lynch.